ETHICAL LEADERSHIP AND DECISION MAKING IN EDUCATION

The fifth edition of the best-selling text, *Ethical Leadership and Decision Making in Education*, continues to address the increasing interest in ethics and assists educational leaders with complex dilemmas in today's challenging, divided, and diverse societies.

Through discussion and analysis, Shapiro and Stefkovich demonstrate the application of four ethical paradigms—the ethics of justice, critique, care, and the profession. After illustrating how the Multiple Ethical Paradigms may be applied to authentic dilemmas, the authors present cases written by graduate students, practitioners, and academics representing dilemmas faced by educational leaders in urban, suburban, and rural public and private schools and universities, in the U.S. and abroad. Following each case are questions that call for thoughtful, complex thinking and help readers apply the Multiple Ethical Paradigms to practical situations.

New in the Fifth Edition are more than ten cases that cover issues of food insufficiency, the pandemic's effects on diverse school populations, a student's sexual orientation, transgender students in the university, lock-down drills for young children, refugees in a Swedish school, boundaries in high school sports, generational differences in an adult diploma school, acceptance of animals on campus, and hate speech in the academy.

This edition also includes teaching notes for the instructor stressing the importance of self-reflection, use of new technologies, and global appeal of ethical paradigms and dilemmas. This book is a critical resource for aspiring and practicing administrators, teacher leaders, and educational policy makers.

Joan Poliner Shapiro is Co-Director Emerita of the New DEEL (Democratic Ethical Educational Leadership) Community Network and Professor Emerita of Higher Education at Temple University, USA.

Jacqueline Stefkovich is an Independent Consultant, Researcher, and Professor Emerita in the Department of Education Policy Studies at the Pennsylvania State University, USA.

"In their fifth edition of this seminal book, the authors skillfully use multiple ethical paradigms to explore complex, real life moral dilemmas. This book is a must-read for educational leaders and those who prepare them for their ethically challenging roles."

Martha M. McCarthy, Presidential Professor,
Loyola Marymount University, and
Chancellor's Professor Emerita, Indiana University

"A significant contribution by two of the most respected and thoughtful scholars in the field of educational ethics. Shapiro and Stefkovich provide the most coherent narrative to date on the significance of ethics for school leaders."

Joseph Murphy, Professor of Educational Leadership,
Emeritus, Peabody College, Vanderbilt University

"Shapiro and Stefkovich facilitate both understanding and application through a set of compelling case studies. This book is, in a word, comprehensive. Few teaching resources in educational leadership come close."

Michelle D. Young, Professor and Dean,
Loyola Marymount University,
Executive Director Emerita, University
Council for Educational Administration

ETHICAL LEADERSHIP AND DECISION MAKING IN EDUCATION

APPLYING THEORETICAL PERSPECTIVES TO COMPLEX DILEMMAS

Fifth Edition

Joan Poliner Shapiro and Jacqueline A. Stefkovich

Routledge
Taylor & Francis Group

NEW YORK AND LONDON

Fifth edition published 2022
by Routledge
605 Third Avenue, New York, NY 10158

and by Routledge
2 Park Square, Milton Park, Abingdon, Oxon, OX14 4RN

Routledge is an imprint of the Taylor & Francis Group, an informa business

© 2022 Taylor & Francis

The right of Joan Poliner Shapiro and Jacqueline A. Stefkovich to be
identified as authors of this work has been asserted by them in accordance
with sections 77 and 78 of the Copyright, Designs and Patents Act 1988.

First edition published by Lawrence Erlbaum Associates, Inc. 2001

Fourth edition published by Routledge 2016

Library of Congress Cataloging-in-Publication Data
Names: Shapiro, Joan Poliner, author. | Stefkovich, Jacqueline Anne,
   1947– author.
Title: Ethical leadership and decision making in education : applying
   theoretical perspectives to complex dilemmas / Joan Poliner Shapiro
   and Jacqueline A. Stefkovich.
Description: 5th edition. | New York, NY : Routledge, 2022. | Includes
   bibliographical references and index.
Identifiers: LCCN 2021025939 (print) | LCCN 2021025940 (ebook) |
   ISBN 9780367898076 (hardback) | ISBN 9780367901394 (paperback) |
   ISBN 9781003022862 (ebook)
Subjects: LCSH: Educational leadership—Moral and ethical aspects—
   United States. | School administrators—Professional ethics—
   United States. | School management and organization—Moral and
   ethical aspects—United States. | Ethics—Study and teaching—
   United States. | Decision making—United States.
Classification: LCC LB1779 .S416 2022 (print) | LCC LB1779 (ebook) |
   DDC 371.2/011—dc23
LC record available at https://lccn.loc.gov/2021025939
LC ebook record available at https://lccn.loc.gov/2021025940

ISBN: 978-0-367-89807-6 (hbk)
ISBN: 978-0-367-90139-4 (pbk)
ISBN: 978-1-003-02286-2 (ebk)

DOI: 10.4324/9781003022862

Typeset in New Baskerville
by Apex CoVantage, LLC

Contents

Preface

Since the publication of the first edition of this book in 2001, the world has become increasingly unstable owing to a global pandemic, financial uncertainty, climate change, racial and social inequality, terrorism, wars, the rise of populism and the increasing fragility of democracy. Additionally, different cultures and religions as well as the increase of misinformation, the rise of hate speech and the growth of new technologies have all impacted our societies. Education is not immune to these changes, and they do affect our ethics. Do we turn to our better angels of our nature (Lincoln, 1861) or to our worse instincts (Meacham, 2018)? In recent memory, there has never been a more important time to teach ethics than in this era.

To deal with some of these changes over time, in the second edition of this book, we added two new chapters. One chapter emphasized religious differences and presented the contradictions between religion and culture. The other chapter focused on testing, juxtaposing the paradox of accountability with responsibility. We also added several dilemmas focusing on higher education, recognizing that many educational leadership preparation programs include students with this concentration.

In the third edition, we inserted a chapter on privacy versus safety that focused on ethical issues dealing with drug use, strip searches, and gang membership. This chapter also contained, under the rubric of technology, problems of cyber-bullying on the internet, sexting, and sexual orientation made public via cell phones. We also included early childhood and special education cases in a number of the chapters.

For the fourth edition, we added dilemmas on: teachers with guns; the military and education; children of undocumented immigrants; homeless students; videos in bathrooms; incentive pay; first responders; private alternative high schools; verbal threats; and gaming etiquette. Additionally, we created a new chapter that focused on technology while emphasizing the need for respect for the individual in this increasingly mechanized world. In this chapter, the dilemmas involved sexting as well as various permutations of cyber-bullying and cell phone use.

Finally, for this fifth edition, as usual our editor asked several faculty members from the U.S. and abroad, who have assigned our book in their classes, what they felt should be included in this current era. In response to their valuable comments, we have added cases on: the coronavirus pandemic and food insufficiency; the coronavirus's effects on diverse school populations; sexual orientation, including transgender students in the university, an international student in a college, and a student's sexual orientation in a Catholic Colombian school; lock-down drills for little children; refugees in a Swedish school; boundaries in high school sports; generational differences in an adult diploma school; acceptance of animals on campus; and hate speech in the Academy.

Beyond these new cases, there are modifications, throughout this book, that make it more up to date. These revisions include citations that will attempt to keep readers current in the field of ethical educational leadership. We have also continued to modify Chapter 12, Teaching as Scholarly Work, to include the use of technology in a time of the coronavirus pandemic. COVID-19 has created whole new approaches to teaching and learning. Whether these approaches will endure, after the virus has finally abated, remains to be seen. But in this interim period, it is important to deal with what we have begun to learn about the importance of online learning. Prior to the coronavirus, our delivery systems for the teaching of ethics had already begun to change, and we thought instructors using this book might find our experiences with hybrid and online teaching of value. Additionally, we do our best to explain why ethical dilemmas, coming from English-speaking schools and institutions, might be interesting and meaningful to aspiring educational leaders in countries where English is not the major language.

Initially, the impetus for writing this book came from three developments in the field of educational leadership: (1) a burgeoning interest in the study of ethics among educational leaders; (2) a rising tendency to use case studies as a method of reflection on administrative problems; and (3) the introduction of licensure standards for school leaders that require an understanding of ethical issues.

THE PURPOSE OF THIS BOOK

This book has several purposes. First, it demonstrates the application of different ethical paradigms through the discussion and analysis of real-life moral dilemmas. Second, it addresses some of the practical, pedagogical, and curricular issues related to the teaching of ethics for educational leaders. Third, it emphasizes the importance of ethics instruction from a variety of theoretical approaches. Finally, this book provides a process that instructors might follow to develop their own ethics unit or course.

CONTENTS AND ORGANIZATION

This book discusses how students and practitioners should consider each of four paradigms presented (i.e., the ethic of justice, the ethic of critique, the ethic of care, and the ethic of the profession) to help solve authentic dilemmas. We have structured these dilemmas with key questions to assist the readers to think in ways that they may not have considered in the past. These questions may also help to open the minds of students, practitioners, or both when introduced to the paradigms. If they are presented as options, these paradigms may help students and practitioners to better solve complex dilemmas in today's challenging and diverse society.

Part I, comprising the first two chapters of this book, provides an overview of why ethics is so important, especially for today's educational leaders, and describes the Multiple Ethical Paradigms' framework that can be essential to practitioners as they grapple with ethical dilemmas.

Part II deals with the dilemmas themselves. After a brief introduction as to how the cases were constructed, an illustration is provided of how the multi-paradigm approach may be applied to a real dilemma. This example is followed by Chapters 3 through 11, which contain ethical dilemmas written primarily by graduate students, most of whom have experience as practitioners, and by some colleagues. These are the kinds of dilemmas faced by practicing educational leaders in urban, suburban, and rural settings in an era full of complexities and contradictions.

Part III focuses on pedagogy. Chapter 12 provides teaching notes to the instructor. To do this, we, as professors and authors,[1] discuss the importance of self-reflection on the part of instructors as well as students. We model how we thought through our own personal and professional ethical codes as well as reflected on the critical incidents in our lives that shaped our teaching and frequently determined what we privileged or emphasized in class.

THE CASE STUDY APPROACH TO TEACHING ETHICS

The case study approach to teaching educators has garnered considerable interest. Much of this interest has been stimulated by educational theories focusing on the merits of reflective practice (Dewey, 1902) and prompted by the successful use of cases for the training of business leaders, an effort spearheaded by Harvard University's Business School. Indeed, Nash (1996), in his book on professional ethics, pointed out that "a good case can be a provocative, almost indispensable tool for teaching the relevant moral concepts" (p. 64).

In response to this interest, numerous authors have written case books aimed at teaching and educational leadership (Hozien, 2017; Kruse & Gray, 2019; Levinson & Fay, 2019; Strike, Haller & Soltis, 2005; Strike & Soltis, 2009, 2015) and at general aspects of educational administration (Gorski & Pothini, 2018; Gray & Smith, 2007; Northouse & Lee, 2018). A few others have written texts with case studies in ethics focused on higher education (Strike & Moss, 2007) and a general population (Kramer & Enomoto, 2014; Niesche & Keddie, 2016). There is even the Journal of Cases in Educational Leadership (JCEL) that is sponsored by the University Council of Educational Administration (UCEA).

There are also many fine scholarly ethics books aimed at educational administrators (e.g., Beck, 1994; Beckner, 2004; Begley & Johansson, 2003; Branson & Gross, 2014; Davies, 2009; Duignan, 2007; Faddis, 2020; Fullan, 2003; Harris, Carrington & Ainscow, 2018; Jenlink, 2014; Johnson, 2020; Normore & Brooks, 2017; Rebore, 2013; Starratt, 1994; 2003, 2004; Strike, 2007; Wagner & Simpson, 2008).

Thus, it is evident from the plethora of publications that there has been a resurgence of interest in, and recognition of the importance of, ethics for educational leaders. Here, the justice perspective has been joined by other approaches, such as care (Gilligan, 1982; Noddings, 2003, 2012, 2013) and critique (Apple, 2010, 2011, 2013; Purpel, 2004; Starratt, 2003, 2009). More recently, the four ethics of justice, critique, care and the profession have been combined with the concept of school law (Stefkovich, 2014; Stefkovich & Frick, 2021) and with turbulence theory (Gross, 2014, 2020; Gross & Shapiro, 2004; Shapiro & Gross, 2013; Shapiro, Gross, & Shapiro, 2008). In addition, the profession of educational leadership has recognized a need for ethics' competencies and standards (Bass, Frick & Young, 2018; Murphy, 2017). Such developments have exposed gaps in the knowledge base that cry out for a response.

GAPS IN THE KNOWLEDGE BASE

The idea for the first edition of this book germinated over a nine-year period during which we taught ethics to diverse educational leaders. During this time, we noticed the dearth of materials available for our training. We advocate reflective practice and, thus, saw the benefits of including a case study approach as part of our instruction. However, most of the case books that we could find either focused broadly on educators in general and did not consider the unique problems of educational leaders, or they concentrated on the preparation of educational administrators, seldom mentioning ethical issues. However, one book, *The Ethics of School Administration* (Strike, Haller, & Soltis, 1988) did both, but discussed ethics primarily from a justice perspective.

Viewing ethics through different paradigms is a relatively recent phenomenon. Hence, few texts have discussed ethical dilemmas from multiple perspectives (i.e., to include the ethics of care and critique as well as justice). When we began our work in 2001, scholars and practitioners were concerned with issues of professional ethics, but none had grappled with the concept of professional ethics as a separate paradigm. More than twenty years later, as we publish this fifth edition of our book, many faculty as well as doctoral students throughout the United States and abroad have incorporated the concept of the ethic of the profession into their teaching and doctoral dissertations.

Thus, we see this book as complementing others that have gone before it by filling a real gap in the knowledge base of ethics' preparation for educational leaders. It provides a conceptual model for the analysis of professional ethics and then includes dilemmas and questions designed to stimulate discussion and apply the ethics of justice, critique, care, and the profession.

We believe our approach is an authentic one, incorporating the voices of our students and using many dilemmas that they have written in our classes. We believe that this approach, although somewhat unorthodox, responds to Nash's (1996, p. 64) concerns and observations when he said:

> The difficulty I have with some textbook cases . . . is that they are oftentimes so overly dramatic they make no claim to verisimilitude.... I have found over the years that the best provenance for cases is in my students' own work lives.

Finally, we believe there is merit in providing a process by which professors and practitioners alike can come to grips with their own ethical codes and then apply these codes to practical situations. We have incorporated this approach into our own teaching and have found it most helpful.

TEACHING NOTES TO THE INSTRUCTOR

We have taken considerable time to design this book so that it can be easily used for instructional purposes. In Chapter 2, we give an overview of multiple ethical perspectives that instructors might wish to present to their students.

Additionally, in each of the chapters that contain ethical dilemmas, we offer a series of questions to assist the instructor in facilitating discussion.

In the teaching of ethics, we not only ask instructors to help students reflect on their own personal values and professional beliefs, but we strongly encourage instructors to do the same. We believe it is imperative that we all become reflective practitioners when attempting to solve ethical dilemmas. We do not advocate one best way to accomplish this task, but we do provide some detailed information in Chapter 12 as to how we have taught ethics to our students by engaging in a process of self-reflection and, most recently, by using technology. We not only invite instructors to read this chapter but hope that students will find this section of interest as well.

We have designed this book so that it is easily adaptable for a variety of uses with a wide range of audiences. It may be utilized either as a basic or supplementary text for university courses related to the preparation of educational leaders, including, but not limited to, principals, superintendents, curriculum coordinators, personnel administrators, school counselors, business administrators, higher education administrators and faculty, teacher leaders, and early childhood directors. It is appropriate for either introductory or advanced levels of educational leadership programs and may be infused into almost all educational leadership curricula or taught in a discrete ethics course in any educational area.

In addition, this book may be used as a professional reference for aspiring and practicing school leaders, central office personnel, educational policy makers, state department personnel, and regional- and federal-level education staff. Others interested in the book as a reference might include school board members, parents' organizations, and professional associations. Moreover, we do not see this casebook as limited to the United States; educational professionals working in other countries have responded positively to the dilemmas we have presented. For example, South Korea has published the third edition of this book (Shapiro & Stefkovich, 2011) in Korean, and we have heard from numerous colleagues throughout the world who are using our book in their classrooms.

NOTE

1. The authorship of this book is in alphabetical order. Both authors contributed equally to the writing of this book.

REFERENCES

Apple, M.W. (2010). *Global crises, social justice, and education.* New York, NY: Routledge.
Apple, M.W. (2011). *Education and power* (3rd ed.). New York, NY: Routledge.

Apple, M.W. (2013). *Can education change society?* New York, NY: Routledge.

Bass, L., Frick, W.C., & Young, M.D. (Eds.) (2018). *Developing ethical principles for school leadership: PSEL standard two.* New York, NY: Routledge.

Beck, L.G. (1994). *Reclaiming educational administration as a caring profession.* New York, NY: Teachers College Press.

Beckner, W. (2004). *Ethics for educational leaders.* Boston, MA: Pearson Education.

Begley, P.T. & Johansson, O. (Eds.) (2003). *The ethical dimensions of school leadership.* Boston, MA: Kluwer.

Branson, C.M. & Gross, S.J. (Eds.) (2014). *Handbook of ethical educational leadership.* New York, NY: Routledge.

Cooper, T.L. (2012). *The responsible administrator: An approach to ethics for the administrator* (6th ed.). San Francisco, CA: Jossey-Bass.

Davies, B. (Ed.) (2009). *The essentials of school leadership* (2nd ed.). London, England: Sage.

Dewey, J. (1902). *The school and society.* Chicago, IL: University of Chicago Press.

Duignan, P. (2007). *Educational leadership: Key challenges and ethical tensions.* Cambridge, England: Cambridge University Press.

Faddis, T. (2020). *The ethical line: 10 leadership strategies for effective decision making.* Thousand Oaks, CA: Corwin.

Fullan, M. (2003). *The moral imperative of school leadership.* Thousand Oaks, CA: Corwin Press.

Gilligan, C. (1982). *In a different voice.* Cambridge, MA: Harvard University Press.

Gorski, P.C. & Pothini, S. (2018). *Case studies on diversity and social justice education.* New York, NY: Routledge.

Gray, D.L. & Smith, A.E. (2007). *Case studies in 21ˢᵗ century school administration: Addressing challenges for educational leadership.* Thousand Oaks, CA: Sage Publications.

Gross, S.J. (2014). Using turbulence theory to guide actions. In C.M. Branson & S.J. Gross (Eds), *Handbook of ethical leadership* (pp. 246–262). New York, NY: Routledge.

Gross, S.J. (2020). *Applying turbulence theory to educational leadership in challenging times: A case-based approach.* New York. NY: Routledge.

Gross, S.J. & Shapiro, J.P. (2004). Using multiple ethical paradigms and turbulence theory in response to administrative dilemmas. *International Studies in Educational Administration, 32*(2), 47–62.

Harris, J., Carrington, S. & Ainscow, M. (Eds.) (2018). *Promoting equity in schools: Collaboration, inquiry and ethical leadership.* London, England: Routledge.

Hozien, W. (2017). *Elementary principals in action: Resolving case studies in leadership.* Lanham, MD: Rowman & Littlefield.

Jenlink, P. (Ed.) (2014). *Educational leadership and moral literacy: The dispositional aims of moral leaders.* Lanham, MD: Rowman & Littlefield Education.

Johnson, C.E. (2020). *Meeting the ethical challenges of leadership: Casting light or shadow* (7th ed.). Thousand Oaks, CA: Sage Publications.

Kramer, B.H. & Enomoto, E.K. (2014). *Leading ethically in schools and other organizations: Inquiry, case studies, and decision making.* Lanham, MD: Rowman & Littlefield.

Kruse, S.D. & Gray, J.A. (2019). *A case study approach to educational leadership.* New York, NY: Routledge.

Levinson, M. & Fay, J. (Eds.) (2019). *Democratic discord in schools: Cases and commentaries in educational ethics.* Cambridge, MA: Harvard Education Press.

Lincoln, A. (1861, March 4). *First Inaugural Address.*

Meacham, J. (2018). *The soul of America: The battle for our better angels.* New York, NY: Random House.

Murphy, J.F. (2017). *Professional standards for educational leaders: The empirical, moral, and experiential foundations.* Thousand Oaks, CA: Corwin.

Nash, R.J. (1996). *"Real world" ethics: Frameworks for educators and human service professionals.* New York, NY: Teachers College Press.

Niesche, R. & Keddie, A. (2016). *Leadership, ethics, and schooling for social justice.* Abingdon, Oxon, England: Routledge.

Noddings, N. (2003). *Caring: A feminine approach to ethics and moral education* (2nd ed.). Berkeley, CA: University of California Press.

Noddings, N. (2012) The caring relation in teaching. *Oxford Review of Education, 38*(6), 771–781.

Noddings, N. (2013). *Caring: A relational approach to ethics and moral education* (2nd ed.). Oakland, CA: University of California Press.

Normore, A.H., & Brooks, J. S. (2017). *The dark side of leadership: Identifying and overcoming unethical practice in organizations.* Bingley, England: Emerald Group Publishing.

Northouse, P.G. & Lee, M. (2018). *Leadership case studies in education* (2nd ed.). Thousand Oaks, CA: Sage Publications.

Purpel, D.E. (2004). *Reflections on the moral and spiritual crisis in education.* New York, NY: Peter Lang.

Rebore, R. (2013). *The Ethics of educational leadership* (2nd ed.). Upper Saddle River, NJ: Prentice Hall.

Shapiro, J.P. & Gross, S.J. (2013). *Ethical educational leadership in turbulent times: (Re)solving moral dilemmas* (2nd ed.). New York, NY: Routledge.

Shapiro, J.P., Gross, S.J., & Shapiro, S.H. (2008, May). Ethical decisions in turbulent times. *The School Administrator,* 18–21.

Shapiro, J.P. & Stefkovich, J.A. (2011). *Ethical leadership and decision making in education* (3rd ed.). Mapogu, Seoul Korea: Hakjisa Publisher, Inc.

Starratt, R.J. (1994). *Building an ethical school: A practical response to the moral crisis in schools.* London, England: Falmer Press.

Starratt, R.J. (2003). *Centering educational administration: Cultivating meaning, community, responsibility.* Mahwah, NJ: Lawrence Erlbaum Associates.

Starratt, R.J. (2004). *Ethical leadership.* San Francisco, CA: Jossey-Bass.

Starratt, R.J. (2009). Ethical leadership. In B. Davies (Ed.), *The essentials of school leadership* (2nd ed.) (pp. 74–90). London, England: Sage.

Stefkovich, J.A. (2014). *Best interests of the student: Applying ethical constructs to legal cases in education* (2nd ed.). New York, NY: Routledge.

Stefkovich, J.A. & Frick, W.C. (2021). *Best interests of the student: Applying ethical constructs to legal cases* (3rd ed.). New York, NY: Routledge.

Strike, K.A. (2007). *Ethical leadership in schools: Creating community in an environment of accountability.* Thousand Oaks, CA: Corwin Press.

Strike, K.A. & Moss, P.A. (2007). *Ethics and college student life: A case study approach* (3rd ed.). Upper Saddle River, NJ: Prentice Hall.

Strike, K.A., Haller, E.J., & Soltis, J.F. (1988). *The ethics of school administration*. New York, NY: Teachers College Press.

Strike, K.A., Haller, E.J., & Soltis, J.F. (2005). *The ethics of school administration* (3rd ed.). New York, NY: Teachers College Press.

Strike, K.A. & Soltis, J.F. (2009). *The ethics of teaching* (4th ed.). New York, NY: Teachers College Press.

Strike, K. & Soltis, J.F. (2015). *The ethics of teaching* (5th ed.). New York, NY: Teachers College Press.

Wagner, P.A. & Simpson, D.J. (2008). *Ethical decision making in school administration: Leadership as moral architecture*. Thousand Oaks, CA: Sage.

Acknowledgments

We wish to extend our sincere thanks to Heather Jarrow, Publisher for Routledge's U.S. Education Book Program, who has guided and supported us so well through the various editions of this book. We also wish to thank Naomi Silverman, formerly from Routledge, for her helpful and insightful suggestions for our first edition. Additionally, we thank the following reviewers who provided worthwhile and useful feedback on our first through fourth editions: Patricia A.L. Ehrensal, Cabrini University; William P. Foster, University of Indiana; Brett Geier, Western Michigan University; William D. Greenfield, Portland State University; Anne Hornak, Central Michigan University; Larry W. Hughes, University of Houston; Marla Israel, Loyola University, Chicago; Sharon D. Kruse, University of Akron; Carl Lashley, University of North Carolina, Greensboro; Steve McCafferty, College of Mount Saint Joseph; Hayley Mayall, Northern Illinois University; Nel Noddings, Stanford University; Katarina Norberg, Umea University; Anthony Normore, California State University—Dominguez Hills; Shawn Powers, Plymouth State University; Ellen Reames, Auburn University; H. Svi Shapiro, University of North Carolina, Greensboro; Kimberly Williams, Plymouth University; and Ronald Williamson, Eastern Michigan University.

We appreciate the valuable input from the following: all our students and colleagues who have contributed dilemmas to this edition and former editions of the book; Judy Leonard, Staff Assistant at Penn State's Department of Educational Policy Studies, who provided detailed and meticulous assistance in the final editing and formatting stages of the second and third editions; Temple University's Educational Leadership & Policy Studies (ELPS) 1998 and 1999 doctoral cohorts, who piloted earlier drafts of our cases; Robert D. McCaig and Lynn Cheddar for their preliminary editing of the first edition; and chapter coordinators in the first edition; Patricia Ehrensal, Kathrine Gutierrez, James Krause, Hollie Mackey, Michaele (O'Brien) Ruzow, Leon Poeske, and Deborah Weaver, who contributed through their writing and spent endless hours coordinating the work of their co-contributors into a coherent chapter; and all our students who, throughout the years, have helped us not only to formulate our professional ethical paradigm but also to grow as professors.

PRACTICE AND PARADIGMS IN THE STUDY OF ETHICS

Part I sets the stage for exploring and solving the ethical dilemmas that make up a central portion (Part II) of this book. It serves as an introduction and consists of Chapters 1 and 2.

Chapter 1 offers a brief overview of the Multiple Ethical Paradigms. It also deals with their applicability and importance in view of the complexities and diversity of this current era. It incorporates the voices of our students, who support our assertion that the study of ethics is needed for all school leaders, particularly considering changes in society. This chapter explores implications for practice and for programs aimed at the preparation of educational leaders.

Chapter 2 describes the conceptual framework underlying our teaching and scholarship in ethical decision making. Here, we stress the importance of preparation for educational leaders in the ethics of justice, critique and care. To these we add a fourth ethic: that of the profession. It is in this chapter that we explain our framework for understanding and using ethics. The discussion of the four paradigms is meant to encourage the reader to deal with the ethical dilemmas, which follow in Part II, in a multi-dimensional way.

We believe it is important to try out diverse approaches for the solving of ethical cases even for those of us who usually respond to dilemmas as moral absolutists or as moral relativists or react to cases using only one or two ethical paradigms. Practice in working through a multiple ethical paradigm process should provide current and future educational leaders with options for dealing with complex and difficult ethical dilemmas that they will face daily.

DOI: 10.4324/9781003022862-1

Multiple Ethical Paradigms and the Preparation of Educational Leaders in a Diverse, Divided, and Complex Era

Foster (1986) expressed the seriousness and importance of ethics in educational leadership when he wrote: "Each administrative decision carries with it a restructuring of human life: that is why administration at its heart is the resolution of moral dilemmas" (p. 33). In a complex, unstable, and ethically polarized era, we think that there is a need to offer differing perspectives to help educational leaders solve authentic moral dilemmas that they frequently face in their schools and in their communities. To assist these educational leaders in making hard choices, in our ethics courses, we offer multiple ethical perspectives to solve and/or resolve moral dilemmas.

A graduate student, in one of our courses, added to Foster's above quotation that focused on administrative decisions. She stated that the material in an ethics course is important not only for educational administrators, but also for professionals and for citizens. Her comment follows:

> Of all the courses I have taken, at all levels, this course has no boundaries. What I mean is all the materials we have read, the discussions we have had and the lessons I have learned, directly impact all I will study and all I will do.... Ethics courses should not be only for students who are interested in going on to law school or medical school. [They] should be for students who are interested in becoming citizens.... If anyone ever challenges the relevance of a course such as this in an educational leadership curriculum, [he or she is] not an educated individual.

ETHICAL LEADERSHIP IN A COMPLEX AND DIVERSE SOCIETY

In the 21st century, as society becomes even more demographically different, educators will, more than ever, need to be able to develop, foster,

DOI: 10.4324/9781003022862-2

and lead tolerant and democratic schools. We believe that, through the study of ethics, educational leaders of tomorrow will be better prepared to recognize, reflect on, and appreciate diversity. This need for ethical preparation is perhaps best expressed by our own graduate students, many of who are practitioners in schools and in colleges and in universities.

Many of our students made direct connections between what was taught in our ethics class and the importance of difference. Here, we use a broad definition of diversity that encompasses the cultural categories of race/ethnicity, religion, social class, gender, disability, and sexual orientation as well as individual differences in learning styles, exceptionalities, and age (Banks, 2019; 2020; Banks & Banks, 2006; Cushner, McClelland, & Safford, 2011; Gay, 2010; Gollnick & Chinn, 2017; Grant & Portera, 2013; Nieto, 2018; Nieto & Bode, 2018; Shapiro, Sewell & DuCette, 2001; Sleeter & Grant, 2003; Sleeter & Zavala, 2020).

As one of our students, a White, male biology professor in a rural setting, pointed out:

> I believe that there is strength in diversity. Diverse biological ecosystems are more stable, might this also be true of social systems? How can we prevent institutions from co-opting women and other minorities and instead cherish the diversity they provide? As educators, we must strive to foster diversity as a source of variability enabling our society to adapt and contribute constructively in a rapidly changing world.

During our teaching of ethics, we also began to recognize that diversity occurred not only across a student population, but also within each group of students as well. For example, our classes contained a number of students of color; yet, in some instances, race seemed to be their only commonality. Although of the same race, some of these students were male and others were female. Some were in their twenties, whereas others were closer to 50. Some were African-American; others were from non-American countries. Some were from urban areas; others lived and worked in suburbia. Some came from poverty; others from affluence. Therefore, many of the perspectives that these particular students of color held were not race-bound, but were influenced just as much or more so by demographics, culture, age, gender or by a combination of these factors.

Illustrative of this concept is a comment from an African-American female who observed issues relative to age, race, and gender:

> It has been my experience that younger women in my classes think this feminist thing is blown out of proportion because they have not faced any of the glass ceilings society can impose. The historical perspective is essential in order that males and females have some basis for challenging themselves and their assumptions with respect to race and gender. Perhaps the

humanistic, caring leader is the answer, or at least the best possibility on the horizon. Politics and social reforms have not solved the problem, so educators—with the eventual help of parents—must.

Similarly, division across gender lines was not always the case. In all of our classes, there were often differences of opinion between women, with some taking a more traditional justice perspective and others favoring feminist approaches (e.g., Clement, 2018; Gilligan, 1982; Gilligan and Richards, 2009; Noddings, 2003, 2012, 2013; Vinney, 2020). In addition, there were always men who made sure the class understood that women did not corner the market on caring. A number of men and women alike asserted that caring was not gender-specific, especially in professions such as education. As one such student said: "We are all in the caring business, so how can we not consider what is best for all people concerned in these situations?"

Religion, too, in combination with other factors such as gender and age, influenced students' perceptions. Consider the comments of this White, male teacher in his thirties who expressed his reactions on reading Gilligan's (1982) abortion dilemmas. He wrote:

> I found myself considering the different feelings that women must go through in considering an issue such as abortion. Even though my own personal belief is one that centers around my religious upbringing, I felt myself struggling with the decisions that had to be made.

Thus, in considering themes of diversity, we found that no one characteristic of students (e.g., race, gender, age, religion, professional experience) resulted in a monolithic view of ethics. Rather, students' views of ethics emanated from a combination of different influences and cut across factors, such as race and gender. A Black, female international student in her late fifties summed up the importance of ethics in a diverse society when she presented this global, cross-cultural view:

> I think the effort of finding our voice(s) is going to continue for a long time, and it will also continue along lines of class, race, ethnicity, and other divisiveness; we will in no way speak with almost one voice until the pendulum swings again in the opposite direction. But with each shift, we pick up more and more contentious issues.

However, perhaps this urban-based, African-American male, best captured an issue related to our complex and diverse society when he made this profound observation:

> I work with a colleague who prides himself on being able to treat all of his students the same way. Regardless of race, economic status, or ability, he

claims to have the means to maintain a completely unbiased view on all. After working with him for six years, I have noticed that he does not have this ability. On a regular basis, I see him playing favorites, making exceptions, and generally doing the exact thing he claims he does not do. As an administrator, he cannot afford to be so rigid. There must be some room for partiality. And he shows it (though he would not admit to it) daily. It seems to me that this inability to be impartial grows out of his position and, in fact, would evolve from any position of administration when the interests of minorities and the oppressed have to be served. A 21st Century administrator must be ready to bend, adjust, and, when necessary, show partiality to those he/she serves if equity and justice are to be served.

The quotation above provides an illustration of one type of paradox that educators must grapple with in making ethical decisions in this era. In this case, justice versus equity is a paradox. This administrator wants to believe he acts with fairness and with no bias, even if he is dealing with a student in need. However, his colleague sees that the administrator does the opposite. Should this administrator continue to believe that he relies solely on the ethic of justice, focusing on impartiality and utilizing the same laws and rules for all students despite their circumstances? Or should this educator be encouraged to understand that there is nothing wrong with dealing with an ethic other than that of justice? Will he ever understand that despite his assumed reliance on the ethic of justice, he is often turning to the ethic of care in the cases of students who need this kind of special help and attention?

This is only one illustration of a paradox that educators grapple with in making ethical decisions. To assist in the analysis and resolution of such dilemmas, we advocate combining various approaches to ethics by using Multiple Ethical Paradigms. The approach offers educators choices and enables them to be flexible and deal wisely with a myriad of educational ethical problems.

THE IMPORTANCE OF THE MULTIPLE ETHICAL PARADIGMS

Throughout this book, the reader is asked to consider current and challenging real-life ethical dilemmas using four paradigms. The four paradigms include the ethics of justice, critique, care, and the profession. Justice, critique, and care are familiar to many in the field of educational leadership. All too often, however, professional ethics is seen as an extension of another paradigm and not thought to stand alone. That is why, in this book, we spend considerable time on the ethic of the profession rather than on the other three forms of ethics. We are convinced that this paradigm deserves to be treated as an independent entity. We think that it is extremely important and complements the other paradigms.

We believe that it makes sense, when dealing with the ethic of the profession, for graduate students and practitioners to take the time to locate the formal codes of the profession and the standards of the field (Bass, Frick & Young, 2018; Murphy, 2017). Along with these activities, we strongly recommend that everyone writes out personal and professional ethical codes and compares and contrasts their two codes. In this way, educators can determine where consistencies exist between the codes and where clashes of codes might appear. These exercises lead to a much better understanding of "self" both as a professional and as a person. The four perspectives or paradigms should help educational leaders solve the real-life, complex dilemmas that they frequently face in their institutions and in their communities.

By using the different paradigms, educators should become aware of the perspective or perspectives that they tend to use most often when solving ethical issues. For example, if an individual has a strong religious upbringing, then, depending on the religious persuasion, the ethic of justice with an emphasis on rights and laws may be the favored approach, or perhaps the ethic of care with its emphasis on compassion and empathy may be the paradigm of choice. In addition, as just mentioned, factors such as age, gender, race, or more likely a confluence of factors may influence the paradigm one prefers.

However, despite any inclinations toward one perspective, the intent of this book is to ask students and practitioners to open their minds by combining a variety of approaches, not simply one or two. Dilemmas in educational institutions can be complicated and may lead naturally to the use of two or more paradigms to solve problems. Today, with the complexity of situations and cultures, it seems more important than ever for educational leaders to think more broadly and go beyond "self" in an attempt to understand others.

In Chapter 12, we discuss our own experiences of self-reflection to provide some concrete examples of this process. Learning to be self-reflective is not easy. It requires a concentrated effort on the part of individuals. This can be accomplished privately. It can also be encouraged in a staff development program or as part of an educational leadership preparation program. Along with self-reflection, we also discuss briefly the ways we deliver the content and the global implications of this kind of work.

THE PREPARATION OF ETHICAL EDUCATIONAL LEADERS

In many ways, the teaching of ethics diverges from the traditional paths employed by many educational leadership programs. Although we do not necessarily advocate that standard courses be changed, we do believe that the teaching of ethics can be a welcome and important addition to those programs. As one of our students wrote in her class journal:

> This course has been very enlightening. It has been a thought-provoking break from the practical mundane courses of educational administration.... My vision has increased and multiplied. Even though I still view the world with racial vision, I am now more in tune with my feminist "ear." I will investigate, read, and learn more and react more critically to my environment.

Others, through our classes, began to recognize the importance of ethics and its contribution to our larger society. This student, in particular, seemed to show a grasp of this bigger picture as it related to the issue of social justice:

> Social justice or equity really seems very obvious as a concept, but it apparently is necessary to make this topic a large part of the doctoral program because it is brought up so often in the readings and discussion. The result is that I am keenly aware of equity as an issue now, and I doubt that I will look at such issues the same as before I started the doctoral program. It is hard to know exactly what my thoughts were about equity before I started the program. I really can't say because the awareness has come so gradually.

Clearly, the majority of students in our courses wanted ethics taught as part of the educational leadership curriculum. In fact, there was no ambivalence in their wish that it be continued and even expanded as a disciplinary area in their program. This student's thoughts illustrate the types of comments that we have heard through the years:

> I feel it imperative for the administrator to be cognizant of . . . the need for institutions of higher learning to maintain a careful balance between those courses that are offered for some instrumental end and those which are offered merely for the sake of obtaining knowledge. I perceive that there is a greater societal pressure on the university for more of the former and less of the latter. We seem to place a much greater focus on acquiring knowledge for the sake of gaining employment than for the sheer joy of knowing. [Yet,] there is a special feeling, indescribable though it may be, in learning something that is new, different, and stimulating.

IN SUMMARY

In this book, we propose that there should not be one best ethical paradigm. Instead, we believe that by using different approaches, students and practitioners will be able to work through their own personal and professional ethical codes, try out what they discovered about themselves by reflecting on the solutions they reach as they analyze diverse ethical dilemmas, and gain greater insights into the conceptual underpinnings of the ethical paradigm or paradigms they have chosen.

While analyzing the dilemmas in Chapters 3 through 11, educational graduate students and practitioners should consciously reflect on the processes used to find solutions to cases. Along with the analysis related to a case, each individual should be able to do a great deal of reflection and soul-searching about his or her private code and professional code, and should be open-minded enough to revise either of them as self-awareness and growth occur.

It is our hope that this book will empower educational leaders, including, but not limited to, principals, superintendents, curriculum coordinators, school counselors, personnel administrators, business administrators, higher education administrators, early childhood directors, faculty, and teacher leaders to make wise ethical decisions in a complex, chaotic, and contradictory era.

REFERENCES

Banks, J.A. (2019). *An introduction to multicultural education* (6th ed.). New York, NY: Pearson.

Banks, J.A (2020). *Diversity, transformative knowledge, and civic education: Selected essays.* New York, NY: Routledge.

Banks, J.A. & Banks, C.A.M. (2006). *Multicultural education: Issues and perspectives* (6th ed.). San Francisco, CA: Jossey-Bass.

Bass, L., Frick, W.C., & Young, M.D. (Eds.) (2018). *Developing ethical principles for school leadership: PSEL standard two.* New York, NY: Routledge.

Clement, G. (2018). *Care, autonomy, and justice: Feminism and the ethic of care.* New York, NY: Routledge.

Cushner, K., McClelland, A., & Safford, P. (2011). *Human diversity in education: An integrative approach* (7th ed.). New York, NY: McGraw-Hill.

Foster, W. (1986). *Paradigms and promises: New approaches to educational administration.* Buffalo, NY: Prometheus Books.

Gay, G. (2010). *Culturally responsive teaching: Theory, research, and practice* (2nd ed.). New York, NY: Teachers College Press.

Gilligan, C. (1982). *In a different voice.* Cambridge, MA: Harvard University Press.

Gilligan, C. & Richards, D.A.J. (2009). *The deepening darkness: Patriarchy, resistance, and democracy's future.* New York, NY: Cambridge University Press.

Gollnick, D.M. & Chinn, P.C. (2017). *Multicultural education in a pluralistic society* (10th ed.). New York, NY: Pearson.

Grant, C.A. & Portera, A. (2013). *Intercultural and multicultural education: Enhancing global interconnectedness.* New York, NY: Routledge.

Murphy, J.F. (2017). *Professional standards for educational leaders: The empirical, moral, and experiential foundations.* Thousand Oaks, CA: Corwin.

Nieto, S. (2018). *Language, culture, and teaching: Critical perspectives for a new century* (3rd ed.). New York, NY: Routledge.

Nieto, S. & Bode, P. (2018). *Affirming diversity: The sociopolitical context of multicultural education (7th ed.). Boston, MA: Pearson.*

Noddings, N. (2003). *Caring: A feminine approach to ethics and moral education* (2nd ed.). Berkeley, CA: University of California Press.

Noddings, N. (2012) The caring relation in teaching. *Oxford Review of Education, 38*(6), 771–781.

Noddings, N. (2013). *Caring: A relational approach to ethics and moral education* (2nd ed.). Oakland, CA: University of California Press.

Shapiro, J.P. Sewell, T.E., & DuCette, J.P. (2001). *Reframing diversity in education.* Lanham, MD: Rowman & Littlefield.

Sleeter, C.E. & Grant, C.A. (2003). *Making choices for multicultural education: Five approaches to race, class, and gender* (4th ed.). New York, NY: Wiley.

Sleeter, C.E. & Zavala, M. (2020). *Transformative ethic studies in schools: Curriculum, pedagogy and research.* New York, NY: Teachers College Press.

Vinney, C. (2020, February 11). *Gilligan's ethics of care.* Retrieved from www.thoughtco.com/ethics-of-care-4691476

Chapter 2

Viewing Ethical Dilemmas through Multiple Paradigms

According to John Dewey (1902), ethics is the science that deals with conduct insofar as this is considered to be right or wrong, good or bad. Ethics comes from the Greek word *ethos*, which means customs or usages, especially belonging to one group as distinguished from another. Later, ethics came to mean disposition or character, customs, and approved ways of acting. Looking at this definition from a critical perspective, one might ask: Ethics approved by whom? Right or wrong according to whom?

In this chapter, in an attempt to answer these and other important questions, we turn to three kinds of ethics that have long and diverse traditions. They are the ethics of justice, critique, and care. We would like you to keep in mind that these are broad descriptions. Our intent for these three kinds of ethics is to provide enough of an introduction to these paradigms to enable you to receive a general sense of each of them. In an effort to be brief, we have had to leave out some outstanding scholars whose works are related to each of the paradigms. For in-depth coverage of scholars and their work regarding the ethics of justice, critique, and care, we suggest that you read beyond these introductory remarks, turn to our references in this book, and locate other writings related to these ethics.

To our multiple ethical paradigms, we have added a fourth, the ethic of the profession. Unlike the other three paradigms, we give special attention to the latter. We do this because we believe there has been a gap in the educational leadership literature in using the paradigm of professional ethics to help solve moral dilemmas. All too frequently, the ethic of the profession is seen as simply a part of the justice paradigm. We do not believe this is so. We want to make the argument that this form of ethics can be used separately to reflect upon and deal with dilemmas faced by educational leaders. Therefore, what we present in this chapter is a more

DOI: 10.4324/9781003022862-3

involved discussion of the ethic of the profession than of the other three paradigms.

THE ETHIC OF JUSTICE

The ethic of justice focuses on rights and law and is part of a liberal democratic tradition that, according to Delgado (1995), "is characterized by incrementalism, faith in the legal system, and hope for progress" (p. 1). The liberal part of this tradition is defined as a "commitment to human freedom," and the democratic aspect implies "procedures for making decisions that respect the equal sovereignty of the people" (Strike, 1991, p. 415).

Starratt (1994a) described the ethic of justice as emanating from two schools of thought, one originating in the 17th century, including the work of Hobbes and Kant and more contemporary scholars such as Rawls and Kohlberg; the other rooted in the works of philosophers such as Aristotle, Rousseau, Hegel, Marx, and Dewey. The former school considers the individual as central and sees social relationships as a type of a social contract where the individual, using human reason, gives up some rights for the good of the whole or for social justice. The latter tends to see society, rather than the individual, as central and seeks to teach individuals how to behave throughout their lives within communities. In this tradition, justice emerges from "communal understandings" (p. 50).

Philosophers and writers coming from a justice perspective frequently deal with issues such as the nature of the universe, the nature of God, fate versus free will, good and evil, and the relationship between human beings and their state. Beauchamp and Childress (1984) and Crittenden (1984) describe competitive concepts related to the ethic of justice. Although acknowledging other perspectives and their positive aspects in their writings, Beauchamp and Childress, and Crittenden return to the ethic of justice and argue that educational leaders in societies whose governments are committed to certain fundamental principles, such as tolerance and respect for the fair treatment of all individuals, can and should look to laws and public policies for ethical guidance (Beck & Murphy, 1994b, p. 7).

Educators and ethicists from the ethic of justice have had a profound impact on approaches to education and educational leadership. Contemporary ethical writings in education, using the foundational principle of the ethic of justice, include, among others, works by Beauchamp and Childress (1984); Goodlad, Soder & McDaniel (2008); Gurley & Dagley (2020); Hester & Killian (2010); Kohlberg (1981); Sergiovanni (1992); Strike (2007); and Strike, Haller, & Soltis (2005).

Kohlberg (1981) argued that, within the liberal tradition, "there is a great concern not only to make schools more just—that is, to provide equality of educational opportunity and to allow freedom of belief—but also to educate so that free and just people emerge from schools" (p. 74). For Kohlberg, "justice is not a rule or set of rules, it is a moral principle . . . a mode of choosing that is universal, a rule of choosing that we want all people to adopt always in all situations" (p. 39). From this perspective, education is not "value-free." This model also indicates that schools should teach principles, especially those of justice, equality, and respect for liberty.

From the late 1960s through the early 1980s, Kohlberg introduced his "just community" approach to the schools. In institutions as diverse as Roosevelt High, a comprehensive school in Manhattan, The Bronx High School of Science, and an alternative high school in Cambridge, Massachusetts, students and teachers handled school discipline and sometimes even the running of the school together. In a civil and thoughtful manner, students were taught to deal with problems within the school, turning to rules, rights, and laws for guidance (Hersh, Paolitto, & Reimer, 1979).

Building on Kohlberg's "just community," Sergiovanni (1992) called for moral leadership and, in particular, the principle of justice in the establishment of "virtuous schools." Sergiovanni viewed educational leadership as a stewardship and asked educational administrators to create institutions that are just and beneficent. By beneficence, Sergiovanni meant that there should be deep concern for the welfare of the school as a community, a concept that extends beyond the school walls and into the local community, considering not only students, teachers, and administrators, but also families.

Unlike many educators in the field, Sergiovanni (1992) placed the principle of justice at the center of his concept of school: "Accepting this principle meant that every parent, teacher, student, administrator, and other member of the school community must be treated with the same equality, dignity, and fair play" (pp. 105–106).

The ethic of justice, from either a traditional or contemporary perspective, may consider a wide variety of issues. Viewing ethical dilemmas from this vantage point, one might ask questions related to the rule of law and the more abstract concepts of fairness, equality, and justice. These may include, but are certainly not limited to, questions related to issues of equity and equality; the fairness of rules, laws, and policies; the absolutism versus the exceptions of laws; and the rights of individuals versus the greater good of the community.

Moreover, the ethic of justice frequently serves as a foundation for legal principles and ideals. This important function is evident in laws related to education. In many instances, courts have been reluctant to impose restrictions on school officials, thus allowing them considerable discretion in making important administrative decisions (*Board of Education v. Pico*, 1981). At the same time, court opinions often reflect the values of the education community and society at large (Stefkovich & Guba, 1998). For example, it was not until the early 1990s that courts upheld the use of metal detectors in schools to screen for weapons (*People v. Dukes*, 1992). In addition, what is legal in some places may be considered illegal in others. For instance, corporal punishment is still legal in 19 states (The Center for Effective Discipline, 2020) and strip searching is legal in all but seven (Stefkovich, Brady, Ballard & Rossow, 2021). In those states, it is left up to school officials, and the community, whether such practices are to be supported or not. Here, ethical issues such as due process and privacy rights are often balanced against the need for civility and the good of the majority.

Finally, what is to be done when a law is wrong, such as earlier Jim Crow laws supporting racial segregation (Starratt, 1994c; Stefkovich, 2014)? Under these circumstances, one must turn to ethics to make fair and just decisions. It is also in such instances that the ethic of justice may overlap with other paradigms such as the ethics of critique (Gurley & Dagley, 2020; Purpel, 2004) and care (Gilligan, 1982; Noddings, 2013). Overall, the ethic of justice considers questions such as: Is there a law, right, or policy that relates to a particular case? If there is a law, right, or policy, should it be enforced? And if there is not a law, right, or policy, should there be one?

THE ETHIC OF CRITIQUE

Many writers and activists (e.g., Apple, 2010, 2011, 2013; Capper, 1993, 2019; Foucault, 1983; Freire, 1998; Giroux, 1994, 2000, 2003, 2020; McLaren, 2020; Price, 2020; Shapiro, 2009; Shapiro & Purpel, 2005) are not convinced by the analytic and rational approach of the justice paradigm. Some of these scholars find a tension between the ethic of justice, rights, and laws and the concept of democracy. In response, they raise difficult questions by critiquing both the laws themselves and the process used to determine if the laws are just.

Rather than accepting the ethic of those in power, these scholars challenge the status quo by seeking an ethic that will deal with inconsistencies, formulate the hard questions, and debate and challenge the issues. Their intent is to awaken us to our own unstated values and make us realize how frequently our own morals may have been modified and possibly even corrupted over time. Not only do they force us to rethink important concepts such as democracy, but they also ask us to redefine and reframe other concepts such as privilege, power, culture, language, and even justice.

The ethic of critique is based on critical theory, which has, at its heart, an analysis of social class and its inequities. According to Foster (1986): "Critical theorists are scholars who have approached social analysis in an investigative and critical manner and who have conducted investigations of social structure from perspectives originating in a modified Marxian analysis" (p. 71). More recently, critical theorists have turned to the intersection of race and gender as well as social class in their analyses.

An example of the work of critical theorists may be found in their arguments, occurring over many decades, that schools reproduce inequities similar to those in society (Bourdieu, 2001; Lareau, 1987, 2011). Tracking, for example, may be seen as one way to make certain that working-class children know their place (Oakes, 1993, 2005). Generally designed so that students are exposed to different knowledge in each track, schools "[make] decisions about the appropriateness of various topics and skills and, in doing so . . . [limit] . . . sharply what some students would learn" (1993, p. 87). Recognizing this inequity, Carnoy and Levin (1985) pointed to an important contradiction in educational institutions, in that schools also represent the major force in the United States for expanding economic opportunity as well as the extension of democratic rights. Herein lies one of many inconsistencies to be addressed through the ethic of critique.

Along with critical theory, the ethic of critique is also frequently linked to critical pedagogy (Freire, 1998). Giroux (1991) asked educators to understand that their classrooms are political as well as educational locations and, as such, ethics is not a matter of individual choice or relativism but a "social discourse grounded in struggles that refuse to accept needless human suffering and exploitation" (p. 48). In this respect, the ethic of critique provides "a discourse for expanding basic human rights" (p. 48) and may serve as a vehicle in the struggle against inequality. In this vein, critical theorists are often concerned with making known the voices of those who are silenced, particularly students (Giroux, 2003; Weis & Fine, 1993).

For Giroux (2000, 2003, 2006, 2012, 2013, 2020) and other critical educators, the language of critique is central, but discourse alone will not suffice. These scholars are also activists who believe discourse should be a beginning leading to action—preferably political. For example, Shapiro and Purpel (1993, 2005) emphasized empowering people through the discussion of options. Such a dialogue would hopefully provide what Giroux and Aronowitz (1985) called a "language of possibility" that, when applied to educational institutions, might enable them to avoid reproducing the "isms" in society (i.e., classism, racism, sexism, heterosexism).

Turning to educational leadership in particular, Parker and Shapiro (1993) argued that one way to rectify some wrongs in school and in society would be to give more attention to the analysis of social class in the preparation of principals and superintendents. They believed that social class analysis "is crucial given the growing divisions of wealth and power in the United States, and their impact on inequitable distribution of resources both within and among school districts" (pp. 39–40). Through the critical analysis of social class, there is the possibility that more knowledgeable, moral, and sensitive educational leaders might be prepared.

Capper (1993), in her writings on educational leadership, stressed the need for moral leaders to be concerned with "freedom, equality, and the principles of a democratic society" (p. 14). She provided a useful summary of the roots of, and philosophy supporting, the ethic of critique as it pertains to educational leaders. She spoke of the Frankfurt school in the United States in the 1920s, in which immigrants tried to make sense of the oppression they had endured in Europe. This school provided not only a Marxist critique but also considered psychology and its effect on the individual. Capper (1993, p. 15) wrote:

> Grounded in the work of the Frankfurt school, critical theorists in educational administration are ultimately concerned with suffering and oppression, and critically reflect on current and historical social inequities. They believe in the imperative of leadership and authority and work toward the empowerment and transformation of followers, while grounding decisions in morals and values.

Thus, by demystifying and questioning what is happening in society and in schools, critical theorists may help educators rectify wrongs while identifying key morals and values.

In summary, the ethic of critique, inherent in critical theory, is aimed at awakening educators to inequities in society and, in particular, in schools. This ethic asks educators to deal with the hard questions regarding social class, race, gender, and other areas of difference, such as: Who makes the laws? Who benefits from the law, rule, or policy? Who has the power? Who are the silenced voices? This approach to ethical dilemmas then asks educators to go beyond questioning and critical analysis to examine and grapple with those possibilities that could enable all children, whatever their social class, race, or gender, to have opportunities to grow, learn, and achieve. Such a process should lead to the development of options related to important concepts such as oppression, power, privilege, authority, voice, language, and empowerment.

THE ETHIC OF CARE

Juxtaposing an ethic of care with an ethic of justice, Roland Martin (1993, p. 144) wrote the following:

> One of the most important findings of contemporary scholarship is that our culture embraces a hierarchy of value that places the productive processes of society and their associated traits above society's reproductive processes and the associated traits of care and nurturance. There is nothing new about this. We are the inheritors of a tradition of Western thought according to which the functions, tasks, and traits associated with females are deemed less valuable than those associated with males.

Some feminist scholars (e.g., Bass, 2020; Beck, 1994; Belenky, Clinchy, Goldberger, & Tarule, 1986; Gilligan, 1982; Gilligan & Richards, 2009; Ginsberg, Shapiro, & Brown, 2004; Goldberger, Tarule, Clinchy, & Belenky, 1996; Grogan & Shakeshaft, 2011; Larson & Murtadha, 2002; Marshall & Gerstl-Pepin, 2005; Marshall & Oliva, 2009; Marshall & Young, 2013; Noddings, 1992, 2003, 2013; Noddings, Stengel, & Alan, 2006; Shapiro, Ginsberg, & Brown, 2003; Vinney, 2020) have challenged this dominant, and what they consider to be often patriarchal, ethic of justice in our society by turning to the ethic of care for moral decision making. Attention to this ethic can lead to other discussions of concepts such as loyalty, trust, and empowerment. Like critical theorists, these feminist scholars emphasize social responsibility, frequently discussed in the light of injustice, as a pivotal concept related to the ethic of care.

In her classic book *In a Different Voice*, Gilligan (1982) introduced the ethic of care by discussing a definition of justice different from Kohlberg's in the resolution of moral dilemmas (see the ethic of justice section in this chapter). In her research, Gilligan discovered that, unlike the males in Kohlberg's studies who adopted rights and laws for the resolution of moral issues, women and girls frequently turned to another voice, that of care, concern, and connection, in finding answers to their moral dilemmas. Growing out of the ethic of justice, the ethic of care, as it relates to education, has been described well by Noddings (1992), who created a new educational hierarchy placing "care" at the top when she wrote: "The first job of the schools is to care for our children" (p. xiv). To Noddings, and to many other ethicists and educators who advocate the use of the ethic of care, students are at the center of the educational process and need to be nurtured and encouraged, a concept that likely goes against the grain of those attempting to make "achievement" the top priority. Noddings believes that holding on to a competitive edge in achievement means that some children may see themselves merely as pawns in a nation of demanding and uncaring adults. In school buildings that more often resemble large, bureaucratic, physical plants, a major complaint of young people regarding adults is: "They don't care!" (Comer, 1988). For Noddings, "Caring is the very bedrock of all successful education and . . . contemporary schooling can be revitalized in its light" (1992, p. 27).

Noddings and Gilligan are not alone in believing that the ethic of care is essential in education. In relation to the curriculum, Roland Martin (1993) wrote of the three Cs of caring, concern, and connection. Although she did not ask educators to teach "Compassion 101a" or to offer "Objectivity 101a," she did implore them to broaden the curriculum to include the experiences of both sexes, not just one, and to stop leaving out the ethic of care. For Roland Martin, education is an "integration of reason and emotion, self and other" (p. 144).

Although the ethic of care has been associated with feminists, men and women alike attest to its importance and relevancy (Smylie, Murphy & Louis, 2016). Beck (1994) pointed out that "caring—as a foundational ethic—addresses concerns and needs as expressed by many persons; that it, in a sense, transcends ideological boundaries" (p. 3). Male ethicists and educators, such as Buber (1965), Normore (2008), Normore & Lahera, 2017, and Sergiovanni (1992), have expressed high regard for this paradigm. These scholars have sought to make education a "human enterprise" (Starratt, 1991, p. 195).

Some scholars have associated the ethic of care with the philosophy of utilitarianism. For example, Blackburn (2006) believes that Bentham, Mills, and Hume spoke of the ethic of care as part of the public sphere. The concept of the greatest happiness of the greatest number, according to Blackburn (2001, p. 93), moved care into the civic realm. He wrote:

> An ethic of care and benevolence, which is essentially what utilitarianism is, gives less scope to a kind of moral philosophy modeled on law, with its hidden and complex structures and formulae known only to the initiates.

The ethic of care is important not only to scholars but also to educational leaders who are often asked to make moral decisions. If the ethic of care is used to resolve dilemmas, then there is a need to revise how educational leaders are prepared. In the past, educational leaders were trained using military and business models. This meant that they were taught about the importance of the hierarchy and the need to follow those at the top, and, at the same time, to be in command and in charge of subordinates (Guthrie, 1990). They led by developing "rules, policies, standard operating procedures, information systems . . . or a variety of more informal techniques" (Bolman & Deal, 1991, p. 48). These techniques and rules may have worked well when the ethic of justice, rights, and laws was the primary basis for leaders making moral decisions; however, they are inadequate when considering other ethical paradigms, such as the ethic of care, that require leaders to consider multiple voices in the decision-making process.

Beck (1994) stressed that it is essential for educational leaders to move away from a top-down, hierarchical model for making moral and other decisions and, instead, to turn to a leadership style that emphasizes relationships and connections. Administrators need to "encourage collaborative efforts between faculty, staff, and students [which would serve] . . . to promote interpersonal interactions, to deemphasize competition, to facilitate a sense of belonging, and to increase individuals' skills as they learn from one another" (p. 85).

When an ethic of care is valued, educational leaders can become what Barth (1990) called, "head learner(s)" (p. 513). What Barth meant by that term was the making of outstanding leaders and learners who wish to listen to others when facing the need to make important moral decisions. The preparation of these individuals, then, must more heavily focus on the knowledge of cultures and of diversity, with a special emphasis on learning how to listen, observe, and respond to others. For example, Shapiro, Sewell, DuCette, and Myrick (1997), in their study of inner-city youth, identified three different kinds of caring: attention and support; discipline; and "staying on them," or prodding them over time. Although prodding students to complete homework might be viewed as nagging, the students these researchers studied saw prodding as an indication that someone cared about them.

Thus, the ethic of care offers another perspective and other ways to respond to complex moral problems facing educational leaders in their daily work. One aspect of its intricacy is that this lens tends to sometimes deal with emotions. Highlighting this complexity, Paul Begley, an educational ethicist, raised the question: Is the ethic of care an emotional or rational model? Thinking through this important question, it became clear that aspects of this ethic could be considered rational, such as providing discipline and attention to students; however, empathy and compassion toward others are also part of this paradigm and tend to demonstrate emotions. Hence, portions of this model coincide well with the emerging brain research regarding decision making, in general, in which emotions and reason are blended in intricate ways (Lehrer, 2009).

Viewing ethical dilemmas through the ethic of care may prompt questions related to how educators may assist young people in meeting their needs and desires and will reflect solutions that show a concern for others as part of decision making. This ethic asks that individuals consider the consequences of their decisions and actions. It asks them to consider questions such as: Who will benefit from what I decide? Who will be hurt by my actions? What are the long-term effects of a decision I make today? And if I am helped by someone now, what should I do in the future about giving back to this individual or to society in general? This paradigm also asks individuals to grapple with values such as loyalty and trust.

THE ETHIC OF THE PROFESSION

Starratt (1994a) postulated that the ethics of justice, care, and critique are not incompatible, but rather, complementary, the combination of which results in a richer, more complete, ethic. He visualized these ethics as themes, interwoven much like a tapestry:

> An ethical consciousness that is not interpenetrated by each theme can be captured either by sentimentality, by rationalistic simplification, or by social naivete. The blending of each theme encourages a rich human response to the many uncertain ethical situations the school community faces every day, both in the learning tasks as well as in its attempt to govern itself. (p. 57)

We agree with Starratt; but we have also come to believe that, even taken together, the ethics of justice, critique, and care do not provide an adequate picture of the factors that must be taken into consideration as leaders strive to make ethical decisions within the context of educational settings. What is missing—that is, what these paradigms tend to ignore—is a consideration of those moral aspects unique to the profession and the questions that arise as educational leaders become more aware of their own personal and professional codes of ethics. To fill this gap, we add a fourth to the three ethical frameworks described in this chapter: a paradigm of professional ethics.

Although the idea of professional ethics has been with us for some time, identifying the process as we have and presenting it in the form of a paradigm represents an innovative way of conceptualizing this ethic. Because this approach is relatively new—one that we have developed through more than two decades of collaborative research, writing, and teaching ethics—we devote more time to explaining this ethic than was given to others. The remainder of this chapter includes some brief background information on the emergence of professional ethics and the need for a professional ethics paradigm. Following these introductory remarks, we describe our model of professional ethics and how it works. This chapter concludes with a discussion of how the paradigm of professional ethics fits in with the other three ethics of justice, critique, and care.

PROFESSIONAL ETHICS AND THE NEED FOR A PROFESSIONAL PARADIGM

When discussing ethics in relation to the professionalization of educational leaders, the tendency is to look toward professions such as law, medicine, dentistry, and business, which require their graduate students to take at least one ethics course before graduation as a way of socializing them into the profession. The field of educational administration has no such ethics course requirement.

However, since the mid-1990s, there has been an interest in ethics in relation to educational decision making. Several writers in educational administration (Beck, 1994; Beck & Murphy, 1994a, 1994b; Beckner, 2004; Begley & Johansson, 2003; Greenfield, 2004; Lashley, 2007; Murphy, 2006; Normore & Brooks, 2017; Pazey & Cole 2015; Starratt, 1994b) believe it is important to provide prospective administrators with some training in ethics. As Greenfield (1993) pointed out, this preparation could "enable a prospective principal or superintendent to develop the attitudes, beliefs, knowledge, and skills associated with competence in moral reasoning" (p. 285). Stressing the importance of such preparation, Greenfield left us with a warning of sorts:

> A failure to provide the opportunity for school administrators to develop such competence constitutes a failure to serve the children we are obligated to serve as public educators. As a profession, educational administration thus has a moral obligation to train prospective administrators to be able to apply the principles, rules, ideals, and virtues associated with the development of ethical schools. (p. 285)

Recognizing this need, ethics was identified as one of the competencies necessary for school leaders in the document, *Interstate School Leaders Licensure Consortium: Standards for School Leavers* (NPBEA, 1996). This document, developed by the consortium, under the auspices of the Council of Chief State School Officers (CCSSO) and in collaboration with the National Policy Board for Educational Administration (NPBEA), was produced by representatives from 24 states and nine associations related to the educational administration profession. This original document was followed by a revised one (NPBEA, 2008). School leaders again set forth six standards for the profession. Of these, Standard 5 remained: "An education leader promotes the success of every student by acting with integrity, fairness, and in an ethical manner." It was slightly modified from its 1996 document.

More recently, the Professional Standards for Educational Leaders have been adopted. These standards were developed by a working group of educators from schools, universities and organizations related to educational administration. The standards reflect an emphasis on student learning. They also try to prepare educational leaders for the future. They are aspirational and yet realistic.

In these standards, ethics is in a prominent position. It is now listed as Standard 2. This standard is called Ethics and Professional Norms and it states: "Effective educational leaders act ethically and according to professional norms to promote *each* student's academic success and well-being" (NPBEA, 2015, p.10).

Standard 2 continues,

Effective leaders:

  a. Act ethically and professionally in personal conduct, relationships with others, decision-making, stewardship of the school's resources, and all aspects of school leadership.
  b. Act according to and promote the professional norms of integrity, fairness, transparency, trust, collaboration, perseverance, learning, and continuous improvement.
  c. Place children at the center of education and accept responsibility for each student's academic success and well-being.
  d. Safeguard and promote the values of democracy, individual freedom and responsibility, equity, social justice, community, and diversity.
  e. Lead with interpersonal and communication skill, social-emotional insight, and understanding of all students' and staff members' backgrounds and cultures.
  f. Provide moral direction for the school and promote ethical and professional behavior among faculty and staff. (NPBEA, 2015, p. 10)

In this latest version, not only is ethics a stand-alone standard, but it is also infused in other standards. In those infused standards, however, ethics is sometimes explicitly stated while at other times it is more implicit. For example, in Standard 1, core values are explicitly emphasized. While in Standard 3, the ethic of care is implicit as it focuses on equity and cultural responsiveness. Standard 5 also threads in an ethic of care while emphasizing community and the support of students. Standards 6 and 7 turn to the ethic of the profession while supporting school personnel and community.

In the past, professional ethics has generally been viewed as a subset of the justice paradigm. This is likely the case because professional ethics is often equated with codes, rules, and principles, all of which fit neatly into traditional concepts of justice (Beauchamp & Childress, 1984). For example, many states established their own sets of standards. The Pennsylvania Code of Professional Practice and Conduct for Educators (1992) is an 11-point code of conduct that was subsequently enacted into state law. Texas has a similar code of ethics, standards, and practices (Texas Administrative Code, 1998) for its educators that, among other things, expects them to deal justly with students and protect them from "disparagement."

In addition, several education-related professional organizations have developed their own professional ethical codes. Defined by Beauchamp and Childress (1984) as "an articulated statement of role morality as seen by members of the profession" (p. 41), some of these ethical codes are relatively new and others are long-standing. Examples of these organizations include, but are certainly not limited to, the American Association of School Administrators, the American Association of University Professors, the American Psychological Association, the Association of School Business Officials, the Association for Supervision and Curriculum Development, and the National Education Association.

On the one hand, ethical codes set forth by the states and professional associations tend to be limited in their responsiveness in that they are somewhat removed from the day-to-day personal and professional dilemmas that educational leaders face. Nash (1996), in his book on professional ethics for educators and human service professionals, recognized these limitations as he observed his students' lack of interest in such codes:

> What are we to make of this almost universal disparagement of professional codes of ethics? What does the nearly total disregard of professional codes mean? For years, I thought it was something in my delivery that evoked such strong, antagonistic responses. For example, whenever I ask students to bring their codes to class, few knew where to locate them, and most get utterly surly when I make such a request. I understand, now, however, that they do not want to be bothered with what they consider a trivial, irrelevant assignment, because they simply do not see a correlation between learning how to make ethical decisions and appealing to a code of ethics. (p. 95)

On the other hand, professional codes of ethics serve as guideposts for the profession, giving statements about its image and character (Lebacqz, 1985). They embody "the highest moral ideals of the profession," thus "presenting an ideal image of the moral character of both the profession and the professional" (Nash, 1996, p. 96). Seen in this light, standardized codes provide a most valuable function. Thus, the problem lies not so much in the codes themselves, but in the fact that we sometimes expect too much from them regarding moral decision making (Lebacqz, 1985; Nash, 1996, 2002).

The University Council for Educational Administration (UCEA) recognized the need for a code that was developed in a participatory fashion and was not meant to be static (Code of Ethics for the Preparation of Educational Leaders, 2011). Over a six-year period, UCEA created a code utilizing the internet and continual committee meetings for input. The code provides a set of principles that is meant to be inclusive and on-going.

Recognizing the importance of standardized codes, the contributions they make, and their limitations, we believe the time has come to view professional ethics from a broader, more inclusive, and more contemporary perspective (Galloway & Ishimaru, 2015; Murphy, 2017; Shapiro & Gross, 2017; Young & Perrone, 2016). This type of approach is reflected in the Professional Standards for Educational Leaders ((NPBEA, 2015). While there is a focus on rules, principles, and identification of competencies, at the same time, the standards acknowledge the importance of different ethical paradigms and of viewing ethics in a broader perspective. This is noticeable in the infusion of professional ethics in several of the standards. Beyond the standards, competence for the profession is frequently assessed through an examination based on a case study approach; that is, an analysis of vignettes asking what factors a school leader should consider in making an educational decision.

A PARADIGM FOR PROFESSIONAL ETHICS

Our concept of professional ethics as an ethical paradigm includes ethical principles and codes of ethics embodied in the justice paradigm, but is much broader, taking into account other paradigms, as well as professional judgment and decision-making. We recognize professional ethics as a dynamic process requiring administrators to develop their own personal and professional codes.

We believe this process is important and, like Nash, we observed a dissonance between students' own codes and those set forth by states or professional groups. For the most part, our students were not aware of these codes or, if they were, such formalized professional codes had little impact on them; most found it more valuable to create their own codes. As one of our students, a department chair, pointed out after his involvement in this process:

> Surprisingly to me, I even enjoyed doing the personal and professional ethics statements. I have been in union meetings where professional ethical codes were discussed. They were so bland and general as to be meaningless. Doing these statements forced me to think about what I do and how I live, whereas the previous discussions did not. It was a very positive experience. I also subscribe to the notion that [standardized] professional ethical codes are of limited value. I look to myself to determine what decisions I can live with. Outside attempts at control have little impact on me and what I do.

Through our work, we have come to believe that educational leaders should be given the opportunity to take the time to develop their own personal codes of ethics based on life stories and critical incidents. They should also create their own professional codes based on the experiences and expectations of their working lives as well as a consideration of their personal codes.

Underlying such a process is an understanding of oneself as well as others. These understandings necessitate that administrators reflect on concepts such as what they perceive to be right or wrong and good or bad, who they are as professionals and as human beings, how they make decisions, and why they make the decisions they do. This process recognizes that preparing students to live and work in the 21st century requires very special leaders who have grappled with their own personal and professional codes of ethics and have reflected on diverse forms of ethics, taking into account the differing backgrounds of the students enrolled in U.S. schools and universities today. By grappling, we mean that these educational leaders have struggled over issues of justice, critique, and care related to the education of children and youth and, through this process, have gained a sense of who they are and what they believe personally and professionally. It means coming to grips with clashes that may arise among ethical codes and making ethical decisions based on their best professional judgment, a judgment that places the best interests of the student at the center of all ethical decision making (Stefkovich, 2014, Stefkovich & Frick, 2021).

Thus, actions by school officials are likely to be strongly influenced by personal values (Begley & Johansson, 2003), and personal codes of ethics build on these values and experiences (Shapiro & Stefkovich, 1997, 1998). As many of our students found, it is not always easy to separate professional from personal ethical codes. The observations of this superintendent of a large rural district aptly sum up our own experiences and the sentiments of many of our practitioner-students:

> A professional ethical code cannot be established without linkage and reference to one's personal code of ethics and thereby acknowledges such influencing factors. In retrospect, and as a result of . . . [developing my own ethical codes], I can see the influence professional responsibilities have upon my personal values, priorities, and behavior. It seems there is an unmistakable "co-influence" of the two codes. One cannot be completely independent of the other. (Shapiro & Stefkovich, 1998, p. 137)

Other factors that play into the development of professional codes involve consideration of community standards, including both the professional community and the community in which the leader works; formal codes of ethics established by professional associations; and written standards of the profession (ISLLC).

As educational leaders develop their professional (and personal) codes, they consider various ethical models, either focusing on specific paradigms or, optimally, integrating the ethics of justice, care, and critique. This filtering process provides the basis for professional judgments and professional ethical decision making; it may also result in clashes among codes.

Through our work, we have identified four possible clashes, three of which have been discussed earlier (Shapiro & Stefkovich, 1998). First, there may be clashes between an individual's personal and professional codes of ethics. This may occur when an individual's personal ethical code conflicts with an ethical code set forth by the profession. Second, there may be clashes within professional codes. This may happen when the individual has been prepared in two or more professions. Codes of one profession may be different from another. Hence, a code that serves an individual well in one career may not in another. Third, there may be clashes of professional codes among educational leaders; what one administrator sees as ethical, another may not. Fourth, there may be clashes between a leader's personal and professional code of ethics and custom and practices set forth by the community (either the professional community, the school community, or the community where the educational leader works). For example, several of our students noted that some behavior that may be considered unethical in one community, in another community, may be seen merely as a matter of personal preference.

Furman (2002, 2003, 2004; Furman & Shields, 2005), expanding on what she characterizes as a separate "ethic of the community" and defining it as a process, asks leaders to move away from heroic (solo) decision making and to make decisions with the assistance of the community. Her definition of community is broad and all-encompassing, relating to a distributive model of leadership (Drysdale & Gurr, 2017; Spillane, Halverson, & Diamond, 2001) as well as to participatory democracy.

To resolve the four clashes, we hark back to Greenfield's earlier (1993) quote that grounded the "moral dimension" for the preparation of school administrators in the needs of children. Greenfield contended that schools, particularly public schools, should be the central sites for "preparing children to assume the roles and responsibilities of citizenship in a democratic society" (p. 268). To achieve Greenfield's goal, we must also turn to teachers, in leadership positions, and their ethics (Burant, Chubbuck, & Whipp, 2007; Campbell, 2000, 2004; Hansen, 2001; Maxwell, Tanchuk & Cramsted, 2018; Strike & Soltis, 2015). Teacher leaders, such as heads of charter schools and learning communities or teacher coaches, need to be prepared as ethical professionals.

Not all those who write about the importance of the study of ethics in educational leadership discuss the needs of children; however, this focus on students is clearly consistent with the backbone of our profession. Other professions often have one basic principle driving its field. In medicine, for example, it is "First, do no harm." In law, it is the assertion that all clients deserve "zealous representation." In educational leadership, we believe that if there is a moral imperative for the profession, it is to serve the "best interests of the student." Consequently, this ideal must lie at the center of any professional paradigm for educational leaders.

This focus is also reflected in most professional association codes. For example, the AASA's Statement of Ethics for Educational Leaders (American Association of School Administrators, 2007) begins with the assertion: "An educational leader's professional conduct must conform to an ethical code of behavior and the code must set high standards for all educational leaders." It has as its first tenet the statement: "The educational leader makes the education and well-being of students the fundamental value of all decision making." It is in concert with Noddings' (2003) ethic of care, which places students at the top of the educational hierarchy and is reflective of the concerns of many critical theorists who see students' voices as silenced (Giroux, 1988, 2003; Weis & Fine, 2005). In addition, serving the best interests of the student is consistent with the most recent National Policy Board's standards for the profession. Standard 2, for example, states: "Effective educational leaders act ethically and according to professional norms to promote each student's academic success and well-being" (NPBEA, 2015, p.10).

Frequent confrontations with moral dilemmas become even more complex as dilemmas increasingly involve a variety of student populations, parents, and communities comprising diversity in broad terms that extend well beyond categories of race and ethnicity. In this respect, differences encompassing cultural categories of race and ethnicity, religion, social class, gender, disability, and sexual orientation as well as individual differences that account for learning styles, exceptionalities, and age often cannot be ignored (Banks, 2014; Banks & Banks, 2006; Cushner, McClelland, & Safford, 2011; Gollnick & Chinn, 2012; Shapiro, Sewell, & DuCette, 2001; Sleeter & Grant, 2003).

The literature does not have a uniform definition for "best interests of the student" (Stefkovich, 2014; Stefkovich, O'Brien, & Moore, 2002). In the absence of such clarification, school leaders have often referred to a student's best interests to justify adults' interests (Walker, 1998). Attempts have been made, however, to fill this gap (Stefkovich, 2014; Stefkovich & Frick, 2021; Stefkovich & O'Brien, 2004). Stefkovich conceptualizes decisions related to a student's best interests as those incorporating individual rights; accepting and teaching students to accept responsibility for one's actions; and respecting students. These three Rs—rights, responsibility, and respect—are key to making ethical decisions that are in a student's best interests and, in turn, to fulfilling one's professional obligations as educational leaders.

In sum, we have described a paradigm for the profession that expects its leaders to formulate and examine their own professional codes of ethics in light of individual personal codes of ethics, as well as standards set forth by the profession, and then calls on them to place students at the center of the ethical decision-making process. It also asks them to consider the wishes of the community. As such, the professional paradigm we are proposing is dynamic—not static—and multidimensional, recognizing the complexities of being an educational leader in today's society. (See Figure 2.1 for a visual representation of this model.)

Thus, taking all these factors into consideration, this ethic of the profession would ask questions related to justice, critique, and care posed by the

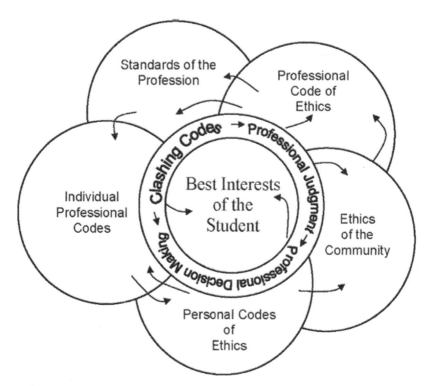

Figure 2.1 *Diagrammatic representation of the ethic of the profession.*

Notes
The circles indicate major factors that converge to create the professional paradigm. The circles shown are: Standards of the Profession; Professional Code of Ethics; Ethics of the Community; Personal Codes of Ethics; Individual Professional Codes, and Best Interests of the Student. Other factors also play a part in the professional paradigm. They are found surrounding the Best Interests of the Student circle and include: Clashing Codes; Professional Judgment; and Professional Decision Making. The arrows indicate the various ways in which the factors interact and overlap with each other.

other ethical paradigms but would go beyond these questions to inquire: What would the profession expect me to do? What does the community expect me to do? And what should I do based on the best interests of the students, who may be diverse in their composition and their needs?

REFERENCES

American Association of School Administrators. (2007). *AASA's statement of ethics for educational administrators.* Arlington, VA: Author.

Apple, M.W. (2010). *Global crises, social justice, and education.* New York, NY: Routledge.

Apple, M.W. (2011). *Education and power* (3rd ed.). New York, NY: Routledge.

Apple, M.W. (2013). *Can education change society?* New York, NY: Routledge.

Banks, J.A. (2014). *An introduction to multicultural education* (5th ed.). Boston, MA: Pearson, Allyn & Bacon.

Banks, J.A (2020). Diversity, transformative knowledge, and civic education: Selected essays. New York, NY: Routledge.

Banks, J.A. & Banks, C.A.M. (2006). *Multicultural education: Issues and perspectives* (6th ed.). San Francisco, CA: Jossey-Bass.

Barth, R.J. (1990). *Improving schools from within: Teachers, parents, and principals can make the difference.* San Francisco, CA: Jossey-Bass.

Bass, L. (2020). Black male leaders care too: An introduction to black masculine caring in educational leadership. *Educational Administration Quarterly, 56*(3), 353–395.

Beauchamp, T.L. & Childress, J.F. (1984). Morality, ethics, and ethical theories. In P. Sola (Ed.), *Ethics, education, and administrative decisions: A book of readings* (pp. 39–67). New York, NY: Peter Lang.

Beck, L.G. (1994). *Reclaiming educational administration as a caring profession.* New York, NY: Teachers College Press.

Beck, L.G. & Murphy, J. (1994a, April 6). A deeper analysis: Examining courses devoted to ethics. Paper presented at the annual meeting of the American Educational Research Association, New Orleans.

Beck, L.G. & Murphy, J. (1994b). *Ethics in educational leadership programs: An expanding role.* Thousand Oaks, CA: Corwin Press.

Beckner, W. (2004). *Ethics for educational leaders.* Boston, MA: Pearson Education.

Begley, P.T. & Johansson, O. (Eds.) (2003). *The ethical dimensions of school leadership.* Boston, MA: Kluwer.

Belenky, M.F., Clinchy, B.M., Goldberger, N.R., & Tarule, J.M. (1986). *Women's ways of knowing.* New York, NY: Basic Books.

Blackburn, S. (2001). *Being good: A short introduction to ethics.* Oxford, England: Oxford University Press.

Board of Education, Island Trees Union Free School District No. 26 v. Pico, 457 U.S. 853 (1981).

Bolman, L.G. & Deal, T.E. (1991). *Reframing organizations: Artistry, choice, and leadership.* San Francisco, CA: Jossey-Bass.

Bourdieu, P. (2001). *Masculine domination.* Stanford, CA: Stanford University Press.

Buber, M. (1965). Education. In M. Buber (Ed.), *Between man and man* (pp. 83–103). New York, NY: Macmillan.

Burant, T.J., Chubbuck, S.M., & Whipp, J.L. (2007). Reclaiming the moral in the dispositions debate. *Journal of Teacher Education, 58*(5), 397–411.

Campbell, E. (2000). Professional ethics in teaching: towards the development of a code of practice. *Cambridge Journal of Education, 30*(2), 203–221.

Campbell, E. (2004). *The ethical teacher.* Maidenhead, England: Open University Press.

Capper, C.A. (1993). Educational administration in a pluralistic society: a multi-paradigm approach. In C.A. Capper (Ed.), *Educational administration in a pluralistic society* (pp. 7–35). Albany, NY: State University of New York Press.

Capper, C.A. (2019). *Organizational theory for equity and diversity: Leading integrated socially just education.* New York, NY: Routledge.

Carnoy, M. & Levin, H. (1985). *Schooling and work in the democratic state.* Palo Alto, CA: Stanford University Press.

The Center for Effective Discipline (2020). http://endcorporalpunishment.org/reports-on-every-state-and-territory/usa/

Comer, J.P. (1988). Is "parenting" essential to good teaching? *NEA Today, 6,* 34–40.

Council of Chief State School Officers (2014). *2014 ISLLC Standards.* Washington, DC: Author.

Crittenden, B. (1984). Morality, ethics, and ethical theories. In P. Sola (Ed.), *Ethics, education, and administrative decisions: A book of readings* (pp. 15–38). New York, NY: Peter Lang.

Cushner, K., McClelland, A., & Safford, P. (2011). *Human diversity in education: An integrative approach* (7th ed.). New York, NY: McGraw-Hill.

Delgado, R. (1995). *Critical race theory: The cutting edge.* Philadelphia, PA: Temple University Press.

Dewey, J. (1902). *The school and society.* Chicago, IL: University of Chicago Press.

Drysdale, L. & Gurr, D. (2017). Leadership in uncertain times. *International Journal of Educational Administration, 45*(2), 131–158.

Foster, W. (1986). *Paradigms and promises: New approaches to educational administration.* Buffalo, NY: Prometheus Books.

Foucault, M. (1983). On the genealogy of ethics: An overview of work in progress. In H.L. Dreyfus & P. Rabinow (Eds.). *Michel Foucault: Beyond structuralism and hermeneutics* (2nd ed., pp. 229–252). Chicago: University of Chicago Press.

Freire, P. (1998). *Pedagogy of freedom: Ethics, democracy, and civic courage* (P. Clarke, trans). Lanham, MD: Rowman & Littlefield.

Furman, G. (Ed.) (2002). School as community: From promise to practice. Albany, NY. State University of New York Press.

Furman, G.C. (2003). The 2002 UCEA presidential address: toward a new scholarship of educational leadership. *UCEA Review, 45*(1), 1–6.

Furman, G.C. (2004). The ethic of community. *Journal of Educational Administration, 42*(2), 215–235.

Furman, G. C., & Shields, C. M. (2005). How can educational leaders promote and support social justice and democratic community in schools? In W. A. Firestone and C. Riehl (Eds.). *A new agenda for research in educational leadership* (pp. 119–137). New York, NY: Teachers College Press.

Galloway, M.K., & Ishimaru, A.M. (2015). Radical recentering: Equity in educational leadership standards. *Educational Administration Quarterly,* 51(3), 372–408.

Gilligan, C. (1982). *In a Different Voice.* Cambridge, MA: Harvard University Press.

Gilligan, C. & Richards, D.A.J. (2009). *The deepening darkness: Patriarchy, resistance, and democracy's future.* New York, NY: Cambridge University Press.

Ginsberg, A.E., Shapiro, J.P., & Brown, S.P. (2004). *Gender in urban education: Strategies for student achievement.* Portsmouth, NH: Heinemann.

Giroux, H.A. (Ed.) (1991). *Postmodernism, feminism, and cultural politics: Redrawing educational boundaries.* Albany, NY: State University of New York Press.

Giroux, H.A. (2000). *Stealing innocence: Youth, corporate power, and the politics of culture.* New York, NY: St. Martin's Press.

Giroux, H.A. (2003). *The abandoned generation: Democracy beyond the culture of fear.* New York, NY: Palgrave Macmillan.

Giroux, H.A. (2006). *America on the edge: Henry Giroux on politics, education, and culture.* New York. NY: Palgrave Macmillan.

Giroux, H.A. (2012). *Disposable youth: Radicalized memories and the culture of cruelty.* New York, NY: Routledge.

Giroux, H.A. (2013). *Youth in revolt: Reclaiming a democratic future.* Boulder, CO: Paradigm Publishers.

Giroux, H.A. (2020). *On critical pedagogy* (2nd ed.). London, England: Bloomsbury Academic.

Giroux, H.A. & Aronowitz, S. (1985). *Education under siege.* South Hadley, MA: Bergin & Garvey.

Goldberger, N., Tarule, J., Clinchy, B., & Belenky, M. (Eds.) (1996). *Knowledge, difference, and power.* New York, NY: Basic Books.

Gollnick, D.M. & Chinn, P.C. (2012). *Multicultural education in a pluralistic society* (9th ed.). Boston, MA: Pearson.

Goodlad, J.I., Soder, R., & McDaniel, B.L. (2008). *Education and the making of a democratic people.* Boulder, CO: Paradigm Publishers.

Greenfield, W.D. (1993). Articulating values and ethics in administrator preparation. In C.A. Capper (Ed.), *Educational administration in a pluralistic society* (pp. 267–287). Albany, NY: State University of New York Press.

Greenfield, W.D. (2004). Moral leadership in schools. *Journal of Educational Administration, 42*(2), 174–196.

Grogan, M. & Shakeshaft, C. (2011). *Women and educational leadership.* San Francisco, CA: Jossey-Bass.

Gurley, D.K. & Dagley, A. (2020). Pulling back the curtain on moral reasoning and ethical leadership development for k-12 school leaders. *Journal of Research on Leadership Education.* https://doi.org/10.1177/1942775120921213

Guthrie, J.W. (1990). The evolution of educational management: Eroding myths and emerging models. In B. Mitchell & L. Cunningham (Eds.), *Educational leadership and changing contexts of families, communities, and schools. Eighty-ninth Yearbook of the National Society for the Study of Education* (pp. 210–231). Chicago, IL: University of Chicago Press.

Hansen, D.T. (2001). Teaching as a moral activity. In V. Richardson (Ed.), *Handbook of research on teaching* (4th ed.) (pp. 826–857). Washington, DC: American Educational Research Association.

Hersh, R.H., Paolitto, D.P., & Reimer, J. (1979). *Promoting moral growth: From Piaget to Kohlberg*. New York, NY: Longman.

Hester, J. & Killian, D.R. (2010). The moral foundations of ethical leadership. *The Journal of Values-Based Leadership, 1*(3), pp.1–10.

Kohlberg, L. (1981). *The philosophy of moral development: Moral stages and the idea of justice* (Vol. *1*). San Francisco, CA: Harper & Row.

Lareau, A. (1987). Social class differences in family school relationships: The importance of cultural capital. *Sociology of Education, 60*, 73–85.

Lareau, A. (2011). *Unequal childhoods: Class, race, and family life* (2nd ed.). Berkeley, CA: University of California Press.

Larson, C. & Murtadha, K. (2002). Leadership for social justice. In J. Murphy (Ed.), *The educational leadership challenge: Redefining leadership for the 21st century* (pp. 134–161). Chicago, IL: University of Chicago Press.

Lashley, C. (2007). Principal leadership for special education: An ethical framework. *Exceptionality, 15*(3), 177–187.

Lebacqz, K. (1985). *Professional ethics: Power and paradox*. Nashville, TN: Abingdon. Boston, MA: Houghton Mifflin Harcourt.

McLaren, P. (2020). *Life in schools: An introduction to critical pedagogy in the foundations of education* (6th ed.). New York, NY: Routledge.

Marshall, C. & Gerstl-Pepin, C. (2005). *Re-framing educational politics for social justice*. Boston, MA: Allyn & Bacon.

Marshall, C. & Oliva, M. (2009). *Leadership for social justice: Making revolutions in education* (2nd ed.). Boston, MA: Allyn & Bacon.

Marshall, C. & Young, M. (2013). Policy inroads undermining women in education. *International Journal of Leadership in Education, 16*(2), 205–219.

Maxwell, B., Tanchuk, N. & Cramsted, C. (Eds.) (2018). *Professional ethics education and law for Canadian teachers*. Ottawa, Canada: Canadian Association for Teacher Education Polygraph Series.

Murphy, J. (2006). *Preparing school leaders: Defining a new research and action agenda*. Lanham, MA: Rowman & Littlefield.

Murphy, J.F. (2017). *Professional standards educational leaders: The empirical, moral, and experiential foundations*. Thousand Oaks, CA: Corwin.

Nash, R.J. (1996). *"Real world" ethics: Frameworks for educators and human service professionals*. New York, NY: Teachers College Press.

Nash, R.J. (2002). *"Real world" ethics: Frameworks for educators and human service professionals* (2nd ed.). New York, NY: Teachers College Press.

Noddings, N. (1992). *The challenge to care in schools: An alternative approach to education*. New York, NY: Teachers College Press.

Noddings, N. (2003). *Caring: A feminine approach to ethics and moral education* (2nd ed.). Berkeley, CA: University of California Press.

Noddings, N. (2013). *Caring: A relational approach to ethics and moral education* (2nd ed.) Oakland, CA: University of California Press.

Noddings, N., Stengel, B.S., & Alan, R.T. (2006). *Moral matters: Five ways to develop the moral life of schools*. New York, NY: Teachers College Press.

Normore, A.H. (Ed.) (2008). *Leadership for social justice: Promoting equity and excellence through inquiry and reflective practice*. Charlotte, NC: Information Age Publishing Inc.

Normore, A.H., & Brooks, J. S. (2017). The dark side of leadership: Identifying and overcoming unethical practice in organizations. Bingley, England: Emerald Group Publishing.

Normore, A.H., & Issa Lahera, A. (2017). Restorative practice meets social justice: Un-silencing the voices of "at promise" student populations. Charlotte, NC: Information Age Publishing.

NPBEA. (1996). *Interstate school leaders' licensure consortium: Standards for school leaders.* Washington, DC: Council of Chief School Officers.

NPBEA. (2008). *Educational leadership policy standards: ISLLC 2008.* Washington, DC: Council of Chief State School Officers, pp. 1–5. Retrieved from www.ccsso.org/Documents/2008/Educational_Leadership_Policy_Standards_2008.pdf

NPBEA. (2015). *The professional standards for educational leaders.* Retrieved from www.ucea.org/new-professional-standards-released-for-educational-leaders

Oakes, J. (1993). Tracking, inequality, and the rhetoric of reform: Why schools don't change. In S.H. Shapiro & D.E. Purpel (Eds.), *Critical social issues in American education: Toward the 21st century* (pp. 85–102). White Plains, NY: Longman.

Oakes, J. (2005). *Keeping track: How schools structure inequality.* New Haven, CT: Yale University Press.

Parker, L. & Shapiro, J.P. (1993). The context of educational administration and social class. In C.A. Capper (Ed.), *Educational administration in a pluralistic society* (pp. 36–65). Albany, NY: State University of New York Press.

Pazey, B.L. & Cole, H. (2015). Tensions and transformations: Using an ethical framework to teach a course on disability law to future educational leaders. *Journal of School Leadership, 25*(6), 1130–1168.

Pennsylvania Code of Professional Practice and Conduct for Educators, 22 Pa. Code, §§ 235.1–235.11 (1992).

People v. Dukes, 580 N.Y.S.2d 850 (N.Y. Criminal Court 1992).

Price, T.L. (2020). *Leadership and ethics of influence.* New York, NY: Routledge.

Purpel, D.E. (1989). *The moral and spiritual crisis in education: A curriculum for justice and compassion in education.* New York, NY: Bergin & Garvey.

Purpel, D.E. (2004). *Reflections on the moral and spiritual crisis in education.* New York, NY: Peter Lang.

Roland Martin, J. (1993). Becoming educated: a journey of alienation or integration? In S.H. Shapiro & D.E. Purpel (Eds.), *Critical social issues in American education: Toward the 21st century* (pp. 137–148). New York, NY: Longman.

Sergiovanni, T.J. (1992). *Moral leadership: Getting to the heart of school improvement.* San Francisco, CA: Jossey-Bass.

Shapiro, H.S. (Ed.) (2009). *Education and hope in troubled times: Visions of change for our children's world.* New York, NY: Routledge.

Shapiro, H.S. & Purpel, D.E. (Eds.) (2005). *Social issues in American education: Democracy and meaning in a globalized world* (3rd ed.). Mahwah, NJ: Lawrence Erlbaum Associates.

Shapiro, J. & Gross, S.J. (2017). Ethics and professional norms. In J.F. Murphy, *Professional standards for educational leaders: The empirical, moral and experiential foundations* (pp. 21–37). Thousand Oaks, CA: Corwin.

Shapiro, J.P. & Stefkovich, J.A. (1997). The ethics of justice, critique and care: Preparing educational administrators to lead democratic and diverse schools. In

J. Murphy, L.G. Beck, & Associates (Eds.), *Ethics in educational administration: Emerging models* (pp. 109–140). Columbia, MO: University Council for Educational Administration.

Shapiro, J.P. & Stefkovich, J.A. (1998). Dealing with dilemmas in a morally polarized era: the conflicting ethical codes of educational leaders. *Journal for a Just and Caring Education, 4*(2), 117–141.

Shapiro, J.P., Ginsberg, A.E., & Brown, S.P. (2003). The ethic of care in urban schools: Family and community involvement. *Leading & Managing, 9*(2), 45–50.

Shapiro, J.P. Sewell, T.E., & DuCette, J.P. (2001). *Reframing diversity in education.* Lanham, MD: Rowman & Littlefield.

Shapiro, J.P., Sewell, T.E., DuCette, J.P., & Myrick, H. (1997, March). Socio-cultural and school factors in achievement: Lessons from tuition guarantee programs. Paper presented at *the annual meeting of the American Educational Research Association,* Chicago, IL.

Sleeter, C.E. & Grant, C.A. (2003). *Making choices for multicultural education: Five approaches to race, class, and gender* (4th ed.). New York, NY: Wiley.

Smylie, M., Murphy, J. & Louis, K.S. (2016). Caring school leadership: A multidisciplinary, cross-occupational model. *American Journal of Education, 123*(1), 1–35.

Spillane, J., Halverson, R., & Diamond, J.B. (2001). Investigating school leadership practice: A distributed perspective. *Educational Researcher, 30*(3), 23–28.

Starratt, R.J. (1991). Building an ethical school: A theory for practice in educational leadership. *Educational Administration Quarterly, 27*(2), 185–202.

Starratt, R.J. (1994a). *Building an ethical school: A practical response to the moral crisis in schools.* London, England: Falmer Press.

Starratt, R.J. (1994b, April 6). Preparing administrators for ethical practice: State of the art. Presentation at *the annual meeting of the American Educational Research Association,* New Orleans.

Stefkovich, J.A. (2014). *Best interests of the student: Applying ethical constructs to legal cases in education* (2nd ed.). New York, NY: Routledge.

Stefkovich, J.A., Brady, K.P., Ballard, T.N.W., & Rossow, L.F. (2021). *The law and education: Cases and materials* (3rd ed.). Durham, NC: Carolina Press.

Stefkovich, J.A. & Frick, W.C. (2021). *Best interests of the student: Applying ethical constructs to legal cases* (3rd ed.). New York, NY: Routledge.

Stefkovich, J.A. & Guba, G.J. (1998). School violence, school reform, and the fourth amendment in public schools. *International Journal of Educational Reform, 7*(3), 217–225.

Stefkovich, J.A., O'Brien, G.M., & Moore, J. (2002, October). School leaders' ethical decision making and the "best interests of students." Paper presented at *the 7th Annual Values and Leadership Conference,* Toronto, Ontario, Canada.

Stengel, B. & Alan, T. (2006). *Moral matters: Five ways to develop the moral life of schools.* New York, NY: Teachers College Press.

Strike, K.A. (1991). The moral role of schooling in liberal democratic society. In G. Grant (Ed.), *Review of Research in Education* (pp. 413–483). Washington, DC: American Educational Research Association.

Strike, K.A. (2007). *Ethical leadership in schools: Creating community in an environment of accountability.* Thousand Oaks, CA: Corwin Press.

Strike, K.A., Haller, E.J., & Soltis, J.F. (2005). *The ethics of school administration* (3rd ed.). New York, NY: Teachers College Press.

Strike, K. & Soltis, J.F. (2015). *The ethics of teaching* (5th ed.). New York, NY: Teachers College Press.

UCEA Code of Ethics for the Preparation of Educational Leaders (2011). University Council for Educational Administration (UCEA). Charlottesville, VA: University of Virginia. Retrieved from www.ucealee.squarespace.com/ucea-code-of-ethics/

Vinney, C. (2020, February 11). *Gilligan's ethics of care.* Retrieved from www.thoughtco.com/ethics-of-care-4691476

Walker, K. (1998). Jurisprudential and ethical perspectives on "the best interests of children." *Interchange, 29*(3), 283–304.

Weis, L. & Fine, M. (2005). *Beyond silent voices: Class, race, and gender in United States schools* (2nd ed.). Albany, NY: State University of New York Press.

Young, M.D. & Perrone, F. (2016). How are standards used, by whom and to what end? *Journal of Research on Leadership Education, 11*(1), 3–11.

PART II

A MULTIPARADIGM APPROACH TO ANALYZING PARADOXICAL DILEMMAS

Chapters 3 to 11 present ethical dilemmas that lend themselves to analysis through a multiparadigm approach. They highlight inherent inconsistencies existing within education in particular, and our communities in general, that tend to give rise to dilemmas. Thus, we have framed each chapter as a paradox, and the cases included illustrate the tensions that surround the concept. The paradoxes highlighted are individual rights versus community standards; the traditional curriculum versus the hidden curriculum; personal codes versus professional codes; the melting pot versus the Chinese hot pot; religion versus culture; equality versus equity; accountability versus responsibility; privacy versus safety; and technology versus respect.

Purpel (1989, 2004), in describing the moral and spiritual crisis in contemporary education, turned to paradoxes to bring out current problems and tensions. We agree with him that many of today's strains and stresses have occurred owing to the contradictions that exist in our society. When these paradoxes are brought to the reader's attention, through the discussion of real-life dilemmas, we hope that they will not only lead to stimulating conversations, but that they will also encourage reflection and guidance for wise decision making in the future.

Because many of the dilemmas are based on true experiences, there has been a genuine effort to make sure that anonymity and confidentiality have been maintained. The cases are meant to be used in educational administration classes and in other courses related to education or leadership in general. They are intended to make certain that students and other readers are exposed to differing paradigms and diverse voices—of justice, rights, and law; care, concern, and connectedness; critique and possibility;

DOI: 10.4324/9781003022862-4

and professionalism. They also reflect the diversity of students and of communities in a complex and turbulent era.

These cases focus on persons holding a variety of positions in schools and in higher education. In constructing the scenarios, we purposely tried to balance the gender, race, ethnicity, and age of both the persons confronting the dilemmas and those with whom they had to deal. In this respect, we gave these persons names that would reflect this diversity. We feel that in view of our diverse, multicultural school communities, this was the most appropriate approach. We were very conscious of the risks in not giving everyone Anglo-sounding names, as is the usual practice in case studies, and consciously tried to avoid reinforcing or adopting stereotypes. We apologize in advance for any stereotyping that may have occurred inadvertently.

Before we turn to the cases in the next few chapters, we would like to provide a brief illustration of how an ethical dilemma may be viewed by applying the Multiple Ethical Paradigms. We turn to a dilemma that we developed and used toward the beginning of our course called **The School Uniform Case**. When we first discussed this case, we raised issues associated with the ethic of justice dealing with the legal ramifications of school uniforms. Although our students understood the concepts associated with the justice paradigm and learned much from this analysis, they also seemed frustrated, and we began to think that the discussion was incomplete. Instinctively, we and our students began to bring in other analyses related to the ethics of care, critique, and the profession. These paradigms tended to complement the justice perspective and no longer limited the discussion.

It was by reflecting on this process, and other subsequent similar situations, that we came to realize that dilemmas are best viewed in a multidimensional or kaleidoscopic fashion, as through a series of lenses. What follows is a brief synopsis of **The School Uniform Case**, some of the issues presented in this dilemma, and some suggestions for analysis using four paradigms. This is not meant to be a complete analysis of the case, as such an endeavor would take up more time and space than we feel is necessary for the intent of this introduction. Instead, we use this case and the suggested approaches only as an illustration as to how to reflect on an ethical dilemma through the use of multiple paradigms.

The School Uniform Case is about a poor, inner-city teenager named Tom, who came to school wearing a new pair of tennis shoes. The shoes were expensive, and he said that he had saved three weeks of his salary from his after-school job to pay for them. Tom was extremely proud of his shoes and showed them off to everyone. The next day, the school was in an uproar when the news came that Tom had been killed. Only a few days later, a 17-year-old classmate of Tom's was seen wearing a new pair of tennis shoes identical to those which Tom had worn.

Prior to the murder, the school's principal, Dr. Smith, had suffered minor irritations regarding students' dress. She became tired of overhearing students complaining that they had nothing new to wear, and she was annoyed at their tardiness due to taking hours to dress for school; but the killing of a student only indicated how severe the problem really had become. There were many issues related to this terrible situation, but in an effort to do something quickly, Dr. Smith decided to consider a disarmingly simple solution for dealing with the problem of envy over other students' possessions. She decided to take seriously the idea of requiring that each student wear a school uniform.

Although this solution sounded simple and appropriate to Dr. Smith, we recommend that she pause and reflect on this dilemma, taking into account four ethical paradigms before deciding that school uniforms are the answer. If, for example, Dr. Smith analyzed the case using the ethic of justice, she would have to look closely at laws, rules, and principles regarding dress codes. These reflections must take into account the laws regarding public schools and students' rights. Dr. Smith would need to consider the First Amendment and the free speech clause within it. A dress code, it may be argued, would come under symbolic free speech.

However, despite the law, students might be regulated, particularly if they were indecent or immodest in dress or disrupted the learning process in some way. Under the ethic of justice, then, Dr. Smith might ask the following: In a public school, do students have a right to choose what they want to wear? How far does this right extend, or are there any limits on their dress? Do the parents have rights in this situation?

Turning to the ethic of care, it is clear that Dr. Smith is concerned about her students' safety. She believes that school uniforms would be a great equalizer and would protect individual students from future dangers caused by others' envy of their clothes. In addition, aware of the poverty in her area, she cares about her students' finances. School uniforms would no doubt be a great saving for her students and their families. In this regard, using the lens of care and concern, some questions she could raise for reflection and discussion include: Shouldn't the school uniform be required because it will serve as an equalizer and, hence, help to make students safe? Won't the requirement of a school uniform assist students in a poverty area who currently pay too much money for designer clothes and jewelry?

If Dr. Smith focuses on the ethic of critique, questions of a broader nature could be asked, such as: What kind of system encourages young people to compete over clothes and fosters envy to such a degree that a young person would kill over what another student wears? How can this system be made better, enabling students to focus on learning rather than on spending money and effort on clothes and jewelry?

Finally, if Dr. Smith turns to the professional ethical paradigm, she might consider all these questions and then go beyond them to determine if there were inconsistencies. To accomplish this, she might ask: What would the profession expect her to do? According to her personal and professional codes of ethics, what should she do? And what would the school and local communities expect her to decide? Still keeping in mind the professional paradigm, she might also ask this key question: Is it in the best interests of students to require that they be dressed in school uniforms?

Thus, what at the outset appears to be a simple solution to a disturbing problem becomes something quite different and far more complex. This type of questioning, using four different ethical paradigms, would hopefully provide Dr. Smith with in-depth and detailed knowledge and sensitivities regarding school uniforms. Although it might take longer than she originally intended to reach a decision, what Dr. Smith decided to do would no doubt be wiser and more informed owing to the different perspectives she had used, and various questions she had explored.

Now let us turn to Chapter 3, which contains the first of the paradoxes and the cases that illustrate some of the tensions as they relate to schooling. This paradox focuses on individual rights versus community standards.

REFERENCES

Purpel, D.E. (1989). *The moral and spiritual crisis in education: A curriculum for justice and compassion in education.* New York, NY: Bergin & Garvey.

Purpel, D.E. (2004). *Reflections on the moral and spiritual crisis in education.* New York, NY: Peter Lang.

Chapter 3

Individual Rights versus Community Standards

John A. Schlegel, Loree P. Guthrie, Jeannette McGill-Harris, Kevin A. Peters, C. Esteban Pérez, and Hector L. Sambolin, Jr.

One of the paradoxes that American society faces is that of individual rights versus community standards. This dichotomy emanates from individuals' desires to be unique, independent, and hold a strong self-identity. Yet, at the same time, people seek interdependence by developing strong human and symbolic relationships (Purpel, 1989, 2004). This need for a group identity compels communities to develop their own identities, ultimately creating community standards. However, moral dilemmas can arise when community standards conflict with individual rights.

The balance between the needs of both the individual and the greater community go back to the foundations of the American republic. It is natural that the education of our nation's students has always fueled this debate. The "special position of trust and responsibility" that educators hold, given their proximity to youth, makes their situation unique (DeMitchell, 1993, p. 217). Educational leaders are a natural buffer as this juxtaposition manifests itself in daily situations, especially in public-school settings. Specifically, the view of educators as role models for students, based on an ethical foundation of different communities, contrasts with the principle of individual rights (Eckes, DeMitchell, & Fossey, 2018; DeMitchell, Eckes, & Fossey, 2009).

This tension between the community and individual rights must be faced frequently by those educational leaders working at the very heart of the debate. Since the move away from the common school to the establishment of the school system and profession of teaching, administrators have had to balance community ethics with teachers' privacy rights.

Early schooling in America was characterized by teacher conduct as a matter of public concern (Tyack, 1974). Throughout the first half of the nineteenth century, schools fell largely under local community control

DOI: 10.4324/9781003022862-5

(DeMitchell, 1993). As such, most details of teachers' lives were placed under the rules, regulations, and scrutiny of local community members. Matters such as marital status, dress, and living arrangements were often direct conditions of employment (Apple, 1986; Hoffman, 1981; Tyack, 1974).

As reformers after 1850 began to make progress toward the establishment of bureaucratized school systems, the "rise of professionalism" began to "counterbalance community control" (DeMitchell, 1993, p. 217). Certainly, teachers were still responsible to the public for life outside of the classroom. However, the prominence of a school bureaucracy often made this scrutiny less intense. The picture of teacher as role model began to be joined by a vision of the teacher as private individual.

Despite the shift away from direct community control, it was not until the 1960s and 1970s that there was any significant movement toward acceptance of greater personal freedom for teachers. Along with the courts, school leaders and boards of education often looked for a direct relationship between teacher action and adverse effect on students (*Morrison v. Board of Education*, 1969).

Yet, in many cases, the selection and retention of teachers continued to remain intertwined based on community values and expectations. Even into the latter half of the twentieth century, dismissal of teachers for conduct outside of school was practiced by various communities (*McBroom v. Board of Education*, 1986).

The following discussion took place during proceedings of the Supreme Court of Pennsylvania in 1993:

> Immorality is not essentially confined to deviation from sex morality; it may be such a course of action as offends the morals of the community and is a bad example to the youth whose ideals a teacher is supposed to foster and to elevate.... It has always been the recognized duty of the teacher to conduct himself in such a way as to command the respect and good will of the community, though one result of the choice of a teacher's vocation may be to deprive him of the same freedom of action enjoyed by persons in other vocations. (DeMitchell, 1993, p. 221)

Although court cases may illuminate the issues surrounding the dispute between teacher as exemplar and teacher as private citizen, administrators must continue to fill a unique role. They must frequently deal with the move to objectify criteria that may be used to balance the community view of teachers as role models and the idea of teachers as professionals.

While there have been moves away from communities monitoring teachers' private lives, the paradox between community control and individual rights continues to exist. With expansion of technology and on-line capabilities, it is much easier for community members to learn about educators' private lives (as discussed in Chapter 10). In addition, with schools becoming increasingly bureaucratic, the concept of role model and exemplar for children still includes teachers but has expanded beyond this role to encompass other school and higher education personnel. For example, two of the dilemmas in this chapter address teachers' rights. Others focus on a school security guard, a coach, a school administrator, and a College Vice President for Student Affairs/Dean of Students.

Moreover, with our increasingly complex society, employees are not the only persons whose rights clash with the community. Although limited, students have rights and, for a school to run effectively and ethically, their voices need to be heard (Mitra, 2018; Mitra & McCormick, 2017). In addition, generations of more involved and less compliant parents seem increasingly comfortable in exerting their rights and those of their children (Cutler, 2000). The days of parents passively accepting the school's authority have receded and seem to be disappearing.

Thus, the nature of community influence has expanded. Two of this chapter's dilemmas involve international students and their parents and three of the six dilemmas in this chapter address sexual orientation with the latter attracting community concerns, whether it be the school community or the greater community. Some community members, including parents, have objected to the rights of LGBT students. Mayo (2020) concluded that parents' fundamentalist religious beliefs often influence a school's reticence to provide bathroom and locker room accommodations for transgender students.

Dawson (2019) mentions that at least seven states have passed laws explicitly prohibiting teachers from: "positively speaking about or correcting misconceptions on homosexuality" (p. 435). Other states have attempted to pass similar legislation and failed. Finally, a sizeable number of local school districts have comparable policies (Hamed-Troyansky, 2016). Legal commentators have referred to such efforts as "No Promo Homo" laws and policies. At the very least, it appears that some communities are ignoring, accepting, supporting, and possibly initiating these mandates.

In this chapter, individual rights and personal liberties are juxtaposed against the standards of the community. Important questions to be asked include: Are there values and moral standards that are absolute or fixed? Do the ends ever justify the means? In considering these questions, this chapter examines the changing face of ethics in different communities.

In **Artificial Insemination** (Case Study 3.1), an unmarried teacher in her late thirties confides to her friend, the district's personnel director, that she wants to have a baby using artificial insemination. In this small, rural community that is largely Christian fundamentalist, the personnel director is concerned about the teacher's personal plan as well as the community's reactions to it.

In **The Trouble with** *Daddy's Roommate* (Case Study 3.2), a parent complains about a children's book, assigned in a high school classroom, dealing with sexual orientation and other sensitive issues. Initially, the book is banned, but that is not the end of the problem. In this dilemma one might ask: Does it matter whether there is a consensus regarding values within a local community and even within a school community?

The School of Hard Knocks (Case Study 3.3) focuses on a school bully and a security guard, who may be abusing his authority (Shaver & Decker, 2017). It pits the voices of young children against the wishes of a school superintendent. In this case, two communities are affected—the students in the school and the district administration. Do the voices of the student community count or does the superintendent have the last word?

Glory and Fame: Determining its Worth (Case Study 3.4) grapples with the desires of the community regarding a winning basketball team, the needs of a student (Jason) who is a star player, and what the law requires. It is a win-win for both the student and the community, but the family has moved out of the district and Jason cannot legally play. Does the end justify the means? Should winning be the goal?

Who Comes First, The Student? The Parents? The School? The Teachers? (Case Study 3.5) addresses the needs of a student, Camila, who is questioning her sexuality despite concerns from her family and the church psychologist who want to "cure her" or even "fix her." Various aspects of community come into play here, the small town where the family came from and where they still have relatives, their new urban setting, the church, and the Catholic school community where the school psychologist and other educators disagree as to appropriate treatment and whether Camila should be stopped from seeing her only friend, with whom she has a close relationship. In the meantime, Camila is hospitalized with depression and an eating disorder.

In the last scenario, **The Cultural Sensitivity of Competing Values** (Case Study 3.6), a college administrator must decide between the institution's rules and the needs of a student who has violated drinking prohibitions that would be legal in his own country. At his coming-out party, Emiliano, a 19-year-old student from Spain became so intoxicated that he ended up in the hospital. Knowing that Emiliano's parents would insist that he return to Spain, and would react badly to his sexual orientation, college officials are torn between disciplining this international student and informing his parents (the standard procedure) or responding to individual needs and cultural differences.

In all the above cases, the educational leader must attempt to view each dilemma from the vantage point of the individual and from that of the community, asking questions such as: When do community standards take precedence over individual rights and liberties? Is the ethical character of educators set at a higher level than those of other citizens in the community? Does the community have a right to place educators at a higher ethical level than its other citizens? Should the community have input into matters regarding school employees' individual liberties? These questions are at the heart of the case studies in this chapter.

CASE STUDY 3.1 ARTIFICIAL INSEMINATION

Sally Fabian is a competent senior high school art teacher with ten years of teaching experience. She is an advisor to the high school cheerleading squad and volunteers her time to serve on several school curriculum committees. She is single and, during the past year, had shared with the district's personnel director the fact that she wanted to have a baby using artificial insemination. Her goal was to parent a child of her own whom she intended to raise as a single mother.

Having thought about being a single parent for several years, Ms. Fabian went through the required process of counseling for a year. Although she did not maintain a steady relationship with any man, she had dated during her ten years as a teacher at North High. Sally had been raised in New York City. She chose to attend a small rural college located about 30 miles from North High School. She decided on this college because of its excellent academic reputation as well as the advice from one of her high school teachers. During her four years in college, Sally fell in love with the area. She felt fortunate when she was hired as a teacher at North High. Sally is a resident of the school district where she taught. In fact, she had recently bought a house directly across from the high school.

Sally's political views could be labeled moderate. She is a registered independent voter. During college, she had done an internship in the local Planned Parenthood Clinic. The community the school district serves is conservative with a small, but unified, group of fundamentalist Christians who are politically active and vitally interested in educational matters. The community has a rich German heritage along with some traces of ethnic and racial diversity.

As the ethnic and racial composition of the community diversified, the community needed to address the accusation that the lifelong residents were prejudiced and refused to include all community residents in the mainstream of town life. The increase in the diversity of the community was attributed partly to the increase in advertisement in larger urban settings for people to move into the area to take advantage of low-income housing. This was a venture taken on by several local businessmen who sought to make substantial financial gains.

Last year, to meet the demands of this growing, rapidly changing, and often contentious population, the school board approved a new administrative position: Director of Personnel and Community Relations. John Edwards was the individual selected to fill this slot. All of Mr. Edwards' teaching experience came from his tenure at a large urban high school where he had taught social studies. Directly before assuming this new position, he had been principal at North High, where he had established himself as an effective leader who worked well with students, teachers, and the community.

Mr. Edwards was committed to school reform and believed that all stakeholders should be able to provide input into the change process. As principal, Mr. Edwards had formed an advocacy group of stakeholders to engage in the change process. He was respected by the community, and he sought to conduct himself in a manner that was consistent with community values. Consequently, change did not come about in an abrupt fashion.

Mr. Edwards was friendly with Sally Fabian and knew of her dream, but he had wondered if she were serious about it. Now, today, Sally had stopped by Mr. Edwards' office to tell him the "good news." She had decided to go forward with the procedure. Mr. Edwards is in a quandary as to how to handle this delicate situation. As an educational leader in this district, he is concerned with the growing number of teen pregnancies, especially at North High. Nevertheless, he believes that teachers are entitled to a private life outside of school, and what one does in one's own time is no business of anyone so long as it does not harm others.

Mr. Edwards is concerned that the community will be enraged if Ms. Fabian goes through with her plan. Furthermore, he is uneasy about his own stake in this case if it became known that he had done nothing to prevent Sally from pursuing her goal. The question that Mr. Edwards must answer is whether he should, or even if he has the right to, discuss this issue with Ms. Fabian. Moreover, if Mr. Edwards discusses his concerns with Ms. Fabian, should the discussion be an exchange of ideas or should Mr. Edwards demand that she not follow through with her plan? In addition, does he have an obligation to inform the superintendent or the new principal at North High, both of whom are very conservative in their outlook?

Questions for Discussion

1. Does Mr. Edwards have a right to intercede in Ms. Fabian's decision to have a child as an unmarried person? If so, what are the possible approaches he might take? What is his best course of action?

2. Does the community have a right to challenge Sally's decision to have a child? Does the community have a right to ask that she lose her job if she carries forth her plan? In this case, who is the community, and do you think they are all speaking in one voice?

3. Would Ms. Fabian be a poor teacher simply because she had a baby without a partner?

4. Inasmuch as Ms. Fabian is not required to discuss her private life at school, is there any reason that the students would be affected by her actions? Is she setting a poor example for her students? Why or why not? Does it make a difference that she is an adult, and her students are minors? Does it make a difference that she is going to be artificially inseminated and not naturally impregnated? Would you see the situation differently if Ms. Fabian had a long-term live-in relationship with a man and decided to get pregnant? If she became pregnant through the usual means but didn't know who the father of her child was?

CASE STUDY 3.2 THE TROUBLE WITH *DADDY'S ROOMMATE*

Did anyone ever say the job was going to be easy? No, of course not, but one hoped the positives would outweigh the negatives. That, however, did not seem to be the case today.

Wedgewood High School's principal, Mary Evans, a former English teacher (and perhaps more comfortable in that role), had just received a briefing regarding the recent action of her new assistant principal, Howard Brill. Brill's action was precipitated by a problem brought to his attention by Mr. Robert Press, a very irate parent.

The parent of a special education child in the school, Mr. Press was incensed that his son was being exposed to some "trash about queers" presented by his teacher that day in class. Mr. Press complained that his son had come home with the news that another English class was reading the children's book *Daddy's Roommate*. This book is about a gay parent and his relationship with a male friend. The assistant principal promised Mr. Press that he would immediately get to the bottom of the situation and see that it was rectified. Mr. Brill's first call was upstairs to the English Department, at which time he demanded that the chairperson inform him of what was going on.

She told him that Elizabeth Bennett, a senior English teacher who had been with the school district for 15 years and who had an excellent reputation, had decided to do a unit on minority groups and the prejudices encountered by them. Censorship was an additional topic in this unit. To let her class know that there are many minority groups that experience prejudice and censorship, Ms. Bennett assigned a variety of literary works, such as *The Diary of Anne Frank, Animal Farm,* and *Inherit the Wind,* and the two children's books, *Little Black Sambo* and *Daddy's Roommate.* Although each member of the class had a copy of all the classics, they did not have copies of the two children's books. These books were presented in class for discussion.

What happened on the day in question was entirely beyond Ms. Bennett's control. Basil Howard, another English teacher (who is considered poor, at best, by his colleagues), saw the book *Daddy's Roommate* on Ms. Bennett's desk and took it. Without stopping to ask why such a book was in a senior-level English class, Howard, enraged, went to his class where he presented the book to his students, making satirical and angry comments about the content of the book. As the remarks became louder, the special education teacher, Paul Jenkins, came by and joined in the book-bashing session. Jenkins then took the book to his special education class and presented it with less than favorable comments, hence the angry phone call to the assistant principal.

Complaints of parents are taken very seriously by the district's central office administration, and past practice has been to accede to the parents' wishes. Thus, Mr. Brill, the new assistant principal, thought he was taking appropriate action when he banned both *Little Black Sambo* and *Daddy's Roommate* from the curriculum. However, he was hardly prepared for the passionate reaction of Ms. Bennett, who went directly to the principal and stated that Mr. Brill had violated her academic freedom and demanded that the books in question be reinstated.

Principal Evans knew she needed to act quickly before the incident escalated further. She also knew her action had to be fair to all concerned. To complicate matters further, Mary Evans had very strong convictions concerning censorship. She could not ignore these convictions now.

Questions for Discussion

1. Who will be affected by Mary Evans' decision? What would each of these persons like to see done? Is there a solution to this problem that would be fair and just to all those concerned? If so, what is it?

2. Is it important to teach students about prejudice and censorship? Why? Is there anything morally wrong with the way Elizabeth Bennett is presenting this issue? Why or why not? Is Principal Evans' decision regarding the book censorship a moral decision? Why or why not?

3. How do you personally feel about censorship? Are your convictions different when applied to a school setting? Why or why not? Do school personnel have a moral obligation to expose students to a multiplicity of ideas? To protect students from knowing about certain issues? Explain your answers.

4. What would you do if you were in Principal Evans' place? Would your decision be different if the issue were strictly political rather than one dealing with sex or sexual orientation?

CASE STUDY 3.3 THE SCHOOL OF HARD KNOCKS

Ricky Johnson was known as a school bully. During the school year several students suffered from his aggressive and mean behavior. Ricky was only in the first grade and had already developed a reputation among his peers and the school community.

This particular day, during lunch, Ricky decided he was going to challenge every boy in his class to a physical battle. He proceeded to run over to several of his classmates and punch them in the stomach. Unfortunately for Ricky, Mr. Washington, the school security guard, witnessed his behavior and was able to stop him before he struck another student.

Mr. Washington brought Ricky kicking and screaming to the main office where he was received by the school nurse and school counselor. While in the nurse's office, Ricky continued to scream, stating that Mr. Washington had held him down and allowed another student (John Petterson) to punch him in the stomach. After hearing Ricky's allegation, the school counselor immediately located John and questioned him about the incident. John confirmed Ricky's claim and stated that Mr. Washington did give him permission to punch Ricky in the stomach while he held him.

During this incident, Ms. Henry, the school principal, arrived and immediately the school counselor and nurse apprised her of the situation. Not wasting a minute, Ms. Henry spoke to all the parties involved.

- Mr. Washington denied the allegations and stated that John did punch Ricky in the stomach, but it was while he was holding Ricky and trying to prevent him from punching another student. Mr. Washington also stated that he has worked in this school district for over 25 years and would never do anything to intentionally harm a student.
- Ricky was very adamant about the fact that Mr. Washington had held him and allowed John to punch him in the stomach.
- John Petterson confirmed Ricky's allegation and stated for the second time that Mr. Washington gave him permission to punch Ricky in the stomach while he held him.

Ms. Henry questioned additional student witnesses who were sitting in the area where the alleged incident took place. Every witness stated that Mr.

Washington held Ricky and gave John permission to punch him in the stomach.

It was extremely difficult for Ms. Henry to imagine that Mr. Washington would ever do anything intentionally to put a child in a harmful situation. She desperately wanted to believe Mr. Washington. Perhaps there was some misunderstanding. However, all the witness statements seemed to support Ricky's allegations.

Later, on this disturbing day, Ms. Henry received a call from Mr. Green, the Millville District Superintendent. Mr. Green called, off the record, to inquire about the situation with Mr. Washington. Apparently, Mr. Green had worked with Mr. Washington for ten years. He was the security guard in the school where the superintendent began his career as a principal in the district. Mr. Green went on to further explain that something like this could ruin Mr. Washington's 25-year career and reputation.

Mr. Washington had never been involved in this type of incident previously. He was a pillar of the community. After hearing all the facts of the incident, Mr. Green went on to suggest that perhaps Ms. Henry could reprimand him behind closed doors and have him apologize to the student. After all, said the superintendent, people make mistakes and the student did not sustain any serious injury.

Questions for Discussion

1. Is there a law, policy, or guideline to help Ms. Henry make a wise decision?
2. If there is no law, policy, or guideline, should there be one?
3. Was Mr. Green's behavior ethical? Was his call to Ms. Henry, off the record, and his suggestion as to how she should handle the situation ethical? Why or why not?
4. Did Mr. Green exercise the ethic of care? If yes, for whom? And why?
5. How might the ethics of the community be applied to this dilemma?
6. What decision would be in the best interest of Ricky? Of Mr. Washington?

CASE STUDY 3.4 GLORY AND FAME: DETERMINING ITS WORTH

Northeast High School carried a long legacy of sports success. Their programs won several state championships in many sports. No one in their area ever came close to winning against them. They consistently produced athletes that went on to become stars in their post-secondary careers, particularly those involved in the school's basketball programs.

Over the past five years, the basketball teams had been unsuccessful, posting several losing records. Principal Kurtz took a lot of heat from the community, board of school directors, and the superintendent. He grew up in the area and was captain of several winning basketball teams. In more recent years, the expectations for a winning team became increasingly intense. Following a losing season, the influential sports community had enough. Members of the board of school directors began putting pressure on the superintendent and high school principal to make changes. Principal Kurtz knew if the basketball team did not improve and become successful, the pressure from the board of school directors would be overwhelming. He knew exactly what to do. When the basketball coach was fired due to lack of success, Principal Kurtz made a recommendation to the athletic director to hire a good friend of his to coach the program. The athletic director did just that.

The team began the next season winning their first three games. Principal Kurtz was relieved. In the fourth game of the season, the team's star player, Jason, who was already receiving scholarship offers from colleges, was injured. He would miss the next eight games. The team lost seven out of those eight games. The chance the team would make the playoffs was slipping away. Once again, Principal Kurtz felt a lot of pressure.

When Jason returned, the team seemed to be untouchable. They went on a ten-game winning streak, and the hope for making the playoffs returned. If the team won their last two games, a playoff berth, i.e., a secured position in the playoffs, was guaranteed. Principal Kurtz was repeatedly commended for his recommendation of the new coach. Then, for the second time that season, Principal Kurtz received devastating news about Jason. The athletic director told Principal Kurtz he just found out from Jason's mother that they had moved last month and were now living in a neighboring district. She informed the athletic director that her son was staying in the district with his youth coach throughout the week, so he did not have to play for his new school's team.

Principal Kurtz, the athletic director, and the coach met the following day. They discussed Jason's future. They all knew that the state's athletic policy did not permit this kind of arrangement, and Jason was illegally playing on their team. They also agreed that Jason was the only reason they would make the playoffs. There was no way the team could achieve that objective without him. If that happened, all three of them were doomed. In addition, they knew that joining the other team would seriously limit Jason's opportunities to play at the next level. College coaches rarely watched their games, and no player from that district ever played after high school. Jason's academic and athletic future would be significantly jeopardized.

As the conversation came to an end, the athletic director turned to Principal Kurtz and said, "Coach Noah and I talked before this meeting. We really need Jason to continue playing, but we know you have the final call. How do you want to proceed?" Principal Kurtz could not remember facing a challenge as difficult as this one. No matter what he decided, someone was going to suffer from his decision. He realized that if he did not allow Jason to play, it would change Jason's life forever. In addition, Principal Kurtz's professional future might also come to an end. However, allowing Jason to play did not seem right either. He thought for a moment, and then responded.

Questions for Discussion

1. What do you think Principal Kurtz should decide? Which ethic is the most important one for him to consider? Why?

2. What stakeholders (Jason, board of school directors, Principal Kurtz, athletic director, community, etc.) are the most important in this decision? How do the ethics differ based on who the stakeholders are? What effect will this have on the outcome?

3. Do the ethics of critique, care, and the profession conflict with the ethic of justice in determining the decision Principal Kurtz should make? If so, in what ways? If not, why not?

4. Would Principal Kurtz's ethical decision making be different if he learned the decision would not have an impact his own professional future? If so, in what ways?

CASE STUDY 3.5 WHO COMES FIRST: THE STUDENT? THE PARENTS? THE SCHOOL? THE TEACHERS?

Camila was born in Pereira, a small town in Colombia's coffee region. When Camila was three, her father, Antonio, lost his business. Pereira did not offer well-paying employment that would satisfy Antonio's ambitions and, following family traditions, Mariana, Camila's mother, had resigned her job after marriage. Thus, with few viable options, Antonio accepted a position in Medellín. Even though Medellín is the second largest city in Colombia, it is only about a third of the size of Bogotá, and with its many small neighborhoods, seemed, at least to Antonio and Mariana, more traditional and family-oriented than the country's huge cosmopolitan capital.

Antonio and Mariana started to search for a school that would represent their traditional values, beliefs, and culture. Camila's parents enrolled her in a private Catholic school, with high academic standards. For the next ten years, Camila spent time with her peers on the school playgrounds, in classrooms and in the cafeteria, on fieldtrips, and at friends' parties.

During her first year in high school, Camila changed. She seemed to lose her spark, and towards the end of the academic year, was isolating herself from her peers and always looked sad. Teachers had concerns about Camila, which they reported to Andrés, the school's psychologist. Andrés met with Camila and was able to establish a connection. After several sessions, Andrés became increasingly concerned, mostly because Camila kept insisting that she "did not fit at school, at home, or even at church, where everyone is welcome!"

Andrés decided to meet with Camila's parents, but when he shared that decision with Camila, she was upset, and left his office. The day before the appointment, Andrés heard that Camila was troubled and anxious in her classes; he immediately talked with her. Camila told him that her family already knew her problem, and they took her to church to pray for her. After church, her parents said that soon she would be fixed.

Andrés was confused and asked her if there was some way that he could help. Camila said, "I am not like my friends; I think I like girls, but that is going to be solved with the help of good intent."

When Mariana and Antonio met with Andrés, they confirmed what Camila had told him. Concerned with her wellbeing, Andrés insisted that Camila needed outside professional help and gave her parents a list of psychologists that the school usually recommends for these situations.

Two weeks passed and Camila did not visit Andrés. He decided to call her parents as a follow up. Mariana answered and seemed pleased to inform him that they had hired Mabel López, a psychologist from their church, who promised that she could "fix" Camila. Andrés asked for Mabel's phone number so that he could get a copy of her report to inform the school of any accommodations that Camila needed.

Andrés met with Camila's teachers who reported that they continued to have grave concerns that she was despondent and isolated. Paloma, her Art teacher said that Camila's drawings and other artistic expressions had changed to dark, complex, negative, emotions; she had shifted to a different place. Paloma had once had a strong connection with Camila, but for months now Camila had been sharing less and less.

The following week, Camila stopped eating and had to be hospitalized. Camila's mother reported that Ms. Velazquez, a hospital psychiatrist, was working with Camila and would allow her to leave the hospital and return to school in a week. After Camila was discharged, her parents and doctors had a meeting with Andrés and Mr. González, the school principal. The doctors explained that Camila was depressed and was taking medicine. They said that she would be balanced in a few weeks but could start attending school immediately. Mabel López, the psychologist from the church, interrupted this discussion, insisting that Camila change her classroom to a placement where she was as far as possible from her friend, Fernanda. Andrés jumped into the conversation, pointing out that Fernanda was the only friend Camila had in school; she was the only one that Camila talked with or shared some issues of her life.

Mariana stopped Andrés and said, "Fernanda is responsible for Camila having feelings for girls. Fernanda has fallen in love with my daughter and has been harassing her."

Camila's parents demanded that Andrés be removed from the meeting, saying that: "Andrés is endorsing a relationship that wasn't intended under God's creation; he is not a good example for Catholic students." They pressured Mr. González to "fire Andrés and expel Fernanda because neither of them follows the Catholic standards in a Catholic school."

The next day Mr. González got a phone call from Ms. Velazquez, the hospital psychiatrist. She stated that, "Camila's depression is explained by the approach the family and the church psychologist are giving to her case." She argued that this could become child abuse and both the school (Mr. González) and the psychiatrist (Ms. Velazquez) should report it under child protection law.

Mr. González was stunned. Even though he personally agreed with Andrés' approach and thought it was in Camila's best interests, he questioned his own ability to convince Camila's parents and was hesitant to impose his own, somewhat more progressive, beliefs on them. Also, if he took this stand, word would spread fast throughout the school. Knowing that most of the students' parents were not quite as conservative as Camila's, nonetheless, could he, as the school leader, take a stand that would be so controversial in a Catholic school? Should he fire Andrés? Even though he disagreed with Mariana and Antonio, he thought that they were trying to act as responsible parents. Was this child abuse? Should he report them as the psychiatrist urged? What was the most ethical decision that he could make? Mr. González's head was spinning with these concerns.

Questions for Discussion

1. How would you balance the private school's Catholic standards and the student's well-being through a justice lens?

2. What is the role of community in Camila's depression? How would you address it through a lens of caring? Critique?

3. Should Mr. González and Ms. Velazquez report the family to the child protection office? Analyze this decision through the four paradigms. Would your decision be different if you knew that Camila was going to be relocated to live with a close relative?

4. What would the profession expect Mr. González to do in this situation? Andrés? Mabel López? Ms. Velazquez? Paloma (the art teacher)?

CASE STUDY 3.6 THE CULTURAL SENSITIVITY OF COMPETING VALUES

"This is a mess." Dr. Marin Lorne thought to himself again and again as he stared at the headline from the student newspaper: "Discrimination or Inequity: Gate Bridge's Subjective Enforcement of the Student Conduct Policy Favors International Students."

A new arrival to campus, Dr. Lorne had accepted the roles of Vice President for Student Affairs and Dean of Students at Gate Bridge College (GBC), a private residential college with 1,100 students. With over 20 years of experience in Student Affairs at other institutions, Dr. Lorne's holistic student success pedagogy was highly touted by the selection committee (comprised of faculty, staff, and students) and the Board of Trustees.

Approximately 13% of the student population consists of international students from over 33 countries. There are many living-learning communities at Gate Bridge College. The International Student Success Center (ISSC) is the living-learning community for international students. The ISSC functions as a residence hall and has language emersion classrooms for all Gate Bridge students. The ISSC has an Executive Director and five Language Fellows that function as traditional resident assistants, mentors, and teaching assistants.

Every year, GBC welcomes 350 new students to campus. Incoming international students arrive on campus one week earlier than domestic students for International Student Orientation. The orientation offers a variety of workshops and sessions, including self-care and mental health, resources for academic support, review of college policies and procedures, working on campus, and community-building activities with faculty and staff.

Last year, the former Vice President of Student Affairs and Dean of Students disbanded the student-led Judicial Review Board after they overturned several sanctions without providing a clear rationale for doing so and replaced it with three Student Affairs Deans and two student-government representatives, collectively known as the Student Conduct Council.

Student protests erupted on campus following this decision, and a deep sense of mistrust of the administration permeated the student body.

The student newspaper article, that Dr. Lorne was reading, contained testimonials from domestic students alleging that the College's enforcement of the student conduct policy regarding alcohol violations is discriminatory and favors international students over domestic students by issuing fees as a sanction and notifying the parents/guardians of domestic students hospitalized due to intoxication while only issuing a "Conduct Warning" for international students hospitalized from the same on-campus party. The article went on to state that the GBC Student Handbook does not contain a "Conduct Warning" category under the current student conduct policy.

Under the direction of the GBC president, Dr. Lorne met with Dr. Cassandra Ornois, the Executive Director of the ISSC and faculty member in the Foreign Languages Department, to obtain more information on the incident referenced in the article. Dr. Ornois shared that the Language Fellows decided to throw a Coming Out party for one of their residents, Emiliano Solia. Emiliano is a 19-year-old male student from Spain majoring in Computer Science. Coming out was a big step for him, and his community wanted to show their support. Dr. Ornois did not know where the alcohol came from and did not see it as an issue; 18 is the legal drinking age in many other countries. To her, it was unfortunate that domestic students chose to act irresponsibly by consuming too much alcohol. Emiliano was not intoxicated, but the paramedics were directed by campus police to transport him out of an abundance of caution and he was discharged after a few hours.

Dr. Ornois met with Emiliano shortly after his hospitalization. Emiliano was in tears and visibly shaking. He begged Dr. Ornois not to tell his parents. Doing so would guarantee that his parents would demand that he go back to Spain immediately and continue his studies there. Furthermore, his parents would not approve of his sexuality. Dr. Ornois decided not to call his parents and issued a conduct warning with the understanding that if it happens again, she will notify his parents. By a majority vote, the Student Conduct Council supported Dr. Ornois's decision.

Toward the end of their meeting, Dr. Lorne said to Dr. Ornois that the student conduct policy must be applied to all students equally. She respectfully disagreed and cautioned Dr. Lorne not to be culturally insensitive. "These misunderstandings could jeopardize our international students' visas and work authorizations," she said.

Questions for Discussion

1. Does Dr. Ornois have a right to enforce the student conduct policy subjectively? Was her decision ethical? From what ethical frame is she working?

2. What role, if any, does the current campus culture have in assessing this situation? How might the ethic of critique apply to this culture? Justice? Care?

3. What would you do if you were in Dr. Lorne's place? Why? What ethical frame seems to underlie his decision-making process? Explain your answer.

4. Should GBC notify Emiliano's parents? Would this be in the best interest of GBC? Emiliano? Why or why not?

5. Analyze both Dr. Ornois's and Dr. Lorne's decision making according to the ethic of the profession.

REFERENCES

Apple, M.W. (1986). *Teachers and texts: A political economy of class and gender relations in education.* New York, NY: Routledge.

Cutler, W.W. (2000). *Parents and schools: The 150-year struggle for control in American education.* Chicago, IL: The University of Chicago Press.

Dawson, K. (2019). Teaching to the test: Determining the appropriate test for first amendment challenges to "no promo homo" education policies. *Tennessee Journal of Law and Policy, 13,* 435–458.

DeMitchell, T.A. (1993). Private lives: community control vs. professional autonomy. *West's Educational Law Quarterly, 2*(2), 218–226.

DeMitchell, T.A. (2011). Immorality, teacher private conduct, and adverse notoriety: A needed recalculation of Nexis? *Journal of Law and Education, 40,* 327–339.

DeMitchell, T.A., Eckes, S.E., & Fossey, R. (2009). Sexual orientation and the public school teacher. *Boston University Public Interest Law Journal, 19,* 65–79.

Eckes, S.E., DeMitchell, T.A., & Fossey, R. (2018). Teachers' careers up in smoke and viral: Off-duty conduct in modern times. *West's Education Law Reporter, 355,* 633–640.

Hamed-Troyansky, R. (2016). Erasing gay from the blackboard: The unconstitutionality of "no promo homo" education laws. *University of California Davis Journal of Juvenile Law and Policy, 20,* 85–115.

Hoffman, N. (1981). *Woman's "true" profession: Voices from the history of teaching.* Old Westbury, NY: Feminist Press.

Mayo, C. (2020). Distractions and defractions: Using parental rights to fight against the educational rights of transgender, nonbinary, and gender diverse students, *Educational Policy, 35*(2), 368–382.

Mitra, D. (2018). Student voice in secondary schools: the possibility for deeper change, *Journal of Educational Administration, 56*(5), 473–487.

Mitra, D. & McCormick, P. (2017). Ethical dilemmas of youth participatory action research in a democratic setting. *International Journal of Inclusive Education, 21*(3), 248–258. DOI:10.1080/13603116.2016.1260835

McBroom v. Board of Education, District No. 205, 144 Ill. App. 3d 463, 98 Ill. 864, 494 N.E.2d 1191 (1986).

Morrison v. Board of Education, 1 Cal. 3d 214, 82 Cal. Rptr. 175, 461 P.2d 375 (1969).

Purpel, D.E. (1989). *The moral and spiritual crisis in education: A curriculum for justice and compassion in education.* New York, NY: Bergin & Garvey.

Purpel, D.E. (2004). *Reflections on the moral and spiritual crisis in education.* New York, NY: Peter Lang.

Shaver, E.A. & Decker, J.R. (2017). Handcuffing a third grader? Interactions between school resource officers and students with disabilities. *Utah Law Review, 2017*(2), 229–282.

Tyack, D.B. (1974). *The one-best system: A history of urban education.* Cambridge, MA: Harvard University Press.

Chapter 4

Traditional Curriculum versus Hidden Curriculum

Leon D. Poeske, Jane Harstad, James C. Dyson,
Lynn A. Cheddar, Arkadiy Yelman, and
Spencer S. Stober

In American education today, one of the paradoxes that exists has to do with the curriculum. Some scholars (e.g., Bennett, 1988; Bennett, Finn, & Cribb, 2000; Hirsch, 1987, 1996; Ravitch, 2003; Ravitch & Finn, 1987) have emphasized the necessity to keep the traditional curriculum of U.S. schools in place. President Trump went so far as to call for a patriotic education (Crowley, 2020). By this, he and others mean holding on to the classical canon and maintaining meanings and knowledge that they believe have stood the test of time.

At the same time, others (e.g., Anyon, 1980, 2005; Apple, 2016, 2018, 2019; Fine, 1991; Freire, 1970, 1993, 1998; Giroux, 1983, 2001, 2020; Greene, 1978, 1988, 2000; McClaren, 2020; Parker & Gillborn, 2020; Ravitch, 2020; Weis & Fine, 2005) have stressed the importance of critiquing the traditional curriculum. In their critiques, these scholars have exposed the hidden curriculum of domination (Purpel & Shapiro, 1995). They have drawn people's attention to traditional education that tends to reproduce the inequalities within society. This curriculum of domination teaches many young people to be competitive, individualistic, and authoritarian. It also labels and places numerous students on educational tracks that lead to limited success in adult life.

Although traditionalists may make the claim that their curriculum is value-free and apolitical, this assumption can be challenged. Schools have consistently conveyed the message of "possessive individualism" and "meritocracy." Implicit in the traditional curriculum is the notion that if one does not succeed, it is one's own fault. Also implicit is the concept that those who are not middle class, White, male, and Eurocentric are frequently considered to be "others" (i.e., different sex, race, ethnicity, sexual orientation, or culture) (Margolis, 2001).

DOI: 10.4324/9781003022862-6

Critical theorists who have exposed the hidden curriculum have done so by using inquiry. They have asked specific questions such as: What should be taught about Christopher Columbus? How should the "discovery" of America be presented to students? What are the "facts," and how should they be explored by students? These critics also know that students learn not only from what is taught in school but also from what is not being taught. They also ask: Should current controversial topics be discussed in schools? If so, how should the new curriculum be delivered? What is the message sent to students if "hot" topics are ignored in today's schools? And what is the message to students if the school budget is shrinking, and new, important instructional material cannot be added to the curriculum owing to the lack of funds?

By asking difficult and challenging questions, educational leaders can expose the hidden curriculum. Armed with this new knowledge, with the help of teachers, staff, parents, and the community, educational leaders have the possibility of developing a curriculum that is truly in the best interests of all their students. Educational leaders can make changes in their schools using several approaches. For example, they can turn to the ethic of care and develop, with the help of Noddings (2002, 2003, 2013), a school with a caring curriculum. Noddings has offered educators a framework for a general education curriculum organized around themes of care rather than the traditional disciplines.

Educational leaders can also turn to the work of Starratt (1994, 2004) and build an ethical school with a curriculum that considers the lenses of justice, critique, and care. This curriculum gives teachers and students ample time for discussions and projects that "will serve to nurture the basic qualities of autonomy, connectedness and transcendence in developmentally appropriate ways" (p. 68).

In addition, educational leaders can consider the real-world ethics advocated by Nash (1996). This kind of ethics "is a complex admixture of personal, social and professional morality" (p. 1) and is grounded in applied ethics. The study of meaningful and current ethical dilemmas could be of importance not only to students but also to teachers, staff, and the community.

This chapter contains six case studies. In Case Study 4.1, **AIDS and Age-appropriate Education**, parents complain about a sixth-grade poster project that is part of a mandated class on AIDS education. State law requires some type of instruction. The posters are very creative, and some have real condoms on them. There are pregnancy problems in the school, but some parents complain to Mr. Thompson, the assistant superintendent for curriculum, that they do not want their children exposed to these posters. Mr. Thompson is in a quandary as to what to do.

Case Study 4.2, **Culturally Responsive Curriculum or an Ethical Dilemma?**, involves an administrator who must navigate the fine line between a teacher's attempts to make the curriculum culturally relevant while inadvertently causing problems for a Native American student in her class, a parent's concerns for the welfare of his child, and the authenticity of what is being taught. Here, one may consider that even the best of intentions may result in problems if there is cultural insensitivity or a lack of understanding.

Case Study 4.3, **School Budget Blues and Copyright**, focuses on a district with a shrinking school budget where teachers cannot order the materials that they need to do their jobs well, and at the same time they are unable to duplicate material because of copyright laws. Recently, the principal had sent out a memo reminding teachers about the copyright legislation. In this case, an outstanding teacher is caught by the principal duplicating materials. The principal is aware of the difficulties placed on the teacher who is desirous of providing her class with current instructional material, and yet he is very concerned about violating the law.

Case Study 4.4, **There's No Place like School**, illustrates problems that happen when regular classroom teachers are reluctant to be involved in inclusion programs which require that students with disabilities be educated in the same classrooms as all other children. The hard decisions that administrators must make in assigning teachers as well as students are stressed.

Case Study 4.5, **Old Enough to be Your Grandmother**, takes place in a high school diploma program for adults who had previously dropped out. The average student age in this school is 34 and there are few, if any, serious conflicts. In this situation, a 60- year-old student, was loudly chastising an 18-year-old who was listening to music in class and speaking rudely to the teacher. Here, issues of age and culture play a part in how the older student should be treated and whether, according to school rules, she should be disciplined.

Case Study 4.6, **No to Pets, Yes to Companion Animals**, is a university-based scenario addressing the development of a policy regarding pets/companion animals on campus. The existing policy is clear as the acceptance of emotional support and service animals, however, there is a dispute as to whether pets should be allowed on campus and, to some students, especially animal rights activists, whether persons should be allowed to have pets at all. How we treat animals, knowingly or otherwise, is at the essence of this argument.

CASE STUDY 4.1 AIDS AND AGE-APPROPRIATE EDUCATION

Eugene Thompson, Assistant Superintendent for Curriculum at the Meadow Woods Consolidated School District, was not sure how Dr. Rose

Jones, the superintendent, would side on this issue. He knew Dr. Jones was supportive of a K–12 sex education program, but Mr. Thompson also understood her desire to "keep the peace" with the public. Mr. Thompson's concern began when a few parents of sixth-grade students at the district's Forest Middle School objected to posters hanging outside the health room. The parents noticed the posters during the school's Back to School Night. They complained about the posters discussing how to have safe sex. The parents told him how some even had real condoms as part of the poster.

Mr. Thompson knew the posters were in that school's hallway, but he did not actually give it much thought, especially because the health education teacher, Marcus Fine, reminded him of the curriculum for the seventh-grade AIDS unit. It stated: "All students shall understand ways to prevent Acquired Immune Deficiency Syndrome (AIDS) without the instructor placing bias on either abstinence or the use of contraceptive devices." It was Dr. Jones who had pushed for this curriculum unit just three years earlier, and it had been unanimously approved by the district's curriculum committee and supported wholeheartedly by the school's principal, Susan Kaplan. Mr. Fine justified the poster project as a creative approach for students to understand the ways to prevent the transmission of the AIDS virus. He also noted that this project was for the seventh grade and not the sixth grade.

Before Mr. Fine left the Back-to-School Night event, Mr. Thompson approached him with the parents' concerns. Marcus Fine asked, "Why are the sixth-grade parents complaining to you? This is a project for the seventh- grade students."

"Look, Marcus, the parents feel their sixth-grade students are too young to be exposed to that type of message. They feel their children do not need to be exposed to such graphic representations of how to prevent AIDS. They also believe we are only promoting the use of condoms while not attempting to promote abstinence. They have already called the superintendent's office, and I'm sure we'll both be getting a call from Dr. Jones soon."

"With all due respect, Mr. Thompson," Marcus replied, "I had approached you regarding this project and you gave me the okay. Look, this poster's message is loud and clear: BE SMART, JUST SAY NO. ABSTINENCE IS THE SAFEST WAY TO PREVENT AIDS. I've attempted to be supportive of students who wish to prevent the spread of AIDS—from both sides of this issue."

"Marcus, I understand that, but I am also concerned about Dr. Jones' response to the parents. The parents are going to focus on the posters that blatantly state, USE CONDOMS. This is the type of poster the parents find offensive. They believe their kids are too young to be exposed to condom posters in the school hallways."

Mr. Thompson left the discussion feeling that Mr. Fine was unwilling to understand the other side of the issue. He realized that Marcus Fine had conducted some controversial lessons in the past but knew that this one could become heated in the community. Even though the state mandated lessons on AIDS education, it was not too long ago that the school board banned some of the library books dealing with sexuality and the human body. The board justified that move by saying they acted on the opinions of the community.

The following day, Mr. Thompson began receiving phone calls from a few parents of current fourth-grade students. They were concerned about this poster project for the following year because their children would be moving into Forest Middle School for fifth grade due to overcrowding at the grade school. Mr. Thompson listened to the parents' complaints. They felt that 10- and 11-year-old children should not be exposed to the explicit message of safe sex. They said it was in "poor taste" and an "obvious decay of moral values in our society." How could the district condone such immorality?

Mr. Thompson listened to the parents and mentioned that he also believed it was a little young for fifth graders to be exposed to such sexual messages. He conveyed to the parents the district's policy on the instruction of sex education to all the grades. He emphasized that discussions on the use of condoms was not in the curriculum for the fifth and sixth grades. Even so, the parents made it perfectly clear that their children should not be subjected to such safe-sex posters for the following year.

Mr. Thompson later heard from the superintendent. Dr. Jones wanted to meet with Mr. Thompson and Mr. Fine the following day to discuss the posters. She gave direct orders that Mr. Thompson take the posters down before she arrived at the school. Although she had heard only the parents' side of the issue, Mr. Thompson realized that Dr. Jones was in no mood to debate, and he felt it was best to follow her orders. He knew Mr. Fine would not be pleased with this directive but understood that it could be considered insubordination if he did not adhere to Dr. Jones' request.

As he walked down to Mr. Fine's room at the end of the day, he passed two seventh-grade girls in the hallway. One was eight months pregnant. He wondered what message was really being sent if the posters came down.

Questions for Discussion

1. Who decides at what age various parts of the curriculum should be introduced? At what age should students be exposed to explicit ways to prevent AIDS and pregnancy?

2. Is there a commonly accepted age when teachers can have students do an assignment such as the one presented? How do teachers or administrators know where to draw the line? Should the community have input into the specifics of the school curriculum? When, if ever, should the concerns of some community members become school policy?

3. If Dr. Jones had not even seen any of the posters, how could she know that the posters were inappropriate for the middle-school students? Does Dr. Jones have legitimate concerns over the following year's incoming fifth-grade class?

CASE STUDY 4.2 CULTURALLY RESPONSIVE CURRICULUM OR AN ETHICAL DILEMMA?

Dr. Adams had been repeating her morning ritual of greeting the students in the hallway as they arrive from their various neighborhoods to start their school day. Her administrative assistant, Delta, came rushing up to speak to her, a tormented look on her face. Delta pulled her over to the side of the hallway and spoke in a whispered rush, "You have a student in your office, and he's not alone! This kid brought trouble with him!" Dr. Adams hurried back to her office, determined to resolve whatever issues her visitors had. As she entered the outer office, she heard raised voices coming from her own open doorway.

Dr. Adams had been enjoying a wonderful morning in her urban middle school. Her 425 students came from a variety of neighborhoods in a sprawling Midwestern city. A wide array of children attended her school from many socio-economic and ethnic backgrounds. She prided herself on the fact that her school was normally a smooth-running operation with only a few behavioral issues; the climate of the school was something she had worked at diligently since becoming the administrator four years previously.

When she entered her office, she found Jeremy Standing Elk, a normally quiet and shy Lakota student, sitting with his father, Harold. It was obvious that Harold was upset, and Jeremy seemed bewildered. Harold was speaking slowly and surely, yet his tone was heated as he explained the situation.

Jeremy, a student in the core American history block, was in class the previous day studying westward expansion when his teacher, Beth, divided the students into three distinct groups: cowboys; settlers; and Indians. Jeremy was grouped with the Indians. Although he felt apprehensive about it, Jeremy didn't want to speak up and say anything in protest. As the lesson proceeded, the group of five boys who were "Indians" complained that they didn't want to be Indians; they felt that they were all going to get killed off, so they started to talk about scalping some cowboys. The father also explained that the boys in the "cowboys" group were in a different clique in the school and that there was a history of tension between the groups. As the lesson proceeded, each group was asked to write about how they felt about the westward expansion and how it had affected their "group." One person from each group was then asked to "share" these ideas in front of the class.

Teacher Beth was at her desk, on her computer, preparing for the next week's lessons. Although present in the room, she was used to the sound of students chattering and discussing the student ideas, so she tuned out the conversations. As the lesson progressed, Jeremy tried to get his group back on track by saying that they needed to write some things down. Unfortunately, his words went unheeded; in fact, the boys in his group chided him about being the one who should do the writing because of his Indian heritage. One of the students went so far as to say that Jeremy should get up and do his "war dance" in front of the class.

Teacher Beth didn't see or hear these conversations go on, and the class did not have enough time to share before the bell rang for the end of the period. Jeremy was relieved, and as Beth finished by saying there had been some wonderful conversations going on, Jeremy was feeling rather disheartened about his group situation. As the class filed out of the door, the other boys in his group patted their hands on their mouths and made the "aye yi yi yi" sound prevalent in so many stereotypical old Hollywood movies. Jeremy chuckled at his pals as they left the classroom.

Jeremy's father, Harold, was clearly upset as he told of his son's experience. Dr. Adams respectfully agreed that the purpose of the lesson was good; however, the practices used to achieve the lesson's objectives could be improved. Dr. Adams, knowing she needed to hear the teacher's side of this incident, set up a meeting with Harold and Beth for after school the following day, giving ample time to notify the teacher of the issues the student and his father had brought up.

Meeting to Resolve the Dilemma

The meeting after school took place in Dr. Adams' office, and as Harold Standing Elk walked in, he was amazed to see five people in the room. Although concerned about the extra people, Harold sat down with Jeremy and placed a book on the table (Lies My Teacher Told Me by James Loewen, 1995). The meeting started with introductions. Harold was surprised to find two curriculum specialists and a social worker among the group.

The teacher then started out emphatically with, "Mr. Standing Elk, I am a good teacher, I've been teaching for 17 years now, and I know I am a good teacher! But let's talk about Jeremy. He comes to class late maybe two or three times a week, and he hardly ever contributes to class discussions, so frankly, I'm surprised to hear he has anything to say at this point in the year! I have brought in the social worker so maybe we can discuss why Jeremy doesn't really speak up in class, but instead he is telling you about what is going on. His grades are mediocre at best, and I'm sure we can all work this out to where Jeremy is going to get a better grade. As a concerned parent, I know you and I can arrive at some agreement."

Dr. Adams was a mildly concerned over the defensive tone of Teacher Beth, and tried to calmly yet assertively interject that Beth was a qualified and professional educator. Harold cut her off abruptly, "Well, I thought I was here to talk about what happened in class yesterday; I am worried about what my son is learning in your class and about how you're teaching about Natives." Harold's voice got louder as he went on. "My boy doesn't like to get up in front of others and say things, and he has few friends as it is. He doesn't want to rock the boat, and he's even mad at me for coming in. I just want to know what you're teaching here in this school, and why my son has to put up with racism in class!" Almost shouting, he added, "And just what in the heck are these folks doing here?" as he gestured at the two curriculum specialists.

Dr. Adams then drew attention to the fact that the curriculum had been recently revised to include ideas other than the Western perspective so prevalent in American history curricula. The specialists told Harold that the lesson was designed to enable Native students to have a say in the history curriculum. They also suggested that if Jeremy was upset by what went on in the classroom, perhaps there was a way that he could speak up during the class rather than deal with it after the incident occurred; this was why the social worker was present. Everyone could see that Harold was very upset by now.

"Doesn't anyone here care about my son? Don't you know what it's like for him trying to get along with kids who make fun of him and his culture every day? All you care about is some silly curriculum that doesn't even teach the real history, or that someone's a good teacher even when they don't notice the racism in their own classroom, but you all don't even know my son or what he's about or how he thinks!"

Dr. Adams was finding out just how little she knew about how to address this issue.

Questions for Discussion

1. Were the educators in this dilemma caring? Why or why not? How could each of these individuals have worked to resolve this dilemma in a more caring manner?

2. What would be the most just course of action for Jeremy? For the teacher? For the other students in the class?

3. To what extent is the teacher responsible for implementing a culturally responsive curriculum and culturally responsive pedagogy?

4. What is a culturally sensitive curriculum? How might this classroom activity be viewed through a lens of critique?

5. How would the profession expect each of these educators to handle this situation? Did they act in a professional manner? Why or why not?

CASE STUDY 4.3 SCHOOL BUDGET BLUES AND COPYRIGHT

The Pierpoint School District had undergone major changes in the past five years. The student population had more than doubled with no signs of slowing down. A new superintendent had come on board, and construction had begun on three more buildings. The additional students, materials, buildings, and staff needed each year to accommodate the overwhelming growth was staggering. Each year, the budget process grew more tense and territorial as departments fought for the few available dollars. Dr. Sharif, principal of Valley View High School, knew this year's budget would again be tough and bare bones. What the board and superintendent were demanding seemed impossible.

In compliance with the central administration's request, the following year's school budget was originally submitted without any allowances for inflation, additional students, or the expenses that accompany them. Now central administration was mandating further cuts from every school. The faculty had been complaining about the concessions they were already forced to make. Dr. Sharif knew he would bear the brunt of the teachers' anger and criticism for this new round of cuts. As far as the cuts for his school were concerned, the only fair thing to do would be to take an equal amount from each department.

Throughout the past few years, cost-cutting measures had been put in place in all the district's operations, presumably to ease the need for additional funds. One major and highly controversial cost-cutting measure was the introduction of a central copying center to be used by the entire district. Although there would still be a copier housed in each building, the large, multiple classroom copying needs were to be sent to the central copying center. Teachers were reminded that even though there had been cuts in instructional materials, they were not to make copies of copyrighted material.

Dr. Sharif was continuing to agonize over which items to cut from each department's budget request when he began to hear noises in the outer office. It had been hours since the office staff had gone home, and the custodians had already cleaned the offices. Dr. Sharif immediately went to investigate and found Jane Tharp, one of the school's most dedicated and well-respected teachers, in the outer office. An instructor of instrumental music, Ms. Tharp had stopped in after a band rehearsal to use the office copier. She was startled by Dr. Sharif's sudden appearance.

As Dr. Sharif drew closer, Ms. Tharp appeared to be trying to hide what she was doing. When he was close enough, Dr. Sharif could see that Ms. Tharp was copying music for one of her bands. Dr. Sharif was dumbfounded. Not only was this against district policy, it was illegal. The superintendent had recently sent a memo to all district employees reminding them about the legalities and liabilities of making photocopies of copyrighted materials.

Ms. Tharp immediately began to try to rationalize her deed by pointing to the rising cost of music, the number of students in her bands, and the declining budget money.

Questions for Discussion

1. Is anything truly wrong with what Ms. Tharp is doing? Is she being dishonest? Is she stealing? Explain your answer.

2. Do you think Dr. Sharif is concerned because the superintendent might uncover what is happening? Because the publishing company might possibly find out and he would be held personally liable? What other reasons might there be for Dr. Sharif to be concerned? Would your answer as to what Dr. Sharif should do change depending on his motivations? How would it change?

3. What do you see as the reasoning behind copyright laws? Who do they protect? What are the consequences of violating them? Are they just laws?

4. What action do you think Dr. Sharif should take? What is your reasoning? What would be the fairest decision Dr. Sharif could make? Fairest for whom? What would be the most caring decision? What parties should Dr. Sharif consider in making a caring decision? Explain your logic.

5. Do you think Ms. Tharp's actions would be easier, or harder, to justify if she made multiple copies of music for personal use, to give to her friends? If she were not a good teacher? Why?

CASE STUDY 4.4 THERE'S NO PLACE LIKE SCHOOL

Mrs. Stell sighed, considering her task. As Director of Special Education, she needed to guide the assignment of students receiving special education services to class lists for the upcoming year. Her task was considerably more difficult at Kessler Elementary due to the number of children with identified difficulties moving from third grade to fourth. Further complicating her task was the number of teachers less than eager to take on added responsibilities without direct help from learning support teachers. She had only one special education teacher per grade available.

During the past 13 years, the district had had seven different superintendents during eight periods of leadership. While in another district, one superintendent had been instrumental in implementing inclusive practices. Therefore, at Kessler School District he decreed that all children, to the maximum extent possible, would be taught in regular education classrooms. Disturbingly, the district had an unusually high proportion of identified students with IEPs, suggesting a pointed belief in the "placement" of students with special needs. This radical change to inclusive practices caused substantial dissension within the district.

Indeed, during the past four years, Kessler Elementary had special education populations double that of the national average. As a result of the superintendent's mandate, most labeled students were placed in regular education while learning support teachers ran from classroom to classroom trying to deliver one-on-one instruction to identified students. As a result of this lack of continuity of leadership, each school within the district has been handling special education services in differing ways with little congruency of practices among the schools.

Following its initial impact, progress toward the implementation of an inclusive philosophy at Kessler Elementary was slow and only partially successful. For the past several years, all children with disabilities were placed with the two most agreeable and cooperative teachers at each grade level. A special education teacher provided direct support. Children in need of more extensive services were placed outside the district. Certainly, the teachers involved felt that identified students belonged in regular education classrooms, but there was still little co-teaching and much pullout, with instruction occurring in small groups in a separate room for a large proportion of core subjects. As a few teachers became more comfortable with modifications, their use increased.

Unfortunately, this practice did not spread through the entire faculty. Still, teachers recommended that their students be placed in these classrooms each year. As a result, two teachers at each grade level taught a disproportionate number of children who were at risk of failure. Mrs. Stell wondered when teachers would think about a systematic process of achieving IEP goals within the context of typical classroom instruction and understand that not all students had to do the same thing at the same time or through one-on-one instruction.

Finally, the situation became intolerable for two teachers. Mrs. Brandle had five children with IEPs and several other children who were at risk. Mrs. Carou had seven children of 25, with IEPs. Both found that the children had significant academic, behavioral and emotional difficulties.

Mrs. Carou, initially an emotional support teacher, was devoted to her students and enthusiastically endeavored to ensure their success. She very ably articulated what each student was capable of achieving and provided differentiated instruction ensuring that all the children would succeed. Despite the challenges of meeting the needs of her students, it was obvious that each child had made progress. Yet, the year had been exhausting. She began early to advocate for a change in how students were placed. Although her students were making progress, keeping the students with IEPs in just two classrooms the following year would do them and the other students a disservice. She was clear and emphatic about these beliefs.

Mrs. Stell convened a meeting with the 3rd and 4th grade teams. The discussion was how best to serve the needs of all students the following year. It was clear that all felt that there were not enough personnel to meet the needs of the students with IEPs, but there wasn't enough money to hire more.

It was evident from the start that most fourth-grade teachers did not agree with Mrs. Carou's recommendation. No, maintain status quo. When Ms. Marco, the new IS teacher, questioned why spreading the students among all the classrooms was not considered, Mrs. Chemsky exclaimed, "We did that before, and it didn't work. The students were all at different levels; it was a nightmare for the learning support teacher to teach reading and math. She simply couldn't get around to all the students."

Ms. Marco seemed puzzled. "Modifications can be made in a methodical manner allowing most of our students to have their educational needs met within the context of regular classroom instruction." Most of the teachers greeted her statement with a blank stare. She tried again: "When planning for instruction, we can look at using the least intrusive modifications first." Many in the group started talking at once. "There is no time to co-teach." "When could we plan?" "The kids can't read, in the first place, how could they do any of the worksheets?" "The kids need one-on-one instruction."

At this point, Mrs. Stell indicated that most special education students did not necessarily need one-on-one instruction. Rather, whenever appropriate, instruction should be blended with instruction for the entire class. Co-teaching allowed, even encouraged, this to occur. Still most disagreed.

When discussion focused on placement in two classes versus all classes, Mrs. Stell's comment to the team was that placement should be based on students' needs. The team struggled to optimize placement of students at risk and with IEPs for the following year. After much research and debate, it became clear that to best increase learning for all, students should be spread among the six fourth-grade classes, which had been separated into two groups. One containing children with IEPs who had more intensive needs and would receive direct service from the special education teacher with the other containing the children whose IEP goals could be met by the regular education teacher in consultation with the special education teacher.

There remained a problem. Mrs. Clay had taught fourth grade for 27 years. She felt that students should be held to high standards and students who could not meet the standards should be placed elsewhere. She felt that inclusion perpetrated a grave disservice to all students, placing undue pressure on the identified students and slowing instruction for the rest. She disagreed vehemently with the inclusive philosophy, stating that those children did not belong in her classroom.

Mrs. Stell considered her options. She could place the students in all fourth-grade classrooms and tell Mrs. Clay that she was responsible for teaching all children. Remembering reading that one bad year can affect a student's academic career long afterward, could she consign a child to that possibility? If she did place children with IEPs with Mrs. Clay, she had two options. She could give her the children who would need more intensive adaptations and the part-time help of the learning support teacher.

Alternatively, she could give her a class where the children's needs were not as intensive, but in which case she would receive very little direct support. Otherwise, she could choose not to give her any children who were at risk or had IEPs. This last option would probably ensure that students who were at risk would have good fourth-grade experiences. It would also make the other teachers' jobs more difficult. In addition, it did nothing to move the school toward the philosophy by which all children can learn and all children belong.

Questions for Discussion

1. What are the benefits and drawbacks of placing students in need of learning support in classrooms other than Mrs. Clay?

2. If Mrs. Stell refrains from placing students receiving learning support in Mrs. Clay's classroom, how might that affect the school community? How do the students' and parents' wishes play into this problem?

3. If Mrs. Clay is assigned students with learning support, what support should the principal and Mrs. Stell offer? If Mrs. Clay is not assigned students with learning support, what role will she play to effect change toward a more inclusive philosophy? Does Mrs. Stell need to consider Mrs. Clay's professional beliefs before placing students in her classroom? Why or why not?

4. What does the law say about placing students receiving special education services in regular classrooms? What decision is in the best interests of the student?

CASE STUDY 4.5 OLD ENOUGH TO BE YOUR GRANDMOTHER

Principal Goldman's ears had always been uniquely attuned to the sound of commotion in the school hallway. Considering that Principal Goldman worked at the Twilight School, a high school diploma program for adults who had previously dropped out, he rarely got to use his almost super-human hearing abilities. Conflicts between students were rare in a place where the average age was 34 and where most of 150 students were genuinely eager to return to school to improve their career prospects. In nearly two years as the Principal of the Twilight School, Principal Goldman had never broken up a fight.

When Principal Goldman walked by the Spanish class and heard a ruckus, the thought of a student conflict did not even cross his mind. Maybe they are moving the desks? Maybe they are excited to practice some new vocabulary? It wasn't until three students came out of the class to ask for help that he realized what was happening. This was the scene in the classroom: a 60-year-old woman was standing over the desk of an eighteen-year-old man and loudly berating him for his poor behavior in class.

"How dare you act this way," she hollered. "Your behavior is disgusting, and you should be ashamed of yourself," she added. "You better respect this teacher if you know what's good for you," she warned. "I am old enough to be your grandmother, and I will not tolerate this in class," she cautioned. "You're acting like an idiot with no self-respect," she admonished. The eighteen-year-old man sat at his desk with his head lowered in shame. Tears welled up in his eyes and began to roll down his cheeks.

Principal Goldman motioned for the woman to meet him in the hallway while the Spanish teacher, her mouth still agape with shock, came over to comfort the young man. By the time they made it back to his office, Denise, the older woman, had given him her side of the story. Jackson, the young man, was especially rude in class this evening. He was playing music on his phone. He made a rude comment to the teacher when she asked him to stop. He refused to leave his seat to participate in a classroom activity. He told the teacher to mind her own business when she redirected him a second time. According to Denise, it was her right and her duty as an elder in the school community to correct his behavior and she insisted that she did absolutely nothing wrong. It's part of the culture, she said. When she was growing up, everyone took responsibility for everyone else's kids and they told them right from wrong.

Speaking with Jackson yielded similar results. He immediately confessed that he had been playing music on his phone and that he was rude to the teacher. Shockingly, his story matched Denise's almost verbatim. Even more surprising was the fact that he didn't want Denise punished and he believed that she had acted appropriately in chastising him in front of the class. "It's no big deal," Jackson said. "Older people are supposed to do that when younger people get out of line."

Considering that both involved parties saw the situation the same way, everything seemed to be resolved. No harm, no foul was Principal Goldman's mindset until he received a visit from the Spanish teacher, Alexis, the next day. She wanted to know what the Principal was going to do about Denise's outrageous behavior. She disrupted the class, she insulted and threatened a vulnerable student, and she completely undermined the teacher as the source of authority in the room. Alexis said that students who witnessed the event felt the same way, and they demand there be swift and severe action.

Principal Goldman conferenced with every student who wanted the opportunity, and the reactions were mixed. Some of the students took the same position as the Spanish teacher. Denise's actions were inappropriate for class and that she had no right to talk to another student that way. In their eyes, the school was a place where everyone was treated equally and fairly—in fact, the student code of conduct said as much! What would happen to the school if we just let any older student treat a younger student this way? Other students disagreed. To them, the interaction between Jackson and Denise was part of the culture and the community they came from. It was perfectly normal for an elder to chastise someone younger and they were surprised by the restraint that Denise had shown.

Principal Goldman had a difficult decision to make. If he followed the student code of conduct, then Denise would surely be suspended from school for several days and it is unlikely that she would want to return. If he did nothing, was he simply teaching all the students that it is okay to berate someone younger than you if you think they are acting inappropriately? Furthermore, Jackson didn't want Denise punished and neither did many of the students. What message would Principal Goldman be sending about the value of the students' cultural beliefs if he punished Denise?

Questions for Discussion

1. What does the ethic of justice dictate that Principal Goldman do in this circumstance, and what does he risk by doing this?
2. One of the students said, "Denise only did that because she cares about Jackson." Through which ethical paradigm do you believe Denise viewed her actions? How is that similar to, or different from the way Alexis, the Spanish teacher, viewed her actions?
3. Discuss how the ethic of the profession intersects with cultural competency in this case, and whether it should have any impact on Principal Goldman's decision.
4. Consider the various personal and demographic factors that might influence Principal Goldman's decision in this case. How might the code of conduct look different if it were written by the students rather than the administration?

CASE STUDY 4.6 NO TO PETS, YES TO COMPANION ANIMALS

Beachfront University, like many colleges and universities, is exploring a pet policy to regularize the presence of animals on campus. Emotional support and service animals are common on the campus, but a growing number of commuter students and staff are bringing animals to campus for other reasons. Resident students would like the same opportunity since their pets remain at home. Provost Donna Smith asked the president of the student government, Roger, to be her co-chair for a campus-wide committee to develop the pet policy. The Provost is concerned that an animal rights group on campus will disrupt this process.

Anya is the group's leader, and she believes that pet ownership is unacceptable. Her group argues that the words we use have consequences—the pet policy should instead be called a "companion animal" policy. Without checking with Roger, Provost Smith decided to preemptively invite Anya to join the committee. She thought that a minority voice was needed. Roger has a different perspective than Anya. He believes that human rights trump animal rights. The action begins at a pet-friendly party hosted in the Campus Commons by Roger and members of the pet policy committee. Upon receiving an invitation to Roger's party because of her status as a committee member, Anya decides to make a grand entrance wearing a surgical mask and holding a stack of "free the animals" signs.

Pet-Friendly Party in the Campus Commons

Anya announces her arrival. "I am here to free the animals that you are holding against their will. These dogs and cats must be free to roam and play without tether." She proceeded to place animal liberation signs throughout the Campus Commons, and then quietly opened the front door. The cats were quick to run free. Anya's actions dumbfounded Roger and his friends. Laughter and a cacophony of canine and feline voices confounded the situation. Roger struggled to remain calm while slamming the front door and yelling, "These pets belong to us!" Cats were running free, and owners struggled to restrain their dogs. Roger was dragging Renaldo, his pet Chihuahua, across the room, with what appeared to be a choke collar, as he attempted to corral the untethered animals.

Alarmed, Provost Smith jumped on top of her St. Bernard to restrain him. Anya realized that her actions were inflammatory, but she did not hesitate to fuel the already chaotic situation by taking a video of what she saw as a pet-friendly party that was not very friendly to pets, including a scene where the Provost appears to be riding a St. Bernard. In Anya's view, these pet owners, many of whom were members of the pet policy committee, abused their pets with unwarranted restraint. Anya had the video to prove it.

Anya and Roger are Planning for the Next Pet Policy Meeting

Anya needed to prepare for the upcoming pet policy meeting. She knew that laws exist to prevent cruelty to animals by pet owners and that an important legal perspective on pet ownership was emerging. Several states prevent convicted animal abusers from owning or possessing an animal. Now, all she had to do was prove animal abuse by the committee members. Anya realized that this one incident, caused in part by her actions, would probably not stand up in court, and such a claim would be costly and time-consuming. Instead, she planned to go public with the video in support of her fight for animal rights, particularly if she does not get her way at the next pet policy meeting.

Provost Smith and Roger, while recovering from the pet-friendly party, realized that they were in a tight spot because of Anya's video. They believed that it misrepresented their love for animals and could be used to discredit the committee, and the University. Provost Smith, in consultation with the University President, Francis Williams, decided that the committee should work harder to address Anya's concerns for the rights of animals while drafting the campus pet policy at the next meeting.

The Campus Pet Policy Meeting

Roger, with Provost Smith as co-chair, called the meeting to order with a moment of silence for both Misty and Muffin, two cats who are now roaming the campus since Anya set them free at the party. Anya was respectfully silent, but with a smile on her face. Roger then uttered a few words, hoping to appease Anya. "Perhaps Misty and Muffin will be happier running free."

Anya did not respond even though Roger's comment revealed some sensitivity to her perspective. Roger then read a few general statements that he and Provost Smith prepared to guide the development of the pet policy. "Beachside University recognizes the positive benefits that well-behaved pets bring to the academic community, but the University also recognizes a need to consider staff and students with animal allergies and/ or a fear of some kinds of animals."

Roger described a well-behaved pet as "not too vocal or aggressive, and fully house-trained." This statement caused several of the committee members to realize that a liability waiver was also needed to protect the University. A lengthy discussion followed, but Anya remained quiet because, in her mind, this policy was more about protecting the University than animals.

Anya then asked to address the committee. "Permission granted," quipped Roger while rolling his eyes. Anya began by distributing educational materials prepared by the Animal Legal Defense Fund (ALDF). She weighed her words carefully. "As many of you know, I see my role on this committee as an advocate for the rights of animals. I take that role very seriously. We humans see ourselves as superior, but the differences between humans and other animals might be, as Darwin suggested, simply a matter of degree and not kind."

A productive discussion followed, and then Anya continued. "Our policy needs to incorporate ALDF guidelines to protect our companion animals from abuse. I believe that words have consequences. The word 'pet' should be replaced with the phrase 'companion animal' in the policy title, and throughout the document." Anya believed that this "sleight of terms" will carry a hidden message—we are animals, with animal friends. Words do matter, and so do pictures! Binging phones were heard across the room as a truncated version of the infamous video went viral, and Provost Smith was seen riding a St. Bernard.

Questions for Discussion

1. What should Provost Smith do? (What ethic/s should Provost Smith turn to for guidance?)

2. What are the challenges for the University in this circumstance? Which ethic would be most helpful in addressing these challenges?

3. Was Anya justified in her actions? From your perspective, what was Anya's ethical perspective?

4. Is pet ownership problematic from a justice perspective? From a care perspective? From a critical theory perspective? Why or why not?

5. What are some of the hidden messages in this case and what ethical frame(s) best explain them?

6. Are humans special? Justify your answer from an ethical perspective.

7. What solution to this problem would be in the best interests of the students at the university? Explain.

REFERENCES

Anyon, J. (1980). Social class and the hidden curriculum of work. *Journal of Education*, *162*(1), 67–92.

Anyon, J. (2005). *Radical possibilities: Public policy, urban education, and a new social movement*. New York, NY: Routledge.

Apple, M.W. (2016). *Official knowledge: Democratic education in a conservative age* (3rd ed.). New York, NY: Routledge.

Apple, M.W. (2018). *The struggle for democracy in education* (3rd ed.). New York, NY: Routledge.

Apple, M.W. (2019). *Ideology and curriculum* (4th ed.). New York, NY: Routledge.

Bennett, W.J. (1988). *Our children and our country: Improving America's schools and affirming the common culture*. New York, NY: Simon & Schuster.

Bennett, W.J., Finn, C.E., & Cribb, J.T.E., Jr. (2000). *The educated child: A parent's guide from preschool through eighth grade*. New York, NY: Simon & Schuster.

Crowley, M. (2020, September 18). Trump calls for a patriotic education for American children. *NY Times*, p. A19.

Fine, M. (1991). *Framing dropouts*. Albany, NY: State University of New York Press.

Freire, P. (1970). *Pedagogy of the oppressed* (M.B. Ramos, Trans.). New York: NY Continuum.

Freire, P. (1993). *Pedagogy of the city* (D. Macedo, Trans.). New York, NY: Continuum.

Freire, P. (1998). *Pedagogy of freedom: Ethics, democracy, and civic courage* (P. Clarke, Trans.). Lanham, MD: Rowman & Littlefield.

Giroux, H.A. (Ed.). (1983). *Hidden curriculum and moral education: Deception of discovery*. San Pablo, CA: McCutchan Publishing Corp.

Giroux, H.A. (Ed.). (2001). *Theory and resistance in education: Towards a pedagogy for the opposition*. Westport, CT: Bergin & Garvey.

Giroux, H.A. (2020). *On critical pedagogy* (2nd ed.). London, England: Bloomsbury Academic.

Greene, M. (1978). *Landscapes of learning*. New York, NY: Teachers College Press.

Greene, M. (1988). *The Dialectic of Freedom*. New York, NY: Teachers College Press.

Greene, M. (Ed.). (2000). *Releasing the imagination: Essays on education, the arts and social change.* New York, NY: John Wiley & Sons.

Hirsch, E.D. (1987). *Cultural literacy.* Boston: Houghton Mifflin.

Hirsch, E.D. (1996). *The schools we need and why we don't have them.* New York, NY: Doubleday.

Margolis, E. (Ed.) (2001). *The hidden curriculum in higher education.* London, England: Routledge.

McLaren, P. (2020). *Life in schools: An introduction to critical pedagogy in the foundations of education* (6th ed.). New York, NY: Routledge.

Nash, R.J. (1996). *"Real world" ethics: Frameworks for educators and human service professionals.* New York, NY: Teachers College Press.

Noddings, N. (2002). *Educating moral people: A caring alternative to character education.* New York, NY: Teachers College Press.

Noddings, N. (2003). *Caring: A feminine approach to ethics and moral education* (2nd ed.). Berkeley, CA: University of California Press.

Noddings, N. (2013). *Caring: A relational approach to ethics and moral education* (2nd ed.). Oakland, CA: University of California Press.

Parker, L. & Gillborn, D. (Eds.). (2020). *Critical race theory in education.* New York, NY: Routledge.

Purpel, D.E. & Shapiro, S. (1995). *Beyond liberation and excellence: Reconstructing the public discourse on education.* Westport, CT: Bergin & Garvey.

Ravitch, D. (2003). *The language police: How pressure groups restrict what students learn.* New York, NY: Knopf.

Ravitch, D. (2020). *Slaying Goliath: The passionate resistance to privatization and the fight to save American schools.* New York, NY: Knopf.

Ravitch, D. & Finn, C.E. (1987). *What do our 17-year-olds know?* New York, NY: Harper & Row.

Starratt, R.J. (1994). *Building an ethical school: A practical response to the moral crisis in schools.* London, England: Falmer Press.

Starratt, R.J. (2004). *Ethical leadership.* San Francisco: Jossey-Bass.

Weis, L. & Fine, M. (2005). *Beyond silent voices: Class, race, and gender in United States schools* (2nd ed.). Albany, NY: State University of New York Press.

Chapter 5

Personal Codes versus Professional Codes

Deborah Weaver, William W. Watts, Patricia A. Maloney, Susan Hope Shapiro, James F. Montgomery, Taryn J. Conroy, and Toni Faddis

In Chapter 2, the ethic of the profession was introduced as a paradigm and described in some detail as a way of viewing and solving ethical dilemmas along with the ethics of justice, critique, and care. The last three ethics and their applications, first articulated by Starratt (1991, 1994), have been cited and researched by many scholars in the U.S. and internationally (Arar, Haj, Abramovitz, & Oplatka, 2016; Berkovich & Eyal, 2018; Gurley & Dagley, 2020; Normore and Brooks, 2017).

Langlois & LaPointe (2010, 2014) have gone so far as to create and validate (Langlois, Lapointe, Valois, & De Leeuw, 2014) an Ethical Leadership Questionnaire, that quantifies educational leaders' answers based on these three ethics and propose a typology of ethical culture that relates to degrees of organizational support for ethical leadership (Lapointe, Langlois, & Tanguay, 2020).

Rarely, however, has the profession been treated as a separate and discrete ethic. In this book, we make an argument for a fourth paradigm, that of professional ethics, which includes ethical principles, codes of ethics, the ethics of the community, professional judgment, and professional decision making.

Shapiro and Stefkovich (1998) stress the importance of asking educational leadership faculty and students to formulate and examine their professional codes relative to their personal codes, the standards of professional practice (Johnson, 2020; Shapira-Lishchinsky, 2018; Young & Perrone, 2016) and the codes of national, state, and local organizations. They are not alone in this emphasis. Duke and Grogan (1997), Mertz (1997), and O'Keefe (1997), to name but a few, have also encouraged a similar process.

While the ethic of the profession is based on the integration of personal and professional codes, it is important to note that an individual's personal

DOI: 10.4324/9781003022862-7

and professional codes frequently collide, a situation which makes ethical decision making difficult for educational leaders. Shapiro and Stefkovich (1998), in their research of doctoral students in an educational leadership program, found that there were many conflicts both between and among students based on their professional and personal ethics.

Not only were the conflicts among students, but they were within oneself. In analyzing codes, Shapiro and Stefkovich and their students thought it was important for educational leaders to look for consistencies and inconsistencies between and within their own personal and professional codes (Bass, Frick, & Young, 2018; Murphy, 2017). Clashes were also discovered when an individual had been prepared in two or more professions. In this situation, codes of one profession might be different from another; thus, what serves an individual well in one career may not help him or her well in another.

The seven cases presented in this chapter offer the reader an opportunity to think through the decision-making process involving dilemmas that arise when an individual's personal ethics conflict with the professional ethics associated with public education. These cases highlight the paradoxes between personal and professional codes. In addition, the questions posed at the end of the cases encourage the discussion of other paradigms in relation to personal and professional codes. The ethics of justice, critique, and care may be applied to the dilemmas described in this chapter. Educational leaders sometimes incorporate more than one perspective in their personal and professional codes but are not aware of this crossover until they spend the time developing and reflecting on their beliefs.

In the first ethical dilemma, **Drunkenness or Disease?** (Case Study 5.1), a director of special education has been convicted of drunk driving. He is an alcoholic and the community wants him fired. Legally, the school district can do this because the state law says that school personnel may be fired for criminal convictions. However, the assistant superintendent for personnel is ambivalent because the individual is very effective in his work and has been so for a long time. In addition, the assistant superintendent believes this individual is suffering from a disease requiring support and assistance, not punishment.

Case Study 5.2, **Rising Star or Wife Beater?**, focuses on a health and physical education teacher and coach of high school football, wrestling, and baseball who is well regarded by the school superintendent and is in line for a new and important position. The administrator finds that the teacher has been brought up on charges of domestic abuse. Although he has had the greatest respect for the teacher professionally, the superintendent is now beginning to feel differently about the teacher on a personal level. Many angry parents have heard about the teacher's domestic behavior, even though charges were dropped, and ask for his dismissal at a school board meeting. The superintendent is faced with a difficult decision that he is asked to make in a public forum.

The third ethical dilemma, **Job Sharing: Some Real Benefits** (Case Study 5.3), introduces us to a school leader who must balance the needs of employees and the guidelines of her board of education. This case involves a pilot job-sharing program in a district where the teachers' union now demands full-time benefits for a year of part-time work. The union makes the case that currently only married people can afford to job share without a proper benefits package. This case resonates with the assistant superintendent for personnel on a personal level because she is single and would like to support benefits for unmarried people. However, professionally, she is aware that the job-sharing arrangement could establish a precedent enabling all part-time workers to request benefits. For the assistant superintendent, any decision made in this case may have repercussions that will affect her at the personal, and especially at the professional, level in her relatively young career.

In Case Study 5.4, **When Teachers Fight**, the administrator, in a preschool setting, must grapple with teachers disrupting the school owing to personal disputes. Despite what most would consider to be highly unprofessional behavior, the director cannot help but feel some sympathy toward a teacher who has worked hard to save her family from homelessness. For this administrator, the ethic of care conflicts with the ethic of the profession.

Case Study 5.5, **A Soldier and Family in Distress**, addresses the poignant problems faced by a military family when the father, a war hero, and an amputee, returns home. Here, the brutal ravages of war disrupt a soldier's ability to cope both physically and mentally and have a profound effect on his wife and twin boys, which, in turn, causes the boys to act out in school and affects their grades. This dilemma is especially difficult for the school leader who is sympathetic to the family but has a history of involvement in anti-war protests.

In Case Study 5.6, **Who Gets the Support?**, a principal is torn between allocating scarce resources for much-needed assistance in his office and an extra school counselor. Mr. Martins, the principal, is suffering health issues related to the stress of the job and desperately needs a second assistant principal to lighten the load. On the other hand, the school's one counselor is severely over-worked as she deals with an increasing number of students in crisis. Whether this principal should consider himself and his health first or whether he should put his students and support staff above his own needs stretches the limits of personal and professional codes.

Finally, Case Study 5.7, **An Empty Stomach or a Full Belly?**, is set during a national pandemic when school buildings are closed to instruction and teaching is online, but lunches for low-income students are available for pick-up. According to school policy, students must be accompanied by a parent to receive a lunch. Hence, a cafeteria worker refuses a student, sending him away to return with his parent who is at home. The boy never returns, and the school principal is wondering if she should contact the family and possibly bend the rule.

CASE STUDY 5.1 DRUNKENNESS OR DISEASE?

Dr. Mari Wang sat in her office long after the school day had ended, contemplating the most recent problem that had occurred in the Harrison City School District. Since becoming an assistant superintendent for personnel five years earlier, she had had her share of problems, but never one involving a key administrator, especially one whom she had supported for the position.

Mr. Kidder currently held the central office position of Director of Special Education and had done so for the past four years. He had been a superstar special education teacher and had earned a Masters' degree and a supervisory certificate some years previously that qualified him for the position when it fell vacant through a retirement. Mr. Kidder not only interviewed well but was also the teachers' first choice, having earned their respect and support during his 20-year service to the district as a classroom teacher as well as chairperson of several special assignments. In addition to his ability, Mr. Kidder possessed a charming and gregarious personality that often made it easy for him to develop an instant rapport with staff as well as parents. Dr. Wang had to admit that Mr. Kidder often brightened up her day with his stories, jokes, and optimistic attitude about life in general.

How sad that this was not the case today. In fact, just two hours previously, Mr. Kidder looked like the world had come to an end, and Dr. Wang was the only link saving him from a fate worse than death. Mr. Kidder's career was in jeopardy; he was about to go to jail because he had been arrested a few weeks earlier for drunk driving. It was his third conviction, punishable by a three-month imprisonment in the local county jail.

The court decided that due to his position in the School District, his character witnesses during the trial, and the lack of any other illegal convictions, he would be eligible for the work-release program, pending approval from his place of employment. Mr. Kidder explained that he would arrange to have someone pick him up at the prison in the morning and bring him to work. He would be able to work until 5:30 p.m. each day, when someone would take him back to the prison by the required curfew of 6 p.m. This would be the arrangement for the next three months, which would take him to the end of May.

After the specifics of the court's recommendations and subsequent plans of Mr. Kidder, Dr. Wang felt it necessary to question him about his actions and why he would allow himself to be put in such a situation in the first place. Obviously embarrassed and ashamed, Mr. Kidder revealed that he had finally admitted to himself that he was an alcoholic. He was not sure when it had all started, but the pressures of the job and an unstable marriage had been a lot to handle on a daily basis, so he had gotten into the habit of stopping at a local tavern for a drink or two after work. After the first two arrests, he sloughed it off as just being unlucky that he was caught and paid the fine. He had had a couple of drinks but was certainly able to drive safely. He really felt that he was not doing anything wrong and that the law was unfair, too strict, and the result of political pressure groups.

The third arrest, coupled with the seriousness of the consequences, made him take a hard look at what he was doing to himself. He went on to say that he had taken the first step to recovery by attending an AA meeting and had recently stood up and admitted that he had an alcohol problem. It was his intention to sign himself into an alcohol recovery program, through the district's employee assistance benefit program, after the school year ended. This would involve six weeks during the summer, which also happened to be his vacation allotment.

Mr. Kidder was confident that he would be able to return to work, well on his way to recovery, and that this type of incident would never reoccur. He was extremely apologetic for his actions and any embarrassment it might cause the school administration and was hopeful that the district would support his plans for recovery from this disease. Dr. Wang thanked Mr. Kidder for his candidness and told him she would get back to him with the decision of what action she would recommend to the superintendent and board of school directors the following day.

Dr. Wang realized that this problem had many facets to review before she could come to a decision. She knew she was in for a long night.

Questions for Discussion

1. Do you see Mr. Kidder's problem mainly as a disease or a lack of moral fiber? Explain your answer. Do you believe that as a teacher Mr. Kidder should be held to a higher moral standard than ordinary citizens? Why or why not? Should what Mr. Kidder does in his private life make a difference in his job status? Why or why not? Does it make a difference that he is a good teacher? A good administrator?

A good colleague? Where would you draw the line between what is of public concern and what is strictly private when considering school employees?

2. Suppose that the law was politically motivated. Does that make a difference as to what Dr. Wang should do? Do you believe the law is unjust? Too strict? Why or why not? Who does the law benefit? If the law were unjust, should that make a difference as to Dr. Wang's decision?

3. What would a caring person do in Dr. Wang's place? To whom should care be directed? Are there others who should be considered in addition to Mr. Kidder? Who?

CASE STUDY 5.2 RISING STAR OR WIFE BEATER?

Alex teaches health and physical education in Maple Grove, an affluent school district. He is also a very successful high school football, wrestling, and baseball coach for the district and is recognized by many coaches throughout the state as an exceptional coach. Many of Alex's teams have won conference and state titles during his tenure. His athletes admire and respect him, and revere him as a father figure and role model. A large percentage of his athletes earn athletic scholarships to attend major colleges and universities. Some have gone on to careers as professional athletes. Many people—parents and students alike—feel great deal of gratitude toward Alex for his time and effort in coaching, particularly Superintendent Brown.

Alex began his career as a substitute teacher in Maple Grove, always making himself available to the school district. He substituted in all subject areas as well as in physical education classes. He worked with all grades, and even volunteered his services to chaperone school activities such as dances, class trips, and any athletic event he was not coaching. He gave up his evenings and weekends to do what he could for the district in the hope of earning a permanent teaching position that would provide him with a contract and stability in his chosen profession. He was motivated and determined to earn a teaching position as soon as possible.

After three years of substitute teaching, Alex began to experience frustration and depression because he had not attained a full-time teaching position. However, a position was soon to open, and a contract would be awarded as well. In the interim, Alex continued to substitute as well as to coach football, wrestling, and baseball. Alex was particularly fond of coaching football and was considered an expert. Not only was Alex a talented coach, but he was very committed to coaching a winning program.

At the end of the school term, the teaching position Alex desired would be advertised, and applicants would start interviewing for the position. All of Alex's hard work and effort would soon pay off. A permanent teaching position and head coaching job were imminent. Even the assistant principal of the high school phoned him and offered his endorsement for the position. The interview process proceeded as scheduled. Alex's interview was nearly flawless.

The following day, Alex received a phone call from the high school principal, Mr. Young, and was offered the position. Alex was ecstatic. Alex thought Monica, his wife, would be pleased as well. The couple had two children. They lived in a lovely home in the district and both children attended the district's schools. Their older child attended the high school and was actively involved in many activities, and their younger child attended one of the elementary schools. Monica had a teaching degree in special education and worked for the district as a substitute teacher. There had been days when both Alex and Monica taught together in the same building and had their older daughter in class. On these days, both Alex and Monica acted very professionally and went about their responsibilities as usual.

By all appearances, Alex and Monica seemed to be the ideal couple and consummate professionals. Alex continued to excel at coaching, and the students in his classes all liked him very much. Superintendent Brown and Principal Young were very pleased with his recent evaluation and considered making plans to train and groom him for a future administrative position.

Monica seemed content to substitute regularly and was willing to start coaching a sport if the opportunity presented itself. Administrators were beginning to take notice of her positive teaching style and her ability to work well with students. However, although Alex and Monica's professional lives appeared stable and happy, their private life, especially their marital relationship, was undergoing serious difficulties.

In the ensuing weeks, Alex and Monica had many fights and arguments at home. Their marital problems continued to escalate, and the stress began to effect Alex's professional obligations and responsibilities. Alex was exhibiting a short temper with his students, colleagues, and even some parents. His physical appearance was disheveled, and rumors that alcohol could be smelled on his breath were circulating. Colleagues noticed that he often arrived late to school and late to some of his classes. His athletes also saw a change in his behavior at practices and were very concerned.

Principal Young also noticed these changes and immediately requested a conference with Alex. In their meeting, Alex confided to Principal Young that he and his wife had separated. He said it was a temporary situation and he felt a reconciliation was soon to occur. Alex apologized for his lack of professionalism over the past few weeks and assured Principal Young that it would not happen again. Superintendent Brown was informed of the matter but was not overly concerned.

The following week, Superintendent Brown received a phone call from the school district solicitor, who informed him that Alex had been arrested the previous night for assault and battery of his wife. She was not seriously injured during this incident and, therefore, decided not to press charges against her husband. Because the school year was coming to an end, Principal Young and Superintendent Brown decided not to make an issue of the incident. They also felt that the summer break would ease any community concerns about what had happened. Besides, Alex's reputation in the district was very positive, and he was the football coach. He did not need any bad publicity.

During the summer break, Alex had another altercation with his wife and was again arrested for assault and battery. This time his wife decided to file and press criminal charges against Alex. She even contacted her attorney to begin divorce proceedings. Her decision to press charges resulted in headlines in the local newspaper, thus alerting the community, school board members, and school officials to the situation.

The news of Alex's arrest spread quickly throughout the school district. Many parents were angry and very concerned about the situation. A group of parents organized to discuss their concerns and agreed to go to the school board to demand the resignation or firing of Alex. Reports indicated that more than 100 parents signed a petition supporting Alex's dismissal and that they planned to storm the next school board meeting in protest.

Shortly after Alex's arrest, his wife once again decided to drop the charges. District officials took the news at face value. They did not think about the cycle of battering as it affected this case. They even put aside their concerns about the community discord over the matter. School officials felt that at the upcoming board meeting a few parents would voice their opinions over this incident and then the meeting would proceed as scheduled. School officials, however, underestimated the outrage that community members were experiencing.

More than 100 parents attended the board meeting. There was standing room only, and the line of people outside the door continued to grow longer. A feeling of tension permeated the room as parents discussed their anger about the situation. School officials and board members were getting nervous and were quite concerned with what would take place at the meeting.

As the meeting got under way, one parent blurted out, "Get rid of Coach Alex; we don't want this type of person teaching our children." The other parents in the room started to cheer and yell their concerns. The president of the school board quickly hammered his gavel on the desk in an effort to bring the meeting back to order.

As the voices of angry parents lowered and the meeting came to order, the president of the Parent–Teacher Association (PTA), Mrs. Lewis, stood up and spoke on behalf of the concerned parents. In a calm, soft, articulate manner, she praised the accomplishments of Coach Alex. She was careful to address all the positive things he contributed to the success of the school, students, and the athletic program. She even mentioned how he had helped her son earn an athletic scholarship to college, but she stated firmly, "Regardless of his past record, we cannot tolerate such acts of violence from any of our teachers."

She continued by saying that teachers are role models to students, and parents entrust their children to people who are believed to be of high moral character. She concluded, "It is very clear that Coach Alex has violated our trust, and therefore, we ask for his dismissal." With that, she turned toward Superintendent Brown and asked, "What are you going to do about this?" The people in the auditorium instantly became silent. Superintendent Brown knew that these people were very upset and wanted a response. It was obvious that Superintendent Brown had an extremely difficult decision to make.

Questions for Discussion

1. What is the fairest choice Superintendent Brown could make? The most caring choice?

2. One might decide to allow Alex to keep his job based on a "greater good for the greater number" reasoning in that he has helped so many young athletes. What are the strengths and weaknesses of this argument? Do you agree with it? Why or why not? What course of action would be in the best interests of all students? Of the student athletes at Maple Grove High? As a coach, does Alex have a special responsibility to be a role model for his students? Is this responsibility more than that of a teacher who does not coach?

3. Compare Superintendent Brown's dilemma with that of Dr. Wang in the previous case study. Could it be argued that spousal abuse is a disease as alcoholism is a disease? Why or why not?

4. Alex has yet to strike a student. Is firing him a good preventive strategy? Why or why not? Do you see any ethical problems to this reasoning? If not, why? If so, what are they? Should a person's private life be just that, private? Why or why not?

5. What questions might a critical theorist ask in this situation? On what concerns might she or he focus?

6. What would you do if you were Superintendent Brown? Explain the reasoning behind your answer.

CASE STUDY 5.3 JOB SHARING: SOME REAL BENEFITS

Dr. Marisa Garcia is a single, 35-year-old assistant superintendent for personnel in the Birchwood School District. She has been in her current position for less than a year. Prior to her appointment as assistant superintendent, she was an assistant principal and a classroom teacher in the same district. Dr. Garcia is happy in her current position and usually enjoys the daily challenge of her work. However, today was an exception. As she drove home from a school board meeting, she had to admit that it was difficult to find enjoyment in solving her current dilemma.

The teachers' union had requested a meeting with the school board to negotiate several changes to the school district's employee job-sharing benefit. Before the meeting with the union, Dr. Garcia met with the school board. Bob Johnson, head of the board's personnel committee, made it quite clear that the school board was not interested in any changes at this time. He then noted that Dr. Garcia was expected to make a recommendation to the board following her meeting with the union to enable the district to prepare for negotiations.

Mr. Johnson owned a small business that had not been very profitable, but it had been successful enough to put food on the table. He was always complaining about the cost of insurance and other benefits he had to provide for his own employees. He often voiced his opinion about teachers being "spoiled," especially when he compared education to the business world. He had been known to say: "This is a small town and the taxpayers are getting real angry about how much the teachers get, compared to other workers."

Because contract negotiation was one of Dr. Garcia's responsibilities, she was the administrator who would be meeting with the teachers' union. Although she had never been involved in a contract negotiation from the administrative side of the table, she knew the teachers had no bargaining power. The job-sharing benefit had been presented by the union the previous year. The board adopted it as a one-year pilot program; therefore, it was not officially negotiated into the contract, and the current contract was still in effect for another year.

The meeting began with a review of the current guidelines for job sharing. Although James Jacobs, the union president, was extremely intelligent and an excellent teacher, he often argued for the sake of a good argument, especially with Marisa Garcia. Mr. Jacobs had a problem with Dr. Garcia's quick ascendancy through the hierarchy. It had been rumored that Mr. Jacobs had informed a few union members that this would be an easy sell, insinuating that Dr. Garcia would not be able to hold her ground against him.

After reading the guidelines, Mr. Jacobs requested the first modification. Two other union representatives in attendance remained silent for most of the meeting except to talk among themselves or echo Mr. Jacobs' sentiments. Dr. Garcia agreed to the first modification, as it was merely a change in the wording of a sentence. The second request was not so easy.

Under the current guidelines, a full-time teacher interested in job sharing gives up full-time status for one year. The current teachers' contract states that part-time employees do not receive medical benefits. Therefore, any teacher involved in a job-sharing situation is not eligible for benefits. The union was requesting a revision of this provision. The union felt strongly that the provision was not fair and did not provide equal opportunity to all teachers. The union felt the district was discriminating against teachers based on marital status because only teachers with spouses who were employed and receiving medical coverage would be able to take advantage of the benefit.

Dr. Garcia did not respond to the claim of violating equal opportunity; however, she informed the union representatives that the board would not support the revision of the job-sharing benefit that maintained medical benefits. Part-time employees did not receive benefits in this district. If the district provided benefits for the job-share employees, then all of the part-time employees would expect benefits. The district could not afford to extend benefits to all part-time employees. The union countered by saying that the difference is that the job sharers are full-time, tenured employees and deserve to maintain their benefits: "We don't believe the union can accept it any other way; we represent the entire faculty—not just those who are married with two incomes."

Dr. Garcia then asked, "Are you saying you are rejecting the current proposal?" Although she cared deeply about this issue on a personal level, she knew what her professional strategy should be for this meeting. Thus, she began by explaining that there were three teachers requesting job sharing for the following year.

Absorbing this new piece of information, Mr. Jacobs replied by saying, "Rejecting it would not be fair to those teachers. We will accept it. However, the language should read that the district agrees to extend the pilot for a second year." Despite their personal differences, in Dr. Garcia's opinion, Mr. Jacobs had raised a few valid arguments. Dr. Garcia knew that, on the one hand, she had really wanted to advocate for single people being able to take advantage of this opportunity; on the other hand, she wanted to uphold the guidelines as directed by the school board. Upholding these guidelines would also show Mr. Jacobs who was in charge.

Dr. Garcia knew how important this decision was to her young career as assistant superintendent. What if her recommendation forced a teachers' strike? Or what if her recommendation made the board think she was just another woman who was indecisive and willing to extend job sharing indefinitely under the guise of a pilot program? For Marisa Garcia to clearly understand her own position and make a recommendation to the board, she knew that she had to determine if equal opportunity as well as care and concern were afforded to all teachers in the district.

Questions for Discussion

1. What are the possible courses of action that Dr. Garcia might take? Of these, which is the most just? Why? Which is the most caring? Why? In this situation, must there be a conflict between what is just and what is caring? Explain.

2. Dr. Garcia is a single woman with her own personal convictions regarding this matter. What would you expect these convictions to be? Should they enter into Dr. Garcia's judgment of the situation? Why or why not?

3. If benefits are extended to job-sharing individuals, should they then also be extended to other part-time employees? Why or why not? Who do you suppose initiated the job-sharing program? Who benefits from it? Who is left out?

4. From a caring perspective, how should Dr. Garcia address Mr. Jacobs' concerns? Mr. Johnson's concerns? How would you answer this question from a justice perspective? Must these answers be different? Why or why not? If you were Dr. Garcia, what would you do to resolve this dilemma?

CASE STUDY 5.4 WHEN TEACHERS FIGHT

Carol Johnson is the director of a day-care center in a large metropolis. She has just promoted Tanya, a former assistant teacher, to head teacher of the two-year-old classroom. Although she is not the most highly trained person, the children and parents love her.

Tanya is a single mother with a 3-year-old child. She also cares for her sick elderly mother who suffers from multiple sclerosis. Her family had spent several years living in a shelter, which has been very hard on everyone. Currently, the money Tanya brings home is the family's major income. The head-teaching promotion has given her the ability to move her child and her mother out of the shelter. Ms. Johnson is aware of this situation and has seen the pride Tanya has felt as she was finally able to move her family into a small but safe place that they can call home. Tanya is now able to provide for her family on her own without relying solely on the use of food stamps and welfare, which were so impossibly hard to get by on.

Tanya has tried valiantly to get everyone in her family back on their feet. Because of this, Tanya's little sister, Delta, also works at the school as an assistant teacher. She was hired due to Tanya's high praise of her little sister's work with children. Delta always has a smile on her face each morning and has proved to be a hard-working and caring assistant.

Unfortunately, situations change. Thursday started out like any other day at work. It was a warm spring day and the children were playing outside. They had a good lunch and began to have their rest time. During the children's break, the teachers took their lunch in shifts. One teacher went to lunch while the other watched the sleeping class. Normally it is important for a teacher to eat her lunch within a limited period, and then return to enable the other teacher to eat within the time span of rest time.

On this particular day, Delta took the first shift for lunch in her room. After a long period of time, she did not return. The other teacher in the room became annoyed because she was hungry and needed a break. Tanya heard about her little sister's lateness and volunteered to miss her own lunch and watch the room so that the other teacher could take a break. As time went by, Tanya became more and more upset. When Delta finally arrived back from lunch, an hour late, Tanya was furious. She told her sister that her lateness was a bad reflection of her own standing within the school. She told her she had missed her own lunch. Despite the reprimand, Delta did not seem to care. In fact, she responded by indicating that Tanya should mind her own business and not tell her how to handle her professional life.

Although the children were still sleeping during rest time, the two sisters began shouting at one another in the classroom. Tanya was furious and Delta egged her sister on by telling her to punch her if she was so mad. Their shouting grew so loud that Ms. Johnson could hear it in her office at the other end of the school.

Ms. Johnson ran out of her office to discover the cause of the shouting. But by the time she arrived, Tanya had pushed Delta into a stack of chairs and both teachers were screaming. In fact, Tanya was being held back physically by two other teachers who were trying to prevent the fight from escalating.

In the other classrooms, the teachers were doing their best to shield the children from the altercation but, due to the volume of the shouting, the youngsters in this small school were aware of the fight. Some even witnessed the pushing and shoving.

Ms. Johnson's presence quickly ended the altercation but the damage had been done. She separated both teachers and made them take independent walks outside to cool down. Children and teachers saw and heard the altercation. All of the teachers were upset and worried. Some of the children seemed to be fine, as many of them had slept through the fight, but others looked a little anxious and confused.

Ms. Johnson's immediate reaction was that she should fire Tanya and Delta on the spot. However, it did not seem to be such an easy decision when it came to Tanya. Ms. Johnson knew that if she did this, Tanya, her child, and her ailing mother would end up back in the shelter. Ms. Johnson returned to her office and closed the door while she decided what to do.

Questions for Discussion

1. Can Ms. Johnson justify keeping Tanya in her position? What does the law say regarding this kind of behavior in a preschool situation?
2. If there is no law, should there be one? Why?
3. Should Ms. Johnson consider the problems that Tanya and her family will face if she loses her employment? Should she consider Delta's difficulties?
4. As a professional, if you were in Ms. Johnson's shoes, what would you do in this case? How would you explain your decision? Discuss.

CASE STUDY 5.5 A SOLDIER AND FAMILY IN DISTRESS

Will Duncan, Richardson Middle School's counselor, took an exasperated deep breath and leaned back in his chair. Not 45 minutes ago, he had two brothers in his office. An experienced counselor, Will had worked with middle school students for seven years before moving back to his hometown where he assumed the position of staff counselor for a small charter school. Sometimes, he found himself counseling and helping the families of former school classmates. This was the case today.

As prepared as Will was, he was ill-equipped to deal with his two most recent students. The Dvorin twins were told to report to Mr. Duncan after a particularly significant episode of acting out. The two brothers reportedly pushed a fellow student to the ground after knocking his books out of his hands. They followed this with a string of obscenities. In recent months, the two brothers' behavior had been in steady decline. Their grades, along with many absences and numerous recently failed tests, had damaged both of their class standings.

Mr. Duncan knew the students' mother. He had gone to high school with her. Will also spent time as a baseball coach and knew the boys from after-school sporting events. Following a visit to the school's disciplinarian, they found themselves in Will's office.

Will asked the brothers why their grades were in decline and about their attendance and the incident. Both brothers seemed uninterested in talking about what has happened. Both students dodged Will's questions but were quite forthcoming about their father's career in the military and his heroism. Will had never had the opportunity to meet their father. The only things he knew about him were through the limited contact he had with Mrs. Dvorin.

Will had very little experience with the military and counseling children of service members. He had never had overly negative feelings toward the military. He was, however, especially against the recent wars being conducted by the United States and attended anti-war rallies in the recent past. Will, at heart, was not in favor of any war. As a counselor, he always thought there were better ways to settle disputes than fighting. Nonetheless, Will was a professional and would deal with this situation without letting his political views get in the way.

Mr. Duncan began asking about their father. The two brothers discussed their father's military career, including the Bronze Star for valor he won in Afghanistan. The counselor listened uncomfortably as they described the events leading up to their father's award. Sergeant First Class (SFC) Dvorin was responsible for five enemy killed-in-action as he worked to save another soldier caught in a vehicle that was under enemy fire. Will noted that the story ended quite abruptly after that. When questioned about what happened in the aftermath, the students offered little more detail.

The bell rang and Will inquired if it was ok to make a call to their home to talk with their parents. Seeing the alarm in the boys' eyes, he reassured them that he was old friends with their mom, and he would only be following up on today's incident and how he might be able to help further. Later that day, Mr. Duncan dialed the Dvorin household and Mrs. Dvorin picked up. During the conversation, she apologized for her sons' behavior and attendance. Mrs. Dvorin indicated that her husband had been medically retired and that she spent a great deal of time shuttling him to and from physical therapy. The rest of her time was taken with a part-time job. Otherwise, she avoided speaking about her husband, which reinforced Mr. Duncan's notion that there were larger problems at home.

Her silence was especially troublesome because the local police department had been in contact with the school in recent months concerning domestic problems happening at the home. The report did not feature a lot of detail but simply requested that the children be monitored for signs of abuse. Following his conversation with Mrs. Dvorin, Will conducted an online search of the family and came across a few police blotter reports from the local newspaper. The reports detailed two domestic disputes and another particularly distressing instance of an apparent suicide attempt by SFC Dvorin. The reports indicated that he was an amputee receiving regular treatment at a Veteran's Administration Hospital.

Will was at a loss. He had a great desire to help the boys but was struggling with a way to accomplish that. The family was clearly trying to support SFC Dvorin. In this case, the entire family was devoted to the person who was at the root of the problem. They were unwilling to do anything that would have a negative effect on SFC Dvorin.

The situation took a turn for the worse when both boys found out that Mr. Duncan had been detained by the police several years ago for attending an anti-war rally in Washington D.C. In the intervening days, he attempted to deal with the situation from many different approaches, but each try was met with denial and accusations that Mr. Duncan was unpatriotic because he was a war protestor. Mrs. Dvorin developed a deep distrust of the school counselor and the school. With the students' behavior at a steady low, Will Duncan did not know how to proceed.

Questions for Discussion

1. In this case, what would the ethic of the profession first and foremost require of Will? What are the competing value sets? Do you think it's possible to completely divorce one's personal values from one's professional actions?
2. Are there perhaps other avenues of support where Will could seek assistance?
3. How does the ethic of care apply to this situation?
4. Under the ethic of critique, would you address this situation differently if SFC Dvorin was not a veteran? Was not a war hero? How? Why?
5. Regardless of political leanings, how would you attempt to act in the best interest of the students?

CASE STUDY 5.6 WHO GETS THE SUPPORT?

Mr. Martins has been the principal at Hot Springs Middle School for the past five years. Prior to taking on the role of principal, he served in several other positions at the school, such as assistant principal, site coordinator, and classroom teacher. He lives in the town of Hampshire Hills, where the school is located. During Mr. Martins' time at Hot Springs Middle School, he has seen many changes occur that are taxing both his teachers and support staff in ways that he is unsure how to address.

Currently, the most pressing issue is a thirty percent increase in the school's student population over the past five years. Further, no new teachers or support staff have been hired in the past five years. Central office administrators in the district attribute the increased enrollment to two likely factors. First, many families have moved from a nearby major city to Hampshire Hills in the past few years. Second, South Valley Charter School has recently closed its doors and left 222 students without a place to call home. Many of those students have enrolled in Hot Springs Middle School.

Hot Springs Middle School has always been underfunded compared to other schools in the district. Teachers and administrators have felt the disparity even more since the increase in student population. For example, class sizes are well beyond state and national levels, with more than 30 students in a class at one time. Often there are not enough books or materials for all the students. The school consists of one school counselor, one part-time school psychologist, and one part-time school social worker. The administration team includes one principal and one assistant principal.

Despite having an assistant principal on his leadership team, Mr. Martins realizes the increasing demands at work are having a negative impact on his health. He is often stressed, anxious, has gained quite a bit of weight over the past two years, and has high blood pressure. Mr. Martins does not make time to care for himself because all his attention goes towards addressing the needs of his school. At a recent doctor's visit Mr. Martins was told that if he did not make some serious life changes, he would have to begin taking blood pressure medication.

This year Mr. Martins has been able to delegate a few administrative tasks to an experienced teacher who is in a Masters' program for educational leadership. She is completing her internship hours at Hot Springs Middle under Mr. Martins' supervision. Mr. Martins is impressed with her work ethic and believes she would be a valuable second assistant principal at his school if the opportunity ever presented itself. He knows that having a second assistant principal, especially with a growing student population, would benefit him greatly and allow him to focus more on his own personal health as well.

At the same time, Mr. Martins has been hearing more frequently from teachers that there are several students who appear stressed and anxious during the school day. Teachers note that many of the new students coming to Hot Springs Middle have a variety of mental health issues that appear to have not been previously addressed. Teachers have observed that students will often break down in tears during class and detail experiences from both at home and school that make them feel anxious. Many of the teachers feel ill-equipped to handle the levels of stress and anxiety students are exhibiting in their classrooms. They discuss this concern with Mr. Martins and ask him for more training and support on how to better handle these situations.

The school counselor, school psychologist, and school social worker are often used as resources for students when they are experiencing high levels of stress and anxiety. Unfortunately, due to the part-time status of the school psychologist and social worker, most of the burden of addressing these needs falls to Mrs. Larson, the school counselor. Mrs. Larson is a professional and has been working at Hot Springs Middle for over seven years. Mrs. Larson is becoming increasingly more concerned that the mental health needs of the students require more attention than she alone can provide. She was especially taken off guard when Maia, a student she has been working with for the past two years, showed up in her office one day visibly high.

Mrs. Larson had been aware that Maia was dealing with anxiety and depression, but never knew Maia to self-medicate. After getting Maia to the school nurse, contacting her parents to pick her up from school, and sending her to a local hospital for assessment, Mrs. Larson expressed her concerns to Mr. Martins that more needs to be done to support the mental health needs of the students. After a long discussion between Mrs. Larson, both administrators, and the school psychologist, Mr. Martins agreed this was an issue that needed to be brought to the superintendent.

Mr. Martins called a meeting with the superintendent and reiterated the changes that have taken place at Hot Springs Middle School over the past five years. He briefed the superintendent on the increase in student mental health issues and the lack of support available to his teachers and support staff to address those needs. Further, Mr. Martins explains how his own health has been affected by the changes at his school. After considering all that was shared, the superintendent offers Mr. Martins a solution.

The superintendent will budget for Mr. Martins to hire either another assistant principal or another school counselor. He is very clear that the district cannot afford to hire two additional employees at this time, so Mr. Martins must choose one or the other. Mr. Martins was not expecting this and is unsure how to proceed. On the one hand, having another assistant principal to support curriculum and instruction efforts in the building would directly benefit Mr. Martins and make his workload more manageable. It would also give him time to focus more on his own health.

On the other hand, Mr. Martins cannot ignore the concerns brought forth by his teachers and school counselor. He knows that having another school counselor at Hot Springs Middle School would help address the mental health needs of the students. Mr. Martins has a decision to make and must do so in a very short amount of time. The superintendent is awaiting his response.

Questions for Discussion

1. What factors should Mr. Martins consider so that he makes a fair decision?
2. What considerations would critical theorists consider in this situation? Who are the marginalized voices in this case?
3. What does the ethic of care require of Mr. Martins? What will be the impact of his decision on the students? Teachers? Other administrators?
4. What would the ethic of the profession require Mr. Martins to consider? What is in the best interests of the student in this case?
5. If you were Mr. Martins, what would you do? Would you be inclined to hire another assistant principal, who would benefit you directly or would you hire another school counselor? Provide the reasoning for your decision.

CASE STUDY 5.7 AN EMPTY STOMACH OR A FULL BELLY?

The outbreak of the Covid-19 disease forced many schools to close abruptly, which was the case in the elementary school district where Sarah Keane is in her second year as principal at Topaz Elementary School. Though national events were being monitored that week, Sarah was astonished by the speed of the school shutdowns that occurred on Friday afternoon. There was neither time, nor information available, to prepare 400 children for what would become a school closure for an indefinite amount of time. In addition to the anxiety expressed by staff, Sarah was alarmed by how school closures would affect the Topaz school community as 100% of students qualify for free and reduced lunch.

The United States Department of Agriculture (USDA) operates a Summer Food Service Program (SFSP) to ensure that children from low-income homes continue to receive nutritious meals when school is not in session. National policies dictate the conditions necessary for schools and districts to seek reimbursement for student meals; failure to comply may significantly compromise remittance. While the SFSP typically operates during the summer months, meals may also be provided at schools that are operated on a year-round calendar or during emergency school closures.

Meal service for students aged 1–18 was slated to begin the following Monday at schools in the district where Sarah works. She coordinated with district nutrition managers and the school's cafeteria staff to provide a bagged breakfast and lunch for children to pick up from school and eat at home. The USDA policy that states breakfasts and lunches must be consumed onsite was officially eased due to community health concerns about transmitting Covid-19. However, a local policy, intended for student safety, requires a parent to accompany a child to the school when obtaining a meal from the SFSP. District officials communicated this policy to all staff and school community members through multiple channels, including email, all-calls, and posted information on websites. Sarah's messages to families in the Topaz community also echoed the district's directive that a child must be accompanied by an adult when picking up food from the school.

When food distribution began at Topaz Elementary, Sarah oversaw the process and was pleased with her cafeteria staff's attention to safety measures and the efficiency for providing meals to the students and families that arrived, many of whom came on foot. Once there was a lull in foot traffic, Sarah excused herself to use the restroom in the main office. When she returned, she learned of an incident that had occurred moments prior. Julio, a ten-year-old boy, had heard from a neighbor in his apartment complex that kids could obtain free food from the school. Julio rode his bike to the school to get lunch but was turned away by Ms. Linda, one of the cafeteria workers, because he wasn't accompanied by an adult. When Ms. Linda inquired where his mother was, Julio responded that she was at home. Ms. Linda asked if Julio could come back with his mother to get the food. Julio nodded, got back on his bike, but was not seen again.

After investigating, Sarah felt conflicted because she recognized that Ms. Linda was following the local policy and was not ill-intentioned. However, Julio went home empty-handed, and she was not sure how he received this message. While she had observed Ms. Linda consistently using a kind tone with students, she wondered if Julio felt reprimanded, disregarded, or insignificant.

Questions for Discussion

1. This case study involves moral aspects pertaining to students' physical, social, and emotional care. Should Julio, or any other child, go without food because an adult did not accompany him when he attempted to pick up a government-subsidized school lunch? Should the age of the child matter?

2. Suppose you are the principal of Topaz Elementary School. Do you believe there are times when it is warranted to break an established policy and disrupt the status quo? If so, would you advise or direct Ms. Linda or another employee to provide a government-subsidized lunch to any child, whether or not an adult is present? What, if any, are the downstream consequences that may occur from your actions?

3. When questioned, Julio informed staff that his mother was at home. Could Julio be lying or misrepresenting the truth? If so, what might be some of the reasons he would mislead staff? Does the ethic of the profession compel you to probe Julio for additional information related to his home life? If yes, what are you attempting to accomplish or prove?

4. While the USDA eased SFSP policies due to the Covid-19 school closures, the local policy regarding picking up government-subsidized food was not modified. From an equity perspective, what are some of the broader implications that result from this approach? In what ways might the ethic of justice support or impede a principal's agency to make in-the-moment decisions during a pandemic?

REFERENCES

Arar, K., Haj, I., Abramovitz, R., & Oplatka, I. (2016). Ethical leadership in education and its relation to ethical decision-making: The case of Arab school leaders in Israel. *Journal of Educational Administration, 54*(6), 647–660.

Bass, L., Frick, W.C., & Young, M.D. (Eds.). (2018). *Developing ethical principles for school leadership: PSEL standard two*. New York, NY: Routledge.

Berkovich, I. & Eyal, O. (2018). Ethics education in leadership development: Adopting multiple ethical paradigms. *Educational Management, Administration, and Leadership, 48*(2), 270–285.

Duke, D. & Grogan, M. (1997). The moral and ethical dimensions of leadership. In L. G. Beck, J. Murphy & Associates (Eds.). *Ethics in educational leadership programs: Emerging models* (pp. 141–160). Columbia, MO: University Council for Educational Administration.

Gurley, D.K. & Dagley, A. (2020). Pulling back the curtain on moral reasoning and ethical leadership development for K-12 school leaders. *Journal of Research on Leadership Education*. Retrieved from https://doi.org/10.1177/1942775120921213

Johnson, C.E. (2020). *Meeting the ethical challenges of leadership: Casting light or shadow* (7th ed.). Thousand Oaks, CA: Sage Publications.

Langlois, L. & LaPointe, C. (2010). Can ethics be learned? Results from a three-year action-research project. *Journal of Educational Administration, 48*(2), 147–163.

Langlois, L., & Lapointe, C. (2014). A measure of ethics. In C. M. Branson & S. J. Gross (Eds.), *Handbook of ethical educational leadership* (pp. 337–351). New York, NY: Routledge.

Langlois, L., Lapointe, C., Valois, P., & De Leeuw, A. (2014). Development and validity of the ethical leadership questionnaire. *Journal of Educational Administration, 52*(3). doi: 10.1108/JEA-10-2012-0110.

Lapointe, C., Langlois, L., & Tanguay, D. (2020). How are you managing, ethically speaking? A typology proposal of ethical culture. *Canadian Journal of Educational Administration and Policy, 194,* 64–77.

Mertz, N.T. (1997). Knowing and doing: Exploring the ethical life of educational leaders. In L.G. Beck, J. Murphy, & Associates (Eds.). *Ethics in educational leadership programs: Emerging models* (pp. 77–94). Columbia, MO: University Council for Educational Administration.

Murphy, J.F. (2017). *Professional standards educational leaders: The empirical, moral, and experiential foundations.* Thousand Oaks, CA: Corwin.

Normore, A.H., & Brooks, J. S. (2017). *The dark side of leadership: Identifying and overcoming unethical practice in organizations.* Bingley, UK: Emerald Publishing Limited.

O'Keefe, J. (1997). Preparing ethical leaders for equitable schools. In L.G. Beck, J. Murphy, & Associates (eds), *Ethics in Educational Leadership Programs: Emerging Models* (pp. 161–187). Columbia, MO: University Council for Educational Administration.

Shapira-Lishchinsky, O. (2018). *International aspects of organizational ethics in educational systems.* Bingley, UK: Emerald Publishing Limited.

Shapiro, J. & Gross, S.J. (2017). Ethics and professional norms. In Murphy, J.F. *Professional standards for educational leaders: The empirical, moral, and experiential foundations* (pp. 21–37). Thousand Oaks, CA: Corwin.

Shapiro, J.P. & Stefkovich, J.A. (1998). Dealing with dilemmas in a morally polarized era: the conflicting ethical codes of educational leaders. *Journal for a Just and Caring Education, 4*(2), 117–141.

Starratt, R.J. (1991). Building an ethical school: A theory for practice in educational leadership. *Educational Administration Quarterly, 27*(2), 185–202.

Starratt, R.J. (1994). *Building an ethical school: A practical response to the moral crisis in schools.* London, England: Falmer Press.

Stefkovich, J.A. & Frick, W.C. (2021). *Best interests of the student: Applying ethical constructs to legal cases in education* (3rd ed.). New York, NY: Routledge.

Young, M.D. & Perrone, F. (2016). How are standards used, by whom and to what end? *Journal of Research on Leadership Education, 11*(1), 3–11.

Chapter 6

The Melting Pot versus the Chinese Hot Pot

Emily R. Crawford, Joseph A. Castellucci,
Robert L Crawford, Omar X. Easy,
Monica N. Villafuerte, Katarina Norberg,
and Steven J. Gross

Many of us are familiar with the metaphor of the melting pot. It emerged as an aftermath of the popular play written by Zangwill (1910). The play, *The Melting Pot*, presented an acculturation model molding immigrants into a "predetermined standard of desirability" (Wong, 1993). Along with this concept, the national motto of *e pluribus unum*—from many, one— also conveyed this desire to create Americans from a "dizzying array of peoples, cultures, and races" (Sewell, DuCette, & Shapiro, 1998). The metaphor of the melting pot left it to the schools to educate students from many cultures through a common language, a common history, and common goals, principles, and values. The schools bore the burden of producing the social and cultural integration required to create "real Americans."

But what is meant by real Americans? (Salomone, 2010). What is the ideal American who should emerge from the melting pot? Judging by the writings of Cushner, McClelland, and Safford (1992), this concept seems not to have changed for more than 100 years. They wrote:

> Real Americans are white and they are adults: they are middle-class (or trying very hard to be); they go to church (often Protestant, but sometimes Catholic as well, although that is a bit suspicious); they are married (or aim to be) and they live in single-family houses (which they own, or are trying to); they work hard and stand on "their own two feet"; they wash themselves a good deal, and generally try to "smell good"; they are patriotic and honor the flag; they are heterosexual; they are often charitable, only expecting a certain amount of gratitude and a serious effort to "shape up" from those who are the objects of their charity; they eat well; they see that their children behave themselves. (p. 216)

DOI: 10.4324/9781003022862-8

Despite the emphasis on acculturation through the schools and other institutions, there have also existed other forces such as the distinct languages, histories, goals, principles, and values of different ethnic groups that emerged from the community, the home, and the individuals themselves (Covaleskie, 2016; Cushner et al., 2011, 2018; Salomone, 2000). For most minority groups, then, in this age of diversity, the melting pot metaphor no longer seems viable (Berray, 2019; Calderon Berumen, 2019). Instead, the concept of the Chinese hot pot (Tek Lum, 1987, p. 105) may be a better fit for their view of American culture. In the hot pot, although all the food ingredients are cooked together, each maintains its unique flavor and texture.

The transition from the metaphor of the melting pot to the hot pot has not been easy or smooth. Tensions and inconsistencies exist that can lead to paradoxes or dilemmas. For example, schools, on the one hand, want students to understand and appreciate other cultures while, on the other hand, they want to socialize young people to become American citizens.

As immigration, especially that of refugees, increases, this dilemma is not restricted to the U.S. At the end of 2019, the United Nations Refugee Agency reported that some 79.5 million persons were displaced due to violence, persecution, conflicts, and human rights violations, and 26 million of these persons were refugees, the highest number reported to date (UNHCR, 2021).

In 2017, Nordgren published a mixed methodology study of Sweden's approach to educating refugee children, comparing his findings to that of the U.S. He studied Sweden because it had the highest per capita number of refugees as well as a firm commitment to accepting refugees and educating their children. He compared his findings with that of the United States because "it is a nation with a reputation for being a nation of immigrants and holds great economic and political importance in the world" (p. 80).

Based on the literature as well as the findings in his study, Nordgren concluded that the best way to address the challenges of educating refugees involves cultural competence on the part of teachers and other educational leaders and relational closeness between the refugees and individuals in their new culture. Cultural competence would include hiring educators who understand and are open to immigrants' culture without feelings of superiority. Unlike the U.S., Sweden has long had a national commitment to cultural competence. Relational closeness requires increased interactions between the native and refugee populations.

The cases presented in this chapter illustrate paradoxes between the dominant culture of the melting pot and the different ways of life of the hot pot. They challenge the reader to examine the conflicts that occur when the dominant culture in schools meets subcultures and "other" backgrounds. Recognizing the growing influx of migrants in other counties, we have expanded this idea past the United States and included a dilemma from Sweden. Two questions worth considering are: Which party has the greater share of social capital? What are the assumptions the school leaders have about the "other" and their customs/social classes in each case?

After reading the case studies that follow, it is important to take the time to consider the questions at the end of each case. Hopefully, these questions will challenge the reader to reflect on the dilemmas from the perspectives of the ethics of justice, care, critique, and the profession.

Case Study 6.1, **A Home for Marlon: The Foster-child Case**, serves to demonstrate how difficult it can be to determine where the language of rights is rejected, and a dialect of care is embraced. Here, a school's director of pupil personnel services must choose between laws, responsibilities, and relationships as he determines whether to pass on to his friend, a teacher, harmful information about a foster-child's background for whom the teacher is providing a home.

In **Parents' Rights versus School Imperatives** (Case Study 6.2), a principal from a school in an upper-middle-class community witnesses a father spanking his son at school. The father is working class and well meaning, and the son has many behavioral problems. The parents are divorced, and the father has custody of the son to save him from a bad situation with his mother. The principal is legally bound to report this incident as child abuse to the proper authorities, and yet he questions making the report.

Turning to the ethical dilemma, Case Study 6.3, **Lost in Translation**, an English language learner with special needs is new to the U.S., although born in this country, and has accused his parent of hitting him. The father, who is from South America and illegally living in the U.S., appears to be a caring parent, but he is clearly having trouble managing a challenging child. In this dilemma, the Spanish teacher, who serves as a translator, must decide whether to provide an accurate translation of the youngster's words, which might lead to a child abuse charge for the father or try to deal with the problem in her own way. Even though this dilemma is very different from Case Study 6.2, the possible mistreatment of a child is the issue in both instances.

The theme of immigration and documentation follows through with a different twist in Case Study 6.4, **Legally Permissive but Ethically Responsive? Undocumented Students and Immigration Enforcement**. This situation involves undocumented parents who are in an elementary school and others who will soon be dropping off their children. While such a practice is common in this district with its large immigrant population, the situation becomes complicated when immigration enforcement authorities are spotted in the neighborhood investigating possibly non-compliant businesses. While these government authorities are not empowered to investigate schools, parents are worried about what will happen when they enter or leave the school. With procedures unclear, the school's principal must make a quick decision as to whether to shelter the parents already in the building, warn those parents on their way to school, and/or take other actions.

In Case Study 6.5, **Homeless Student: Discipline Must Be Maintained**, three students are charged with violating state criminal laws, including breaking and entering. As per district policy, the usual sanctions for such offenses include immediate out-of-school suspension pending an exclusionary hearing. Complications arise when the suspected ringleader's advocate requests a referral for special education testing. In these cases, the solution is home schooling—except that the student has no home.

Case Study 6.6, **When Refugee Students Challenge the School's Culture**, describes the case of Richard a principal of a school known for high performance in Seatown in the middle of Sweden. In 2015, for the first time, Richard's school was asked to accept refugee students from the Middle East. On the one hand he wanted to and needed to accept and support these students. Yet, on the other hand, he faced fears from teachers and concerns from parents about the possible impact of these new students on the school's reputation. Additionally, he faced requirements that the school maintain its high level of performance from the Central office. This left Richard with a dilemma: How will he accept these students while at the same time resolve the fear, concern, and demands placed upon him?

CASE STUDY 6.1 A HOME FOR MARLON: THE FOSTER-CHILD CASE

Marlon, a 16-year-old-male classified as emotionally disturbed, enrolled at the Benjamin Franklin High School in September, and was assigned to a self-contained special education classroom. Marlon had been relocated into the district to be placed in a new foster-care home. He had been in various residential placements and foster-care homes since the age of ten. Marlon was removed from his biological parents after it was discovered that he was the victim of their sexual and physical abuse. Marlon's student file contained reports documenting three years of increasingly disturbing behaviors. He was demonstrating an escalating pattern of frequent fire-setting and had reportedly sexually molested two young children with whom he shared a foster-care placement.

Jim Campbell, the school's director of pupil personnel services, is concerned because Marlon's new foster parents are Mr. and Mrs. Kearns, a well-respected, kind couple who fit in well with this conservative, church-going community. Mrs. Kearns is a part-time art aide at the high school. Mr. Kearns is a businessman who travels frequently and works long hours.

They have two young children: a 6-year-old girl and a 3-year-old boy. Mr. Campbell has frequently socialized at the Kearns' home for birthday parties, dinners, and other family activities. He has young children like the Kearns family. As per foster-care state law and policy in this state, Mr. and Mrs. Kearns have not been informed of Marlon's history and behaviors.

Resolving to put things right, Mr. Campbell quickly left school the day he first read Marlon's student file, firmly convinced that he knew the right thing—the only thing—to do. Although sure in his conviction, Jim also knew he should not act immediately. He needed time to evaluate the situation to make a reasoned decision. Walking through the school parking lot that afternoon, he was clear on one thing. No way was he going to permit the Kearns family's two children, children just like his own, to be potential victims of a sexually aggressive, emotionally disturbed youth. Although he felt a need to wait until the following day to make a decision, he felt certain that his desire to protect the Kearns family would primarily inform his decision.

Later that evening, with his children tucked up in bed and his wife asleep early with the flu, Mr. Campbell decided to give the issue deeper consideration. As he settled under the covers, he thought about his own children safely tucked up in their beds. He also hoped for the safety of the Kearns children. Before turning off the bedside lamp, Jim read over the Personal and Professional Code of Ethics he had written down some time ago, now kept as a bookmark in his Bible. What caught his attention was a particular line. It read: "Always be a voice, a presence for the comfort and protection of the weak, the innocent, the defenseless . . . because there but for the grace of God go I." And there but for the grace of God so went his children. However, unlike the Kearns family, they did not have this threat of a stranger in their home as they slept.

Mr. Campbell knew he had to tell Mrs. Kearns about Marlon's past, about the potential danger now posed to her children. Mr. Campbell was a deeply religious family man who valued his children, and all children, immensely. He began his career as a teacher because of his desire to help children. The care and protection of students was central to his moral code.

As he lay thinking of the Kearns' children, Mr. Campbell was confronted with the image of Mrs. Kearns crying in his office, telling him the details of how Marlon one night had done the unspeakable to one of her children.

He then saw himself confessing that he was sorry, that he had known about Marlon all along. Perhaps, if he had revealed to her the truth, her tragedy could have been avoided. Jim saw a tearful Mrs. Kearns challenge him: "You knew, you knew about this all along and you did not tell me! How could you let this happen to my children?"

Then something else began to creep into his thoughts. Even as he imagined Mrs. Kearns condemning him, he remembered that, in addition to being a concerned father, he was also a man with a very serious professional responsibility. In his current role as director of pupil personnel services he began to feel a certain uneasiness. In one sense, this was not an unfamiliar position for Mr. Campbell. He had certainly been aware of other situations in the past that were similar or worse, involving issues such as sexual abuse, incest, drugs, and domestic violence. Although he had been disturbed, he had never been tempted to violate students' privacy and confidentiality, even though some of the situations had been much worse than the Kearns family's current situation. His thoughts about confidentiality led him to consider the consequences. "And what about the consequences of my actions?" thought Mr. Campbell. "I've never violated a student's confidentiality before. Credibility demands honesty. If word got out that I told the Kearns about Marlon, how would my teachers and the other students feel? Would they feel confident that they could talk with me confidentially? Would I still be credible in their eyes?"

"Beyond credibility," his thoughts continued, "are there any legal ramifications if I violate the laws governing student privacy? Would this jeopardize my current position? Would I be passed over if I ever wanted to become superintendent?"

"Foolish!" he screamed inside. "We're talking about children here. Maybe all these confidentiality laws protecting juvenile criminals weren't good laws in the first place!"

Mr. Campbell was growing increasingly concerned and physically upset at this seemingly unsolvable dilemma. He did not even want to look at the clock, knowing all too well that it was much too late to claim a good night's sleep. He again recalled his Personal and Professional Code of Ethics: "Always be a voice." But for whom was he supposed to be a voice? Who was supposed to receive the charity, mercy, forbearance, and benevolence that he mentioned in his Code? What did these words really mean anyway? Mr. Campbell began to wonder about Marlon. Was he asleep, or was it a sleepless night for him also? Mr. Campbell wondered how many sleepless nights—nights of turmoil and fear—Marlon had suffered in his young 16 years. Wasn't Marlon a victim too? Perhaps it was Marlon who really was the weakest, most defenseless voice in this whole mess. The Kearns' children, like Mr. Campbell's own children, had warm, stable, loving homes, but what was it like to be moved from home to home as a child? The reality of the situation, beyond all the worries, was that only one child had been repeatedly victimized. That child was Marlon.

Mr. Campbell, under his warm covers, felt thankful for the security and comforts of his own home. "If I told Mrs. Kearns, she would immediately have Marlon removed from her house." So where would Marlon go next: another move, another school, another strange room during another sleepless night? A sinking feeling hit Jim; a deeper sadness, not anger, just sadness for Marlon. The youngster did not seem such a monster now. In fact, he did not really know Marlon at all, just what Marlon's records said and what his own fears had portrayed him to be.

Mr. Campbell imagined Marlon reporting to his office prior to leaving the school due to another move, another transfer into another foster home. He saw himself seated at his desk in his office. Before him stood Marlon, who with tired eyes simply said, "You told them about my past. They weren't supposed to know. I wanted to start all over again. I just wanted what every other kid has, a home. I've already been hurt too many times by adults I trusted. How could you do this to me?" As he continued to reflect, Jim did not know what bothered him the most, his own anger or his own tears.

Despite the difficulty, Mr. Campbell knew he must view the current dilemma from a more objective perspective. Thus, a fundamental question remained: Did Marlon's presence in the Kearns' home pose a grave danger to the Kearns family? First and foremost, he considered that although Marlon may have a past history of dangerous behaviors, including fire setting and sexual molestation, he had not yet demonstrated harmful behavior or expressed intent to engage in harmful conduct. Marlon had not yet crossed the line to suggest that he posed a grave risk to the Kearns family.

The dilemma for Mr. Campbell was based partly on emotional identification and affinity for the Kearns family and the projection of his own fears concerning Marlon. The situation that objectively confronted him at this juncture involved only the potential of dangerous behavior and his own fears. Marlon had not shown any indications to warrant concern for the Kearns family.

Mr. Campbell clearly agonized over this decision. Neither course of action relieved him of responsibility for potential adverse consequences. All night, he tossed and turned, and as he did so he constantly asked: What would be the best way to resolve this dilemma? How could I reach a decision that would be in harmony both professionally and personally?

When the morning dawned, Mr. Campbell finally made his decision. He decided not to tell Mrs. Kearns about Marlon's past. His reward was simply a sense of relief stemming from the feeling that his decision was in harmony with who he knew himself to be, as both an administrator and a person.

Questions for Discussion

1. Do you think Mr. Campbell made the best decision? Why or why not? If you were in his place, what would you have done?
2. Assume that Mr. Campbell did not personally know the Kearns family. Would that factor make a difference, in your opinion, as to the best course of action? Why or why not? What if Mr. Campbell did not know the Kearns family but knew Marlon very well? Should that factor make a difference in his decision?
3. Consider this case from the point of view espoused by Kohlberg (1981), Gilligan (1982), Gilligan & Richards (2009) and Noddings (2003, 2013). How might the decision have played out considering each of these theorists?
4. Mr. Campbell chose not to break his state's law regarding the confidentiality of foster-children's records. Do you agree with his decision? Is it ever justifiable to break a law when making an administrative decision? When? Do you see any way that breaking the law might have been justifiable in this case?
5. Was Mr. Campbell's decision in Marlon's best interests? In the best interests of the other students? In the best interests of the community? What community? Do you see any conflict between what appear to be Mr. Campbell's personal and professional codes of ethics? Between his codes of ethics and his actions? Explain.

CASE STUDY 6.2 PARENTS' RIGHTS VERSUS SCHOOL IMPERATIVES

It was 4 p.m. on Friday afternoon, and Ned Parker was still at his desk. In front of him was the pamphlet distributed by the state's Division of Youth and Family Services that detailed the school's role in preventing child abuse. Among other things, the pamphlet was very specific regarding school officials' responsibilities. Any school official or teacher who fails to report suspected child abuse, the pamphlet read, could be held criminally liable.

Of course, Ned Parker was aware of the legal responsibilities of school officials regarding possible child abuse cases. Indeed, he had presented in-service training to his teaching staff on just that subject. As principal at Sandalwood Elementary School, Ned had reported dozens of suspected child abuse cases over his eight-year tenure even though the school was situated in a mostly upper-middle-class community. He understood his responsibilities all too well. Yet, on this Friday afternoon, he felt very unsure of himself. Earlier that day, he had witnessed a parent beating his child but was hesitant to report this incident as child abuse.

The child in this case was Robert Buck, a sixth grader who was both small in stature and emotionally immature for his age. He had transferred to Sandalwood earlier in the school year from a district in another state, following the bitter divorce of his parents. Robert's father, Frank Buck, had been awarded full custody, and the transition was anything but smooth.

Robert was a discipline problem from almost the first day he arrived. He was constantly disrupting his classes, disrespectful to his teachers, and both physically and verbally abusive to his classmates. Needless to say, his academic achievements were few. Robert had been a frequent visitor to Ned Parker's office and had been rapidly progressing through the various levels of the school discipline policy.

Frank had also been a frequent visitor to the school. He was a rough and relatively uneducated working-class man who had dropped out of high school to marry his pregnant girlfriend. He lived on one of the few streets in the community that had escaped gentrification, a street very close to the school district's boundary line. However, he was glad to live in this district, hoping that a good education might make up for all the problems in his son's life.

When his marriage went sour, Mr. Buck made every effort to gain full custody of his only child to remove him from what he called the "unhealthy influence of his mother." In his dealings with Frank, Ned had believed him to be a concerned parent who was doing his best with the child under very difficult circumstances. He had personally come to the school each time there was a problem with his son. His meetings with the principal and each of Robert's teachers had always been cordial, and he had often expressed support for the school's efforts toward his son. He regularly attended parent back-to-school nights and was one of the few fathers who was active in the PTA.

It was becoming apparent that Robert was not responding to the typical disciplinary practices of the school. After a series of disruptive behavior reports from teachers, Mr. Parker suggested to Frank that he implement a remediating program suggested by the school psychologist. All indications were that Frank was dutifully following this program.

The final straw came early on Friday when Robert was sent to the principal's office for what his teacher described as behavior that was out of control. Ned called Frank to inform him of the problem. Angry, Frank said, "This has gone too far. That boy needs to be taught once and for all how to behave." With that, he abruptly hung up the phone.

Ned did not quite know what to make of that phone conversation until Frank appeared at his office door no more than 20 minutes later. With a facial expression clearly displaying anger and frustration, he apologized to Ned for the trouble his son had caused. "Now I'm going to do what I promised if I had to come out to this school again," he said to the boy. With that he grabbed his son's arm and jerked him out of the office and down the corridor. Ned followed him out and was horrified at what followed.

When they got to the end of the corridor, Frank threw his son up against the wall and began thrusting a pointed finger in his chest. Ned could barely make out what was being said, but it sounded angry and threatening. Then Frank forcefully turned his son around and began spanking the boy across the backside no fewer than eight times. Pain and embarrassment were evident on Robert's face as tears streaked down his cheeks. Ned shouted down the hall, "Please, sir. That is not necessary." Frank bellowed back, "I'll decide what is necessary for my son." With that, he grabbed Robert by his shirt collar and marched him out of the door.

Now, Ned Parker sat in his office contemplating whether he should report the incident as child abuse. On the one hand, he thought, he had clearly witnessed behavior he himself would never condone in himself or any of his teachers. The brutal nature of the spanking was also disconcerting and clearly painful to the boy, and who knows what kind of beating Robert might receive in the privacy of his father's home.

On the other hand, it was only a spanking. As a boy, Ned himself had been spanked by his father for misbehavior; yet he would never consider his father to be a child abuser. Many parents spank their children routinely and would be appalled at any suggestion that they were committing child abuse. Anyway, what business does the school have interfering with parents' rights to discipline their own children as they see fit?

Ned knew what the consequences would be if he reported this incident to his state's Division of Youth and Family Services. The division routinely filed child abuse charges against parents for cases with less evidence than this one. The children were typically placed in a foster home until the case was resolved in court. Parents were usually fined and forced to undergo counseling and parenting classes. In the most extreme cases, the child could be removed from the home permanently.

Ned also knew the consequences of not reporting a suspected child abuse case. He remembered an incident from a few years before in a neighboring school district where a man mercilessly beat his 10-year-old daughter to death for accidentally breaking a dish. School officials were accused of neglecting to report suspicions of abuse that they held for months before the child's death. Ned did not want to be held responsible for another such atrocity.

Nevertheless, Ned believed that Robert's father was a concerned and loving parent who had given in to personal frustration over the continued misbehavior of his son. After all the other disciplinary alternatives had failed, he probably resorted to carrying out a standing threat. Was it really child abuse or merely a thorough and well-deserved spanking? Is it right to make this father answer for his actions in a court of law and possibly face losing his son? Is it ethical to ignore this incident and possibly enable this father to severely hurt his son? Ned stared at the phone on his desk and wondered whether he should make that call.

Questions for Discussion

1. Do schools have the right to determine how parents may discipline their children? Do you believe that Mr. Buck's actions constitute child abuse? Why or why not? How do your state laws define child abuse? Should Mr. Parker report this incident to the authorities? Why or why not? If Ned thought Mr. Buck's actions were not child abuse, but feared that Mr. Buck was, or could become, more violent at home, should he report the incident to the authorities? Discuss the pros and cons of taking action against an anticipated wrongdoing.

2. What do you suppose was the purpose of states instituting child abuse laws? Who likely supported or rallied for such laws? Who do these laws benefit? Do you believe that such laws are fair? Why or why not? If there was a class difference between those who fought for the law and those whom the law affected, would that change your opinion of the laws? Why or why not? Should exceptions be made in these types of cases, or should the law be followed literally? Explain your answer. Should professional judgment be a consideration in reporting such incidents? Why or why not? How would this work? Whose professional judgment should be considered and why those persons as opposed to others?

3. What is the most caring solution to this problem? Would it be caring to report Mr. Buck? What solution would be in Robert's best interests? The best interests of all students?

4. Some 31 states have passed laws forbidding corporal punishment in schools (Center for Effective Discipline, 2020), and many, if not most, school districts have policies opposing this type of discipline. Discuss the pros and cons of corporal punishment in schools. Is there a difference between corporal punishment in schools and similar types of discipline at home? Explain. Is there a difference between corporal punishment and child abuse? How are they the same? How are they different?

CASE STUDY 6.3 LOST IN TRANSLATION

It was 8:25 a.m. and the day was just beginning at the primary school. Each teacher met her students outside to escort them to the classroom. From the onset of the day, the co-teachers of one of the second-grade classrooms knew this wasn't going to be an ordinary day when Pablo walked into the school sobbing. The young boy could barely utter a few Spanish words when he was warmly greeted by his English-speaking teachers. Both the general education teacher and the special education teacher looked at each other with bewilderment, not knowing how to begin to assist the upset 8-year-old boy.

The child in this case is Pablo Guzman, a new English language learner (ELL) recently arrived from Ecuador. Pablo, born in the United States, has lived with his mother and older brother in South America since the parents' deportation four years ago. Currently the boy and his father rent a room from a neighborhood family as the two adjust to their new living arrangements, getting to know each other on a daily basis. The parents agreed that it was in the child's best interest to return to the U.S. because his schoolteachers were physically abusing Pablo due to his inappropriate behavior at the Ecuadorian public school. The father recounted that he could no longer afford to send his wife enough money to cover his son's medical expenses, since the boy was seeing therapists regularly. On several occasions Pablo had also mentioned that his older brother didn't love him and would often beat him when their mother wasn't home.

Pablo's transition has been anything but smooth, particularly because he has difficulty communicating in his native language, doesn't speak any English, has trouble following directions, trusting others, and socializing with his peers. Pablo disrupts his class several times a day, is disrespectful to his teachers, has pulled down his pants in class, and has shown aggressive behavior towards his classmates. While many of the Spanish-speaking children in class are eager to translate for Pablo and his teachers, the amount of off-task time for all the students is immense.

To assist the classroom teachers, both the English as a Second Language (ESL) and Spanish teachers have been serving as translators/school counselors/deans on a daily basis. At the teachers' requests, the father has been extremely cooperative in providing previous school records, medical documentation, and demonstrating complete willingness to work collaboratively with the school to assess the child's educational and neurological needs. Within the few short months Pablo has been at the primary school, the young boy is showing willingness to learn English and has shown some academic and social progress in small groups.

Early that Monday morning, the special education teacher shuffled Pablo into the building, and coincidentally ran into the Spanish teacher in the stairwell. She kindly requested a translation to understand her student. Pablo told the Spanish teacher that his father had hit him with a belt the night before and again that morning because he wouldn't eat his meals. Although the boy's speech wasn't very clear, the teacher could decipher the child's accusation. The Spanish teacher knew for a fact that Pablo had never expressed this concern since his arrival at the primary school. As a Latina and mother, she understood the Hispanic culture's acceptance of spanking, empathized with the father's frustrations, and recognized that this could be an isolated incident. Based on her encounters with the father, she strongly believed that this was not a suspected case of child abuse. However, she also acknowledged that her colleague was expecting to hear a true translation of what the boy had stated.

The Spanish teacher knew what the consequences would be upon translating the boy's accusation and she feared what the father's reaction would be if this case was reported to the Department of Youth and Family Services (DYFS). She immediately recalled that during a previous meeting, Mr. Guzman had appeared defeated by the challenges of raising a special needs child alone in this country. He was so distraught that he had mentioned the possibility of sending Pablo back to live with his mother in Ecuador. Fearing for the boy's ultimate safety, she hesitated before translating her conversation with the little boy.

The Spanish teacher wondered if the father's illegal immigrant status might indeed cause him to send the boy back to Ecuador if he felt threatened after the school reported the case to the DYFS. Besides, what constituted "real" child abuse—an occasional spanking from his concerned father or the daily abuse at the hands of his Ecuadorian schoolteachers and older brother? She was sure that if she addressed this concern with the father herself, it could be handled without reporting it to the DYFS.

Questions for Discussion

1. How might this dilemma be viewed through the lens of justice? Are there laws, policies, guidelines, or issues of fairness that the teacher might consider?
2. How might this dilemma be viewed through the lens of critique? Consider the student, the Latina teacher, and the father.
3. Taking into account school/family relations, has the family been treated in a caring manner?

4. What would the education profession expect of the teachers and the principal? How could an understanding of the Latino culture serve to meet the student's best interests?

5. What would you have done in this situation if you were the Spanish-speaking teacher?

CASE STUDY 6.4 LEGALLY PERMISSIVE BUT ETHICALLY RESPONSIVE? UNDOCUMENTED STUDENTS AND IMMIGRATION ENFORCEMENT

"Buenos días, Principal Valle!" a second grader calls out as she enters César Chávez Elementary with her mother.

"Buenos días," Principal Valle replies to the little girl and a dozen other families going into the school.

The chorus of greetings from student after student reflects the school environment as a warm, nurturing, and safe place for learning. As the lead administrator, Principal Valle takes her professional role and the education of children seriously.

Principal Valle can see Officer Wilkinson, the school's resource officer, casually talking to parents and students. Officer Wilkinson knows the local residents and has developed a trusting relationship with them. The residents help Officer Wilkinson keep an eye on the school. Wilkinson's presence reassures school staff, students, and residents, especially as there is increased gang activity in the area.

Principal Valle and Officer Wilkinson trade pleasantries and small talk with community members in a mix of English and Spanish, and they reflect on the school community. The school has its challenges, but it also has a lot of heart and potential. Many students come from low-income backgrounds. Most are on a free or reduced lunch program. The school has also failed to make Annual Yearly Progress (AYP) two years running, but test scores are rising. Parent involvement at the school is growing. There is mutual trust between the school and community, and parents like Principal Valle.

There are undocumented students at César Chávez, but these students are not treated differently from other students. Their education is equally vital to Principal Valle and her staff; it is also her legal obligation. In her principal preparation program, she learned about a Supreme Court decision that stated that children of undocumented parents are legally guaranteed a K–12 education. Anyway, a student's legal status is rarely discussed in the school, although some undocumented parents have confided in teachers. Occasionally a child's parent is deported. Principal Valle feels a strong sense of responsibility for what goes on in her school; she tries to stay aware of what is happening in students' academic and home lives.

Principal Valle walks toward her office. In the hallway she notices adults crowded in the front office. They are speaking urgently with the office assistant, Ms. Bianca, and they look incredibly worried. She hears the words "la migra," several times—and knows it means immigration enforcement authority.

The parents tell Principal Valle that immigration enforcement vehicles are down the road from the school. They don't want to leave the school building out of fear. Principal Valle knows this fear intimately; her uncle was undocumented. Further, some of the school's teachers come from families with undocumented members. Many think the U.S. immigration system is broken and prejudiced against Latinos. Principal Valle feels similarly, but her personal beliefs about immigration should not cloud her judgment in this situation.

Principal Valle urges everyone to stay calm, and she reassures the parents they are safe and can stay in the school. She thinks about the students. Officer Wilkinson walks into the office, and they have a quick, hushed conversation. He returns outside to patrol the school grounds.

Ms. Bianca answers the ringing phone. Principal Rob Carson from Fairview Elementary is calling. Principal Valle picks up the phone.

"Hi, Rob. It's Maria Valle."

"Hi, Maria. I'll keep this quick. Some of our parents say that immigration is in the vicinity of Fairview. Anything happening near you?"

"I just walked to the front office. Several parents are here saying immigration is around. Two people said they spotted white vans, which is typical of immigration enforcement. I'd heard rumors immigration authorities are ramping up raids on businesses hiring undocumented workers, but enforcement hasn't been close to school. What's happening at Fairview?"

"Same thing. No parents are in my office, but I've received multiple calls from parents concerned that agents will pick them on up on their way to school. A few worry agents will come into school looking for undocumented kids. What bad timing, too. Like yours, our kids are in the middle of testing."

"Right. Bad timing. I don't think enforcement would come into an elementary school. Not sure whether it's legal or not, but I can't imagine they'd go after young children. I'll call our district legal department to see what they know. Meanwhile, as a precaution I'll call for a school lockdown. I'll call you back shortly."

"Ok. Thanks, Maria."

Principal Valle uses the PA system to alert teachers of the lockdown. Students somehow heard immigration was around and are worried for their parents. Principal Valle soon calls Principal Carson back.

"Rob, legal said they can't say anything about immigration enforcement in the area. We need to decide how to proceed. Legal said we can call parents to say there's talk that immigration is around, and parents might have someone else pick their child up from school."

"That sounds sensible. Thanks. Call me if anything else happens or if you want to talk further."

"Certainly, Rob. Thanks. Good luck."

Principal Valle looks for the school counselor to confer with her. She also needs help to call parents. Her plan is to walk through the hallways to ensure all classroom doors are shut, in keeping with school lockdown procedures. She is still uncertain whether she should have let parents stay in the school. If immigration authorities come looking for a parent, it would place her in an awkward position. She wouldn't want to betray the trust of her students' parents but lying to government officials could have severe consequences, something that seems beyond the scope of her position as a school leader.

Questions for Discussion

1. Do you agree with Principal Valle's course of action? Why or why not?
2. What is Principal Valle's responsibility toward the community? Was it in students' best interests to let adults stay in the school?
3. Should Principal Valle's personal feelings about U.S. immigration color her decision making?
4. How much and what kind of information should be shared with students in this situation?
5. What would the profession expect of Principal Valle in this context?

CASE STUDY 6.5 HOMELESS STUDENT: DISCIPLINE MUST BE MAINTAINED

As the fall season rolls in—one of the best times of the year in the northeastern region of the country—it is always accompanied by more troubling acts by teenagers. Critics seems to think it is how society is these days, but from a school leader's point of view it is just the changing of the season and youngsters are trying to find things to replace the ever-so-busy summer days.

It was one of those typical bi-weekly Friday morning meetings with all of the principals from the elementary schools, the principal and vice-principal of the high school, the school resource officer, a representative from the district attorney's office, and the superintendent of schools. The meeting normally began by going over the juvenile and adult driven court cases from weeks before, proceedings where participants would review the new arrangements of both juveniles and adults.

This morning, however, was a little different. The meeting began with an arraignment of a case that involved two freshmen. These students were charged with violating state criminal laws: Daytime Breaking and Entering (B&E) with Intent and Elderly in Fear (placing a person of 60 years of age or older in fear generally by assault and/or battery). They were immediately suspended for ten days pending an exclusionary hearing.

Principal Mr. McDonald and Vice-Principal Mr. Ernest met with both high school students individually. Based on the felony charges for both students, the principal and vice-principal had the right to exclude these students from school, which would end their high school careers before they even began. Mr. McDonald and Mr. Ernest met with student number one, Douglas Roberts, and his parent, a single mother. Douglas and his mother were in tears after they realized that he was on the verge of being excluded from school. Douglas then stated that he did not enter the house of the elderly woman; it was his friend, student number two, Kevin Nulls.

The police report indeed stated that one student entered the house and the other stood watch outside. Mr. McDonald and Mr. Ernest decided to keep Douglas suspended for the ten days and then bring him back to school under stipulations, including: checking in with the vice-principal once a week, joining a club and/or sports team, and maintaining a clean conduct record. Also, he could not be absent from school without a note.

That same afternoon Kevin Nulls was brought in for his meeting; he had with him his mother, grandmother, attorney, and Department of Children and Families (DCF) worker. Immediately, the administration realized that this was not going to be easy. Naturally, the school attorney was present; the meeting began by the principal explaining to Kevin and his team the charges and the position of the school. Kevin had no reaction; his mother blurted out that she told him this would happen if he didn't behave himself. She also stated that he never listens to her, but instead, tells her to shut up, and pushes her down. Kevin's mother proceeded to say that she was not working, had lost her apartment in the city of the school's location, and was now staying in a room of a friend in another city.

"I don't know what to do, I can't take care of him, I am afraid of him. His dad is not around so he won't listen to me!" said Kevin's mother.

Out of nowhere Kevin yelled out, "Shut your mouth!" His DCF worker moved over to him quickly and held his hand to calm him down. The next move by the DCF worker was the game changer. She simply said that she wanted Kevin Nulls to be tested for Special Education (SPED).

When Kevin and his team left the meeting, Mr. McDonald and Mr. Ernest knew that they had a very difficult decision to make. They both realized that Kevin was likely the one who orchestrated the entire B&E and probably would be charged with the crime. According to school policy and based on past practice, this student should be excluded from school. With the introduction of SPED, however, the district may be required to home school him. These school leaders are left wondering how this situation can be resolved in an ethical matter knowing that Kevin does not have a place to call home.

Questions for Discussion

1. What legal restrictions bind these school leaders? What actions would be most just? Most fair?
2. How could the ethic of care be applied to this situation?
3. Under the ethic of critique, how should Mr. McDonald and Mr. Ernest discipline Kevin Nulls as compared to Douglas Roberts? More or less harshly? The same? Explain your answer.
4. What would the profession expect of Mr. McDonald and Mr. Ernest?

CASE STUDY 6.6 WHEN REFUGEE STUDENTS CHALLENGE THE SCHOOL'S CULTURE

In 2015 there was a great refugee migration towards and within Europe. In Sweden, with its ten million inhabitants, the number of asylum seekers doubled from 81,301 asylum seekers in 2014 to 162,877 in 2015. Consequently, the situation made heavy demands on municipalities, school leaders and educators who experienced increasing diversity followed by new and complex challenges.

All children in Sweden between 7 and 16 years of age and registered in a municipality are subject to compulsory school attendance, regardless of their legal status. Newly arrived[1] students have a right to education, whether they have a residence permit or not. Richard, a principal with 15 years of experience as a school administrator and his first year in Blue School was faced with a dilemma: on the one hand he wanted to and was required to accept these refugee students yet on the other hand he had to respond to the qualms of teachers and parents who were concerned about the impact such a new influx might make to the school and its community. The thorny question of what constituted "Swedishness" i.e., speaking Swedish, sharing the same traditions, and knowing the same national history, further complicated the issue as did the district's demand that school performance sustain its heretofore high level of achievement.

Richard described the challenge facing him in this way:

> I've been working as a principal since 2002. First as a deputy and since 2005 as principal for compulsory schools and upper secondary schools, public and independent schools. Today I run a public compulsory school, grades P-9, with around 500 students in total. It is quite exciting since I now have returned to my childhood's school; I was a pupil here 30 years ago.
>
> Blue School is situated in a socio-economic advantaged school district and there are high demands and expectations regarding the students' outcomes. The school has almost no history of migrant students; it is in contrast to my earlier experiences. I have, for instance, opened a school with 85% migrant students. I learned a lot during those years. We had nowhere to go with our questions, no literature to learn from; we had to solve our challenges ad hoc. I have graduated from the National Principal Training Program but school leadership for diversity was not an issue in the program.
>
> When I came to Blue School in August 2015, I asked for newly arrived students. The first group of eight students arrived in October 2015. The reaction from the staff and parents was not long in coming. Several of the parents phoned and posed frank questions "What was I thinking?", and "How could I guarantee their children's safety?" This new situation awakened emotions, a turbulence, and an insecurity among a quite conservative and comfy group in the school where Swedishness is extremely over-represented.
>
> I did not have the opportunity to select my educators as I could when I opened the school I mentioned earlier. Several of the staff members displayed a resistance to work differently, to cooperate and help each other in this new situation. None of the staff members left the school but I had those who cried. The teachers asked: "What do I do now? What material shall I use? Who will take care of this group of students? How am I supposed to cope with this?" They wanted to send the students to the special education teacher, in order to transfer them to a different group. They had several suggestions all aiming to exclude the newly arrived students from ordinary classes. It was the same reaction as if it concerned students with learning disabilities. They did not know how to handle the situation and became nervous and unsure as educators. I would like to believe that their perspectives were limited due to their lack of knowledge and relevant experience.

Adding to this tense situation, Blue School was under pressure due to demands for high grades from the central office. This school is a high-status school and is expected to have good student outcomes. The results had declined so better grades were the goal. That in turn increased our teachers' stress.

Richard was no stranger to the needs of newly arrived students, yet he found himself in a school community where this was a dramatic departure from the norms of the past. There were faculty members and parents who felt ill at ease and the demands for increased academic performance certainly made the situation more complex and turbulent. As he reflected on his past positive experience with similar situations in his previous school, Richard weighed the challenges and potentials in his head.

How would he reconcile the need to serve his new students while at the same time help teachers and parents accept and respond positively to them? How could he help his traditional faculty and community see that Swedishness was a concept that could possibly be expanded to include new members of that country's population? Without conceptual as well as concrete answers to these questions, Richard knew that the chances of success were remote. As his mind drifted over the facts and possibilities of this new situation Richard knew he needed to consider this dilemma from multiple points of view.

Questions for Discussion

1. The Ethic of Justice: Richard is required to support the refugee students' entry and success in his school. Can he share the requirements in such a way with parents, students, and their families that they understand what is expected of him and the school by the government?

2. The Ethic of Critique: The concept of Swedishness is at the heart of the resistance to refugee students for some teachers and parents. Clearly a narrow use of this word privileges some at the expense of others. What can Richard do to make this concept more inclusive?

3. The Ethic of Care: Is it possible for Richard to care for all the parties? If so, how? If not, why not?

4. The Ethic of the Profession: What would the profession expect from Richard? What actions are truly in the interests of all students?

NOTE

1. Newly arrived students i.e., newly arrived asylum seekers or those who have arrived to Sweden within the last four years.

REFERENCES

Berray, M. (2019). A critical literary review of the melting pot and salad bowl assimilation and integration theories. *Journal of Ethnic and Cultural Studies* 6(1), 142–151.

The Center for Effective Discipline. (2020). Retrieved from http://endcorporal-punishment.org/reports-on-every-state-and-territory/usa/

Calderon Berumen, F. (2019). Resisting assimilation to the melting pot. *Journal of Culture and Values in Education, 2*(1), 81–95.

Covaleskie, J. F. (2016). Moral vision in a world of diversity. *Values and Ethics in Educational Administration, 12,* 1–8.

Cushner, K., McClelland, A. & Safford, P. (1992). *Human diversity in education: An integrative approach.* New York, NY: McGraw-Hill.

Cushner, K., McClelland, A. & Safford, P. (2011). *Human diversity in education: An integrative approach* (7th ed.). New York, NY: McGraw-Hill.

Cushner, K., McClelland, A. & Safford, P. (2018). *Human diversity in education: An integrative approach* (9th ed.). New York, NY: McGraw-Hill.

Gilligan, C. (1982). *In a different voice.* Cambridge, MA: Harvard University Press.

Gilligan, C. & Richards, D.A.J. (2009). *The deepening darkness: Patriarchy, resistance, and democracy's future.* New York, NY: Cambridge University Press.

Kohlberg, L. (1981). *The philosophy of moral development: Moral stages and the idea of justice* (Vol. 1). San Francisco, CA: Harper & Row.

Noddings, N. (2003). *Caring: A feminine approach to ethics and moral education* (2nd ed.). Berkeley, CA: University of California Press.

Noddings, N. (2013). *Caring: A relational approach to ethics and moral education* (2nd ed.). Oakland, CA: University of California Press.

Nordgren, R.D. (2017). Cultural competence and relational closeness: examining refugee education. *Journal of Research in Innovative Teaching and Learning, 10*(1), 79-92. Retrieved from https://doi.org/10.1108/JRIT-08-2016-0001

Salomone, R.C. (2000). *Visions of schooling: Conscience, community, and common education.* New Haven, CT: Yale University Press.

Salomone, R.C. (2010). *True American: Language, identity, and the education of immigrant children.* Cambridge, MA: Harvard University Press.

Sewell, T.E., DuCette, J.P., & Shapiro, J.P. (1998). Educational assessment and diversity. In N.M. Lambert & B.L. McCombs (Eds.), *How students learn: Reforming schools through learner-centered education* (pp. 311–338). Washington, DC: American Psychological Association.

Tek Lum, W. (1987). *Chinese hot pot.* Honolulu, HI: Bamboo Ridge Press.

United Nations High Commissioner for Refugees (UNHCR), USA for UNHCR, The UN Refugee Agency. Retrieved from www.unrefugees.org/refugee-facts/statistics/

Wong, S.C. (1993). Promises, pitfalls, and principles of text selection in curricular diversification: the Asian-American case. In T. Perry & J.W. Fraser (Eds.), *Freedom's plow: Teaching in the multicultural classroom* (pp. 109–120). New York, NY: Routledge.

Zangwill, I. (1910). *The Melting Pot.* New York, NY: Macmillan.

Chapter 7

Religion versus Culture

Kathrine J. Gutierrez. Susan C. Faircloth, Tamarah Pfeiffer, Amelia Foy Buonanno, Aisha Salim Ali Al-Harthi, Kuan-Pei Lin, and Patricia A.L. Ehrensal

Religion and culture can exert a powerful influence on ethics (Miller, 2016). Accordingly, religion, culture, and ethical decision making among school leaders are often intertwined and can either oppose each other or grow as a society becomes increasingly diverse. For example, Arar, Haj, Abramovitz, & Oplatka (2016) have studied the ethical decision making of Arab School leaders in Israel, revealing connections between religion and culture, but also showing more tendencies to apply a critical framework among younger educators.

In countries, such as England and France, where religion is regularly taught as an academic subject, Bouchard (2020) identified strong ethical components in the religion course curricula. These include: 1) personal identification (knowledge and care of self, e.g., identity, moral ideal, critical thinking and values, existential questioning, self-esteem, liberty); 2) education for otherness (knowledge about distinctiveness of others, e.g., diversity, differences, group's identity, community, cultures, and ethnicities); and 3) education for society (e.g., common good, common values, rights, legal and social standards, civic mindedness). Bouchard combined these various categories to form four additional groups. She believes this analytical model could be adopted worldwide.

While such courses can be offered in United States' public schools, their occurrence is less common than in some other countries. Since the origins of the public-school movement in the U.S., the issue of religion in public schools has been a concern, if not outright contentious (Yudof, Kirp, Levin & Moran, 2002). The U.S. Supreme Court has ruled that certain practices in public schools are clearly illegal. For example, we know that teachers or other school officials may not begin the day with school prayer or Bible readings, as was past practice. They may not lead prayers

DOI: 10.4324/9781003022862-9

at school athletic events or have a religious speaker at graduation ceremonies. These practices all violate the Establishment Clause of the First Amendment to the U.S. Constitution (Stefkovich, Brady, Ballard & Rossow, 2021).

Not only are school officials prohibited from endorsing one religion over another they may not endorse religion over non-religion. As far as the curriculum is concerned, teachers may teach about religion (as in a comparative religion class), but they may not teach religion or proselytize in public schools. While public school officials shall not endorse religion, neither can they be hostile toward it. Thus, if a public school runs non-curricular clubs or opens its facilities to non-religious groups, then it must treat religious groups in the same manner. In addition, it is legal for public schools to provide transportation, books, and other materials and support services to religious schools. Accordingly, parents may take advantage of state voucher systems, when available, to help support their children's education in non-public schools (Stefkovich et al., 2021).

At the same time, lower courts disagree on the legality of student-led prayer and whether students may use their in-class or homework assignments as a vehicle for proselytizing about their religion. In some states, laws permitting moments of silence in schools have been declared unconstitutional when it was found that their intent was for prayer. These conflicting aspects of the law combined with larger issues of cultural diversity and what we expect our public schools to look like give rise to serious ethical dilemmas on the part of educational leaders (Stefkovich et al., 2021; Stefkovich & Frick, 2021).

For example, it is generally legal but not usually mandatory (depending on various state laws and school policies) that schools provide "opt-outs" for students who have religious conflicts with different aspects of the curriculum or for students or teachers who require time off for religious holidays. However, the more diverse our school community, the more complicated this situation can become.

Blankenship-Knox and Geier (2018) use New York City as an example. As of 2018, in addition to numerous federal holidays including Martin Luther King Day, Memorial Day, Thanksgiving, and Christmas, the school district gave the day off for the Lunar New Year (a major cultural holiday for Chinese and Koreans), Good Friday (a Christian holiday), Yom Kippur and Rosh Hashanah (Jewish holidays), Ramadan and Eid al-Adha (Muslim holidays). Herein lies the crux of both a legal and ethical dilemma:

> Incongruously, the holiday Diwali, the festival of lights celebrated by Hindus, Sikhs, and Jains in India, has not yet been included on the list of holidays celebrated by New York Schools despite prominent populations of Hindus, Sikhs, and Jains. (Blankenship-Knox and Geier, 2018, p. 7)

As mentioned in Chapter 6, we contend that diversity strengthens public schools, and exposure to different views better prepares all students to take their place in our increasingly diverse and pluralistic society. Educational historian David Tyack (1974) reminds us that our public schools were established as common schools with a goal of educating all students. Therefore, while we respect the rights of parents to send their children to religious schools (with the possible help of vouchers) or to home school, as a rising number of parents have done, we recognize the importance of all types of difference, including cultural and religious diversity, in our public schools.

At the same time, diversity brings challenges, and it is these challenges that represent the focus of this chapter. Oftentimes, ethical dilemmas occur when religion and respect for diverse cultures are pitted against the values and norms of the school and, sometimes, the curriculum being taught in the classroom. Strike, Haller, and Soltis (2005) caution us that "schools would need to be careful to help students understand that they need to tolerate views and lifestyles even if they disapprove of them. But they [the schools] would also have to respect students' right to disapproval" (p. 127).

This chapter includes six ethical dilemmas. The first four take place in K–12 school settings. The fifth and sixth come from higher education, but their underlying concepts could well fit a K–12 situation. Although the characters and situations presented in this chapter are mostly fictionalized, the content of each dilemma is based in part on a practice or belief characterized by certain cultures, religions, or both.

In these dilemmas, we have purposely focused on situations where religion and culture are so intertwined that they are difficult to separate. We have also chosen a few of the many important racial, ethnic, and religious groups who are either an emerging part of the culture of 21st-century schools and universities or have previously been ignored as part of this culture (or both). We have done this not only to illustrate the breadth of perspectives that school officials may confront in an increasingly diverse society but also to show possible connections with how we have historically treated more "traditional" religions. With limited space, we could not be totally inclusive and apologize in advance for any of the great number of religious beliefs that we have omitted. We were fortunate to have been able to work with students and colleagues who represent the diverse cultures/religions described in this chapter and who were willing to give generously of their time in writing these dilemmas.

Case Study 7.1, **Buddhism and the Caring of Animals**, shows an ethical conflict between teaching an approved curriculum and respecting the religious beliefs of students. In this dilemma, a third-grade student disagrees with the science curriculum that allows students to keep pets in class and feed them live animals. The teacher and school principal must decide how to adhere to the school's science curriculum while caring for and considering a student's religious beliefs.

In Case Study 7.2, **Ceremonial Rights**, an American Indian principal is planning to open the new school library with a local ceremonial celebration. The principal is challenged by one of her teachers as to the appropriateness of this celebration in a public school. Here, we urge our readers to grapple with ethical problems related to cultural traditions and religious beliefs as well as to examine possible ethical implications related to the beliefs of the majority and the rights of individuals. One might ask whether this situation is comparable to student-led prayers in school communities that are predominately Christian and, if it is not, why it is different.

Case Study 7.3, **Time Off for Religious Services**, involves two relatively new teachers who are troubled by the school's leave policy concerning attendance at religious services. The school principal is confronted with honoring the cultural tradition of the school and its community members or agreeing with the merits of the school's leave policy. Although this dilemma is set in Guam, a U.S. territory with a predominately Catholic population, we ask our readers to compare, and contrast, other instances where religious holidays have been integrated into "vacations" when large segments of the school community would otherwise be absent or when students, teachers, or both have been given "opt-outs" to attend religious functions.

Case Study 7.4, **Moral Empathy, Vulnerability, and Discipline in the Digital Age**, explores the relationship between school discipline, sexuality, and parents' religious beliefs at a time when privacy rights seem to have reached an all-time low. In this dilemma, a student's classmates take a compromising picture of the student masturbating in a stall in the boys' bathroom. Now, the school leader must decide how to deal with the classmates' actions, the offended student's inappropriate behavior, and the conservative religious beliefs of the student's parents, which will likely result in them pressing for severe disciplinary sanctions.

Turning to Case Study 7.5, **Religion and Social/Personal Contradictions**, a professor faces the dilemma of whether to continue teaching course content about homosexuality that some students find offensive on religious grounds. The professor grapples with the situation of how best to teach what is important content for the course while still respecting issues of diversity. This situation involves a female Muslim student, but a similar situation might occur with other religions, such as fundamentalist Christians or certain sects of Orthodox Jews.

In these situations, Strike, Haller, and Soltis (1988) have suggested that:

> Schools might explain to students whose religion teaches that homosexuality is a sin that homosexuals are entitled to equal rights regardless of whether homosexuality is a sin. But schools need not insist that these students view homosexuality as merely an alternative lifestyle. (p. 127)

We ask our readers to consider this viewpoint as well as to examine the scenario through other ethical paradigms, such as care, critique, and the profession.

Our final dilemma, Case Study 7.6, **A Secreted Culture of Religious Intolerance**, takes place on a university campus that has experienced substantial upheaval during the past year. These incidents centered on hate speech and protests related to race, ethnicity, and sexual orientation, all of which met with quick responses from central administration. Now, when the same type of animosity is directed at Jewish students and faculty, the reaction from institutional leaders is different, more measured, leaving this group feeling increasingly fearful, alone, and unsupported in the midst of a crisis.

CASE STUDY 7.1 BUDDHISM AND THE CARING OF ANIMALS

Green Hill Elementary School is an urban school in the Brighton School District. Green Hill houses grades K-6 and has 600 students. The socio-economic status of most students is middle class. Brighton School District has a diverse community representing a mixture of ethnicities, which include White (non-Hispanic), Hispanic, and some immigrants from China, Taiwan, Japan, and Korea. Hence, the community also represents various religious beliefs and cultural backgrounds.

The school's mission statement reads as follows:

> Green Hill Elementary School, in partnership with parents and the community, encourages each student to develop individual abilities to become a life-long learner. Green Hill has several goals: (1) to increase every student's reading and writing proficiency, (2) to increase every student's math reasoning and problem-solving skills, (3) to increase student interest in science and math, (4) to encourage all students to learn to respect each other and value diversity, (5) to offer curricula that help students progress through developmental learning stages and develop appropriate social skills, and (6) to foster student understanding of different worldviews and to encourage life-long learning.

Sophia Shin Liang is an eight-year-old female student of Taiwanese descent enrolled in Green Hill Elementary School. Her family relocated to the Brighton School District from Taiwan before Sophia was born. Sophia was born and raised in the town of Brighton. Although Sophia is a U.S. citizen, her family values their heritage and religious beliefs. Buddhism is the religious belief and practice of the Liang family. A central tenet to the practice of Buddhism is the caring and welfare of all creatures of the Earth. The belief discourages any human being from harming any living creature.

In the fall of August 2003, Sophia Shin Liang became a third-grade student in Mrs. Cullen's science class. All science classes at Green Hill Elementary keep frogs in an aquarium as part of their curriculum to teach the life cycle of prey and predator. As such, live bugs are fed to the frogs. Frogs have been part of the third-grade science curriculum at Green Hill Elementary School for the past five years, under the supervision of Principal Gary Goodman. The school board approved the science curriculum that supports keeping live animals to aid in the learning and development of elementary science.

On the first day of class, Mrs. Cullen introduced the curriculum for the semester that involved showing and talking about the class frog and the live bugs for its food. Each student had been assigned one week to care for and feed the frog the live bugs. Sophia Shin Liang grimaced at the fact that she would have to feed the frog live bugs because this goes against her Buddhist belief of not harming any living creature. Thankfully, Sophia was not scheduled to feed the class frog until the first week of October. This, in her mind, was sufficient time to talk with both her teacher and parents about the situation and to see if she could be excused from her class obligation to feed the frog.

However, after three weeks into the school year, Sophia witnessed several of her classmates feeding live bugs to the frog. She was appalled, disgusted, hurt, and discouraged that such an awful act was being committed in her presence. On Friday, the third week in September, Sophia set both the frog and the bugs free by carrying the animals outside during recess when no one was in the classroom. She thought no one had witnessed her act of kindness. However, two of her classmates saw her setting the animals free and confronted her about the situation.

Raul: Hey Sophia, what did you do? I saw you set the bugs and frog free.

Stacey: Yes, I saw it too. You are a thief. . . . You stole them from our class and now they are gone! I am going to tell Mrs. Cullen.

Sophia: No! I am not a thief. I just set them free to go where they belong. It is not right to feed the bugs to the frog. We are killing the bugs, protected creatures of the Earth. It is not right and against my religious beliefs! I felt sorry for them. I needed to set them free.

After recess had ended, Raul and Stacey reported the incident to Mrs. Cullen. Mrs. Cullen asked Sophia to talk with her outside the classroom about what happened.

Mrs. Cullen: Sophia, could you please tell me what happened during recess? Is it true you set the class animals free?

Sophia: I am sorry Mrs. Cullen. I did set the animals free because my Buddhist belief does not allow any harm to any living creature. It is not right to feed bugs to the frog because this is killing creatures of the Earth. My belief does not allow killing or harming any living thing.

Mrs. Cullen: I understand your concern for not wanting to harm any animal, but the frog and bugs belong to everyone in the class and are for learning purposes. Now the class is without these animals, and it is highly unlikely that we will be able to purchase another set for our class. I am very disappointed in you. You are a good student and should have talked with me before taking action on your own. I have no other choice but to send you to see Principal Goodman.

Sophia was sent to Principal Goodman's office. Principal Goodman was upset that Sophia had let the animals go and decided to call her parents to speak with him and to take Sophia home for the day. Both Mr. and Mrs. Kuan Lee Liang were upset and confused at the phone call from Mr. Goodman.

"How could our Sophia be in trouble?" they asked one another. "She is such an obedient child and a good student," Sophia's mother told her husband. Within 20 minutes of Principal Goodman's phone call, Sophia's parents arrived at Green Hill Elementary School.

Principal Goodman: Thank you both for coming in so quickly. Sophia explained to me why she set the science class animals free, but I still need to have you talk to her about what she did wrong.

Mr. and Mrs. Kuan Lee Liang: Sophia is just a child and she is just following our religious beliefs without thinking about the big picture of the purpose of these animals in the classroom. We believe that all creatures should be unharmed and even a small bug has the right to survive. Yes, the frog needs to eat food, but if humans get involved in the process to feed the bugs to the frog, we are aiding in the killing of these bugs, rather than the frog surviving, and seeking food on its own in a natural habitat.

Principal Goodman: I understand your devotion to your religious beliefs, Mr. and Mrs. Liang. But these animals are an important part of the science curriculum, and I doubt that this situation will be taken lightly by the other parents and the school board.

Mr. and Mrs. Kuan Lee Liang: We understand the importance of the science curriculum. But we will not punish Sophia for embracing the tenets of Buddhism. The school and you, Principal Goodman, should support the school's mission, especially its focus "to encourage all students to learn to respect each other and value diversity." You should respect our belief and value our family's diversity. We ask that Sophia not be punished for what she did and that her classmates are told the truth about why Sophia set the animals free.

Principal Goodman: I empathize with you both. But the school board approved keeping animals in the classroom as part of the science curriculum five years ago, and I have not had any complaints until now. On the contrary, several parents have spoken highly of their children's enthusiasm and increased interest in science because of their experiences with the animals in the classroom. Given my position as principal, I will explain to the school board that this incident is a rare case and that I still encourage the use of animals for the science curriculum. After all, it is in the best interests of the majority of students to foster their learning in science. However, as a resident of this community, I am torn between my own personal beliefs of embracing diversity and respecting and valuing different religious beliefs. I will take a couple of days to think about this situation and then determine the best decision. Until then, I will ask Mrs. Cullen not to have Sophia watch the other students feeding the frog. Sophia will not be punished in any way, but I feel you should take her home for the rest of the day.

Questions for Discussion

1. What are the benefits of students feeding the frog as part of the science curriculum? Does the science curriculum consider the greater good for all students over individual rights? Should it? Why or why not? What would a caring principal do in this situation?

2. Who is determining the curriculum? What do you think other parents with different religious beliefs would say against not having the students feed the frog live bugs?

3. How does the ethic of the profession factor into Principal Goodman's decision? What in this scenario leads you to your decision?

4. Do you see any conflict between Principal Goodman's professional beliefs, the ethic of care, and the community's interests?

5. Considering all the ethical frameworks, is there a resolution that could support both sides, that is, Principal Goodman backing the current science curriculum and the Liang family's Buddhist belief of not harming any living creature? Explain your answer.

CASE STUDY 7.2 CEREMONIAL RIGHTS

Diné High School (DHS) sits at the bottom of a mesa surrounded by native vegetation of yucca and sagebrush. It is a public high school on a Navajo reservation and is one of 35 public schools within a 160-mile radius. The closest school to Diné is a Bureau of Indian Affairs school serving grades K–8.

The student population at DHS is approximately 90% Navajo and Hopi; the other 10% of the students are Anglo. The community is made up of a post office, a church, a chapter house (a community center where tribal council officials hold meetings and gatherings such as dinners and special elections), a hospital, and a tribal housing authority funded by the U.S. Department of Housing and Urban Development.

On August 7, with a new school year scheduled to begin in less than a week, Ms. Tsosie, the principal, was working on the agenda and pre-service schedule for the returning staff. Teachers were returning to the building daily, and the rest of the staff would be in full force within the week. As with most other schools, the beginning of the school year was quite hectic.

On this day, Mr. Bia, a graduate of the school, came to register his ninth-grade son. On entering the school, he saw that the new library had been completed and wanted to take a tour. Seeing that the principal, Ms. Tsosie, was in her office and had just hung up the phone, he knocked on her door and introduced himself. "Ya'ateeh Abini [good morning], Ms. Tsosie. Shei ei Ted Bia Yinishye. Shi ei Todichinii nishili, Tohtsoni bashichiin [My name is Ted Bia. I'm of the Bitterwater clan born for the Redhouse people]." After his formal introduction, he told Ms. Tsosie that he was very happy to see her. He then complimented her on the new library:

"As a graduate of Diné High School I am so pleased to see the library addition. I know that a lot of hard work went into making the high school library a place for the kids here and also a special place for the entire community. I especially hope you were able to add some new technology into the library. I was wondering if I might take a look inside while I'm here?"

Mr. Bia stepped into the hallway and Ms. Tsosie unlocked the library so that he could sneak a peek. Ms. Tsosie was happy to visit and show Mr. Bia around, since this was not the first time that he had shown interest in the school. She remembered that on several occasions he had made a point to attend meetings in which community participation was sought. In fact, Mr. Bia, as a parent, was an important advocate in promoting the idea of a community library initiative.

On exiting the library, Mr. Bia addressed Ms. Tsosie and asked in a very low, deliberate tone, "So, Ms. Tsosie, when will a Blessing Way Ceremony be held for the library?" (Blessing Way is a traditional Navajo ceremony that is most often observed to bring about goodness and harmony to an individual and extended families.)

Ms. Tsosie stopped, looked around, and replied, "The day before the students arrive next week." Mr. Bia walked down the hall with Ms. Tsosie and then stopped and said, "That's nice, I hope it is at a time that both my son and I can attend."

Mr. Bia then picked up his son and headed out of the door. Ms. Tsosie returned to her office thinking about her conversation with Mr. Bia. Sitting at her desk she looked down and saw a sticky note. She had placed the note there to remind her to be at school at dawn on August 11 to greet the medicine man and his wife along with all other invited community members who would be attending the Blessing Way Ceremony.

She remembered that early morning was the time of day the medicine man, a Navajo elder who would be traveling some distance to perform the ceremony, had set for the Blessing Way Ceremony. Ms. Tsosie was eager to meet the requests of those who would be participating in the ceremony. Although the Blessing Way is traditionally a four-day event, she was pleased that the medicine man, the superintendent, and the community members had agreed to participate in a shortened version of the ceremony. She was excited to know that the school year would begin with a blessing of the new library and good feelings for the upcoming school year.

After going home for the evening, Ms. Tsosie thought again about her conversation with Mr. Bia. Feeling a little anxious about the ceremony, she called the superintendent, Dr. Begay, and requested to meet with him the following morning.

The next morning, Ms. Tsosie waited patiently to meet with Dr. Begay at his office. When they were finally together, Ms. Tsosie began with a simple question to the superintendent: "We did decide to have a Blessing Way Ceremony for the new library and the beginning of the new year, right?"

Dr. Begay flipped open his calendar, looked at it very seriously, and replied, "I have it right here, August 11 in the library. Correct?"

"Well, that's what I have on my calendar, but I wanted to make sure that I had the right day scheduled," Ms. Tsosie replied.

Ms. Tsosie then asked, "Has the medicine man been contacted?"

The superintendent said in his low, deliberate voice, "Yes, in fact I'll be going out to get him and his wife early that morning. When they arrive, will you and some of your staff members please be at the high school with coffee and food ready for the medicine man and a few guests? We will probably need enough food to feed maybe 50 people."

Ms. Tsosie quietly responded with a "Yes."

Following the meeting with the superintendent, Ms. Tsosie returned to her office. Less than ten minutes later, her phone rang. "Good morning. This is Ms. Tsosie. What can I do for you?"

"Ms. Tsosie, this is Ms. Dee." (Ms. Dee is a teacher who was at the district office getting a signature on a trip when she saw the notice about the Blessing Way Ceremony.) "I just wanted to ask you a question. I'm at the district office and saw that you are going to have a Blessing Way Ceremony for the new library. I want you to know that I don't think what you are doing is right."

Ms. Tsosie waited for Ms. Dee to pause and then asked, "Why?"

Ms. Dee continued, "I believe that the Blessing Way Ceremonies should not be conducted in schools. I don't believe in this type of practice, and I don't understand why you are having this ceremony at school. My child goes to school here too, and this is not what we believe in at home. Why are you making the students go to this?"

Ms. Tsosie clarified: "There are community members and other district staff who will attend. Invitations have also gone out to all high school personnel and the student council. But, no one has to come if they don't feel like it."

Ms. Dee, sounding a little flustered, continued: "Well, this is not something I believe in and I'm not alone in my beliefs. I think you know, Ms. Tsosie, that there are a lot of staff and faculty who attend local churches of different faiths and don't believe in traditional ceremonies like the Blessing Way Ceremony. And many of the younger people here don't believe that traditional practices should be part of the school. If people want their children to learn about this type of thing, or participate in these ceremonies, then they should do this stuff at home or in the community— but not in the school."

Thinking that it would be more appropriate to discuss this matter in person rather than over the phone, Ms. Tsosie waited for Ms. Dee to pause before suggesting that they meet in person to discuss this matter further.

"I've told you how I feel, and I don't think there is a need to discuss this further." Without saying goodbye or waiting for Ms. Tsosie to respond, Ms. Dee slammed down the receiver.

Feeling that she had done her best to resolve this dilemma, Ms. Tsosie turned to her desk calendar and wrote in big letters, BLESSING WAY CEREMONY, in the box marked August 11. She then drew a smiley face on the calendar and retired for the night.

Questions for Discussion

1. Does the Blessing Way Ceremony violate the principle of separation of church and state? If so, how, and why? If not, why not? What

impact should culture have upon decisions to include or exclude religious activities from school?

2. Do you agree with the principal's decision to proceed with the Blessing Way Ceremony? If you were the principal, how would you have handled this dilemma? Explain your reasoning.

3. What would be the most caring resolution to this dilemma?

4. Who is making the rules here? Whose values do these rules represent? Would this situation be different if the school community was predominately Christian? If students initiated and led the ceremony?

5. To what extent should student voice/perspective influence the selection and scheduling of activities and ceremonies in school? To what extent should faculty/staff voice/perspective influence the selection and scheduling of activities and ceremonies in school?

6. How do you distinguish between cultural and religious activities in a school setting?

7. Given the ethical frameworks discussed in this text, are there one or more elements or constructs of ethics that would be most applicable in resolving this dilemma? If so, which one(s) would you suggest? Why?

CASE STUDY 7.3 TIME OFF FOR RELIGIOUS SERVICES

Guam, a U.S. territory, is a small island community with a population of approximately 165,000 people (Guam Economic Development Authority, 2014a). Residents comprise a melting pot of ethnicities: Chamorros (the indigenous people of the island), Japanese, Koreans, Filipinos, Vietnamese, Chinese, Palauans, Micronesians (people from the Federated States of Micronesia: Chuuk, Yap, Pohnpei, Kosrae), White Americans (non-Hispanic), African Americans, Indians, and others. Specifically, the ethnic groups represented on the island, according to the 2000 census, were: Chamorro 37.1%, Filipino 26.3%, other Pacific islander 11.3%, White 6.9%, other Asian 6.3%, other ethnic origin or race 2.3%, mixed 9.8% (Central Intelligence Agency, 2014a).

The cultural diversity on the island of Guam is typified by the existence of the various ethnic groups who make up the residents of the island. The nationality of individuals born on Guam is classified as Guamanian (Central Intelligence Agency, 2014b). "Guam's culture has also been influenced and enriched over the last 50 years by the American, Filipino, Japanese, Korean, Chinese and Micronesian immigrants that have each added their unique cultural contributions" (Guam Economic Development Authority, 2014b). The island is also home to both a U.S. Air Force Base and Naval Base, which work in a partnership known as Joint Region Marianas.

Public education on Guam is overseen by the Guam Department of Education, which is a single unified school district for grades Kindergarten through 12 with 26 elementary schools, 8 middle schools, 5 high schools, and an alternative school, serving over 30,000 students (Guam Department of Education, n.d.). Public schools on Guam are patterned after school systems in the continental United States and "the Chinese and Japanese communities each support schools to preserve their respective language and culture" (Guam Economic Development Authority, 2014c).

The teachers in each of the schools are as diverse as the community residents. Like the community, many of the public-school teachers are Chamorro or of Chamorro ancestry and devout Catholics. According to the Central Intelligence Agency (2014c), 85% of the community residents are Roman Catholics. In any given week of the year, Catholic rosary services are held in cathedrals, residents' homes, or both. What follows is a hypothetical case scenario that considers the realities of an island community in which most of the population follow the same faith.

On May 30, the day after the Memorial Day weekend and just 2 weeks shy of the end of the school year, teachers and administrators were busily preparing for year-end testing and budget review. At Central Elementary School, teachers had just been notified that one of their recent retiree colleagues, Mrs. Maria Cruz, had passed away over the weekend. A well-liked teacher, Mrs. Cruz had worked at Central Elementary for 30 years. On this Tuesday, Catholic rosary services for Mrs. Cruz were to take place at noon and 6 p.m. at the town cathedral.

Principal Robert Perez circulated a written notice to all teachers regarding the rosary services for Mrs. Cruz. The notice read:

> One of our former teachers, Mrs. Maria Cruz, sadly passed away over the weekend. Noon rosary services for Mrs. Cruz will be held at the cathedral. Any teachers wishing to attend the noon rosary service for Maria may do so as long as their classes are covered by other teachers for the time they are away. No official leave form is required to attend the rosary services. Kindly inform my secretary, Ms. Anita Baza, of your intentions and who will be covering your class.

Later that morning, Principal Perez saw first-grade teacher Ms. Rose Torres in the hallway. "Hi Rose! Are you planning to attend the rosary for Maria anytime this week?"

Ms. Torres replied, "Yes, I am. Tina Mafnas (another first-grade teacher) and I are combining our classes and will take turns covering for the hour."

Principal Perez responded, "Great. As always, you do not have to sign a leave form if you stagger the coverage of your classes. Just be sure the kids are working on the set curriculum for that time period and let my secretary, Ms. Baza, know your schedule."

On receipt of the notice, fourth-grade teachers Mrs. Sashi Takagumi (a Japanese resident in the community) and Ms. Meifeng Wei (a Chinese resident, originally from Hong Kong) fumed over the notice in the teachers' lounge. "The fact is that Principal Perez has practiced a no leave deduction policy during our entire 5 years of employment here," Mrs. Takagumi complained. "Just last week, I wanted to visit the Shinto shrine, and I signed annual leave to do so—in which I returned back to work within one hour." She continued, "Meifeng, this is really unfair! Maybe I should say that I am going to attend a rosary service next time so that I do not have to sign annual leave."

"Yeah, but what can we do? We are in the minority when it comes to religious beliefs in this community. And the fact that Principal Perez is a devout Catholic only perpetuates this 'school culture' of taking care of your own kind," retorted Ms. Wei.

"We need to stand up for what is right," replied Mrs. Takagumi. "We are foolish to let it escalate further. We are no longer new teachers trying to pass our probationary period. We do not need to keep a low tone about this any longer. Either we are allowed the same no leave policy to attend our religious services or else everyone has to sign for annual leave for any kind of absence related to attending a religious event."

"I see your point, Sashi," said Ms. Wei. "But the real focus should be on what is the appropriate action to take as professionals. I mean, shouldn't church and state issues stay out of our public schools? I don't think that central office, in particular Superintendent Salas, will be happy to know that classes are being combined even if it is only for one hour. And what about the parents of these children in combined classes; what will they think? You know that regardless of what religion these children practice, their parents will be upset over lumping two classes into one huge classroom. It really has become more of a break period than a focus on teaching the curriculum for that hour. It is too difficult to oversee so many students and keep their concentration. By the time the classes combine, which usually means going to the library or study hall room, 30 minutes have gone by," explains Ms. Wei.

"Yes, I agree with you, Meifeng," Mrs. Takagumi firmly stated. "We need to petition Superintendent Salas to investigate this 'time off without leave' practice. The children are the ones at a disadvantage with this practice, not us. We really should focus on doing our best job to educate our students."

Mrs. Takagumi and Ms. Wei decided to write a formal letter to Superintendent Salas concerning this dilemma. In addition, they planned to attach a petition containing signatures of other teachers from Central

Elementary School who were opposed to Principal Perez's "time off without leave" practice.

Four teachers in favor of the "time off without leave" practice heard about the petition and stormed into Principal Perez's office. One of these teachers, Mrs. Baza, began: "Principal Perez, you have to talk with Mrs. Takagumi and Ms. Wei. If their petition ends up in Superintendent Salas' office, we all lose out on the practice of taking time off to show respect and attend ceremonies and events for our specific religious beliefs."

"Yes," agreed Joe Cruz, another teacher, and cousin of the deceased teacher, Maria. "You need to communicate our culture of caring and concern for others."

"Joe is right. However, Mrs. Takagumi and Ms. Wei are still relatively new to our island and our school. We need to embrace their concerns too and let them know that the school respects their religious beliefs and practices," replied teacher Cecilia Mafnas.

"They have nothing to complain about," a fourth teacher observed. "You let them take time off when they need to pick up their children. It is not your fault, Principal Perez, if they submit a leave form to the payroll officer for taking time to attend a funeral service. They never asked not to sign one for their services. They do not understand the culture and tradition of the school. We care about our colleagues. That is the kind of teachers we are. Regardless of the type of religious funeral services, we care enough to pay our last respects to the families of our deceased teacher."

On hearing the comments of these four teachers, Principal Perez called Mrs. Takagumi and Ms. Wei into his office for a chat. "Sashi and Meifeng, thank you for coming to my office. I know you are upset about the 'time off without leave' practice to attend religious services. You have been part of our school for five years. You should understand and be aware of the cultural tradition of paying last respects to a deceased teacher of our school. I understand your strong resolve to obey the rules and regulations of the profession and that any absence away from work should require signing a leave form. On the other hand, I am committed to the concern and caring nature of this community and the traditions of our school. I ask that you give me two days to think over how to best handle this situation before you submit your petition to Superintendent Salas."

Mrs. Sashi Takagumi and Ms. Meifeng Wei were quite cordial with Principal Perez and respected him as the school leader. They agreed to wait two days to submit the letter and petition to Superintendent Salas. Now, Principal Perez needs to decide how to address this dilemma as he sees the merits of both those in favor of and those against the "time off without leave" practice.

Questions for Discussion

1. Is there a legal issue here? If not, why not? If so, what is it and how would you resolve it? What is the fairest way to handle this situation? The most caring?

2. Why do you think the "time off without leave" practice has been allowed to go unnoticed for five years? Do you think the "culture" of the community and/or school should determine policy and/or practice? Explain your answer.

3. Does the ethic of the profession support Principal Perez in carrying out his "time off without leave" practice? Why or why not? How should Superintendent Salas respond to this dilemma, keeping in mind the best interests of the students?

4. What action would you take as a teacher who does not agree with the practice? Do you think Mrs. Takagumi and Ms. Wei chose an appropriate strategy to address this dilemma? Why or why not? What else could they have done?

5. How do you think Principal Perez should respond to possible negative reactions from the parents of the children being placed in a so-called break hour period? Do you see an ethical issue here? If so, what is it and how would you resolve it? If not, why not?

CASE STUDY 7.4 MORAL EMPATHY, VULNERABILITY, AND DISCIPLINE IN THE DIGITAL AGE

Roger is noticeably different than the other students. His stutter, mannerisms, and social awkwardness make him a target for harassment by his peers. Despite his differences, seeing bullying of Roger is rare. His charming personality helps him forge acceptance from the most intolerant of peers. Honestly, it is difficult not to like Roger.

Earlier in the year, however, an incident left him at a loss to contain his frustration. He was upset, somewhat incoherent, and pacing around Assistant Principal Souza's office mumbling. Mr. Souza met with Roger and his father to deescalate and resolve the problem, which was minor. Soon after, Roger gained his composure and returned to class. Though Roger appeared to perform within the average of his peers academically, there were noticeable differences developmentally.

A comprehensive evaluation was recommended to ensure that the school was providing enough support for Roger. The parents, within their rights, declined the evaluation; the primary reason being fear of stigmatization if the outcome identified any differences from that of typical peers his age or even his siblings. Essentially, the parents did not want to recognize that Roger's mannerism presented as atypical. Unfortunately, another situation involving Roger had occurred later in the year. This time, the school team needed to consider Roger's uniqueness when determining appropriate disciplinary action.

Fridays carry powerful energy in a school. Mondays, the students chatter about weekend drama. Fridays, the school administrators try to keep from being Saturdays. On one particular Friday, the office was buzzing, teachers were shuffling students into classrooms, and Assistant Principal Souza was preparing a fire drill. Roger approached saying, "I really need to talk to you, Dr. Souza." As the assistant principal tested his "walkie," he looked around the office. It was cluttered with commotion and he knew Roger's conversation needed privacy. "Can it wait until after the fire drill?" he asked. Roger couldn't give Dr. Souza a straight answer, but he said that he did not want to go to class or be seen because he was embarrassed about an incident that happened. Hearing those words, Roger and Dr. Souze left for his office.

Roger explained the incident. He began with references to puberty and uncontrollable urges. Dr. Souza thought to himself that he should have participated in the fire drill. But as Roger continued to explain an incident that happened yesterday at school, this dialogue soon became more than "the birds and bees" conversation about sexual development. Roger had an "uncontrollable urge" during class. He asked permission to go the bathroom where he proceeded to masturbate in a bathroom stall. Unbeknownst to Roger, Aaron, one of Roger's classmates, entered the bathroom. Upon arrival, Aaron quickly gathered what was happening. Within moments, Aaron heartlessly held his phone over the stall and recorded Roger in the act.

Roger did not share the incident with anyone that day, including his parents. Dr. Souza later realized that there were two factors driving Roger's decision: embarrassment and religion. The assistant principal told Roger, who was sobbing in his office, that he understood it was not his intention for this situation to unfold. Dr. Souza knew a conversation must be had around the inappropriate use of public space, but his priority was to find Aaron's phone and tell the principal about what happened. But before calling, Dr. Souza want to make Roger feel comfortable with the next steps. Roger became anxious, understandably, because he knew that it could no longer be a private conversation given the nature of the incident. Dr. Souza also knew from past discussions that Roger's parents were very religious and conservative as to sexual matters. It was not beyond this family to press for severe disciplinary action against their own son based on religious grounds of moral indecency.

Dr. Souza met with the principal. The school leaders took swift action, found Aaron and confirmed the cell phone was in his possession. Aaron did not cooperate, which meant that the administrators needed to exercise caution and be clear as to their limitations. Aaron had rights and Roger's story had yet to be verified. Moving forward, the administrators consulted with school police, who quickly contacted their deputy given the nature of the incident. Since state law bans cell phones from entering the building, the school could share fault over the event; something the school leaders did not foresee as an issue. Regardless, however, this incident bordered on sexual assault, providing leverage in pursuit of the phone. With this new knowledge, the school leaders called the police department who transferred the incident to the Special Victims Unit. Aaron was ultimately given a lateral transfer to another school in the same district.

Questions for Discussion

1. To what extent might gender influence the outcome of this incident with consideration as to the context of the dominant culture of American society? To what extent might the context also influence the ethical paradigm of the school leader and how it is applied?
2. Were the school leaders' decisions just? Fair for all parties involved?
3. How might the outcome of this dilemma have been different if Aaron's lateral transfer was not possible? To what extent might the inability to remove the student influence the ethical actions taken? Might a different paradigm be used?
4. The dilemma does not mention the extent to which culture was discussed by the school team. To what extent would you consider religious beliefs given this scenario? How might Dr. Souza operate through the ethic of profession in this respect?
5. How might considering one's own culture and the culture of others influence a school leader's ethical paradigm and decision-making?

**CASE STUDY 7.5 RELIGION AND SOCIAL/PERSONAL
CONTRADICTIONS**

The day before the beginning of fall semester at State University, Dr. Diane Morgan, a professor in the Department of Women's Studies, was busily preparing for her introductory class to women's studies. As the course progressed, the class has been challenging at times owing to the great diversity of students. Even though Diane tried to provide a safe environment for all her students despite their backgrounds, sometimes she felt student resistance to discuss certain controversial social justice issues. She included these issues in her course to help students ask hard questions and arrive at their own conclusions.

One morning, the class had been discussing homosexual marriage. Students were sitting in groups of four to a table. They were about to start discussing an article they had to read on the topic. Each group was required to present their reaction to the class after discussion. Diane interrupted the group work, remarking, "I know each of you has an opinion about this. However, please keep an open mind and respect for others' points of views. You might want to consider issues such as sex discrimination, identity development, gender social construction, legal regulations, and current social, political, and cultural changes."

Diane walked around the class to listen and to facilitate group discussions. One group attracted her attention owing to its diversity. It consisted of four students: Fatmah, an Arab Muslim woman interested in the oppression of women; Mike, a gay campus activist involved in a diversity initiative on campus that supports lesbian, gay, bisexual, and transgender students, faculty, and staff; Susan, a White American majoring in women's studies and interested in women's right to choose; and David, a fundamentalist Christian pastor and graduate student in religious studies, interested in developing community capacity to create venues for healthy adolescence gender identity development.

Their group discussion started slowly but quickly heated up as a result of clashing backgrounds and opinions. Diane noticed that Fatmah, who is usually active in group discussions, was strangely quiet. When Diane asked her after class about the reasons for her lack of participation, she requested an appointment to talk to her privately about this. Curious to know Fatmah's reasons, Diane agreed to see her at 3:00 p.m. that same day. When Fatmah arrived at her office, she immediately asked her, "I was surprised at your unusual silence today in class."

Fatmah [Hesitating.]: I don't know how to tell you this, but today's class discussion made me feel very uncomfortable.

Diane: That's great! I don't want you to feel "comfortable" in this class. I think if you feel "uncomfortable," then you're actually learning. We talk about controversial issues in this course and if they are not troubling to you, then you probably shouldn't take the class. Having said that, tell me what is uncomfortable for you.

Fatmah: I am really interested in the class. I think there are a lot of social injustices for women, especially in my part of the world, and I am troubled by that. However, Dr. Morgan, the issue of gays and lesbians in my society is something that is not a subject for discussion.

Diane: Well, in this country this topic is still controversial for many people.

Fatmah: Yes. I could tell from one of my group members' opinion. But I feel that this issue is putting me personally in both cultural and religious conflict. Culturally, it's outrageous to talk about sex in general in my society, let alone a topic like this. Today's topic is very problematic for me because the issue is more than cultural; it's religious. In Islam, we believe that homosexuality is against human nature, and it's a great sin. We believe that people choose to become homosexual and are not born that way. The environment plays a great role in shaping such identities.

Diane: Let me ask you this: Do you think this is not an issue in your society as well?

Fatmah: I don't know, BUT it is not something that my religion would allow me to talk about, let alone fight for social justice on its behalf. Islam is very strict about this issue. I totally understand the purpose of this discussion for the class, but for ME this is against everything that I was raised to believe in, and just by participating in this discussion I might be committing a "sin." I'm facing a tough conflict.

Diane was feeling a little hurt that somebody could view a gay person in this way. It made her think of the many times her son had faced similar opposition. She reminded herself that she is in the position of an instructor who is willing to offer help to her students with a possibility of hope in transforming their perspectives. Diane sighed inwardly and responded, "Fatmah, the course is not about changing your social or religious beliefs. The course is about examining them and broadening your understanding of social justice. In this country, this is a big issue right now, and there are many people in the class who are interested in it."

Fatmah gazed at Diane in silence as she thought to herself, "You don't understand my situation. I think you're oppressing me by making it a course issue! The course is supposed to focus on women's issues, not gays and lesbians."

Diane never had a Muslim student before in any of her courses. She was not aware of the concept of "sin" in Islam and its possible consequences for Fatmah's performance in her class. She asked Fatmah to sit out the next class and to come to see her at the end of the week, as she tries to think of ways to help her deal with her. Eventually, when Fatmah came to see her by the end of the next class, she said, "I remember your interest in women's oppression. I think one way for you to think about this is to focus on how this movement has socially and historically developed in the United States and apply what you learn from it to your country, as the topic for your course paper."

As Diane spoke, Fatmah was thinking that this could be a reasonable assignment. However, she still felt strongly about issues of homosexuality being discussed in the class. Fatmah thanked her and said she would have to think about this option for a few days since the deadline for dropping a course was in one week. Diane struggled with Fatmah's comments about possibly dropping the course. She felt that the issue of homosexuality was an important topic for her class. She was aware that her decision "carries with it a restructuring of human life" (Foster, 1986, p. 33), and hoped that Fatmah could reach a point of religious tolerance. She tried to find a solution for her, but she could not discard the topic from the course.

Questions for Discussion

1. Discuss the multidimensions of Diane's ethical dilemma: Discuss your reaction to Diane's decision to include gay marriage and homosexuality as issues for discussion in her women's studies class. Explain what influence Diane's personal life and values had on her decision to include the topic of homosexuality in her course.
2. From an ethical perspective, why do you think Diane decided to continue to use a controversial issue in the course despite the fact that she had observed the discomfort of some students with this topic? Was she considering the greater good for the majority of her students? The best interests of each student?
3. What would be the most caring way to resolve this dilemma? Why? Do you think Diane's suggestion solves Fatmah's religious concern?
4. In light of the various ethical paradigms, what would you do if you were Diane? What alternative solutions might you offer the student?

CASE STUDY 7.6 A SECRETED CULTURE OF RELIGIOUS INTOLERANCE

Provost Johnston closed his office door and now that no one could observe him finally let out the long sigh he had been holding in. It had been a difficult and contentious meeting, but then it has been a difficult and contentious year. The academic year seemed to get off to a good start. There were no major issues in the first few weeks, but that changed in October.

It started with white supremacists' leaflets being posted on public bulletin boards around the campus. While it still was not known if a student or staff member posted these, the material was unsettling to the campus community. The Student Government Association (SGA) quickly posted "Hate has no place at State University." Dr. Pierce, a professor in the English Department, organized an anti-racism "teach in," which was well attended. Several weeks later, anti-immigrant leaflets were posted on the bulletin boards (again the source was unknown), and many Latinx students complained that some students were heckling them, saying, "Go back to your own country."

Again, SGA posted anti-hate posters and this time Dr. Garcia of the Spanish Department and Dr. Logan, an economist in the Business School, offered a well-attended "teach in" on economic and cultural advantages of immigrants. Early in the spring semester a local conservative and activist Christian church was granted permission (under the Equal Access Act) to hold an anti-abortion demonstration on the campus. During the demonstration, Church members also had anti-LGBTQ posters and literature. Additionally, they harassed any student whom they thought was "gay." SGA joined forces with the University's Alliance chapter and held a "Rainbow Rally" demonstrating that LGBTQ students and staff are an esteemed and vital member of the campus community.

The meeting on this day was with the ten members of the faculty who are Jewish and the student leadership of Hillel to voice their concerns over the recent anti-Semitic activity on campus. The day before a group of students marched across the campus chanting, "Jews will not replace us!" mimicking the marchers in Charlottesville. When he learned of the event, Provost Johnston knew that the Jewish faculty and students would want to meet, so he cleared an hour in his calendar anticipating their request. The meeting began with cordial greetings, but quickly became contentious.

Dr. Friedman, a former vice president of the faculty senate, took the lead and simply asked what the administration was planning to do to address the students' behavior. Provost Johnston responded, "there isn't anything that administration can actually do." He continued, "The marchers were students, but their actions didn't break any university rules."

"So," replied Dr. Friedman, "the university rules allow anti-Semitic speech?"

The Provost responded, "This is a State university; therefore, student's free speech is protected by the Constitution. Much as we may dislike what they say, they have a right to say it."

"That's interesting," responded Dr. Goodman, "yet the University was quick to condemn racists and homophobic speech, and even allowed rallies and teach-ins in response!"

The Provost thought for a moment, then responded, "But in those cases there was a perceived threat to the Black, Latinx, and LGBTQ students."

"And a group of students chanting 'Jews will not replace us' is not seen as a threat to Jewish students and faculty?" asked Dr. Friedman rather heatedly.

Attempting to bring down the temperature of the conversation, the Provost responded, "It was only one incident in this case, while there were several incidents of hate-speech in the other cases."

At this point Sarah Levi, the student president of Hillel International (the largest Jewish campus organization in the world), stated, "But this isn't the first incident. Anti-Semitic flyers have been posted on the Hillel bulletin board several times. Our flyers posted on various bulletin boards around announcing upcoming events have been defaced with anti-Semitic epithets including swastikas. It became so frequent last semester that, out of fear, we held our Sukkot celebration indoors and didn't put a Menorah in the window as we usually do for Chanukah. Now many of our members are beginning to believe that they are not safe on campus."

Provost Johnston gently responded, "Did you report these events to campus security?"

"Yes," responded Sarah, "but they said there was nothing they could do unless one of us was directly threatened."

Trying a different tact, Provost Johnston asked Sara, "Have you talked to the SGA leadership? Perhaps you could organize a joint activity to address your group's concerns."

"I reached out to them on several occasions, including yesterday after the march, but they are not interested in helping. Not surprising as one of the marchers was the vice president of SGA!"

Provost Johnston was taken aback at the last statement, but after some thought responded to all in the meeting, "Perhaps it would be best not to draw any more attention to it. I'm not sure another rally or teach-in would be helpful; the campus community is exhausted at this point. Also, it may have the unfortunate consequence of drawing attention to which members of the student body are Jewish, which might lead to individuals being harassed. Maybe it's best to keep a low profile."

Dr. Friedman responded in a low seething manner, "I've been a member of the faculty here for 30 years. In that time, I and other Jewish members of the faculty have heard anti-Semitic jokes and comments from students, faculty, staff and yes administration. Yet every time we raised this issue with administration or tried to have it put on the Faculty Senate agenda no one wants to address it. The University is quick to respond to hate speech targeted to other minority groups, but anti-Semitism gets swept under the carpet! This, however, is different. It goes far beyond jokes and comments in bad taste. That march yesterday was meant to harass the Jews on this campus—telling us we have no place here; we aren't real members of the 'campus community.' What you are telling us is that, as in the past, Jews on this campus cannot depend on Administration for anything more than offering advice to 'keep our heads down!'"

Provost Johnston protested saying "That isn't what I'm advising. I take what happened yesterday very seriously, therefore I need to carefully consider how to proceed. Remember, I need to consider the entire campus community. I have already called a meeting with Mr. Rodriguez (the equity officer) and the university counsel to discuss how we should respond to the march. I will inform you of our decision." With that the meeting ended.

Discussion Questions

1. The First Amendment of the U.S. Constitution does guarantee Free Speech Rights. Yet, the free speech rights of the marchers result in the Jewish members of the campus experiencing injustice. What issues does Provost Johnston need to consider in addressing these tensions?

2. The ethic of care places a primacy on relationships. Is Provost Johnston's concern about the campus community's "exhaustion" consistent with the ethic of care? Does this care for the broader campus community harm the relationship of the Jewish faculty and students with that community?

3. The ethic of critique is concerned with uncovering and dismantling systematic injustices towards, and the marginalization of, groups. Is Provost Johnston's reluctance to address concerns of Jewish members of the campus community perpetuating institutionalized anti-Semitism and silencing the voices of Jews on campus? Is this consistent with the ethic of critique? If so, how so or why not?

4. Thinking about the ethic of the profession and considering the tensions within and among the ethics of justice, care, and critique in this dilemma, is there a way to act in the best interest of *all* students? What are the intended and unintended consequences for all students if the university does not address anti-Semitism on campus?

REFERENCES

Arar, K., Haj, I., Abramovitz, R., & Oplatka, I. (2016). Ethical leadership in education and its relation to ethical decision-making: The case of Arab school leaders in Israel. *Journal of Educational Administration, 54*(6), 647–660.

Blankenship-Knox, A.E. & Geier, B.A. (2018). Taking a day off to pray: Closing schools for religious observance in increasingly diverse schools. *Brigham Young*

University Education and Law Journal, 2018(2), 1–51. Retrieved from https://digitalcommons.law.byu.edu/elj/vol2018/iss2/2

Bouchard, N. (2020). Ethics education in religious education: Analysis of the major orientations found in England's national framework for religious education. *McGill Journal of Education, 55*(1), 127–150. Retrieved from https://doi.org/10.7202/1075723ar

Central Intelligence Agency (2014a). People and society: Guam ethnic groups. Retrieved from www.cia.gov/library/publications/the-world-factbook/geos/gq.html

Central Intelligence Agency (2014b). People and society: Guam nationality. Retrieved from www.cia.gov/library/publications/the-world-factbook/geos/gq.html

Central Intelligence Agency (2014c). People and society: Guam religions. Retrieved from www.cia.gov/library/publications/the-world-factbook/geos/gq.html

Guam Department of Education (n.d.) Home[page]. Retrieved from https://sites.google.com/a/gdoe.net/gdoe/

Guam Economic Development Authority (2014a). Guam: American in Asia. Retrieved from www.investguam.com/guam/

Guam Economic Development Authority (2014b). Guam: Guam quick facts. Retrieved from www.investguam.com/guam/

Guam Economic Development Authority (2014c). Guam: quality of life: education. Retrieved from www.investguam.com/guam/

Miller, R.B. (2016). *Friends and other strangers: Studies in religion, ethics, and culture.* New York, NY: Colombia University Press.

Stefkovich, J.A. & Frick, W.C. (2021). *Best interests of the student: Applying ethical constructs to legal cases in education* (3rd ed.). New York, NY: Routledge.

Stefkovich, J.A., Brady, K.P., Ballard, T.H., & Rossow, L.F. (2021). *The law and education: Cases and materials* (3rd ed.). Durham, NC: Carolina Press.

Strike, K.A., Haller, E.J., & Soltis, J.F. (2005). *The ethics of school administration* (3rd ed.). New York, NY: Teachers College Press.

Tyack, D.B. (1974). *The one-best system: A history of urban education.* Cambridge, MA: Harvard University Press.

Yudof, M.G., Kirp, D.L., Levin, B., & Moran, R.F. (2002). *Educational policy and the law* (4th ed.). Belmont, CA: Wadsworth.

Chapter 8

Equality versus Equity

James K. Krause, David J. Traini, Beatrice H. Mickey, Daniel L. Dukes, Carly Ackley, Jennifer Antoni, and Laura L. Randolph

In today's diverse and complex society, a paradox exists between the concepts of equality and equity. We define equality under the rubric of equal or even-handed treatment as discussed by Strike, Haller, and Soltis (1988). They provided this definition: "In any given circumstances, people who are the same in those respects relevant to how they are treated in those circumstances should receive the same treatment" (p. 45). On the one hand, equality, defined in this way, looks at the individual and the circumstances surrounding him or her. It does not focus on group differences based on categories such as race, sex, social class, and ethnicity. This view is one of assimilation because it assumes that individuals, once socialized into society, have the right "to do anything they want, to choose their own lives and not be hampered by traditional expectations and stereotypes" (Young, 1990, p. 157). It is a positive and inspiring concept—an ideal that is well worth attaining.

Equity, on the other hand, as we define it here, deals with difference and takes into consideration the fact that this society contains many groups that have not always been given equal treatment and/or have not had a level field on which to play. These groups have frequently been made to feel inferior to those in the mainstream, and some have even been oppressed. To achieve equity, according to Young (1990), "Social policy should sometimes accord special treatment to groups" (p. 158). Thus, the concept of equity provides a case for unequal treatment for those who have been disadvantaged over time. It can provide compensatory kinds of treatment, offering it in the form of special programs and benefits for those who have been discriminated against and need opportunity.

Movements have had a profound effect in fighting for equity or social justice. In the case of the Native American movement, a battle took place

DOI: 10.4324/9781003022862-10

against the concept of assimilation. This fight was for "a right to self-government on Indian lands" (Young, 1990, p. 160). It was also a desire to retain the language, customs, and crafts that gave this group its special identity.

Pressure from group movements has often led to legislation that has provided opportunity. To give an example of this, the women's movement fought for and eventually obtained the passage of Title IX of the Education Amendments Act of 1972. Title IX made it known that discrimination on the basis of sex was illegal in any educational program receiving federal funding (American Association of University Women (AAUW), 1992, p. 8). The passage of Title IX opened the door for many gender-equity programs and projects (AAUW, 1995) enabling women and girls to be empowered and learn how to overcome the barriers that still exist today.

Today, Title IX is also being considered in another light, i.e., equity as applied to transgender individuals, a group that comprises only 0.6% of the U.S. adult population, but one that has experienced great discrimination (Stefkovich, Brady, Ballard, & Rossow, 2021). The leading court opinion on this topic is *Bostock v. Clayton County* (2020), an employment case, in which the U.S. Supreme Court said that the wording of Title IX, which prohibits discrimination "on the basis of sex," includes discrimination against transgender persons. The High Court did not decide how or whether this decision applies to schools, but several federal appellate courts have agreed that students meeting specific criteria to be categorized as transgender must be allowed to use bathrooms and/or locker rooms designated for the gender with which they identify and not the gender assigned at birth (Stefkovich et al., 2021).

The law on this topic has many nuances, is rapidly changing, and can vary depending on your state and/or federal jurisdiction (Bohm, Del Duca, Elliott, Holako, & Tanner, 2016; Maier, 2020), therefore it is critical that educational leaders consult with their school attorney and/or professional association regarding their legal obligations. For these reasons and understanding the trauma that transgender students experience every day, it is perhaps even more important that educators make wise ethical decisions. To this extent, we have included a transgender dilemma aimed at the university level, but one that could stimulate wider discussion.

It is not only in racial, ethnic, and gender movements, however, that the paradox of equality versus equity may be found. If one turns to the umbrella term of diversity and defines it broadly, then a range of differences can be explored that includes categories not only of race, ethnicity, and gender but also of social class, disability, sexual orientation, and exceptionalities (Banks, 2014, 2020; Banks & Banks, 2006; Cushner, McClelland, & Safford, 2011; Gay, 2010; Gollnick & Chinn, 2012; Grant &

Portera, 2010; Nieto, 2012, 2018; Shapiro, Sewell & DuCette, 2001; Sleeter & Grant, 2003; Sleeter & Zavala, 2020).

The paradox of equality versus equity is treated differently under each of the four paradigms we use to analyze ethical dilemmas in this book. Turning to the first of the four paradigms, the ethic of justice is broad enough to include both equality and equity. This all-encompassing definition goes back as far as Aristotle, who "held that justice consists in treating equals equally and unequals unequally" (Strike & Soltis, 1992, p. 46). By this, Strike and Soltis felt he meant that "if high-school grades are the basis of admission into a university, then two people with the same grades should receive the same treatment. Either both should be admitted, or both should be rejected" (p. 46).

This illustration demonstrates the use of the justice paradigm for the principle of equality. But Aristotle also recognized that "when people differ on some relevant characteristic they should be treated differently." Strike and Soltis (1992), in this case, provided the example of a visually handicapped student who is not being treated fairly by being given the same book to read as a sighted student. "Here," they said, "fairness requires different treatment" (p. 46). This illustration utilizes the concept of equity in relation to the paradigm of justice. Thus, under the ethic of justice, both equality and equity are acknowledged.

The ethic of care, another of the four paradigms used in this book, challenges the impartiality and detachment of moral reasoning (e.g., Gilligan, 1982; Gilligan & Richards, 2009; Noddings, 2002, 2003, 2013). The concept of impartiality has tended to work by distancing oneself from others to enable an equal weighing of all interests. The caring frame would not be remote, but instead would be compassionate and place equity rather than equality at its center. No doubt, those who care would really listen to the voices of diverse groups—particularly those who have been discriminated against in the past. They would turn away from the ideal of impartiality that is inherent in our society and our beliefs (Young, 1990). Instead, they would recognize differences and the history of unfair treatment to different groups over time by trying to rectify past wrongs.

Under the ethic of critique, hard questions can be raised concerning the treatment of diverse groups in society. These questions consider issues of oppression, domination, and discrimination. The myth of merit (Fishkin, 1983) and the problems of distribution of goods and services to all groups within our society may also be explored. In addition, within this paradigm, current demographic trends can be viewed in critical as well as positive lights. The unprecedented expansion of our nation's racial, ethnic, socio-economic, and cultural groups can be discussed and questioned using this ethic, as can some of the accompanying problems of children of poverty, single-parent homes, and students of exceptionality (Hodgkinson, 1992; Utley & Obiakor, 1995).

Turning to the ethic of the profession, we know that how schools, colleges, and universities address the evolving needs of our students and society will determine, to a large extent, the success of our nation. A great challenge to be faced involves how educators balance the acceptance and support of difference without hurting the collective whole of our society. This is not an easy balance for educational leaders to attain, and the major question in this paradigm remains: Is equality or equity, or a combination of both, in the best interests of the students?

In this chapter, we present seven dilemmas related to ethics, equality, and equity. A range of approaches is addressed in the cases themselves and in the questions that follow each situation. In this edition, we have added two new dilemmas, one considering the needs of a student already in crisis when a pandemic occurs and another involving a transgender student requesting university housing. In all these dilemmas, the administrators and teachers in charge want to do the right thing. However, what is right for one person or group may not be right for others.

Case Study 8.1, **When All Means All**, deals with a problem in a school that is beginning to serve as a model of inclusion for the state. In this dilemma, the problem centers on an emotionally disturbed child in a regular elementary school classroom who has caused chaos. Having worked with the child in the classroom for a time, a teacher has found him to be a constant source of problems. She feels that the youngster is infringing on the rights of others and is also not receiving the kind of attention he needs in an inclusive classroom.

In Case Study 8.2, **Black and White and Shades of Gray**, new minority teachers are to be retrenched owing to economic reasons. The old rule, "last hired, first fired," is presented with all its problems. The principal is placed in a very difficult position in a district in which minority students are increasing in number.

Access to Knowledge (Case Study 8.3) describes a dilemma involving a principal approached by Latino parents who want their child to take courses in the college preparatory track. The student has been discouraged by the school counselor and by his teachers from taking college preparatory work. The principal finds out that the student has not been doing well in his classes. Conflicting feelings on the part of the school leader handling the situation are discussed.

In Case Study 8.4, **Academic Integrity in a Deaf Education Setting**, the assistant principal of a school for students with hearing impairments addresses standardized testing and how it is administered by two very different teachers. He must decide whether teachers should follow test directions, as written, or modify them according to the needs of their students. This case asks: How should directions be administered to provide an equal playing field on standardized testing for students who are deaf?

Case Study 8.5, **When Fundraising and School Policy Collide**, focuses on a small preschool center that depends heavily on donations. A grandfather, who gives money generously, wants his grandson to attend the school, but a child with spina bifida is next on the waiting list. The decision that must be made by the director is to determine who should be invited to enroll in the school, keeping in mind the consequences of that decision.

How we anticipate the needs of discrete populations or singular students who might be especially endangered during a widespread crisis carries with it many ethical questions about those who are cared for and those who are easily forgotten. In Case Study 8.6, **After Thought**, a school counselor is confronted with the problem of how to convince her principal that a student in crisis needs to keep his homebound instruction during a worldwide pandemic when the principal's focus is on the needs of the entire student body—all of whom he sees as homebound.

Our final case study (8.7), **Gender Inclusive or Gender Disability?**, turns to higher education and the housing needs of a transgender female ready to begin her first year at the university. Rose, a university administrator in the housing office, has just learned of this situation at Open House Day when the student and her parents ask about housing accommodations. With resources planned, but not readily available, Rose can allocate space set aside for students with disabilities. Even if this situation were amenable to the new student and her parents, it nonetheless, raises ethical issues as to how to allocate resources among equally deserving groups and individuals.

CASE STUDY 8.1 WHEN ALL MEANS ALL

As Jim Martin headed toward home, thoughts filtered back to better times. He found this occurring more frequently during the past few weeks. Three years had passed since Freedom Elementary School had implemented a full inclusionary model of educating students with disabilities. As director of special education for the school district, and with his office in the Freedom building, Jim had invested a great deal of time in developing the program and, thus, had a special interest in seeing it succeed. He also believed that the process of inclusion was a natural extension of the child-centered, collaborative approach the district and community supported. Here, the regular classroom would be the educational setting of choice for all students. However, after its early success, more recent struggles were now wearing on everyone. "How could something that unified everyone such a short time ago be so divisive now?" he wondered.

Jim had served as director of special education for 11 years. He was well liked and well respected by his staff and co-workers and had an excellent relationship with Rose O'Brien, the building principal. Jim had always prided himself on fostering the development of a highly skilled, caring faculty. He was able to do this by sharing leadership. The idea of establishing an inclusive school stemmed from his work and that of a committed core of teachers. This team truly served as the driving force behind the exploration, development, and implementation of an inclusion model.

It was not easy to build this concept into a functional process, but everyone's hard work and steadfast belief provided the foundation for what would benefit all. Support soon grew from a small pocket of Freedom's staff to widespread support throughout the faculty and community. Most teachers genuinely believed that all children would be best served in a regular education setting with their same-age peers. Eventually, Freedom's effort to include students with disabilities began to draw attention from across the state. Educators from other school districts began to explore the "Freedom Model." Administrators and teachers flocked to the school in droves. Faculty members were asked to present at state-wide conferences on inclusive practices. Jim had just recently received notice of the upcoming publication of an article he had written for a professional journal. It was entitled "Freedom: An Inclusionary Model for All." Advocates of full inclusion held up the Freedom Model as an example of successful practice that developed from the grass-roots effort of caring educators.

Momentum from the early successes, or the "Golden Age" as it later became known, carried staff through the first two years. Inclusion was not an easy process, but challenges were met with effective collaborative efforts. Staff and services were in place to prevent any child from needing to be pulled out of the regular classroom. Students were doing well, and the parents of students with disabilities were happier than ever. Although there were some parents who voiced concern about unfair levels of attention directed toward students with disabilities (and away from their own children), these parents remained the minority in the parent–teacher organization. The school had established its identity as an inclusive school. This was a source of pride to the school and community.

At the start of the third year, Cody Smith, a fourth-grade student with serious emotional difficulties, enrolled at Freedom. Staff had included students with behavior problems in the past, but the level of Cody's conduct disorder was new to most. He had a long history of aggressive acting-out, disruptive behavior, and poor peer–teacher interactions. He had been previously served in a self-contained classroom for students with emotional disabilities. He had met with moderate success in this program, but the program's staff felt the need for continued extensive support.

The team met with Mr. and Mrs. Smith to review the wealth of educational and psychiatric information provided in Cody's file. Although there was some hesitancy, the team agreed that inclusion for all means all. If they were to be true to their established philosophy, they could not segregate certain students. The Smiths were somewhat confused by all this. Early on in Cody's school career, they had tried to fight his removal from the regular classroom. Just as they were becoming comfortable with the separate services, a new set of professionals were saying the regular classroom would be best for their son. They liked the idea of him being with "normal" kids, but would he fit in? They were finally convinced to try an inclusive class after speaking with other parents who advocated strongly for inclusive education.

The team assembled the following week to develop a plan outlining the supports and services necessary to educate Cody in the regular fourth-grade classroom. A range of supports involving additional staffing, curricular and instructional adaptations, and behavior support planning were developed. Jim swelled with pride as the staff met this challenge and developed a quality, individualized program. Cody's parents were fully involved and very pleased with their new-found empowerment. During the first month in his new school, Cody experienced only minor difficulties. Adjustments in supports were made to address his needs, and he responded well. Everyone was excited to be part of another success story. Cody was happy, learning, and making new friends.

As October arrived, however, so did the firestorm of Cody's behavior. Almost overnight, he went from cooperative and pleasant to aggressive and disruptive. He threw books and food, cursed openly at adults, refused to comply with basic requests, and threatened to hurt other students. Mrs. Appleby, his teacher, often found herself at his side or in the hallway trying to calm Cody and prevent further disruption. Everyone now knew what a conduct disorder involved. The team immediately pulled together for the first of seemingly endless team meetings.

The team adjusted Cody's behavior support plan to allow for "calming" time when he became agitated. This proved unsuccessful. Individual aide support was assigned. Cody continued to disrupt class with his verbal outbursts. Teachers began to rotate one-on-one coverage. Unstructured time was studied and structured. The team studied factors in Cody's life that may have precipitated these difficulties. Profanity-laced tirades and non-compliance continued. Positive contingencies proved ineffective, family case management was fruitless, and medical intervention was unsuccessful. Consultation with social workers and psychologists led to little, if any, positive change.

After three months, the roof was about to blow off. Parents throughout the school demanded that Cody be removed. Others requested that their children transfer to other classes away from Cody. An undercurrent opposing inclusion started to surface for the first time. Jim Martin danced from fire to fire, trying to quell the rising displeasure of staff, students, and parents. Throughout all this, Cody and his parents remained pleased with the regular class placement.

Then it happened. The team wearily pulled together for another planning meeting. Jim was presenting his thoughts on the latest plan for intervention when Mrs. Appleby, Cody's teacher, stopped him midsentence and said, "I want him out of my class now! This is no longer fair to Cody or the other children." Two other team members concurred: "We cannot meet his needs in the regular classroom. He is too disruptive to the education of other students. This kind of class is too much for him to handle. He is too much for us to handle." Jim was completely caught off-guard by their comments.

"What about our philosophy that all our students will be included in the regular classroom?" Jim asked.

"Now!" they said with angry glares.

Several other team members, including Cody's mother, wanted to hear more from Jim about possible interventions. Heated arguments began to rise from the team. Accusations, name calling, and blame placing surfaced. Jim thought everyone could use a chance to cool off, so the meeting was rescheduled for the following morning. Members of the team stormed out, spewing threats involving the local teachers' association and disability advocates.

Word spread quickly within the school and community. Jim's office was transformed into a mission control center. Staff marched in to vent their frustrations. Even Principal O'Brien, who had been a steadfast supporter, expressed serious concerns. Parents called to address several rumors that they had heard. Advocates called for reassurance that inclusion would not be sacrificed. Cody's father even called to let Jim know his attorney would be attending the morning conference. What else could go wrong? The phone rang again and Jim recognized the superintendent's voice, and tone, on the other end. He didn't focus on every word, but the message came through clearly: fix this one immediately.

As Jim continued his drive toward home, he began to question his own beliefs regarding inclusion. "If we say inclusion is for all children," he thought, "is it right for us to separate some who are not experiencing success in this setting? Has all this work gone for naught? Is the process worthwhile if anger and resentment become pervasive throughout the school? How can this situation be 'fixed' as the superintendent instructed?" He wondered what would happen at the next morning's meeting and every day thereafter.

Questions for Discussion

1. Considering the support Jim has lost, should he continue the program? Discuss the pros and cons of program continuation that Jim should consider before he makes his decision.

2. Is it fair to sacrifice the needs of the individual even when he or she represents a voice not experienced by the majority? Is it ever fair to sacrifice the greater good for the individual? If so, under what circumstances? Is this the situation that exists with Cody? Does caring extend to the needs of the group, or is it restricted to the needs of the individual? Where and how does one draw the line between individual rights and the common good? In this case, is there an ethical choice that would support both sides? If so, what is it?

3. There are important laws to protect individuals with disabilities, but there are also laws that require teachers to educate all children. Do you see these laws as conflicting? Why or why not? Who made these laws? Who were they designed to protect?

4. Do you see any conflicts between Jim's personal beliefs about inclusion and his professional beliefs? What in this scenario leads you to draw your conclusion?

CASE STUDY 8.2 BLACK AND WHITE AND SHADES OF GRAY

Northern Regional School District had changed dramatically over the past ten years. During that decade, the two townships it served had been transformed by a booming economy from a sleepy, rural, nearly all-White farming region into a bustling, quasi-suburban, multicultural area. One result of this economic expansion was a rapid growth in population and a concomitant change in demographics that had a profound effect on the composition of Northern High's student body. In the space of just ten years, the racial make-up went from 98% White and 2% African American to 70% White, 22% African American, and 8% Asian. There had been little change, however, in the composition of Northern staff. Prior to the boom, all 30 teachers had been White. Now, there were 85 on the staff, and only two were minority: one was African American and the other was Asian.

Things began to change two years previously when Dr. John DiCaprio became principal. A graduate of Northern nearly 20 years before, he had returned with impressive credentials. A Harvard doctorate and five years of administrative experience in the prestigious suburban district of nearby

Monroe City had assured the board of his competence, but it was his record at Northern as a student that had landed him the job. He had been student council president, a member of the National Honor Society, captain of the football team, and the only wrestler ever to win a state championship. His elevation to principal was hailed as the return of a favorite son.

Despite the support he enjoyed, John's tenure had not been without a few bumps. One of the most sensitive issues, and, in DiCaprio's opinion, one of the most critical, was the racial imbalance between the student body and the teaching staff. When he arrived, Northern High School had a staff that was 2.5% minority to educate a student body that was 30% minority. DiCaprio had pushed hard for increased minority hiring, but there was a great deal of resistance. A walkout by minority students in the spring triggered in part by this imbalance, had been a wake-up call. The previous summer three new teachers had been hired, and two of them were African American. Minority representation on the staff now stood at 5.7%. Dr. DiCaprio was happy that the district was moving in the right direction.

According to projections by the state economic development authority, this part of the state of New Sussex had been labeled as the state's leading area of growth. Using data provided by the state, the district had estimated that the student population would continue to grow and eventually double within the next 15 years. Of greater significance was the forecast that a sizable number of new students would be African American and Asian. Dr. DiCaprio had seen in these statistics both a challenge and an opportunity. Increased enrollments translated into increased hiring, and it was through new hiring that Dr. DiCaprio planned to increase the number of minorities on his staff.

DiCaprio's best-laid plans now seemed like pie in the sky. The economic worm had turned. Much of the development in Jefferson County, where Northern's two feeder districts were located, had been fueled by growth in two areas. The first was the expansion of high-tech businesses in Monroe City, less than 20 miles away. The second was the increasing number of casinos in Pacific City, less than 30 miles away. The casinos had made shore property along the southern New Sussex coast too expensive for middle-income professionals, and so they had come to Jefferson County seeking affordable housing. With a recession in full swing, casinos went belly up, and the economic boom in Monroe City went bust.

The impact on Northern was immediate. The student population growth curve was, at best, expected to be flat for the next couple of years. Some even foresaw a decrease. To DiCaprio, the handwriting was on the wall; there would have to be a reduction in force (RIF). RIFing was anathema to the teachers' association because it made vulnerable teachers who had gained tenure and, presumably, job security. In deciding who to let go, the union was adamant that the "last hired, first fired" rule be followed.

For DiCaprio, RIFing was the death-knell of his minority hiring program. He had searched far and wide to find the best qualified candidates, and his efforts had not been in vain. The two new African-American teachers had done a great job in their first year at Northern. He could easily think of a dozen tenured teachers he would rather let go. Although he would have dearly loved to violate the "last hired, first fired" rule, DiCaprio knew that to do so would create such a furor that the staff, usually complaisant, would most likely rise up and take drastic action, possibly even strike.

It was the first week of April, and the district was required to inform all staff by the end of the month of their employment status for the upcoming year. DiCaprio had just met with the superintendent and received a directive: he would have to eliminate one position. As if that were not bad enough, the decision had been made to effect this reduction by increasing class size in either the Math or English Departments. What a setback! Of the two new African-American teachers hired, one was an English teacher, the other a math teacher. One would have to go. DiCaprio was incensed. He had argued for several other options, without success. He knew there had to be another way.

Peter Weiss was finishing up his second year in the Social Studies Department. DiCaprio had frequent conversations with Barbara Meyer, the department head, about him. Peter had been struggling somewhat with his teaching technique and his rapport with the students. One sore point was the fact that, although White, he was teaching the African-American history course that had been implemented the year after the student walkout. There was no hard evidence that he was insensitive to the minority students in the class. Complaints came mainly from parents and were philosophical in nature. "How could a White man understand the struggle of African Americans?" was a query that had been put to him many times.

Beyond this course, DiCaprio and Meyer had some misgivings about Weiss' capability, as evidenced by his mediocre course observations. Despite his concerns, DiCaprio believed that every new teacher should be given a fair chance to learn the craft of teaching. He remembered his own first few years in the classroom. His performance had been less than stellar, and he knew that he had needed those three years to develop into a good, solid teacher. He had intended to give Weiss the same opportunity. Now, however, as a principal, he had a different set of priorities. He certainly had doubts about Weiss' potential but had been willing to give him one more year. Given the need to reduce his staff by one, his thinking now took a different course.

George Taylor was the African-American English teacher who had been hired the year before. Fresh out of college and single, George had done an outstanding job both in and out of the classroom. He was co-advisor for the African-American Culture Club and had volunteered to run the "We the Students" Committee. DiCaprio had founded this group after the walkout to promote understanding among the races at Northern. He had run it the first year but found that his busy schedule did not permit him to continue in this capacity. When George was hired, he was asked to take over and had done a first-rate job. George also had dual certification in social studies.

If Peter Weiss were not rehired, then George could switch from the English Department to the Social Studies Department. DiCaprio would be able to follow his superintendent's directive to reduce staff in the English or Math Department. He would be able to keep a gifted minority teacher, have an African American teaching the course in African-American history, and maintain what meager gains he had made in trying to establish a minority presence on the faculty. Of course, this could be accomplished only if he let Peter Weiss go after his second year; however, this would violate his long-standing belief that teachers should be given at least three years to prove themselves.

As he left the office that day, he was, for the first time in a long time, not quite sure what to do. As he rounded the corner, he bumped into Peter Weiss.

"Hey, Dr. DiCaprio, want to see something?" Peter said, waving a picture in his hand.

"What have you got there, Peter?" Dr. DiCaprio replied. "It's a sonogram. My wife and I are going to have twins."

Questions for Discussion

1. What is the fairest decision Dr. DiCaprio could make? The most caring? Are they different? Is what is fair or caring for Peter Weiss the same as what is fair or caring for George Taylor? Are there others who should be considered in trying to determine fairness or caring? If so, who are they? Why those persons?

2. What do you assume would be the consequences for Dr. DiCaprio if he broke the "last hired, first fired" rule? Are there times when rules or laws must be broken to achieve a higher moral level? Do you think this situation is an example of one of these times? Why or why not? Explain.

3. Where do you suppose the "last hired, first fired" rule came from? Could you speculate as to what its original purpose may have been? Do you believe it is a just rule? If you believe the rule is just, do you believe it is absolute? Or are there circumstances under which the rule might be applied differently or not at all? Whose rule is this?

Who benefits from the rule in this scenario? Who, in general, would benefit from such a rule?

4. What do you believe is the most moral decision that Dr. DiCaprio could make in this situation? What would you do if you were in his place? Why would you take such action? In this circumstance, are your personal beliefs the same or different from your professional beliefs? Explain.

CASE STUDY 8.3 ACCESS TO KNOWLEDGE

Mackenzie High School, the only public high school in Hartford County, has an enrollment of 2,500+ students in Grades 7 through 12 of which 55% are minority. Students enroll in Mackenzie from five economically diverse elementary schools: two schools are in an affluent community; two schools are in a modest socio-economic community; and the last school, at the opposite end of the socio-economic ladder, has a minority population of 90%.

Mackenzie High School is situated in the center of Harford County, an active, politically charged, blue-collar, multi-ethnic community comprised of African, Asian, Hispanic, and European Americans. Harford County is primarily working class with many prosperous businesses.

With the influx of people from diverse backgrounds, Whites have remained in the majority; however, demographic changes have had a powerful impact on cultural life and the high school's educational mission. Despite the diversity among students, the high school faculty remains quite homogeneous. As the racial make-up of the community changed, Mackenzie High School attempted to ease the process of assimilation by emphasizing language instruction, offering remedial classes, instituting multicultural courses and implementing a comprehensive vocational program.

Meanwhile, the White majority see the changing economy and increasing population as signs of a future struggle. Parents in the minority population feel similar. Both groups want their children to make better lives for themselves by attending college; consequently, the demand for access to college-bound programs has intensified. Issues of access to knowledge and equality of educational opportunity have come to the forefront.

Minority students make up the majority enrollment in vocational education classes. Teachers subscribe to Jensen's research, which argues that there is a real genetically determined difference in intellectual ability of minorities. Teachers believe that minority students perform poorly academically because they are below average in intellectual ability.

Ruben and Gabriella Soler moved to Harford County from Puerto Rico a decade ago. The Solers have three children; two have graduated and obtained employment in nearby businesses. Alberto, their youngest son, wants to go to college, and despite numerous meetings with the counseling department regarding placing Alberto in a higher functioning group, Mrs. Soler has little doubt that minority students are not treated fairly. Alberto has been placed in low-functioning groups most of his educational life. Now, he is preparing to enter the upper division of the high school, and he wants to be placed in the college-bound program.

Dr. Meyerowitz, the high school principal for eight years, is fair-minded and committed to high expectations for all students. During the past five years, she observed a change in teacher attitude and performance, noticing that teachers accepted the idea that minority students could not be expected to learn at high levels, which is reflected in the manner in which students are placed in programs as well as in the quality of instruction. Given these circumstances, it is not surprising that Principal Meyerowitz welcomed Mrs. Soler's concern.

Maryanne Polk, widely known in Harford County, heads the counseling department. She has advised most of the students' parents and, her decisions have made it generally impossible for minority students to escape a lifetime of work in the factories surrounding Harford County. Having been denied access to equal educational opportunity, a disproportionate number of Latino and African-American students are enrolled in vocational education courses. Most minority students are advised to enter the workforce, apply for apprenticeship programs, or join the armed services. Few, if any, are recommended for college. Most non-minority students are given a fair chance to prepare for college by their placement in the college-bound program.

Maryanne Polk felt Alberto would not do well in the college-bound track. Mrs. Soler feels that Ms. Polk has no right to thwart Alberto's dream of going to college. She is convinced that minority students do not achieve at high levels because the school culture favors the White majority. Teachers do not create a democratic environment in their classrooms, nor do they exhibit attitudes of caring. Alberto has a fundamental right to the same opportunities afforded to White students, and Mrs. Soler is demanding that her son be given the same opportunity as non-minority students.

Principal Meyerowitz conveyed Mrs. Soler's sentiments to Maryanne Polk, who assured Dr. Meyerowitz that her decision was made in Alberto's best interest. Alberto was recommended for the vocational program based on achievement, standardized test results, and teacher recommendation. Ms. Polk was confident that Alberto lacked the aptitude to do well in college, and it was her professional duty to guide Alberto toward an attainable goal.

Pat Meyerowitz did not doubt Maryanne's sincerity. Nor did she think that Maryanne's decision was in Alberto's best interest. As an educator, Maryanne Polk is in the position of deciding the path Alberto's life will take. This is a job that she has done for years, and as far as many people are concerned, she has done it well. On the other hand, Pat Meyerowitz is the instructional leader. She recognizes that Maryanne is influenced by past practices that have had an unsympathetic outcome for minority students.

Is Alberto entitled equal access to good instruction and equality of opportunity so that he can gain the skills and knowledge necessary to attain his goal? What should Dr. Meyerowitz do?

Questions for Discussion

1. Alberto has been tracked into low ability groups and received an inequitable education since first grade. What should the principal do?
2. What, if any, are the benefits and detriments of tracking?
3. What should a caring administrator and director of student services do?
4. In this scenario, do you agree with Pat or Maryanne? As director of student services or principal, how would you handle this situation in the most ethical manner?
5. If you really believed that Alberto could not make it through a college preparatory program, would you tell him? What would you tell the Solers? Should students be permitted to take whatever courses they wish? Why or why not? If not, how does one decide where to draw the line?

CASE STUDY 8.4 ACADEMIC INTEGRITY IN A DEAF EDUCATION SETTING

Ms. Johnston pulled into the school parking lot earlier than normal on a brisk March morning. This was the first day that the students at Fairway High School, a large public school in a growing suburban area, would be taking the high stakes state assessment. Just like other teachers in her school, Ms. Johnston had been working tirelessly all year to teach and reteach the essential skills covered in the high school graduation test. However, one important difference between other teachers and Ms. Johnston was that she had been using two languages to instruct her students: English (for reading and writing purposes) and American Sign Language

(ASL). As a deaf teacher who is a native signer and a well-known teacher-leader in the field of ASL, Ms. Johnston realizes the importance of her deaf students learning both languages and had established a classroom in which both languages are valued and studied intently.

As she walked into the building to prepare for the arrival of her students on this particularly important morning, Ms. Johnston began to remember a poignant conversation she had with Mr. Humphries, the assistant principal responsible for overseeing the special education programs at the school. During their intense discussion on testing accommodations for deaf students, Ms. Johnston pointed out her concern that the deaf students who use ASL were at a disadvantage over the deaf students in the school in which she had previously taught. In Ms. Johnston's eyes, the biggest struggle had to do with the translation process of English print into sign language, which is viewed as the equivalent of reading aloud the test to hearing students (both accommodations are for those students reading significantly below grade level, as documented in the students' IEPs).

According to the state's testing manual, teachers must sign the questions and answer choices verbatim as they are written in English. Ms. Johnston elaborated that because ASL is not signed English, then signing the print words "verbatim" in English order would be like taking each printed English word and translating it word-for-word into spoken Spanish, instead of using correct Spanish grammar. Ms. Johnston compared this policy with the policy in her previous state, which allowed signing that is consistent with the sign language used during classroom instruction (ASL in Ms. Johnston's class). The premise was to make sure that deaf students had the same accessibility to the printed information that hearing students would have to an exam that was read aloud to them.

By the end of this conversation, Mr. Humphries expressed his understanding of Ms. Johnston's perspective on signing accommodations but emphasized that because the state's policy says "verbatim," they are required to follow this requirement.

As the students began to walk to their rooms on this first morning of testing, Mr. Humphries stood in the hallway near the deaf/hard-of-hearing classrooms and began to think about how truly diverse the deaf students are in this school. Some students would receive their accommodations through spoken English (often called the "oral" approach to deaf education), some would rely on a cued language transliterator (called "cued speech"), and yet another group would receive their accommodations through ASL. It was this last group that raised Mr. Humphries' curiosity.

For this day's testing, the students who use ASL were divided into two classrooms; half were with Ms. Johnston in her classroom and the other half were with Ms. Smith, the other deaf education teacher in the department who uses ASL. Mr. Humphries first stepped into Ms. Smith's classroom to check on their testing progress and could tell that everything was going smoothly. Although he was a beginning signer himself, he was confident that Ms. Smith was signing the test "verbatim." However, when he walked into Ms. Johnston's classroom, he noticed that her signing was very different from Ms. Smith's. Ms. Johnston seemed to spend more time signing each test item, and Mr. Humphries wasn't sure if she was really signing "verbatim," as her signing seemed to create more of a visual picture for the students. Out of fear of offending Ms. Johnston because she is deaf and is a leading expert in the field, he did not say or report anything related to this situation.

Three months later, Mr. Humphries sat in his office closely reviewing the test results for the deaf students in the school. He was stunned to see how significantly better the students in Ms. Johnston's testing room scored, as compared with those in Ms. Smith's. This was especially surprising, considering that all the students were at relatively similar ability levels. Immediately, Mr. Humphries remembered back to the testing day when he noticed what looked like Ms. Johnson giving more of a visual explanation to the students while signing the questions and answer choices.

Mr. Humphries scheduled a meeting with Ms. Johnston to ask her about this. During the meeting, Ms. Johnston admitted that she did sign "conceptually accurate" ASL instead of "verbatim" English word order, because she feels that signing correct ASL gives her students a clearer picture of the questions and helps level the playing field for deaf students who use ASL. She also noted that this is an issue of equity for her students and that their state is behind the times by requiring "verbatim" signing.

Her final comment left Mr. Humphries wide-eyed: "I have a moral obligation to fight for the rights of deaf students, and to ensure that they are given the same opportunities and advantages that are given to hearing students. If you want to report me to the state, then you have my permission. But I know in my heart that I did the right thing."

When Ms. Johnston left the room, Mr. Humphries realized he had a difficult decision to make. He knew that Ms. Johnston had violated policy, and that it appeared to have increased scores. He also knew that Ms. Johnston was not ill-intentioned in her actions, and only wanted the best for her students. Finally, he admitted to himself that because so few public-school educators have any knowledge of deaf education, it is highly likely that no one would ever learn of this situation.

Questions for Discussion

1. Which of the four ethical paradigms is most applicable to this situation?

2. Which solution to this ethical dilemma would be in the best interest of the students in Ms. Johnston's testing room? Ms. Smith's testing room?

3. During his decision-making process, Mr. Humphries brought the situation to the attention of a fellow assistant principal, who then stated, "When in doubt, report! High stakes testing is about following the rules. Period." If you were Mr. Humphries, how would you respond to this statement?

4. Suppose you are the principal of Fairway High School, and Mr. Humphries sat down with you to discuss the situation. You realize that you have very little knowledge about the needs of deaf students. How would you give advice or make decisions in this situation?

5. Do you believe there are times when teachers and administrators have an ethical obligation to make decisions that go against local, state, or federal policy? If yes, do these times include situations involving high stakes testing?

CASE STUDY 8.5 WHEN FUNDRAISING AND SCHOOL POLICY COLLIDE

Ms. Ross had been Director at The Small School for four years and loved the work that took place there. The Small School, a private early childhood center that promised kindergarten readiness for its population, prided itself on creating classrooms of diverse learners. To that end, The Small School offered youngsters from ethnically diverse backgrounds, special needs children, and those who do not come from English-speaking homes priority when determining the potential admission of a given child. The waiting list to get into the center is long, but sometimes a spot other than those for the infant room would open up so that someone on the waiting list could enroll their child.

While the school is well known in the local area for providing high-quality early childhood programs, the center is also staffed with special educators, a school counselor, and a social worker who work individually with children to identify any special learning needs early on in a child's academic life. Parents from the most affluent backgrounds like their children to attend the center, as recent studies by a local university have shown that children who attend the program are more developed cognitively and socially and are generally ahead of their peers upon entrance into kindergarten.

Ms. Ross knew that her school was not like every other preschool in town and that the work she and her teachers were doing with children in their youngest years was something that she found both exhilarating and fulfilling. This was Ms. Ross' first administrative position since leaving the classroom as a teacher at The Small School, and she had made the transition easily, so far.

As Director, Ms. Ross holds many roles, one of which was to be the "face" of the center within the local community. Within the center, Ms. Ross was in charge of not only operational leadership but also supervising teachers, providing professional development to her staff, and maintaining close relationships with the families of children that attended her center. In addition, it was her responsibility to work closely with the development office and to meet with potential donors, since much of the funding for the center came from external gifts.

Because the economy was not what it had been at the beginning of her tenure as an administrator, Ms. Ross was finding that many donors could not give as much as they had in the past. Still, she remained optimistic that the unique mission and population of the center would help the development department reach their goal as usual.

Unfortunately, Ms. Ross received word from the development office that she would need to look over her budget for the coming fiscal year. They did not reach their fundraising goal, and it was going to impact the children if she did not make some changes. Ms. Ross had just brought up her budget on the school computer when she heard three heavy knocks on the door. "Come on in," Ms. Ross called.

In walked Mr. Simmons, grandfather of a past student at The Small School, and reoccurring donor. Ms. Ross was surprised to see Mr. Simmons, though he did come by from time to time with good news about a significant gift he had just given to the school. By the look on the man's face she could see that this was not one of those conversations.

"Hi, Ms. Ross, I am going to get right down to business," Mr. Simmons explained as he sat down in the chair across from her desk without being asked.

"No problem, what can I help you with today? Would you like some coffee or something to drink?" Ms. Ross faked cheer as she tried to lift the negative feeling in the room.

Mr. Simmons replied, "No, I am fine, I am going to make this quick. I saw one of your teachers at the grocery store last week and she informed me that there is a spot opening in your two-year-old classroom. First, I do not know why this information was not provided to the donors. Why wasn't it in the newsletter? Second, I want my grandson, Harrison, to be put in that position. His mother is ready for him to enter an early childhood program, and obviously we want him here."

Ms. Ross was furious: which of her teachers would have done that? One of the issues she talked to the teachers about in their staff meetings was the need for confidentiality, especially when it comes to enrollment. The waiting list for the Small School was very long, and the next child on the list, Caleb, had visited the school twice, and, as a child with spina bifida, would benefit from the social interaction, resources, and opportunities at the school.

"I completely understand, what you are saying Mr. Simmons, but we do have a waiting list and I would need to look that over again to see where Harrison is on the list, I'm sure you understand that."

"No, actually I do not understand that, Ms. Ross. I have given over three million dollars to this school in the past two years, and I need to make sure that this happens."

Ms. Ross had never seen Mr. Simmons quite this hostile before. "It's just that we have another child on the list who, because of certain circumstances, cannot get into another program like this one. He has visited the school twice with his family and plans to enroll in two weeks when the other child leaves."

Mr. Simmons paused to think for a minute then rose to his feet and walked to the door. He turned back toward Ms. Ross while grabbing the door handle. "Well, I understand your situation, Ms. Ross, and here is mine. I usually give a lot of money to this school, you know this, and if Harrison gets in, I will give you double what I gave last year. If he does not, please take me off your donor list because I will not be giving to this organization any longer."

As Ms. Ross watched Mr. Simmons leave the office, she put her head in her hands and considered her options. She could call Caleb's family and say that she was wrong and that the position was filled and allow Harrison to enroll or she could call Harrison's mother and tell her that the position was filled and work closely with the development department to try and make up for the lost resources.

On the one hand, if Ms. Ross chose to put Caleb in the class, she knew that he would immediately receive the attention and services he needed. She had previously seen children with special needs grow and develop because of their experience in this center and that was what she wanted to do.

On the other hand, if she did not put Harrison into the class, she could risk losing a substantial amount of money for the school. This kind of money ultimately allows the school to provide these exceptional services to children. Without Mr. Simmons' money, many of those services may have to be cut, which would influence all the children. No matter what happened next, Ms. Ross knew that she was in a dilemma for which she had no immediate answers.

Questions for Discussion

1. Does Mr. Simmons have a right to expect that his grandson will be enrolled in the school? If there are no clear expectations for a donor's role in the school, how should Ms. Ross address these concerns? Through a justice paradigm? Through the ethic of care?

2. Should Ms. Ross follow the waiting list policy and enroll the next child on the list, namely Caleb? Why or why not?

3. If Ms. Ross chooses to place Caleb in the classroom and the school is negatively impacted because of this, do you think this will affect whether Ms. Ross should keep her job? Why or why not?

4. How could Ms. Ross' decision impact and/or change the culture of the school? How would this dilemma be viewed through the ethic of critique?

5. When a decision is made, what is at stake for The Small School? Ms. Ross? Mr. Simmons? Caleb? Harrison?

CASE STUDY 8.6 AFTER THOUGHT

It had been an exhausting, last day for Janelle, a school counselor at Benjamin Franklin High School, the only high school of a small district situated in a tiny, historic, city along the Delaware River. The seemingly impossible had happened: Benjamin Franklin, along with every other school in the county, was closing for five weeks due to a global pandemic. The announcement had come about 5pm on a Friday, and faculty had one more day, that Monday, to tie up loose ends and implement a remote learning program for the following school day, Tuesday.

Thus, faculty had spent the day updating their web pages, some of which had not been touched for years, and hurriedly putting five weeks of assignments on-line. "Don't forget to copy an equivalent amount of work in packet form," the principal had reminded them. The packets, Janelle learned, were for students who either lacked a device, Internet connection, or both.

It wasn't so much that the plan that Benjamin Franklin High School (BFHS) had provided differed so vastly from the plans of their higher performing counterparts in the county. No, every high school seemed to have a plan for virtual learning both through an online system and instructional packets. Like many schools within the county, BFHS even had its own 1:1 initiative where senior and junior students were provided laptop computers to complete their schoolwork all year long. While the district couldn't provide laptops to students in all grade levels, at least the juniors and seniors, district leaders would argue, were able to reap the benefit of having their own device. All in all, the message around BFHS that last Monday was that the students were all set. But were all students set, Janelle wondered?

Janelle thought about some of her most vulnerable students. She feared that students who tended to be disengaged from school, for a host of reasons, would fall further behind during the timeframe of remote learning. One such group of students she had not heard any specific guidance on were the homebound students. These were students who were receiving their instruction via teachers meeting them after school hours, at their houses or a meeting spot in the tiny community.

Most of them were on homebound due to serious conduct issues, and a few were in the advanced stages of pregnancy. What will we be doing for our homebound students? pondered Janelle. She glanced out her window, overlooking the row of fast-food restaurants that many of her former students staffed along the highway that divided the tiny city. As she headed over to the vice principal's office, she thought specifically about Tyshawn, a Special Education senior, mere months from graduation, placed on homebound after he was caught in a car with a gun by the police. Although it was Tyshawn's car, his mom passionately assured Janelle that the gun wasn't his, and he had no idea it was under the seat.

Mr. Crespo, a second-year vice principal at BFHS, was hurriedly trying to assemble the next school year's Program of Studies, which was due to the Board for approval that week, virus or no virus. He was the type of administrator, Janelle gleaned, that preferred to handle one task at a time. Janelle made her way to his doorway, and quietly observed a look of distress on Mr. Crespo's face. "Hi Tony. Quick question for you."

Tony looked up quickly. One hand was gripping his forehead like a migraine was about to creep in. "What have you got for me, Janelle?"

"What's the plan for the homebound students?"

Mr. Crespo barely thought a second. "Well, the whole school is on homebound now! Let them get on their teachers' webpages on-line or pick up a packet like everyone else. Right now, I am trying to finish these revisions for the Program of Studies."

Janelle thought a moment, as she leaned her shoulder against Tony's doorway. Tyshawn was the type of student who engaged more when he was nudged with a blend of warmth and humor. No other recipe seemed to work with Tyshawn. Yes, he had a district issued device, and yes, the district could provide a hotspot for him as a socioeconomically disadvantaged student. Additionally, he could be provided a packet. But would a packet, laptop, or hotspot nudge Tyshawn to try one more problem, or get him started on his expository essay?

Tyshawn never let himself look vulnerable in front of teachers, but a skilled teacher could sense where he was struggling and try to address the deficiency, all with warmth, humor, and care. Cut off from teachers, would Tyshawn choose not to engage with this new program? Although Tyshawn had had a good rapport with his original teachers at the beginning of the year, he had since experienced a weapons' charge and subsequently, was excluded from the regular program for months in accordance with district policy. In terms of pace and volume of work, he was now used to his new normal, that of the homebound program.

Not wanting her student, precariously close to graduation, to flounder more than necessary, Janelle pressed. "Could we see about getting his homebound teachers to continue their work with him, one on one, remotely?

By this point, Tony pivoted back to his computer screen. "Sorry, Janelle. The district is not going to want to spend the money on homebound instruction when every student is in the same boat." He began to type quickly. To Janelle, his fingers looked like tiny tap dancers on his keyboard.

"But the district was going to pay them anyway if it weren't for the virus." She tried to keep her voice friendly. Older than Tony, but lacking the positional power he had, she didn't want to seem critical or negative.

"It's a no-go, Janelle. They want to try it this way." His fingers stopped clicking. "Hey, can you send an all-staff email telling all the homebound teachers what I just said? I am not going to get a chance to do that before everyone leaves, and I know I will forget." His fingers started to dance across the keys again, in a frenzy of clicks.

After two decades of counseling work in a high poverty school, Janelle had a knack to "foresee" where students or families would be missed or left behind, despite well intentioned policies and programs. While she tirelessly tried to shine the light on these instances, she sometimes lacked the social capital or influence to get resources to shift.

Still in his doorway, Janelle glanced at the clock above his desk. Thirty-five more minutes until the teachers would need to leave for five or more weeks, and she still had several calls to make about other matters. Tony's supervisor, Principal Paulson, was not even in the building, as he had meetings at district office all day. Janelle pondered how to proceed.

Questions for Discussion

1. What actions might Janelle take, guided by the ethic of critique? Because Tyshawn is a member of multiple subgroups that have traditionally been subjected to discriminatory practices by school

systems, how can school leaders avoid falling prey to applying the "myth of merit" (Fishkin, 1983, as cited by Shapiro & Stefkovich, 2021) to Tyshawn?

2. Does Janelle have the right to broach the conversation with Principal Paulson or beyond? What would the profession expect of Janelle in this case? Of Vice Principal Crespo? Of Principal Paulson?

3. What is the most caring decision that district leadership could make? The fairest? In this case, are the two different?

4. While keeping Tyshawn's program the same as other students supports a narrow concept of equality, it may not achieve the aim of equity. How might this paradox be seen by the array of factors that comprise the professional paradigm? For instance, how would the ethics of the community frame this dilemma? The standards of the profession? The best interests of the student?

5. Because Tyshawn was awaiting adjudication for a weapons' charge, does that change the answerability for his learning that educators and leaders share responsibility for (Shapiro & Stefkovich, 2021)? What actions might Janelle take regarding students with possible criminal involvement if she were the principal?

CASE STUDY 8.7 GENDER INCLUSIVE OR GENDER DISABILITY?

It is Open House Day for Florence Patterson University (FPU), an urban institution in the north-eastern United States. The campus is filled with excited students and families taking in the university environment and wondering if this place and space can be the start of their college journey. Rose is an administrator in the university's housing office and is working sessions answering student and family questions about what it means to live on-campus.

Rose watches as a bubbly, confident, student with both parents flanking either side quickly head in her direction. This student introduces herself as Alexandria and announces that she has quite the challenge for her. Alexandria is an incoming student for the following semester. She went on to explain that while she goes by Alexandria her school records have her listed as Adam and that she identifies as transgender. Where should she live?

Rose was appreciative of this student's direct approach because she had a similar discussion with her supervisor just a few weeks ago. Alexandria wanted to know the possibility of not living with a male. She desired to live with a female or discuss options. Rose's conversation with her supervisor involved requesting permission to pilot a gender-inclusive housing option. It was denied and, worse, additional discussion ceased regarding how the housing office would support students who came forward with this request. Now, Rose was adamant; we couldn't deny them housing.

This was not the first time a student had approached Rose. During the previous Open House Day another, more reserved, student asked Rose the same question. Rose was more direct saying: "We are exploring this option for the future but do not see it as an available option for the upcoming fall." That student, not accompanied by parents, accepted Rose's explanation, stating an interest in being a part of future conversations.

Today's experience was different. Unlike the first student, Alexandria was energetic with a commanding presence. She was also supported by her parents, all wanting to know what would happen next. Rose, remembering her supervisor was present at the Open House, invited him to join the conversation. Collectively, the five of them discussed possible next steps.

During the conversation, Alexandria and her family were extremely open and forthcoming, sharing intimate details about where Alexandria was in her transition, responding to questions such as: Had she gone through reassignment surgery? Was she taking or planning to take hormone drugs? Who in her circle knew? And had she connected with other campus and/or community resources?

Alexandria stated she had not undergone surgery; she was planning to start hormone treatments in the fall that would result in more developmental and external physical changes. She was emphatic that she wanted to live in a traditional residence hall and interact with different people; she wanted the university experience. She didn't want to be relegated to a single room or be surrounded by all men. Alexandria wanted the opportunity to interact with men and women and be able to use a female restroom. While Rose was appreciative of this information, it made it that much harder to tell this family that the university did not have an option. Rose could feel her supervisor not wanting to share that news.

Just when Rose was about to explain the current accommodations offerings, her supervisor interrupted and mentioned the possibility of a disability accommodation. He stated that there had to be an option through the university's Disabilities Resource Office to get them a space. Rose was taken aback that he would provide such a definitive response without first investigating. He was normally more conservative in his approach with students. Rose was hesitant about this alternative. While it was a way to circumvent existing policies with medical documentation, different sets of rooms could become available that were not offered to the general population to support this student. She couldn't help but be concerned. She worried about what message this would send to the student. Were they implicitly stating that being *you* was a disability? Additionally, how would Rose's campus partners who provide accommodations for students with documented medical conditions respond?

Rose left the Open House somewhat dejected and slightly frustrated by her supervisor's approach. She had held several conversations with other students who identified as transgender, and this option was not presented to them. But Rose knew Alexandria was counting on her to find some alternative to live on-campus as Alexandria and not as Adam (as her records stated). Monday morning, after the Open House, she connected with the Disability Resources Office to see if this option was a possibility. Understandably, they were concerned, wondering how all of this would work, knowing that they were having difficulty finding accommodations for a list of other students with legally recognized medical needs.

Once Rose received the Office's process and the necessary steps that Alexandria would have to take, she was hesitant to contact Alexandria. Rose was questioning if this process would guarantee Alexandria a space; also she was hesitant as she thought about the other students she had met during previous Open Houses. Should she reach out to them and offer them the same option?

Questions for Discussion

1. Using an ethic of critique lens, what laws or policies might Rose explore for future discussions with her supervisor and/or Disability Resources Office to re-examine gender-inclusive housing?
2. If Rose was leading with an ethic of care, how might her actions change to be more supportive of Alexandria?
3. If Rose was leading with an ethic of justice, how might she balance the parents' reaction?
4. If Rose was leading with an ethic of the profession, how might she have prepared herself better for the final Open House and the anticipation of other students requesting gender-inclusive housing.
5. What follow-up should Rose have with her supervisor? How might this incident motivate Rose to reintroduce the concept of gender-inclusive housing?

REFERENCES

American Association of University Women (AAUW) (1992). *How schools shortchange girls: A study of major findings on girls and education.* Washington, DC: Author.

American Association of University Women (AAUW) (1995). *Achieving gender equity in the classroom and the campus: The next step.* Washington, DC: Author.

Banks, J.A. (2014). *An introduction to multicultural education* (5th ed.). Boston, MA: Pearson, Allyn & Bacon.

Banks, J.A. (2020). *Diversity, transformative knowledge, and civic education: Selected essays.* New York, NY: Routledge.

Banks, J.A. & Banks, C.A.M. (2006). *Multicultural education: Issues and perspectives* (6th ed.). San Francisco, CA: Jossey-Bass.

Bohm, A.S., Del Duca, S., Elliott, E., Holako, S., & Tanner, A. (2016). Challenges facing LGBT youth. *Georgetown Journal of Gender and the Law, 17,* 125–173.

Bostock v. Clayton County, 590 U.S. __, 140 S. Ct. 1731 (2020).

Cushner, K., McClelland, A., & Safford, P. (2011). *Human diversity in education: An integrative approach* (7th ed.). New York, NY: McGraw-Hill.

Education Amendments Act of 1972, 20 U.S.C. §§1681–1688.

Fishkin, J. (1983). *Justice, equal opportunity, and the family.* New Haven, CT: Yale University Press.

Gay, G. (2010). *Culturally responsive teaching: Theory, research, and practice* (2nd ed.). New York, NY: Teachers College Press.

Gilligan, C. (1982). *In a different voice.* Cambridge, MA: Harvard University Press.

Gilligan, C. & Richards, D.A.J. (2009). *The deepening darkness: Patriarchy, resistance, and democracy's future.* New York, NY: Cambridge University Press.

Gollnick, D.M. & Chinn, P.C. (2012). *Multicultural education in a pluralistic society* (9th ed.). Boston, MA: Pearson.

Grant, C.A. & Portera, A. (2010). Intercultural and multicultural education: Enhancing global interconnectedness. New York, NY: Taylor & Francis.

Hodgkinson, H.L. (1992). *A demographic look at tomorrow.* Washington, DC: Institute for Education Leadership.

Maier, M.B. (2020). Altering gender markers on government identity documents: Unpredictable, burdensome, and oppressive. *University of Pennsylvania Journal of Law and Social Change, 23,* 203–248.

Nieto, S. (2012). *Affirming diversity: The socio-political context of multicultural education* (7th ed.). Boston, MA: Pearson, Allyn & Bacon.

Nieto, S. & Bode, P. (2018). *Language, culture, and teaching: Critical perspectives for a new century* (3rd ed.). New York, NY: Routledge.

Noddings, N. (2002). *Educating moral people: A caring alternative to character education.* New York, NY: Teachers College Press.

Noddings, N. (2003). *Caring: A feminine approach to ethics and moral education* (2nd ed.). Berkeley, CA: University of California Press.

Noddings, N. (2013). *Caring: A relational approach to ethics and moral education* (2nd ed.) Oakland, CA: University of California Press.

Shapiro, J.P. Sewell, T.E., & DuCette, J.P. (2001). *Reframing diversity in education.* Lanham, MD: Rowman & Littlefield.

Sleeter, C.E. & Grant, C.A. (2003). *Making choices for multicultural education: Five approaches to race, class, and gender* (4th ed.). New York, NY: Wiley.

Sleeter, C.E. & Zavala, M. (2020). *Transformative ethic studies in schools: Curriculum, pedagogy, and research.* New York, NY: Teachers College Press.

Stefkovich, J.A., Brady, K.P., Ballard, T.N.W., & Rossow, L.F. (2021). *The law and education: Cases and materials* (3rd ed.). Durham, NC: Carolina Press.

Strike, K.A., Haller, E.J., & Soltis, J.F. (1988). *The Ethics of school administration.* New York, NY: Teachers College Press.

Strike, K. & Soltis, J.F. (1992). *The ethics of teaching* (2nd ed.). New York, NY: Teachers College Press.

Utley, C.A. & Obiakor, F.E. (1995, July). *Scientific and methodological concerns in research perspectives for multicultural learners.* Paper presented at the Office of Special Education Project Direction Conference, Washington, DC.

Young, I.M. (1990). *Justice and the politics of difference.* Princeton, NJ: Princeton University Press.

Chapter 9

Accountability versus Responsibility

Susan A. Rosano, David M. Gates, Lindy Zaretsky, Elizabeth A. Santoro, Mary Beth Kurilko, and Peter Brigg

There is a strong focus on accountability in education. However, this concept is not new. It has been with the U.S. since the 1970s and has increased over time. Some say it was taxpayers in California who led the way to this emphasis when they complained that they were not getting their money's worth in public education and opted out of paying taxes through Proposition 13, passed in 1978 (Shapiro, 1979). Others believe that *A Nation at Risk: The Imperative for Educational Reform* (National Commission on Excellence in Education, 1983) was the cornerstone for the accountability movement.

Additional national reports and federal laws, such as *America 2000: An Education Strategy* (1991), *Goals 2000: Educate America Act* (1993), and *No Child Left Behind* (NCLB) (2002), included accountability with the latter asking for stronger accountability than was previously required, focusing on outcome measures and test scores. The *Every Student Succeeds Act* (ESSA), passed in 2015, replaced NCLB. ESSA allows states more flexibility as to test requirements and stresses equity in dealing with disadvantaged groups, but it still relies on assessment and accountability measures. Furthermore, there has been a dramatic rise in philanthropic efforts to reform education that require standards for reporting (Gomez-Velez, 2016).

Although all these initiatives include accountability, it is important to understand that this concept comes from an accountant's ledger that all too often places the budget at the center of the decision-making process. Despite its derivation, with a stress on the budget, the term itself is complex and has numerous meanings. In fact, there are as many as ten kinds of accountability. They include political, legal, bureaucratic, professional, and market accountabilities (Darling-Hammond & Snyder, 1992). Added to these are parent, student, fiscal, and personal forms of accountability

DOI: 10.4324/9781003022862-11

(Gross & Shapiro, 2002; Gross, Shaw, & Shapiro, 2003). Finally, there is public accountability (Gold & Simon, 2004; Wilson, Hastings, & Moses, 2016).

Despite the diversity inherent in the term, accountability, in all its forms, is seen by many to be a major factor in school improvement. Not only the general public, but also numerous educators, have found it to be a much-needed factor leading to positive changes in the schools. Strict accountability makes certain that budgets are kept in check, meeting the approval of many taxpayers.

High stakes, standardized test results are most often used for accountability purposes to determine how successful an educational institution or district has been in educating its young people. However, it is not only the institution or district that is affected, but also the individual student. For students, the number they receive on a high stakes test can determine their educational opportunities in the future. Over time, tests do more than provide a number for how successful a school or student has been. Frequently, these tests drive the curriculum. Teachers and administrators often turn to the test to guide what they should teach in schools. Some people perceive the continual testing, the reporting of scores in newspapers and magazines, and the tests driving the curriculum to be positive accomplishments, whereas others consider them to be negative activities, publicly punishing students and educators alike and, in some instances, encouraging students and school personnel to cheat (Nichols & Berliner, 2007).

In different parts of the U.S., there is a growing Opt-Out Movement (Mitra, Mann, & Hlavacik, 2016; Wilson & Hastings, 2021). The New York State Allies for Public Education (2021), a coalition of 60 parent and educator groups, is one of the leaders encouraging students not to take the standardized tests. Other grassroots groups include FairTest: National Center for Fair and Open Testing and United Opt-Out National. Kirylo (2018) discusses this movement, mentioning numbers of opt outs rising to six figures. For most parents, this decision is not taken lightly, and they tend to worry about how opting out will affect their children's educational future. But their hope, and that of many others, is that the Opt-Out Movement will lead to alternative forms of assessment of their children's achievement other than high stakes standardized tests.

While accountability is frequently associated with educational achievement, it is also often thought to be a concept that creates a great deal of blame. By turning to numbers alone as guides, through standardized test results, taxpayers, legislators, and the nation believe that they can determine how students are doing, and many are ready to place the blame on schools. All too often, other factors, such as poverty, drugs, environmental pollutants, and crime, with their negative effects on learning, may be ignored. At least one commentator (Anderson, 2016) has pointed out that the U.S. could take a lesson from Canada and what appears to be a less punitive, more pedagogically-sound, approach to standardized testing. (Readers may want to compare this observation with Case Study 9.4 which is based in a Canadian school and authored by a Canadian school leader.)

There is another term, however, that is not used enough regarding school success or lack of it. This concept is responsibility (Gross & Shapiro, 2002). Responsibility, while resembling accountability, may be perceived as more inclusive and places the answerability for the success or failure of young people's learning on all of society—the public, legislators, parents, teachers, and administrators as well as the schools. This term does not always connote blame, nor does it put a budget at the center of the decision-making process. Instead, it offers another concept regarding education that asks everyone to share responsibility for young people's learning and to place students at the center of the educational process. It is a much broader term that not only encompasses the results of high stakes tests but also can include evidence from authentic and alternative types of assessment in determining what students have learned.

The paradox of accountability versus responsibility is highlighted in this chapter's case studies. In each of the six cases, testing is a central issue. However, the cases are different in that five of them are in K–12 settings (one of which takes place in Canada) and the final dilemma occurs on a college campus.

In the first dilemma, **The Secret Society of Test Givers** (Case Study 9.1), a teacher feels under pressure to make certain that students in her class do well on high stakes standardized tests. She has been told by her school administrator that unless her students obtain passing results, there is a good chance of a state takeover, a resulting budget cut, and inevitable loss of jobs. Because of all the accountability pressures on the school principal, he has urged his teachers to do what they need to do to make certain that students do well. Now the teacher faces the decision as to what she should do as a responsible, professional educator.

In Case Study 9.2, **Whose Best Interests? A Testing Dilemma**, a school administrator has been told that while his district is currently doing well on the standardized tests, it has been projected, within the next two years, that many of his students will not pass the exam. In response to this information, the superintendent, with the encouragement of the board of school directors, has been proactive and has devised a new curriculum with test-specific courses. When the principal explains the proposed changes to the department chairs, the idea is met with resistance. The chairs are angry because they have developed courses by turning to research and using best practices, and they believe that these carefully crafted courses are good for the students now and ultimately will be beneficial for their futures. Thus, they are reluctant to make the substantial revisions requested. The principal is facing an ethical decision that pits policy against best practice and pits teachers against administrators and the school board.

Providing rewards for teachers whose students perform well is the theme of Case Study 9.3, **Incentive Pay for Teachers**. Even though the school superintendent is well respected and based her plan on statistics, a first-year principal felt "in his gut" that this was the wrong approach and would affect teacher morale in his building where test scores were already good, just not outstanding.

Case Study 9.4, **Testing High Stakes**, focuses on the administering of a mandatory, high stakes literacy test in Canada and the problems that those students who are slow learners face. In this instance, a principal must deal with parents who demand that their children be given special accommodations for taking the high stakes test. However, she is aware that the test guidelines do not allow for these privileges. The principal is very concerned about the parents' expectations and the reality of the test-taking situation. She is especially worried about the climate change in her school from one of care, cooperation, and respect for all learners to that of performance, efficiency, and economy.

In Case Study 9.5, **Ability, Maturity, and Parental Perspectives**, which is an early childhood dilemma, there is a disagreement between parents and teachers. The parents have conflicted with the administration since their child was in first grade and, now that he is in the third grade, they, on the one hand, want him once again to be retained because of immaturity. The teachers, on the other hand, feel he is ready to move on to the next grade. Should the principal succumb to the demands of the parents and choose education retention or accept the decision of the teachers, which is based on best professional judgment as well as testing results, but still may be viewed as social promotion? In this era focusing on accountability and meeting proficiency requirements, a decision of this nature is not treated lightly.

Case Study 9.6, **A Merit-based Scholarship**, deals with the fractious issue of affirmative action regarding college opportunities. It takes place in a small Midwestern college. It involves a merit-based scholarship with two finalists who are both outstanding. However, there are differences between the candidates: their results on a standardized test for admissions into the college, their race/ethnicity, and their gender. This case pits the college president, pressured by a board member, against the admissions director, who has always made the scholarship decision. Breaking with tradition, the president is attempting to override the professional judgment of the admissions director in the scholarship selection process.

CASE STUDY 9.1 THE SECRET SOCIETY OF TEST GIVERS

June Lopez was a teacher at an urban elementary school, PS 235. Although she was a new faculty member at this school, she was really a seven-year veteran from a private school system. This was her first assignment in a large, urban, public school system, but she felt ready to work in this high poverty area. At the outset, she was greatly impressed with the school's atmosphere and, in a short time, she developed a fine working relationship with her colleagues, the students, their parents, and the administration. However, she was never in this school at testing time. Thus, she was surprised at the amount of anxiety and tension that seemed to be surrounding this event. In the faculty lunchroom, not much was said. In fact, she noticed how quiet it was around the table. However, in some of the classrooms, as she passed by the closed doors and peeped through the windowpanes, she was getting the distinct impression that all was not as it should be.

James Rose was the principal of PS 235 for the past ten years and was a seasoned administrator, having served as an assistant principal and a supervisor of English teachers. He was not new to poverty in education, since he had worked in a couple of schools where there were a substantial number of low-income families, and this school was no exception. In PS 235, all the children qualified for free breakfast and lunch. Many of the youngsters were being raised by single mothers or grandmothers or were in foster care.

Approximately one-quarter of the parents did not appear for report conferences, despite the many outreach activities the school provided to involve them. For example, and most recently, the school received new books, and once the teachers were prepared to handle the material, the principal offered training sessions for the parents. Although few parents or guardians turned up, he knew how important it was to keep teachers and families working together, and he fully recognized the need for parents to be part of their children's education. However, despite his continuing attempts to take the role of instructional leader seriously, his school was thought to be failing based on only one criterion: low test scores.

Although the school was labeled as failing, what Ms. Lopez saw, considering her own background in private education, was that her colleagues in PS 235 provided a supportive and caring environment for students. One indication of this was that attendance was good, usually between 92% and 94%, for both teachers and students. Another reason for her faith in the school was that she had overheard visitors saying that the children seemed happy and appeared to be at ease and secure. Although she felt confident in the abilities and sensibilities of her colleagues and her principal, the problem with the test scores continued to cause concern within the faculty.

Despite their worries, most of the teachers appeared to believe that they were doing the very best they could with the resources and circumstances they had been given. They also felt that they had a responsibility toward the students and community that went well beyond reading, writing, math, and science. Most of them believed in developing the whole child, and that included instructing students in music, art, athletics, and citizenship, to name but a few areas. However, no matter what their beliefs might be, the fact remained that children in the school were doing poorly on standardized tests, and they all knew that something had to be done.

It was at Friday's faculty meeting when the concerns about testing rose to the surface. This occurred when Mr. Rose reminded his staff that the test scores must go up or there would be serious consequences. He stated in a hushed voice, behind the closed meeting room door, "Do what you have to do." The teachers groaned and many started talking among themselves. At June Lopez's table, this is what they said:

Ms. Greene: Last year, Mr. Rose sent tests back that students had not completed, and he told me, "Do what you have to do to get these completed."

Ms. Golden: Oh please, I'm going to leave the calculators out during the test.

Ms. Davis: I'm going to not only read the directions to my students but the questions and the answers as well. I know a teacher at PS 92 who frowns to let the students know which are the wrong answers and smiles for the correct ones.

Ms. Greene: They [the administration] seem to care more about raising the test scores than whether or not the students are actually learning the material. I can't stand it anymore. I'm putting in for a transfer.

Ms. Davis: [Looking at Ms. Lopez]. You heard Mr. Rose say, "Do what you have to do." And that's exactly what you have got to do to survive in this crummy school.

Ms. Lopez: But aren't you concerned that you could lose your job if this got out?

All teachers: [In unison.] No! They don't care. Just raise those scores.

Ms. Golden: Oh June, you may want to leave the dictionaries out on the desks. And, if they [the students] ask questions, don't hesitate to answer them. Remember June, it's all about the test.

Ms. Greene: Besides, do you really believe that some of these other schools are not doing the exact same thing?

Ms. Davis: You know they are.

Ms. Golden: Our school has been playing by the rules for a long time and look where it's gotten us.

Ms. Sanford: [Who has been silently listening to all of this.] You all can do what you want. But this is my teacher's license, and I'm not losing it for anyone. I have heard that one teacher, not here, but in another school, erases answers. This is treading on very dangerous ground. I understand why someone might go to these lengths, but it ain't gonna be me!

June Lopez left the meeting feeling very upset. It appeared that most of the teachers, at least at her table, were planning to cheat, and she did not know what to do. She was not sure how her students would do; in particular, if the other teachers were cutting corners, how would those students' test results affect the scores in general? She could not help but ask: If she followed the letter of the law in giving the test, would her students' results be lower than the others'? How would those results make her look as a teacher?

Questions for Discussion

1. In light of the circumstances described in this dilemma, what would be the fairest course of action for June to take for: The teachers? The principal? The students and their parents? The community? Would it make a difference if she knew that everyone else in other nearby schools was doing the same thing? Does it matter that a state takeover would spell disaster for the district, end in loss of jobs for the teachers, and would likely make matters worse for the students? If this were the case, would the teachers' actions be justified?

2. Would it be more caring for June to report Mr. Rose's and the teachers' actions to someone higher up the chain of command or to remain silent? Why? If you believe she should report the problem, whom should she tell? Explain your rationale.

3. What actions might June take if she were coming from a critical theory perspective? What issues of power and domination might she identify?

4. What would the profession expect of June in this case?

5. What actions on June's part would be in the best interests of the students? Why?

CASE STUDY 9.2 WHOSE BEST INTERESTS?
A TESTING DILEMMA

The meeting could have been worse. That thought provided Central High School Principal Charlie Franken little solace as he sat in his office reflecting on the discord created in the just concluded meeting with his department chairs. Their responses to the proposed curriculum change approached open revolt, and Charlie felt trapped with few good options.

Central High students always performed well on the state's standardized tests by maintaining scores that were equal to or above state averages. The school continued to meet state-defined, adequate yearly progress targets. Unfortunately, it was the school's future performance that most concerned the board of school directors. With each passing year, the state's goals for acceptable scores became more aggressive. Due to such high expectations, it appeared that many districts would not meet state goals in the coming years. The school directors wanted to ensure that their district would not be among them.

If the number of Central High students achieving acceptable scores increased, at the current rate, the school would be placed on the state's "at-risk" list in two years' time. Such an action would eliminate state funding incentives for good performance and open the door for a state takeover of the school district. With such dire consequences looming in the future, the directors thought it prudent to increase student performance on the state test. The board charged the district superintendent, Dr. Carl Horne, to design and implement a curriculum that specifically addressed state standards. Appreciating the gravity of the situation and the serious concern of the board, Dr. Horne developed a plan that he presented to Charlie Franken.

In a meeting with Charlie, Dr. Horne presented an outline of the curriculum changes that the board of directors agreed would address their concerns. Courses designed specifically to address the state standards would be created in each of the four core disciplines for Grades 9 through 12. These eight new courses would provide intensive training in test-taking skills. The curriculum would be centered on the material covered by the state standards and would be mandatory for students who failed to meet acceptable levels of achievement on the state exams. Because there was no federal or state funding provided to support such an initiative, these changes were to be implemented utilizing current staff.

Charlie's reaction to the proposal was less than enthusiastic. Sensing his opposition, Dr. Horne explained how such a curriculum was in the best interest of the school district. The community respected the accomplishments of the district and was proud of its standing in the state. The threat of falling below state expectations and being placed on an "endangered list" would undermine the trust and support of the community. The turmoil that would result from such a situation would be unthinkable; consequently, it was necessary to act before problems developed. Dr. Horne's parting words were clearly etched in Charlie's memory.

He stated, "You're either part of the problem or part of the solution. Keep me informed of your progress."

Now that he had his "marching orders," Charlie's first action would be to meet with his department chairs. Because of their previous work on developing the curriculum, he knew the meeting would not be pleasant.

Under Charlie's collegial style of leadership and with the notable support of the department chairs, especially the respected English chair, Alicia Weston, the faculty developed a curriculum to best serve the needs of all Central High School students. They researched and worked with a strong sense of purpose nurtured by an altruistic desire to give their students "the best." Developed and implemented over a five-year period, the curriculum identified three directions of academic preparation based on students' post-graduation plans. Each discipline offered courses designed to prepare students for college, vocational/technical school, or direct entry into the workforce. At each grade level, an interdisciplinary relation among the core disciplines was established. Students were free to choose from among the offerings to create an individualized plan that best suited their needs. Although subject to ongoing evaluation and revision, the current curriculum appeared to be successful in achieving the desired objectives and was highly regarded by the staff. It was with this in mind that Charlie presented the new curriculum revision plan to the department chairs.

As anticipated, the chairs were not receptive to the proposed change. The impact on the current curriculum would be significant. At first, discussion centered on a practical consideration. With no new staff, the courses offered for vocational/technical school students and those desiring to enter the workforce on graduation would be virtually eliminated, as many of those students would most likely be candidates for the new courses. This trend would be exacerbated in future years with the relentless raising of state targets for successful achievement.

The discussion then took a more philosophical turn. The validity of teaching test-taking skills was questioned. How were such skills useful in the real world? In addition, the practice of "teaching to the test" was anathema to educators interested in providing their students with the knowledge and skills necessary for success in their chosen areas. Furthermore, by identifying which students were assigned to the courses, the school would be eliminating student and parental choice by subjecting them to mandatory tracking. It was no surprise that Alicia Weston was particularly vehement in her objections by suggesting that teachers were not needed to fulfil the processing demanded of the new curriculum; trainers would be sufficient.

What did surprise Charlie was Alicia's threat to resign her position as chair and revert to being a regular classroom teacher if such curriculum changes were mandated. She did not want to be in a leadership position for the implementation of a program that she considered to be unethical. While proffered in the heat of the moment, Charlie knew her well enough to realize that this was not a mere bluff. Trying to gauge the reactions of the other chairs to her pronouncement, Charlie could not discern if any were inclined to follow her lead.

Sitting in his office, Charlie considered his dilemma. He knew he was bound to carry out the mandates of the school board and the superintendent, but what if he believed that a particular directive was not in the best interests of the students? Then he paused to reflect: Who is the ultimate judge of what is in their best interests? The authority certainly resides with the board, but are the directors the best qualified to make curricular and pedagogical decisions? What would be the effect on the school's students, morale, and culture if the curriculum changes were unilaterally mandated? Would siding with his chairs in a unified front delineating the shortcomings of the proposed changes influence Dr. Horne and the board to reconsider their position? These questions preoccupied his mind as Charlie tried to formulate the first report of this progress for Dr. Horne.

Questions for Discussion

1. What actions might Charlie take that would be fair to both the students and the faculty? Would you recommend that he take these actions? Why or why not?

2. Is caring for the school district synonymous with caring for the students? What is the principal's best course of action according to the ethic of care? Should the ethic of care be the primary lens through which to view this dilemma? Why or why not?

3. Why is accountability so important in education today? Who benefits from an educational curriculum and system based on uniform standards?

4. What is Principal Franken's ultimate responsibility? What should be in his first progress report to Dr. Horne? Should he take the chair's side on this issue? Why or why not?

5. What would the profession expect Charlie to do in this case? What action would be in the best interests of the students?

CASE STUDY 9.3 INCENTIVE PAY FOR TEACHERS

Mr. Brightbill sat among his fellow administrators in an Administrative Council meeting on the last day of June. Smiles, handshakes, and small talk filled the room as summer had officially set in. Mr. Brightbill received a few extra congratulatory remarks as he successfully completed his first year as the principal of Fairview Elementary. His first year was a success overall, and the praise was warranted, but he wasn't ready to rest on his laurels. He was bursting with ideas and knew he had to make plenty of improvements.

One of those was reading achievement. Brightbill and the rest of the administrators recently received their state test scores. Brightbill was pleased with the results overall; however, he was eager to diagnostically look at the test scores, specifically reading, to pinpoint focus areas and create goals for the upcoming year. The Fairview staff was enthusiastic and hardworking. He was looking forward to working with them to create these goals.

As conversations concluded, Brightbill peered down at the agenda. He quickly spotted "State Test Scores" as an agenda item, which he could have predicted; however, there was a topic listed that did surprise him—"Merit Pay." The test scores throughout Green Valley School District (GVSD) were certainly acceptable and fell in the above average range. What made this even more confusing to Brightbill was that he had such a dedicated staff—the suggestion that money would be a motivating factor for the teachers wasn't necessary.

Dr. Tallymore, Superintendent of GVSD, started the meeting tackling agenda items and providing valuable insight as she did in every Administrative Council meeting. Mr. Brightbill often said how much he has learned from her leadership including her sensible and astute approach to problem solving. He was sure that the topic of merit pay would make much more sense once she explained her rationale. Dr. Tallymore introduced GVSD's plan for merit pay as a tiered approach to incentivize teachers to assist in putting forth extra effort (with compensation) to help students demonstrate academic growth on the state assessments.

Mr. Brightbill was struggling internally. He has bought into everything that Dr. Ballymore said since he arrived in Green Valley but could only think of how the school's culture and environment might become negative and divisive with incentive pay. There would be obvious potential for detrimental effects on the teachers and their working environment. It would undoubtedly be noticed by the students. He believed that students would be in a position in which the learning environment could be compromised.

Mr. Brightbill was afraid that incentive pay places such a heavy emphasis on state standardized assessments that teachers might be driven to teach with a controlled focus on these standardized tests, and, to him, these test results were truly just one measure of students' academic abilities. Mr. Brightbill's stomach was turning. He silently asked: Is this what is best for kids?

Dr. Tallymore went on to explain that for performance incentives to be effective, they must be based on student performance. Test scores were good, but stagnant. She stated that, "ensuring student success is the goal. Increasing student achievement must be the basis for all fundamental decision making. There must be rewards or consequences tied to our instruction and incentive plan. GVSD's incentive plan is individualized. Merit pay that rewards all teachers based on a district-wide goal has been proven ineffective." Brightbill knew that was true.

Incentive programs that awarded bonuses to very large fractions of teachers were not correlated with higher student achievement. Tallymore continued, "Green Valley School District will include a pay-for-performance incentive for teachers. In the upcoming year, teachers will receive tiered bonuses based on student performance. The merit pay will be based on a student growth model using scores from the state assessments to determine academic growth from year-to-year. We will focus on how much each student improves academically each year as opposed to a percentage of students who perform at a proficient level. Teachers will receive bonuses based on the percentages of students who achieve levels of expected growth predicted by the state and given to us prior to the start of the year. Teachers could receive up to a $3,000 bonus for students meeting expected levels of academic growth."

Tallymore shared a chart illustrating the bonus structure. Teachers would receive a bonus of $500 for 75% of students who meet the anticipated growth predicted by the state, and a gradual increase in bonus monies would be distributed based on the number of students who meet the expected levels of growth. No bonus money would be earned for less than 75% of students achieving anticipated growth expectations.

Mr. Brightbill knew that Dr. Tallymore would have research to support this decision as well as a thorough plan; however, his gut, not his typical diagnostic approach, was telling him this is not the right thing to do. GVSD had experienced much success, but the expectations had increased. Most students were making consistent growth, but to reach the cohort of students not meeting anticipated growth, Dr. Tallymore created the aforementioned incentive plan.

Mr. Brightbill was wide-eyed and ambitious. He believed that motivators to increase desired results from teachers must be intrinsic, not extrinsic. Incentive pay plans were designed to motivate teachers extrinsically to work harder to drive test scores. Brightbill came to GVSD to make a difference in the lives of students. He believed in accountability and measuring progress, but he did not believe the path to do that was through bonuses based on standardized assessments. Mr. Brightbill was not controversial. He was there to help carry out the vision of the superintendent, but is it time for him to speak up?

Questions for Discussion

1. What is Mr. Brightbill's ultimate responsibility? What would be more ethical—to carry out the vision of the superintendent, or to challenge this suggestion and stand up for what he believes? Why?

2. Would it be ethically just to determine performance pay for teachers based on student performance? Why or why not?

3. Merit pay challenges the status quo. Will merit pay positively push teachers to work harder for academic success? Will it promote rigor and higher expectations? Why or why not?

4. Is the ethic of the profession compromised with the implementation of merit pay? Why or why not? Is academic success the most important factor in education? If so, how does merit pay increase the likelihood of ensuring success? If not, how does it inhibit the educational process? How does merit pay fit into the ethic of care? Dr. Tallymore argues that the ethic of care is not removed by placing a monetary value on student growth. Do you agree? Why or why not?

CASE STUDY 9.4 TESTING HIGH STAKES

Gillian Goodwin's head ached. She tossed the four letters from parents into her "priority response" bin. Ms. Goodwin, the principal of Roselawn Secondary School located in a western province of Canada, had just hung up the phone with her superintendent of schools. They had discussed at length the issues the parents had raised in the letters and how the school would strategically be responding to the parents' requests. Although somewhat reluctant, Ms. Goodwin had agreed with her superintendent that they needed to "nip this one in the bud" as quickly as possible. She leaned back in her chair and closed her eyes.

The letters were from four parents of children in the tenth grade who had recently received a memorandum from the school notifying them of the scheduled dates and times of the mandatory Secondary School Literacy Test (SSLT). Each letter asked for special and different privileges for their child regarding the exam.

Passing this test was essential for graduation. It was based on reading and writing skills, and if students did not pass, they could take the examination as many as three times before the end of Grade 12. The four parents, including the chair of the parent council, Carol Johnson, had written the letters after a meeting in Ms. Johnson's home where they discussed the problems their children faced in taking the exam. Ms.

Johnson's son was diagnosed with attention deficit hyperactivity disorder (ADHD), and he had an individual education plan (IEP).

At the meeting, Ms. Johnson told the other parents that she planned to ask the school to administer the examination to her son in two afternoon sessions and not during the one day that the other children had to take the exam. She believed that her son did much better in the early afternoon after he took his medicine. The other children did not have a diagnosis, but they simply did not do well in exams.

After their conversation with Ms. Johnson, each of these parents felt that their child should have some special accommodations, such as additional time, breaks, assistive devices, or technology. Ms. Johnson had told the parents that all their children needed was an IEP to receive these accommodations. To obtain an IEP, each parent was considering hiring a private psychologist to test their child and hopefully make a diagnosis that would require special arrangements for the examination.

After reading the fourth letter, there were many questions racing through Gillian Goodwin's mind. She pondered: How did the principalship become so removed from the instructional and relational leadership role she had so enjoyed in the past that she had already agreed with the superintendent to nip this problem in the bud? When did her role become such a prescriptive and technical data-driven, number-crunching game? Was the role so narrowly defined by and confined to reacting to problematic issues that appeared messier and more taxing with each passing day? Did she, in fact, really have any freedom or professional autonomy left to creatively explore with parents alternative solutions that served the best interests of the students? This latest dilemma had her doubting her capacity, willingness, or ability to muster the energy to engage in this latest round of negotiation and compromise tactics.

Enough reflection, Ms. Goodwin thought. She quickly sat upright in her chair and retrieved the four letters from her response box. It was time to move into action. She contacted each parent and gave them the times she could meet with them the following day. She then asked her special education department head, Mr. Jenkins, to come to her office as soon as he could manage it. Once he arrived, she briefed him on the contents of the letters, explained about the meeting for tomorrow, and gave him time to read the four letters. What follows is part of the conversation Ms. Goodwin had with Mr. Jenkins:

Ms. Goodwin: I can see that you are upset by the letters and rightfully so. However, the superintendent and I have agreed that we will stress that the testing agency's guidelines clearly state that to protect the security of test materials and to ensure the validity and reliability of the results, all students across the province must write the SSLT at the same time, and that includes Ms. Johnson's child. As for the other parents, I have already pulled their children's school records that clearly demonstrate our teachers have been addressing both strengths and needs of these students in their instruction and in the work assigned. There is absolutely no evidence to support the parents' claims that their children need IEPs. To calm the parents' fears, we will remind them that if their children do not do well, they are entitled to retake the test.

Mr. Jenkins: While I am relieved to hear what you have to say, what if the parents will not back down? Who is going to write these IEPs if that happens? It is not the responsibility of my special education teachers since these children are not formally identified through the IPRC [Identification, Placement, and Review Committee] process. We can barely manage to complete the paperwork required of us right now. These accountability measures are just going too far!

Ms. Goodwin: The superintendent and I have played out all the scenarios that you have described. Regarding Mrs. Johnson, we do not believe she will be granted her request through the testing agency. As for the other parents, we will emphasize that all evidence to date does not indicate a need for the development of IEPs or for further accommodations for their children. This will be the primary message we send to them tomorrow. It is of paramount importance that we take a "divide-and-conquer" approach here.

After Mr. Jenkins left, Ms. Goodwin had to admit that she was not looking forward to the confrontational and adversarial approaches she knew would be adopted the following day when she informed each parent that their request was denied. She did not blame the parents for trying. Why shouldn't they try to position themselves at an advantage in this competitive school climate that valued performance, efficiency, and economy over the ones she had worked so hard to cultivate in her school—those of care, cooperation, and respect for all learners?

What had really unsettled her was hearing herself say to both her superintendent and Mr. Jenkins, "We take a 'divide-and-conquer' approach,'" and they had both been very supportive of this stance. How had she arrived at such thinking? It went against all her beliefs and values associated with inclusive leadership that she had tried so hard to live out in her practice.

In thinking through her beliefs once more, one unexplored option came to mind that had not been discussed with the superintendent or with Mr. Jenkins. Ms. Goodwin remembered that she had a small amount of discretionary monies. She could, she realized, consider using these funds to accommodate the concerns of the three vocal parents who did not have IEPs for their children. Those monies could be utilized for some special sessions of test preparation for the students and could even help Ms. Johnson's child as well. But what would other parents say if word got out? What of the needs of their children? What about the multicultural parents, who were not vocal and yet had children in her school, whose first language was not English? Did they not deserve some special consideration too?

Intuitively, she knew that if she did not provide some accommodations, this story was not going to have a very happy ending tomorrow for either the parents or the school system. She knew that more meetings would be requested and coalitions of allies on both sides would argue their respective cases in such meetings. Requests were no longer really requests because "no" was no longer an acceptable response. Demands were only masked as requests with much posturing on both sides regarding honoring differences of perspectives.

Taken aback by her own escalating cynicism, Ms. Goodwin had to ask herself: When exactly had she begun to doubt what had been her unshakable belief in the ability to achieve equity and excellence in education for all through collaborative problem solving among parents, educators, and other stakeholders in education? Called on to handle another school problem, she continued to wonder how she should handle tomorrow's meeting and if she should alert Mr. Jenkins and the superintendent to any change of strategy.

Questions for Discussion

1. How might Gillian Goodwin handle this situation if she were trying to abide by the letter of the law? The spirit of the law? Would these approaches be the same or different? Why?

2. What is the most caring action that Gillian can take? Who should this ethic of care be directed toward? Why that person(s)?

3. Who has determined these guidelines? Why must standardized tests be administered? Why must they count as a requirement for graduation? In this situation, who is in a position to benefit the most? The least? Explain your answer. What, if anything, can be done to equalize this situation?

4. Is it in the best interests of each student to treat everyone the same or to make accommodations for those who need more assistance? Why?

5. What might the profession expect of Gillian? What obligations, if any, does she have to the multicultural community as well as to the community in general?

CASE STUDY 9.5 ABILITY, MATURITY, AND PARENTAL PERSPECTIVES

John Dolan is currently a third-grade student at Happy Times Elementary School, a large suburban district outside of a Mid-Atlantic city. John enrolled in this elementary school in first grade; he attended a Montessori program in his pre-first-grade years. While in first grade, the teacher noticed early in the school year that John was struggling with his readiness skills in reading. John was recommended for services with the reading specialist where he met the eligibility requirements to receive such service. Beginning in mid-October of first grade, John began to receive 30 minutes of remedial help with the reading teacher daily. John began to make small strides with his reading skills. He was proficient or above average in all other subjects.

During a mid-year conference with the teacher and the counselor, Mr. and Mrs. Dolan requested that their son be retained in first grade. Their basis for retention stemmed from their concerns about his immaturity. Mr. and Mrs. Dolan are in their early fifties. John's other siblings are 12 to 14 years apart in age. John has no children in his neighborhood near his age to socialize with after school and on the weekends. The teacher and counselor explained to Mr. and Mrs. Dolan that John was making progress in his reading; they believed the reading support intervention was working. They also shared with the parents how well their son was doing in his other subject areas such as math, science, and social studies. However, the staff did express their concern about his tantrums when he was corrected or did not get his way. To address these concerns, the staff devised a behavior plan. Mr. and Mrs. Dolan supported the behavior plan and indicated that they would partner with the school on the plan. Mrs. Dolan indicated that she had arranged for a teacher in another building (the one where she is employed as a cafeteria worker) to tutor John once a week in reading skills. The team agreed to revisit his progress in late April with a comprehensive review of his data.

At the end of April, the teacher, principal, counselor, reading support teacher, and parents met to review John's progress. The school team provided the parents with reading data reflecting the progress being made; however, the strides were minimal and slow. His teacher could also observe daily John's frustration with his reading and his poor self-esteem concerning his reading ability. The team was beginning to conclude that perhaps John had a specific learning disability in reading since he did very well in other areas but continued to perform below grade level benchmarks in reading.

Mrs. Dolan requested retention for her son while Mr. Dolan was not in agreement with her. The school team was concerned because repeating the grade would serve no benefit to John in the other subject areas, since he was doing well, as indicated by his scores. The principal and the team recommended a psycho-educational evaluation by the school psychologist to rule out any learning disabilities. The parents agreed with the recommendation and signed the permission to evaluate.

John was found to have a specific learning disability in reading comprehension, decoding, and written expression. John's overall IQ was 121. The IEP was developed with the parents, and John began receiving services in the beginning of second grade. During second grade, John started to make steady gains in his reading ability. The outbursts were still occurring, but nothing was at a level to warrant serious concern. The parents continued to "baby" him. Once again, at the end of second grade, the parents wanted to retain John due to his immaturity. The parents did not seem to be aware that they were contributing to his behavior problems.

Now, this school year, the school team is once again faced with the request from both parents to retain their son based on his immaturity. The dilemma for the principal is complicated in a variety of ways. Mr. and Mrs. Dolan requested a meeting with the special education teacher and the regular education teacher to discuss progress and asked the special education teacher not to include the principal in the meeting. Dismayed by the parents' request, the principal advised the special education teacher to include the special education supervisor in the meeting in case the issue of retention was discussed.

The meeting had occurred several weeks before. The parents brought along the teacher, from another building, who is tutoring John. During this meeting, the team reviewed John's progress and shared the gains he has made in reading this year. He is only six months behind in reading. The teachers also shared that John has demonstrated progress in all academic disciplines; they were even pleased with his improved behavior. The teachers believed the special education intervention, coupled with their effort and care, provided for such strong gains. The parents were adamant about the retention to the point of the becoming belligerent. The tutor was also adamant and expressed to the team the idea of retention as the only solution. The supervisor informed the parents of their rights to place their request in writing. She shared with them that after the request is presented to the Child Study Team with data, the principal would make the final decision. However, it was clear at the meeting that the parents believed they had made the final decision based on the information given to them by John's tutor.

The parents are angry, demanding, and now refusing to meet with the principal, special education supervisor, and director of elementary education to discuss their concerns. Numerous attempts have been made to schedule an appointment. The parents continue to ignore the outreach efforts being made by the school.

The dilemma now exists because the parents believe strongly that retaining their son will "make him more mature." The school team has the data to support his gains. The interventions provided academically and behaviorally have worked. Retaining this student would be of no benefit to him. Under these circumstances, questions remain.

Questions for Discussion

1. Do the parents have a right to demand retention based on immaturity?
2. Do you think an exception should be made in this case to grant the parents' request for retention? How does this relate to the ethic of justice for the child, parents, teachers, and administrators?
3. Are all the professionals described in this dilemma operating under the ethic of the profession? If not, explain with examples.
4. Is it fair to retain a student based solely on immaturity? How does this notion relate to the ethic of critique?
5. Are the parents operating under the ethic of care for their child to request the retention? Explain. Have they considered the feelings of their child to be retained and its impact on him?
6. Is the school team (principal and teachers) demonstrating the ethic of care regarding their opinions on retention for this youngster? Explain.
7. What decision should the principal make? State specific reasons for your response.

CASE STUDY 9.6 A MERIT-BASED SCHOLARSHIP

Jessica Walters stared at the two files on her desk. As director of admissions at a small, liberal arts college in the Midwest, she and her staff were faced with tough admissions decisions each day, but this case was the most difficult she had dealt with in her 20-year admissions career, and it was certainly the thorniest she had ever experienced here at Midvale College.

The applications in question were from two top-achieving students competing for a unique scholarship offered to a single high school senior from the town. Each one had attended strong schools, taken challenging courses, led clubs, started organizations, and were in the top 10% of their graduating classes. Despite their similarities, their family situations, their gender, and their racial and ethnic backgrounds were different. The

Hispanic male candidate, Juan Hernandez, came from a single-parent home; however, that single parent, a father, was a lawyer. The White female student, Courtney Rolands, came from an intact home, but both parents were in blue-collar hourly wage jobs and neither had attended college.

Academically, while these students were both strong candidates, there was one key difference: their American College Testing (ACT) scores. The Hispanic male student's score was four points—a substantial difference on the composite ACT scale—below that of the White student. Jessica knew that if she followed the college's written guidelines for this scholarship, Courtney Rolands, the student with the higher ACT score, would get the award. Jessica reviewed the files again. This time she looked for any other serious differences in the students' applications. She could not discover any particular challenges that might be considered as a plus factor in the scholarship consideration. The only significant difference was their ACT scores.

This case was exacerbated by the fact that Jessica's college had been enjoying record enrollment numbers during her tenure. She was a shrewd marketer, and she and her team had been able to attract more and better qualified students. Unfortunately, with increasingly higher ACT scores from their incoming freshmen, more students of color were denied admission. Jennifer's graduate work had been in the area of standardized test differentials, so she was acutely aware of students of color having admission difficulties. Admittedly, the decline in Hispanic numbers was slight, but some people were starting to notice. Student groups and faculty were beginning to agitate about the declining number of Hispanics admitted to Midvale College, and the president of the college was feeling the heat. The issue was compounded by the fact that the town, like many other towns in the Midwest, had been experiencing a Hispanic population boom.

On the one hand, Jessica could understand their concerns. Enrolling a diverse student body was a compelling issue and important enough to allow colleges to consider race as a plus factor in admissions. However, University of Michigan U.S. Supreme Court cases (*Gratz v. Bollinger*, 2003; *Grutter v. Bollinger*, 2003) gave Jessica pause; colleges and universities across the country were re-evaluating their admissions policies to ensure they were legal. These court decisions addressed the use of race in admissions, but much of the discussion surrounding them indicated that minority scholarships and financial aid would be the next targets. In sum, what the decisions said was that race could be a factor in assuring diversity in admissions but that there could not be a quota system to ensure minority representation. The policy needs to be flexible and highly individualized in that several factors are considered. The admissions policy in *Gratz v. Bollinger* (2003) was illegal because, among other things, it automatically gave applicants an additional 20 points if they came from underrepresented minority groups.

Midvale College had never used an affirmative action policy in admissions, and the information distributed to the public indicated that the college did not consider race in admissions decisions. In the case of the Midvale scholarship application, it did ask for race, but the form clearly indicated it was optional and would have no impact on the scholarship decision. If Jessica started to use that piece of information as part of the scholarship decision process it would feel to her to be unethical, and possibly it might even be illegal. However, Jessica wondered if she could consider race in this situation because it had to do with a scholarship award as opposed to admissions. After all, both students would be admitted to the college.

As she was still considering which student should win the scholarship, the college president contacted her to say that he had just received an angry call from a member of the college's board. The Hispanic member was outraged at the possibility that a minority student might be passed over for the scholarship due to a lower test score. He pointed out that a minority student had never received this scholarship (in fact, few had ever applied), and this year it was important that someone who was not in the majority should receive it.

The president was tired of all the pressure and effectively told Jessica that she "should" award the minority student the scholarship. As she put down the phone, Jessica knew she had to make the most ethically challenging decision of her career. Traditionally, it had always been the admissions director who made the decision about the scholarship. Should she allow the president and the board member to determine the recipient of the award, or should she make the decision herself?

Questions for Discussion

1. Which ethical paradigm(s) does the president of Midvale College seem to be most influenced by? Is his directive legal? Is it just?
2. If we only had the ethic of justice as a paradigm, what decision would Jessica have to make?
3. How might Jessica use the ethic of care in this case? Is it possible to care for all parties in this case? If so, how? If not, why not?
4. From a critical perspective, what are the ethical issues in this scenario that relate to social class, racial/ethnic equality, power, and oppression?
5. Imagine that you are the admissions director. Choose the student you think should win the scholarship competition. Carefully consider which ethical paradigm(s) you are using as you make your decision. Explain.

REFERENCES

America 2000: An education strategy (1991). Washington, DC: U.S. Government Printing Office.

Anderson, A. (2016). Education reform policies: How the Canadian government's role in education can influence the United States' education system. *Michigan State International Law Review, 24*, 545–598.

Darling-Hammond, L. & Snyder, J. (1992). Reframing accountability: creating learner-centered schools. In A. Lieberman (Ed.), *The changing contexts of teaching. Ninety-first yearbook of the national society for the study of education* (Pt. 1, pp. 11–36). Chicago, IL: University of Chicago Press.

Every Student Succeeds Act, Pub. L. No. 114-95, § 8038, 129 Stat. 1802 (2015).

Goals 2000: Educate America Act. (1993). Washington, DC: U.S. Government Printing Office.

Gold, E. & Simon, E. (2004, January 14). *Public accountability: School improvement efforts need the active involvement of communities to succeed.* Philadelphia: Research for Action.

Gomez-Velez, N. (2016). Common core state standards and philanthrocapitalism: Can public law norms manage private wealth's influence on public education policymaking? *Michigan State Law Review*, 161–214.

Gross, S.J. & Shapiro, J.P. (2002). Towards ethically responsible leadership in a new era of high stakes accountability. In G. Perrault & F. Lunenberg (Eds.), *The changing world of school administration* (pp. 256–266). Lanham, MA: Scarecrow Press.

Gross, S.J., Shaw, K., & Shapiro, J.P. (2003). Deconstructing accountability through the lens of democratic philosophies: toward a new analytic framework. *Journal of Research for Educational Leadership, 1*(3), 5–27.

Kirylo, J.D. (2018). The opt-out movement and the power of parents. *The Phi Delta Kappan, 99* (8), 36–40.

Mitra, D., Mann, B., & Hlavacik, M. (2016). Opting out: Parents creating contested spaces to challenge standardized tests. *Education Policy Analysis Archives, 24*, 1–23.

National Commission on Excellence in Education (1983). *A nation at risk: The imperative for educational reform.* Washington, DC: U.S. Government Printing Office.

New York State Allies for Public Education (2021). Retrieved from https://nysape.org

Nichols, S.L. & Berliner, D.C. (2007). *Collateral damage: How high stakes testing corrupts America's schools.* Cambridge, MA: Harvard Education Press.

No Child Left Behind, 20 U.S.C. §1751(b) (1) (2002).

Shapiro, J.P. (1979). Accountability: a contagious disease? *Forum for the Discussion of New Trends in Education, 22*(1), 16–18.

Wilson, T.S. & Hastings, M. (2021). Refusing the test: Debating assessment and accountability in public education. *Journal of Cases in Educational Leadership.* Retrieved from: https://journals.sagepub.com/doi/10.1177/1555458921993181

Wilson, T.S., Hastings, M., & Moses, M.S. (2016). Opting out as democratic engagement? The public dimensions and challenges of education activism. *The Good Society 25*(2-3), 231–255.

Chapter 10

Privacy versus Safety

Hollie J. Mackey, Liza Meiris, Addie Daniels-Lane,
Tara H. Collice, Stormy Stark, and Susan H. Shapiro

While educational leaders have as their primary charge to ensure that the students in their schools are provided with high-quality instruction, this goal cannot be achieved if schools are unsafe. Keeping schools safe and providing the school community with a sense of security is an important responsibility, which, if not carried out, can cause serious repercussions. At the same time, most of us would agree that personal privacy is one of the most important rights we possess. Justice Brandeis observed that:

> [T]hey [the framers of the U.S. Constitution] recognized the significance of man's spiritual nature, of his feelings and of his intellect. They knew that only a part of the pain, pleasure and satisfactions of life are to be found in material things. They sought to protect Americans in their beliefs, their thoughts, their emotions and their sensations. They conferred, as against the government, *the right to be let alone—the most comprehensive of rights and the right most valued by civilized men [persons].* To protect that right, every unjustifiable intrusion by the government upon the privacy of the individual, whatever the means employed, must be deemed a violation of the Fourth Amendment. (*Olmstead v. United States*, 1928, p. 478, Brandeis, J. dissenting [emphasis added])

Indeed, our Bill of Rights guarantees individuals the freedom from warrantless searches and self-incrimination; however, the framers of the Constitution could not anticipate how large our public school system would become or the threats to safety that would challenge those fundamental rights (Stefkovich & Miller, 1999). Thus, in the school context, there is a fine line between privacy and safety. Creating this context is the widely accepted fact that school is one of the few places where parents are, for the most part, compelled to send their children for most of their childhood (Levin,

DOI: 10.4324/9781003022862-12

1986). Further blurring this line is the precedent set by Justice Abe Fortas in *Tinker v. Des Moines Independent Community School District* (1969) that "special characteristics of the school environment" (p. 506) provide schools with the ability to limit students' and teachers' rights. This notion of special characteristics "has been central to judicial reasoning about individual rights in schools" (Warnick, 2009, p. 200).

From a practitioner's perspective, educators have always been concerned about maintaining order and discipline in the schools. The issue of school safety, however, reached a peak in the 1990s. The Gun-free School Zones Act of 1990, ruled unconstitutional in *U.S. v. Lopez* (1995), was followed by the Gun-free School Zones Act of 1994, which mandated that states pass legislation requiring schools to expel, for at least a year, students possessing weapons on school property. While exceptions could be permitted on a case-by-case basis, this federal law resulted in states enacting zero-tolerance legislation and policies, which began with guns but often expanded to other student behavior, sometimes including trivial offenses (Shouse, 2005).

Repealed in 2002, the Gun-free School Zones Act was re-enacted under *No Child Left Behind* (2002). Around the same time, the 1999 shootings at Columbine High School in suburban Colorado reminded Americans of the potential horrors of school violence. Here, two high school students killed 12 students and one teacher and injured another 23 people (Epstein, 2019). While not the first incident of its kind at the time, Columbine was one of the most publicized, attracting widespread media attention, which brought up crucial issues of bullying, discipline, and weapons in schools.

Efforts were also ongoing to eradicate drug use in the schools. In 1994, the Elementary and Secondary Education Act (ESEA) authorized The Safe and Drug-free Schools and Communities Act (SDFSCA) State and Local Grants Program. Providing financial support for programs that would prevent drug and alcohol use among youth, this initiative was "a central part of the Federal Government's effort to encourage the creation of safe, disciplined, and drug-free learning environments that will help all children meet challenging academic standards" (Bilchik, 1999).

Within the next seven years, the U.S. States Supreme Court issued two decisions that permitted, under certain circumstances, random drug testing of students in public schools. The first, *Vernonia v. Acton* (1995), allowed schools to randomly drug test student athletes. The second, *Board of Education v. Earls* (2002), ruled as constitutional random drug testing of students involved in extracurricular activities. Language in both opinions viewed drug use as a threat to keeping schools safe.

In 2009, the Supreme Court heard *Safford v. Redding*, a case involving the strip search of a middle-school student for possession of prescription-strength ibuprofen. While the Court ruled for the student, the justices were hesitant to say what they would have decided had the search been for more serious drugs. They did, however, grant the school district immunity from money damages, noting that school authorities would not have necessarily known that the strip search was illegal because the law was unclear.

Indeed, some lower court opinions have condoned such practices as legal and necessary for the safety of the school (*Cornfield v. Consolidated School District*, 1993; *Williams v. Ellington*, 1991). All these decisions are based on a standard of reasonableness set forth in the Supreme Court's ruling in *New Jersey v. T.L.O.* (1985) where the Court balanced the privacy rights of students against school officials' duty to maintain order and discipline, a responsibility that has come to be equated with school safety.

School safety assumed additional widespread significance as more school shootings tragically occurred. These include, but are not limited to: Sandy Hook Elementary School in Newtown, Connecticut where a shooter killed 20 children between six and seven years old and six adults on December 14, 2012 (Morgan, 2016); Marjorie Stoneman Douglas High School in Parkland, Florida where a gunman killed 17 persons and injured another 17 on February 14, 2018 (Chuck, Johnson & Siemaszko, 2018); and Santa Fe High School in Santa Fe, Texas (near Houston) where eight students and two teachers were killed and another 13 persons were wounded on May, 18, 2018 (Fernandez, Fausset, & Bidgood, 2018).

Educators and policy makers have responded to school shootings with increased attention to safety technology, additional law enforcement officers in schools, revised school discipline procedures (Ahranjani, 2017; Torres & Stefkovich, 2009), and lock-down drills (Rygg, 2015). Some schools have gone so far as to simulate actual shootings, unannounced and with real guns but not real bullets and fake blood. At least one commentator has questioned whether this type of drill might be more detrimental than helpful in that it may frighten or desensitize students (Rygg, 2015).

Another researcher (Jacobs, 2000) concluded that none of the measures used to prevent school violence work because the instigators are usually deeply disturbed and. will risk their own lives to kill others. Additionally, school shootings are isolated incidents. Although highly publicized, they are not that common compared to the total number of schools and students. On the other hand, a much larger number of students are deprived of their Constitutional rights as educators attempt to prevent an event that may not happen and may not be preventable.

Similarly, Crews (2014), who interviewed perpetrators of school shootings, found that abuse at home, school bullying, and adverse reactions to prescription drugs (that treat Asperger's syndrome or attention deficit/hyperactivity disorders), among other factors, served as triggers for violence. Crews concluded that early identification and prevention aimed at working with/listening to the student were much more effective than punitive measures or strategies aimed at all students.

In some instances, the "special characteristics" of schools have been used to place safety ahead of individual rights. In this respect, scholars have questioned the necessity for this erosion of rights in the name of security (Casella, 2003; Chen, 2008; Martinez, 2009). In addition, rather than resting blame solely on the perpetrators of a crime, the notion of collective responsibility for ensuring the safety of America's children has emerged (Lickel, Schmader, & Hamilton, 2003).

This chapter contains six case studies dealing with issues of personal privacy versus safety in the schools. Case Study 10.1, **Keeping Children Safe: When Is Enough, Enough?**, addresses the sensitive issue of drug use and the extent to which school leaders are willing to go to keep schools safe and drug free. Here, based on her demeanor and changes in her physical appearance, it seems clear that a student is experiencing some type of crisis in her life. The school counselor and administrators assume that the student is using and possibly distributing illegal drugs. In reaction to the pervasive use of drugs in school and to keep both the student and the school community safe, the counselor conducts a highly intrusive search—one that reveals something very different. This case illustrates how a seemingly pervasive fear of drugs may overshadow other equally if not more important student concerns.

Confidentiality Laws: To Protect or to Betray, Case Study 10.2, follows the theme of privacy versus safety in that a school counselor must decide whether to reveal personal information a student has told her in private. This scenario takes place in an alternative high school for students who have had serious discipline problems and, for the most part, unstable home lives, which have caused a lack of trust in most adults as well as potentially dangerous situations in the school. After spending a great deal of time cultivating a particular student's trust, a counselor must decide whether to reveal information to her principal who is insisting that she break confidentiality for safety's sake. Problems result when the counselor must decide between violating the law and school policy and betraying the student's confidence.

Gangs pose an enormous threat to school safety, an issue that is explored in Case Study 10.3, **Punishment, Rehabilitation, or Mitigating Circumstances?** Here, both the greater community and the school community are committed to eradicating a serious gang problem and have developed policies to address this threat. The school's policy requires, among other things, the suspension of any student promoting gang activity. In this scenario, a middle-school student is trying to recruit some of his classmates for gang membership and is suspended. Before the student can return to school, a parent must be present. School leaders find an even more compelling dilemma when they realize that the student's mother, whom they were counting on for support, has not only been extraordinarily difficult to contact but also may be part of the problem. In addition to disciplinary issues, this situation explores the larger problem of where to draw the line between the privacy of families and the safety of the individual student and of all students.

Case Study 10.4, **Follow Policy or Favor the Connected?**, deals with the issue of threats and whether they are true threats or students simply trying to work out their frustrations in disturbing, but non-violent, ways. The situation becomes more complicated when one of the students is the daughter of a particularly assertive school board member who has had a great deal of contact with the school, and another is a student who has a history that is confidential. Assessing possible danger, keeping student information private, and deciding how to handle situations with somewhat similar fact patterns in a consistent yet equitable manner lie at the heart of resolving this ethical dilemma.

Criminal activity, especially the taking of hostages, near a school is always terrifying. This fear is compounded when students are just beginning to enter the school building and the hostages are a kindergartner and the child's mother. Case Study 10.5, **First Responder: Hostage Situation at School**, addresses how a lone principal handles this situation when there is no emergency plan, cell phone communications are down, and the only working phones are in his office. Deciding whom to respond to first and how much information to provide to anxious parents results in ethical as well as administratively strategic decision making.

The theme of protecting young children follows through in our final case study (10.6), **Lockdown, Leadership, and Little Children**, which addresses the fear that lock-down drills can cause balanced with their original purpose of addressing safety. Here, a school leader must decide between obeying the law that requires these drills and observing the privacy rights of her employees who not only question the wisdom and likely harm this requirement imposes but have refused to participate in these mandated exercises.

CASE STUDY 10.1 KEEPING CHILDREN SAFE: WHEN IS ENOUGH, ENOUGH?

Dr. Matayo walked slowly through the reception area and down the hall to his office before entering and gently closing the door. Hand still resting on the handle, he let his head drop slightly to rest against the back of the door. Nine years of teaching and four years as a principal had not prepared him for the events that had just transpired under his watch. While still a little unclear about what he needed to do, the one thing he knew was that within minutes he would have two angry parents, a contrite school counselor, and one scared high school senior waiting for him outside his office. He took a few deep breaths and recalled what had led to this disastrous day.

Ironside High School was in a relatively well-populated mountain state area. Although the community was technically considered rural, Ironside accommodated over 1,200 students who came primarily from families associated with the mining industry on which the town had been built. This industry provided a tax base that afforded the school district resources well beyond those of most schools in the state. These included an indoor track and swimming pool, enough money in the budget to maintain smaller class sizes, a "serenity garden" for students and staff, and the space and funding for three full-time school counselors specializing in academic advising, emotional support, and drug and alcohol education. Most recently, the school had used surplus budget money to expand and refinish the student parking lot to accommodate the increasing number of students who were driving to school.

With the good always came the bad, it seemed. Many of the students at Ironside had access to a lot of money, not a responsibility that they seemed to take seriously. Dr. Matayo was always mildly surprised when the students arrived in their shiny new cars that made the faculty and staff vehicles look like they belonged in a junk yard. He was also saddened by the number of students who had been caught with illegal drugs in the community. Unfortunately, the town was situated along an interstate corridor known to be used for moving drugs between Mexico and Canada. It seemed that their location was a nice resting spot for some of these dealers and the city was suffering.

Dr. Matayo was thankful that they had not yet discovered any drugs in the school, but he knew it was only a matter of time. His students had both the money and the resources to get just about any drug they wanted. He thought about how times had changed. When he was in school it was obvious which students were involved with drugs and alcohol and those who were not. Now it seemed that it was mostly athletes and honor students. It was a painful memory that just two years ago they lost a student to drug use. He was a good student, an all-conference athlete whose mother had found him dead on the garage floor. He had seemed fine at football practice that day, only to suffer a heart attack 30 minutes after practice due to methamphetamine use.

Dr. Matayo turned back to the matter at hand. Mrs. Teahorn, the extremely competent and caring drug and alcohol counselor, had stepped up her efforts to educate students in the hopes of preventing drug and alcohol use. She had also tried to keep a vigilant eye on the student body to try to recognize signs of drug use and get students help if they needed it. Over the course of the previous month one student, Natasa Kadiev, had shown some classic signs.

Typically, an outgoing and friendly girl, she had become withdrawn and rarely spoke to anyone. Her cutting-edge fashion sense had been traded for a uniform of sweatpants and a hooded sweatshirt. Her haphazard ponytail appeared to have been pulled up as an afterthought and she no longer wore any make-up. Mrs. Teahorn had overheard students talking about Natasa, some even implying that not only was Natasa using drugs, but she was probably getting them for her friends too.

Mrs. Teahorn tried talking with Natasa many times and had even pulled her from class on several occasions to try to develop a closer relationship with her in the hopes that she would disclose the cause of her rapid trans-formation. It appeared that the opposite had occurred. Natasa had complained to Dr. Matayo that she felt "picked on" and that she wished Mrs. Teahorn would leave her alone. She resented being pulled from her favorite class. After talking with Mrs. Teahorn he had decided that, while she needed to ease off Natasa, it was certainly a good idea to keep an eye on her for her own safety. If she was using drugs, she was putting both herself and others at risk.

Dr. Matayo moved the chairs in his office around to accommodate the unplanned meeting between himself and the four people he could hear gathering outside his office. Mrs. Teahorn entered first, making brief eye contact and then quickly averting her gaze to a painting on the back wall as she took her seat. Mr. and Mrs. Kadiev came through the door next, his arm protectively around her shoulder and a look of anger and deter-mination in his dark brown eyes. Mrs. Kadiev cried gently into a handker-chief. Trailing in last was Natasa, whose hand was carefully encircled by the hand her mother had dropped behind her to cement the solidarity of their little family through touch.

Dr. Matayo: Let's start at the beginning. Mrs. Teahorn, would you please explain what happened? Natasa, if you want to add anything you are entitled. Your side of the story is important too. If you feel Mrs. Teahorn is not accurate, please speak up.

Mrs. Teahorn: This morning I passed Natasa in the hallway and her eyes were all sunken in and red like she had been crying or something. I know you told me to give her some space, but my heart just broke for her; so I decided to pull her from third period, her study hall, to talk with her.

Dr. Matayo: Please continue.

Mrs. Teahorn: Once we got to my office, she started yelling at me to mind my own business. I told her what I knew about the signs of drug use and asked her if she had been using drugs. She told me "no," but I didn't think she was telling the truth. I could see I wasn't getting anywhere and decided to send her back to class. She had tossed her backpack against a chair in my office and some of its contents had fallen to the floor. I leaned down to help her when she jerked the bag away and told me to leave her stuff alone. I raised my hand to touch her shoulder to reassure her that I was only trying to help when she quickly moved her bag behind her. That made me think she had drugs, so I asked her to empty the contents of her bag. She refused and said I had no right. I explained to her that I did as per district policy. She then started tugging at her sweatshirt that had gotten twisted with all her jerking around. She kept trying to put it over her hips so I thought she might have drugs in her pockets. I asked her to take off her sweatshirt knowing she had a T-shirt on underneath and to then empty her sweatpants pockets.

Dr. Matayo: So, you were concerned that she was both using drugs and that she had them in her backpack or pockets?

Mrs. Teahorn: Yes, absolutely! We have seen so much devastation due to drugs the past few years, I thought I was doing the right thing.

Dr. Matayo: Please continue.

Mrs. Teahorn: Well, I guess she knew I was not going to let her leave so she pulled off her sweatshirt and dumped her backpack out all over my floor. And then . . .

Natasa: And then I said, "Are you happy now?"

Dr. Matayo: Is that when you called Mr. and Mrs. Kadiev?

Mrs. Teahorn: Yes.

Natasa: Must have been SOME surprise to see that the perfect counselor was WRONG! Tell them what you found Mrs. Teahorn . . . wait, let me . . . she found this stupid big round belly and a pregnancy book in my backpack! Some drugs, right?

Dr. Matayo let this all sink in and wondered what he was going to do. He knew that Mrs. Teahorn was only doing what she had felt she needed to do to protect Natasa and perhaps other students from drugs. He also knew that the Kadievs were a very prominent family and Mr. Kadiev would want heads to roll for this. He glanced up once more and saw before him a counselor who knew she had erred, two parents who just found out that their daughter was pregnant, and one young woman whose troubles had just been compounded by humiliation and broken trust.

Questions for Discussion

1. What is the ethical dilemma presented above? Analyze this scenario through the lenses of justice, care, critique, and profession.
2. Discuss how the scenario illustrates the tension between students' safety and their right to privacy within schools. Which is more important?
3. Was Mrs. Teahorn justified in her assumption that she might find drugs either in Natasa's backpack or her pants pockets? If you were Dr. Matayo, how would you explain this justification to Natasa's parents? The school board?
4. What are the implications for Dr. Matayo should he decide not to strongly reprimand Mrs. Teahorn? Should she be reprimanded?
5. How does this scenario challenge the conflict between personal and professional ethics?

CASE STUDY 10.2 CONFIDENTIALITY LAWS: TO PROTECT OR TO BETRAY?

Danielle Schaeffer's drive to Shady Lane School was a long one, and she used that time to create a mental checklist of what she hoped to accomplish that day. As the school counselor, she worried about one student showing possible signs of drug use, one whose boyfriend punched her in the face this week, and another who would be returning to public school. Shady Lane was a private alternative high school with a vision for providing a therapeutic environment for students who have been removed from the public-school setting. Serving approximately 30 students in such an intimate environment allowed Danielle to run group therapy sessions, individual therapy, and crisis intervention. Given the special population of the school, many of her students had disturbing life stories that led to their behavior problems. At times she felt that she could make a positive impact, other times she felt powerless in the face of such profound odds against her students.

On this day Danielle's chief concern was one student in particular, Tyrone. Teachers had been complaining about Tyrone's behavior more and more at each daily staff meeting; his recent vile use of language, bullying, wandering around the school, and inappropriate flirtation with girls had left teachers frustrated and upset. Principal Snyder's first question was always the same: "Whose caseload is he on?" Of the two counselors on staff, Tyrone's behavior was Danielle's task at hand.

The school year was just over halfway finished, and Danielle finally felt she was making deeper connections with the students. Trust is a difficult thing to gain from students who have been abused in so many ways and seldom praised. She outlined the confidentiality rights to the students often; according to the American Psychological Association, a psychologist's primary obligation is to maintain the privacy of the client unless there is imminent danger to the client or another individual. In many cases, however, her students had learned to be distrustful of adults. So, Danielle felt she was finally getting her job done as students began to open up, and conversations started to begin with, "You're not going to tell the principal/my parents/anyone this, right?" Now she finally was able to reach students regarding their deeper problems and insecurities and was even seeing a difference in their coping skills and behavior.

Tyrone was no exception; he had begun to open up to Danielle in the past about how his mother was in jail, his grandmother kicked him out, and how he felt bullied and alone at the group home he lived in. One day he broke down into tears saying, "I never trust my girlfriends, but it's really that I just need a mom." So when Tyrone's behavior went downhill and he wasn't confiding in Danielle, she had become worried that it was because what he was dealing with was too severe, or illegal, or that he was too ashamed to process his emotions.

Danielle decided to give it one more try and called Tyrone to her room. Tyrone began with his usual detachment and denial, but finally explained that he got a text from a girl who said that she was pregnant. Tyrone questioned whether she was really pregnant and if so, whether it was really his child. This girl had a history of lying and manipulation, so Tyler left her calls and texts unanswered but had been feeling guilty about this and apprehensive about the possibility that he was to be a father. Danielle breathed a sigh of relief; while the possibility of an unwanted pregnancy was not ideal, she could list a thousand more critical issues that would have demanded immediate intervention, so she talked him through it and he left looking more light-hearted than when he came in.

During the faculty meeting that afternoon Danielle was excited to report to the principal that Tyrone's issue was not a dire problem that required outside intervention, and that he may soon be back to normal. She was shocked, however, by Principal Snyder's response when she, as a counselor, declined to provide further details citing Tyrone's right to privacy. Mrs. Snyder, seeing this as a power struggle with a noncompliant employee, became visibly angry during the conversation.

"For safety reasons you are required to inform me of what's going on in my school! You better be careful keeping such information hidden. Don't get in trouble for these kids!" Mrs. Snyder exclaimed.

Danielle wondered what could be causing this sudden burst of emotion. Jealousy? Paranoia? Genuine concern? She began to have the sinking feeling that there was no easy way out of this. Telling the principal meant that she would take matters into her own hands and discuss the situation with Tyrone, and Danielle might lose the hard-won trust of not only Tyrone but also all the students. Not telling the principal, however, considering the aggressive response of Mrs. Snyder, could put her job on the line if she continued to withhold information.

As a teacher and a counselor, Danielle was accustomed to making sacrifices for her students; she had always prided herself on doing what was in the best interests of the student, even when administration stood in the way or it seemed an impossible task. Would Danielle be "doing her job" by supporting students or by complying with the principal? The right thing to do, in Danielle's mind, would be to maintain the privacy of her students. But was it worth the sacrifice?

Questions for Discussion

1. What rules and laws apply in this situation? In what ways are the laws clear and in what ways are they vague? Under the ethic of justice, would Mrs. Snyder be justified in terminating Danielle's employment? If so, for what reason? If not, what recourse would Danielle have?

2. Are at-risk teenagers a special group that should be advocated for? In what ways do they need specialized support? How does a counselor's role differ from that of a teacher?

3. What should a student expect in this situation according to the ethic of care?

4. What factors might be considered under the ethic of critique?

5. What responsibilities does Danielle have to the students? In what situations would it be in the students' best interest to break their trust? Who should have the final say in how to determine the proper actions?

CASE STUDY 10.3 PUNISHMENT, REHABILITATION, OR MITIGATING CIRCUMSTANCES?

Wilbur Meadows Elementary School is in a mid-size urban area. The city population is about 55% African American, 30% Caucasian, and 15% Hispanic and other. Recently the city has seen the proliferation of gang activity and gangs have been identified as being active in the city. An upsurge in violence and drug activity has been recorded. Initially the city leaders denied there was a problem. More recently, they have acknowledged it and begun taking aggressive action against gangs. The Board of Education has also reacted by establishing an anti-gang policy.

This policy requires a five- to nine-day suspension, notification to the local gang task force, a possible legal hearing, and referral to an anti-gang program. The district is also establishing its own anti-gang program under the guise of the Phoenix Curriculum. This program focuses on goal setting, personal choice, and developing responsibility (Youngs, 1989). The curriculum is being used to target students in Grades 4 to 8.

Recognizing that Wilbur Meadows serves a troubled community known for drugs and violence, Ms. Smith, the school's principal, and the School Leadership Team believed it was time for the staff to know as much about gangs as the children. They invited the State Police Gang Unit to conduct an in-service for the staff. They also invited incarcerated gang members who have turned their lives around to engage and dissuade students.

Jamal Sanders, a seventh-grade special needs student at Wilbur Meadows Elementary School, was suspected of flashing (gang-related) signs. Ms. Smith and the school counselor, Mr. Alex, had several conversations with Jamal about gangs. When Jamal's mother was asked to come in for a conference, she sent representatives in her stead. Jamal was eventually caught in the act of trying to encourage other students to become part of a local gang, the Junior Hoods 301 Sect. Consequently, Jamal was suspended, and his name was sent to the local gang task force.

Ms. Smith and Mr. Alex met again with Jamal to impress upon him the seriousness of the situation. Jamal's mother was notified that a mandatory parent conference would be required before Jamal could return to school. Several messages left for her went unreturned. The school's social worker hand-delivered the letter. It was apparent that something had to be done with Jamal, some type of intervention with parent input and support. Ms. Smith wondered if Jamal's family had any idea where he seemed to be heading and how much support she could expect from them.

When Jamal's mother reported to the school office for the conference, Principal Smith and Mr. Alex looked at each other with stunned expressions. Ms. Delores Sanders entered the room wearing a sleeveless, low-cut blouse. The upper part of her arm was encircled by a tattoo of cat paws (the symbol of the Hoods); at the center of her cleavage was an additional cat paw. Principal Smith's head began to spin. Nothing in her training had prepared her for handling this. Where and how to begin? These were just two of the questions looming in front of her. A strategic diplomatic approach would have to be the order of the day. She hoped Mr. Alex had some insightful strategy to contribute or at least was ready to follow her lead.

Questions for Discussion

1. How can Principal Smith protect Jamal given the circumstances? Should she confront Ms. Sanders for her possible involvement in gang activity?
2. What type of disciplinary action should be taken against Jamal? Should Ms. Smith refer Jamal to the district for a hearing to expel him or should she report him, or his mother, to the police?
3. Given the circumstances, is rehabilitation possible for Jamal? What is the most caring way to handle this situation? Should Principal Smith report Ms. Sanders to Child Welfare for possible child endangerment?
4. Is the district's policy fair to students like Jamal? Should there be exceptions to the rule? If so, how would you craft these rules/policies?
5. How might this situation be handled from a critical theory and/or social justice perspective?

CASE STUDY 10.4 FOLLOW POLICY OR FAVOR THE CONNECTED?

Pine Valley School District is a small district in the suburbs of a major metropolitan area. The district serves kindergarten through twelfth grade in three economically diverse municipalities and is run by a school board comprised of nine elected officials.

Pine Valley Middle School (PVMS) serves approximately 1,100 students and is located on the boundaries of the district. It is one of the top-performing schools within the county on state assessments. The teachers, within the school, work in small teams to meet the needs of the multifaceted student population. PVMS has one head principal, Dr. Turner, and two assistant principals, Mr. Brown and Mrs. Livingston. The assistant principals handle disciplinary issues with fair and consistent consequences.

Maxine, the youngest of four, is a seventh-grade student from an upper-middle-class family. Maxine does well in school. Her father, the vice-president of the school board, feels that Maxine can be much more sensitive than his older children and worries about her feelings. He has expressed his concerns regularly with Ms. Carr, Maxine's counselor. Ms. Carr has shared this information with Maxine's teachers. Maxine's father also has expressed concerns with the superintendent about programs within the middle school that he feels are not developmentally appropriate, most often when his daughter was not successful. The superintendent passes this information to the administrative team.

Ms. Carr is the counselor to approximately 376 seventh-grade students. Her day begins by listening to messages from concerned parents and meeting with troubled students. On this one morning, Ms. Carr fielded a phone call from the parent of Eddie Flood, a young, gregarious seventh grader. Eddie's mom was concerned because of comments another student made to her son in class the previous day. Eddie suffers from anxiety and depression. He is medicated and works very hard to hide his insecurities.

Eddie is well-liked by his peers and has many friends. However, in classes he sometimes is distracted and has a difficult time completing work. Mrs. Flood said her son had come home from school extremely upset. In his English class that day a girl at Eddie's table turned to him and said, "If I had one wish, I might bring a knife to school and kill you. My wish is that you were dead." Eddie came home devastated and shared with his mom that this same girl repeatedly called him stupid and slow. Mrs. Flood shared that Maxine was the student. Ms. Carr, knowing that this might be a sensitive issue, immediately brought it to Mrs. Livingston.

Mrs. Livingston began by speaking with Eddie. She also interviewed two other students who confirmed the comment. Mrs. Livingston and Ms. Carr discussed it and decided that the counselor would call Maxine down to talk. Maxine met with Ms. Carr in her office and shared her frustration with Eddie. She said she felt that Eddie purposefully did not participate in group projects and that she needed to do all of the work or her grade would suffer. She also admitted to saying that she would like to stab and kill Eddie. She shared that she said it out of frustration and anger, and then she began to cry. Ms. Carr called Mrs. Livingston in, and Maxine repeated that she was angry and threatened to stab Eddie. Mrs. Livingston informed Maxine that there would be a consequence for her actions but admitted that, she wasn't sure what it would be.

Mrs. Livingston was stumped. Less than two months prior to this she had handled a similar situation. Ruth, an eighth grader, was an extremely aggressive and argumentative student and spent many afternoons in Mrs. Livingston's office. This poor behavior contributed to poor grades. Ruth threatened to have a male classmate shot because she felt he disrespected her. She made the threat verbally in front of witnesses and was immediately suspended for three days and sent for a risk assessment, as per policy. She was unable to just return to school. She had to attend a reinstatement hearing prior to coming back. Her father brought the paperwork from the risk assessment stating that she was not a threat or danger to herself or others. Dr. Turner, the eighth grade counselor, and Mrs. Livingston presented the information garnered from the investigation, and the student apologized for her words before being allowed to resume classes. All these actions strictly adhered to school policy regarding threats.

This situation, although similar, differed in a few ways. Maxine was typically a good student. She was also very quiet, shy, and sensitive. She recently stuck up for a student in one of her classes who was being bullied by confronting the bully. All the teachers have worked to build her self-confidence because of her father's concerns. Ms. Carr regularly reported Maxine's progress to her dad. Most importantly, Maxine was the daughter of a board member—a very vocal board member who had begun to criticize the middle school more and more since his youngest daughter began to attend.

Mrs. Livingston briefly spoke with Dr. Turner and explained the basics of the issue. What would be done next depended on his guidance.

Questions for Discussion

1. How does the ethic of justice apply to this situation?
2. How does the ethic of care relate to this scenario? How might it hinder justice? Why might it be the wrong decision?
3. Should the fact that Maxine's father is the vice-president of the school board matter in the decision-making process? Is there an ethical paradigm that would help the administration explain to her dad the reason for a consequence?
4. Which ethical paradigm would be most helpful in this situation?
5. Is it ethical for Maxine's dad to use his influence as a member of the board and his relationship with the superintendent to sway decisions and policy when it comes to his children?

CASE STUDY 10.5 FIRST RESPONDER: HOSTAGE SITUATION AT SCHOOL

A mother and a six-year-old kindergarten child stop at a convenience store next to the entrance of the child's elementary school at 7:30 a.m. on a school day. The only access for the school is a roadway that runs parallel next to the store. While they are in the store, a gunman enters and announces that everyone in the store has just been taken hostage.

Unaware this is unfolding, buses approach the elementary school and unload students aged five to ten years old. School begins at 7:40 and almost all the students have arrived and are getting ready to begin their classes. The school has a population of five hundred students in kindergarten through fifth grade and a staff of 40 adults including teachers, administrators, and staff. The buses that transport the children to this school are also used to transport students to the middle school and high school located five miles away. The school also has ten students, of varying ages, who are confined to wheelchairs and are only able to be transported on wheelchair accessible school transportation.

Emergency personnel responding to the scene include the sheriff who is serving as the hostage negotiator, sniper and SWAT teams, fire personnel who handle closing the major roadway that passes by the school and store, state police, and local rescue teams. Many of the emergency personnel working the crisis are parents of students or relatives of people in the school. The unified incident command team has to manage the scene and the negotiation process while debating whether it is safer to keep the elementary school on lock down or attempt to evacuate.

An evacuation attempt means driving everyone past the hostage scene, which could create a very dangerous situation. The arrival of school buses to transport everyone away from the scene could also scare the hostage taker and cause him to make erratic and dangerous decisions. The school buses necessary for evacuation are still carrying middle and high school students to their destinations. Logistically, this will mean either delaying an evacuation long enough for the buses to drop off their other students or endangering more students by bringing the buses back as quickly as possible. The bus dispatch radio frequency is also at risk of being silenced because emergency personnel need all communication lines.

Mr. Stewart, the elementary principal, has 12 years of service, but he has no experience in crisis situations. The elementary school is also short of its vice principal because the former vice principal was promoted to middle school principal mid-year and a replacement has not yet been found. The principal is in a building with 16 different door access points, not all of which have video surveillance. The entire front wall of the school is glass, which was designed to complement the atrium and create an open feel in the school. The administrative offices are located across from the glass wall.

With the media arriving on the scene of the hostage crisis, Principal Stewart realizes that the cell phone towers cannot handle the rapid influx of usage because phones within the school cannot get a signal. Mr. Stewart loses all ability to communicate if he leaves the administrative offices and their landline phone connections. He must make an ethical decision whether he should be visible in the school hallways maintaining calm or stay in the administrative offices able to communicate with the outside world, including concerned parents.

Dr. Fraser is in her first year as a superintendent in this district and in the role of superintendent. She has had extensive tabletop and classroom training on crisis management, but this district has no emergency response plan and no emergency communication system. Dr. Fraser's office is three miles from the elementary school. The only way she can communicate with Mr. Stewart is to call his office phone or use e-mail.

Dr. Fraser's staff has concerned parents coming in and calling, asking about the safety of their children, and begging to be allowed access to the school. The public relations staff member is on maternity leave and no one else is trained to respond to the barrage of calls. Dr. Fraser is trying to maintain order while assessing the conditions at the elementary school and coordinating with emergency personnel. The elementary students will need crisis counseling, especially as law enforcement informs her that a student and parent are hostages in the store.

Dr. Fraser, Mr. Stewart, and Deputy Davis, the ranking police officer on scene, begin to talk on the phone. Mr. Stewart says the staff and faculty are trying to appear normal and none of the students are aware that there is an issue. In the school, everyone is safe. All the doors are locked, and other than the phone lines being overwhelmed by frightened parents, the situation is being managed extremely well. Deputy Davis provides an update on the hostage situation.

Davis reports the victims are still being held hostage and are unharmed. He also relates that the suspect is not being very communicative. He explains that a helicopter may be landing on the school soccer field under the orders of the state police. Davis says the primary goal is to safely remove the hostages. His other advice is that he believes any attempt to evacuate the school would be unwise and he requests a district employee come manage the parents who are gathering at the roadblock and trying to reach their elementary school children. Everyone on the phone call hears the sound of gunshots and Deputy Davis abruptly announces the situation has just shifted drastically and the call disconnects. Dr. Fraser now must determine the best course of action.

Questions for Discussion

1. What is the most ethical communication strategy Dr. Fraser can adopt? Why? Explain your answer.

2. What are the pros and cons ethically of evacuating or not evacuating the school? Explain your answer based on the four ethical paradigms.

3. Based on a justice perspective, should Mr. Stewart stay in the office or be in the hallways of his school? From critique? From care? What would the profession expect Mr. Stewart to do?

CASE STUDY 10.6 LOCKDOWN, LEADERSHIP, AND LITTLE CHILDREN

It is a cold and foggy morning in mid-January as Mrs. Kelly flips through her calendar to prepare for her weekly staff meeting. Although it is only Tuesday morning, Mrs. Kelly is already feeling the familiar ache in her back from her morning routine of taking the squirming infants from their parents' arms and giving each baby and little ones a reassuring hug before taking them to their classroom teachers. It is a tough job, but she can't imagine doing anything else. She even went back to school three years ago and completed her online master's degree when the laws changed so she could keep her job and supervise the Universal Pre-Kindergarten program they hope to start in the fall. It was a large investment, but listening to the sounds of the bustling center, she knows it is worth it.

The sounds of babies crying and toddlers laughing fill the halls. The neighborhood has changed since she started working here 18 years ago. The safe little urban neighborhood, where the school began, is now struggling in harder times. Mrs. Kelly finds herself getting a little more nervous when she pulls down the school's metal shutters at night. The neighborhood, once filled with hard-working blue-collar families, is now relying on vouchers to pay their childcare bills and parents often struggle to find enough money to pack a solid lunch or fill up the baby bottles.

At 8 a.m., Mrs. Kelly enters the little gym that also doubles as their meeting room and starts pulling out a few folding chairs to begin the meeting. Her co-workers file in, balancing their coffee cups and clipboards in their arms, as they get ready for the meeting.

"Good morning. I know we are short on time so let's get going." Mrs. Kelly begins. "Oh, I almost forgot, before we start, I want to give everyone a heads-up that at 2 p.m. today we will be holding out first lockdown drill. I know we discussed this briefly over the summer, but I will go over the highlights with you once again. The children are to shelter in place with the lights off and remain as quiet as possible. Also, this is going to be an unannounced drill. The law states we cannot tell the parent about it until it is over. We need to keep it private and work on issues of response among ourselves."

Mrs. Kelly begins to hear some snickering. She looks around and notices several of the staff members whispering to one another.

"Ummm . . . am I missing something?" she queries. She can feel the energy in the room begin to shift. After working with these staff members for so many years, she can sense quickly when trouble is brewing.

"You have got to be kidding me! Do you remember the last time we turned out the lights for Rachel's birthday?" Martha, Head of the Two's

Room begins. She is a large woman who has had four children of her own. She has little formal training, but the other staff members refer to her as the Baby Whisperer and she is a pro at handling even the fussiest toddler. "They all started to scream and cry. It took us over an hour to calm them down and that was even after we had shown them the cake."

"And what about us?" Kayla, Head of the Baby Room, chimed in. She had raised five boys and had only finished high school but was never shy with an opinion. "How do we keep babies quiet? We have half the kids napping at that time and the ones who are awake will scream and keep the others up. We'll never get back on schedule. I don't have enough hands to calm everyone down. This is ridiculous!"

"I know, I know," Mrs. Kelly tries to calm the rising tide of discontentment now flowing through the room. "But it's the law. We must hold these drills now. Those in charge are trying to keep kids safe. Look at what happened in Sandy Hook. It can happen anywhere."

"And what am I supposed to say to the preschoolers?" asks Tamara, the new teacher for the preschoolers. "They are going to ask questions you know. I keep telling them school is a safe place, and we all know how many of these kids need a safe place. So now, do I tell them they can get shot at school? And now we're keeping secrets from the parents. They don't even know we are doing these drills. I am not doing that Mrs. Kelly! You do it!"

"Now wait a minute . . ." Mrs. Kelly struggles to think of a way to regain control. "This is not my idea. The city says the timing of these drills need to be confidential. It's not a secret but it needs to be unannounced and by doing that it will also give us some time to reflect and plan on our own. We have to . . ."

"And what if a shooter comes?" Kayla responds. "We are just sitting ducks. You can hear those babies cry all the way to the street corner. What am I gonna do? They'll know we're here. I can't hide eight babies and I can't pick them up and run. You know I'll be the first one to get shot. No drill is going to help that. You come in and tell those kids to be quiet. And when the parents find out you didn't clear it with them first they will roast us over a hot stove. I am not going to do that drill!"

"Now wait!" Mrs. Kelly takes a deep breath and tries to explain again. "Of course, I'll be there. Of course, I'll help but we have to practice. When we are inspected, they will check our logbook to make sure we did the drill. And what if something happens, and we never prepared or saw what we need to fix. If the parents are involved at this point not only will we be in violation of the law but it will give us no space to plan or to think about how best to keep these children safe."

"It's not right and if you make us do your drill. I am taking it to the parents. They are not going to be happy, little kids preparing to get shot.

You know they'll go crazy if they hear about this especially when you didn't tell them first."

"I'm not doing it! You write in that book of yours that we did or didn't do the drill. I don't care. But we are not doing this drill and I'm not keeping your drill a secret," another teacher exclaimed.

Mrs. Kelly takes a long look at the angry faces surrounding her. She knows if she goes forward with the drill the teachers will not comply and will not participate in it. She also knows they will involve the parents in protesting the drill. Does she go forward risking an altercation with her staff and families or does she alter the drill record putting her own career in jeopardy and perhaps risking the children's safety as well? Mrs. Kelly knows she has a difficult decision to make. What should she do?

Questions for Discussion

1. Using each of the four ethics of justice, critique, care, and the profession, defend Mrs. Kelly's position to hold the drill?
2. Using each of the four ethics of justice, critique, care, and the profession, defend the teachers' decisions to not participate in the drill?
3. Using each of the four ethics of justice, critique, care, and the profession, defend the parent rights to know about these drills ahead of time?
4. How would you handle this dilemma?
5. What is the most ethical way to resolve this dilemma?

REFERENCES

Ahranjani, M. (2017). The prisonization of America's public schools. *Hofstra Law Review 45*(4), 1097–1117.

Bilchik, S. (1999). *Promising strategies to reduce gun violence report.* United States: Department of Justice, Office of Juvenile Justice and Delinquency Prevention. Retrieved from: www.ojjdp.gov/pubs/gun_violence/173950.pdf

Board of Education of Independent School District No. 92 of Pottawatomie County v. Earls, 536 U.S. 822 (2002).

Casella, R. (2003). Zero tolerance policy in schools: rationale, consequences, and alternatives. *Teachers College Record, 105*, 872–892.

Chen, G. (2008). Communities, students, schools, and school crime: a confirmatory study of crime in U.S. high schools. *Urban Education, 43*, 301–318.

Chuck, E., Johnson, A., & Siemaszko, C. (2018, February 15). 17 killed in mass shooting at high school in Parkland, Florida, nbcnews.com. Retrieved from www. nbcnews.com/news/us-news/police-respond-shooting-parkland-florida-high-school-n848101

Cornfield by Lewis v. Consolidated School District No. 230, 991 F.2d 1316 (7th Cir. 1993).

Crews, G.A. (2014). School violence perpetrators speak: An examination of perpetrators' views on school violence offenses. *Journal of the Institute of Justice and International Studies, 2014*, 41–58.

Elementary and Secondary Education Act (ESEA) (1994). Improving America's schools act. Retrieved from: Archived Information: H.R. 6 Improving America's Schools Act of 1994.

Epstein, K. (2019, April 20). Columbine shooting anniversary: Community remembers victims with memorials and vigils. *The Washington Post*. Retrieved from www. bing.com/search?q=columbine+shooting+anniversary%3A+community&form=A NSPH1&refig=01176831c09640909bd669c8093f58cb&pc=U531

Fernandez, M, Fausset, R. & Bidgood, J. (2018, May 18). In Texas Shooting, 10 dead, 10 injured and many not surprised. *The New York Times*. Retrieved from www.nytimes.com/2018/05/18/us/school-shooting-santa-fe-texas.html

Gun-free School Zones Act of 1990, 18 U.S.C. 922 (q)(1)(A).

Gun-free School Zones Act of 1994, 20 U.S.C. § 8921.

Jacobs, T.L. (2000). School violence: An incurable social ill that should not lead to the unconstitutional compromise of students' rights. *Duquesne Law Review, 38* (winter), 617–662.

Levin, B. (1986). Educating youth for citizenship: the conflict between authority and individual rights in the public school. *Yale Law Journal, 95*(8), 1647–1680.

Lickel, B., Schmader, T., & Hamilton, D.L. (2003). A case for collective responsibility: who else was to blame for the Columbine high school shootings? *Personality and Social Psychology Bulletin, 29*(2), 194–204.

Martinez, S. (2009). A system gone berserk: how are zero-tolerance policies really affecting schools? *Preventing School Failure, 53*(4), 153–157.

Morgan, D. (2016, December 14). A look back: Sandy Hook Elementary School shooting - CBS News. Retrieved from:12 https://www.cbsnews.com/pictures/a-look-back-sandy-hook-elementary-school-shooting/

New Jersey v. T.L.O., 469 U.S. 325 (1985).

No Child Left Behind, 20 U.S.C. § 1751(b) (1) (2002).

Olmstead v. United States, 277 U.S. 438 (1928).

Rygg, L. (2015). School shooting simulations: At what point does preparation become more harmful than helpful? *Children's Legal Rights Journal, 35*(3), 215-228.

Safe and Drug-free Schools and Communities Act (SDFSCA), State and Local Grants Program. (1994). Elementary and Secondary Education Act (ESEA) 1994. Title IV, §§ 4111-4116, 20 U.S.C. §§ 7111-7116.

Safford v. Redding, 129 S.Ct. 2633 (2009).

Shouse, R.C. (2005). Some current threats to humanistic pupil control. In W.K. Hoy & C.G. Miskel (Eds.), *Educational leadership and reform* (pp. 301–318). Greenwich, CT: Information Age.

Stefkovich, J.A. & Miller, J.A. (1999). Law enforcement officers in public schools: student citizens in safe havens? *Brigham Young University Education and Law Journal,* (*winter*), 25–69.

Tinker v. Des Moines Independent Community School District, 393 U.S. 503 (1969).

Torres, M.S. & Stefkovich, J.A. (2009). Demographics and police involvement: Implications for student civil liberties and just leadership. *Educational Administration Quarterly, 45*(3), 450–473.

U.S. v. Lopez, 514 U.S. 549 (1995).

Vernonia School District 47J v. Acton, 515 U.S. 646 (1995).

Warnick, B.R. (2009). Student speech rights and the special characteristics of the school environment. *Educational Researcher, 38*(3), 200–215.

Williams by Williams v. Ellington, 936 F.2d. 881 (6th Cir. 1991).

Youngs, B.B. (1989). The phoenix curriculum. *Educational Leadership, 46*(5), 23–24.

Chapter 11

Technology versus Respect

Angela Duncan Montgomery, Dipali Puri,
Christopher S. Weiler, Jason Rosenbaum, and Amy Lavin

The use of technology has grown exponentially in recent years, bringing with it many advances to society, and enhancing the ways in which we learn. It has also spawned new concerns as well as exacerbated old problems, especially those related to the purposes of schooling, which include treating individuals with dignity and teaching respect for others.

Rapidly advancing technology has added to problems affecting the entire school community with issues of cyberbullying, social networking websites, and cell phones with instant messaging, texting, and digital photo-sharing capabilities. Mental, emotional, and physical difficulties associated with unwanted exposure to the public, diminution of privacy, public shaming, sexting, and cyberbullying can result in loss of confidence, depression, anxiety, eating disorders, and sometimes suicide.

Moreover, these issues have reached international significance with researchers, scholars, scientists, social scientists and practicing educators throughout the world asking important questions regarding the ramifications of these rapid changes and searching for solutions. For example, Aziz & Mohamad Amin (2020), who compared approaches to cyberbullying in Malaysia and New Zealand, found that Malaysia took a more legalist, punitive strategy while New Zealand involved a family-centered restorative justice approach recommended by the United Nations. The authors encouraged Malaysia and others to adopt New Zealand's model.

Bhat, Ragan, Selvaraj, & Shultz (2017) conducted quantitative research on cyberbullying in India and recommended preventative approaches and additional counselors and psychologists who could focus on these issues. They also suggested further research including qualitative studies that would examine the nuances of gender and cultural difference of cyberbullying between males and females in India.

DOI: 10.4324/9781003022862-13

Shaheen Shariff (2009, 2015), a Canadian researcher who has written extensively on topics related to technology, is one of many scholars (Gorman & Pauken, 2003; Noddings, 1992, 2013; Starratt, 2003; Stefkovich, 2006, 2014; Stefkovich, Crawford, & Murphy, 2009; Stefkovich & Frick, 2021; Willard, 2000) who sees a moral dilemma beyond the legal dimensions. In her first book on cyberbullying, Shariff describes this challenge for educators and policy makers:

> Maintaining civilization and civil behavior is difficult enough in organized society, even when the rule of traditional law is supposed to prevail and order and authority exist to protect innocent citizens. What happens when traditional rules and the authority are removed? This is the dilemma that schools confront as they attempt to navigate the legal and moral challenges around responding to cyber-bullying [sic] and, ultimately, developing in students appropriate moral compasses for an electronic age. (Shariff, 2009, pp. 2–3)

Finally, legal scholars (Decker, 2014; Eckes, DeMitchell, & Fossey, 2018; DeMitchell, Eckes & Fossey, 2009; MacKenzie, 2016) warn us that teachers' off-duty conduct can easily be exposed through the internet leading sometimes to disastrous consequences for the teachers, administrators, and students. Accordingly, Decker (2014) asserts that schools have legal ways of dealing with teacher misconduct other than instituting strict policies that would deprive them of their First Amendment rights. Such occurrences are evidenced in this chapter's first two cases.

The five scenarios in this chapter address issues that few educational leaders could have anticipated in earlier times. In Case Study 11.1, **After-school Antics**, the leader of a small elementary school attempts to build a cooperative spirit among her staff through professional development. Unfortunately, the new positive relationship extends into "happy hour." On Facebook, a parent in this tight-knit community sees photos of her child's teacher having far too good a time at a local bar. How does the principal deal with a team spirit that moves beyond her teachers' professional codes and into their personal lives?

Case Study 11.2, **All's Fair in Love and School**, concerns a teacher's private life that inadvertently, and suddenly, becomes public. In this dilemma, a young, very popular teacher who has done much for the school in his five years of employment now finds his job in jeopardy after private information is discovered on his cell phone. In this instance, the cell phone dropped out of his pocket as he left the classroom to gather up some papers he had left in the teachers' room. Class had not yet begun but the students had started to arrive. One student found the cell phone, looked inside, and discovered private pictures, which he then shared with other students, revealing the teacher's sexual orientation, an event that caused the teacher to lose control of his class and ultimately affected his teaching, as students and parents alike complained not about the teacher's sexual orientation but about the disruption in the classroom.

Cyberbullying in the Middle, Case Study 11.3, adds a twist to traditional bullying problems as the bullying is done on the internet. This dilemma involves Sam Walsh, a middle-school student who is being harassed by Babe-ah-licious555, an anonymous person who says she is in one of his classes. This student taunts Sam and then takes the humiliation to a public level by photographing and recording him in embarrassing situations and then broadcasting this information and her unkind e-mails to other students in school.

In Case Study 11.4, **School Discipline, Criminal Complaint, or Compassionate Intervention?**, sexting, i.e., the transmission of sexually explicit photos by telephone, is the focus of this dilemma. In this scenario, a middle-school student sends this information in response to what he construes as a dare on the part of a female classmate. Now, the school principal finds herself embroiled in issues of school discipline, morality, and possible violation of child pornography laws.

The last case study in this chapter (11.5), **Gaming Etiquette or Virtual Bullying?**, illustrates how something as seemingly innocent as playing games on the internet can turn into a competitive situation that involves possible harassment, bullying, and disclosure of secretly recorded videos, demonstrating a profound disrespect for an already marginalized student.

CASE STUDY 11.1 AFTER-SCHOOL ANTICS

Dana Hajjar smiled as she left her teachers' lounge. The joys of working in a small school again, she thought to herself as she took the long way back to her office. She enjoyed the happy hum of the hallways on a Monday morning. She had been the principal at several much larger schools in recent years and was starting to remember why she liked leading small schools so much. The people and camaraderie just felt different than at a bigger school. This kind of family atmosphere made it so much easier for everyone to work together as a team. Dana had realized long ago that the key to a happy school often rested in the ability of the staff to get along with one another and to work as a cohesive unit. She prided herself on her ability to always work hard at creating those relationships.

When she started as the new principal of Phelps Elementary at the beginning of the school year, she had gone about the task of implementing numerous social activities and team-building exercises. At first, the staff seemed resistant. Most of them had worked there for several years together and thought that all these "getting to know one another," touchy-feely activities were ridiculous, especially coming from an "outsider from the big city." But slowly, spearheaded by the cooperation and extra efforts of veteran teacher Mr. Kang, the staff was starting to come around. Dana was thankful that Mr. Kang was on board. It was making her job much easier.

One Friday each month, Dana had implemented a professional development workday, in which students had the day off and the staff could spend the day grading, planning units as teams, and working together on projects. Afterward, it seemed that Mr. Kang had instituted a Friday night happy hour at a local restaurant and bar. These evenings were starting to become big staff events, and for that Dana could not have been happier. Even on Fridays without professional development days, members of staff were going out together regularly, enjoying their off-time and beginning to truly become friends.

These friendships were starting to be reflected in the school day. The curriculum was getting stronger, and the teachers were beginning to depend on one another for advice, critique, and collaboration. Dana knew that with so few employees at the school, it was very easy for the staff dynamic to go one of two ways: not getting along at all or being very tightknit. As Dana left the teachers' lounge that morning, watching teachers work together on lesson plans and laugh about Friday night's happy-hour antics, she realized that it had become the latter—she had a tight-knit staff who were getting along quite well and whose work was reflecting this new-found sense of teamwork. She couldn't have been more satisfied.

The smile slowly faded from her face as Dana reached the office and heard the parent of one of her second graders yelling at the office secretary. "What kind of school is she running here? That kind of stuff might fly in her big city, but it is not going to happen in this community!" Slowly, anxiously, Dana entered the office.

"Mrs. Sampson. Hello there. What can I help you with this morning?"

"It's about time you showed up! What do you intend to do about my Jimmy's teacher's ridiculous behavior this weekend?"

Dana was dumbfounded. "Why don't you come into my office, Mrs. Sampson, and we can talk about this."

Mrs. Sampson was one of the most active parents in the community. She had four children come through this elementary school. Her two oldest children had been in Mr. Kang's class, as was her current fifth grader Frankie. Her youngest son, Jimmy, was in Gertrude Voortmann's second-grade class. She had been supportive of the school, and Dana had always had positive interactions with her. This behavior was very uncharacteristic. Visibly angry, Mrs. Sampson stormed into Dana's office.

"Do you know what your teachers did this weekend, Ms. Hajjar? Because I do."

"I'm afraid you've lost me. I know that some of them went out to dinner on Friday night, but I wasn't there for that. I heard they had a nice time."

"Ha! It was a little more than dinner don't you think? So, I assume you haven't seen the photos they took?"

Dana shook her head: "No."

"You really should keep better track of your teachers," mumbled Mrs. Sampson under her breath, as she shook her head incredulously.

Dana was trying to keep up, but couldn't figure out where Mrs. Sampson was going, and she didn't like any of the implications of Mrs. Sampson's questions. True, she didn't typically know what her teachers did on the weekends and, quite frankly, Dana didn't really feel like it was her business. They needed their downtime, and they were entitled to it. But then, thought Dana, if their behaviors were causing this kind of parental uproar, maybe she should be better connected to what was going on.

The longer she sat there, the more frustrated Dana became with Mrs. Sampson's questions and tone. She didn't appreciate Mrs. Sampson's assumption that she was in the dark about issues with her staff. "I'm close to my staff, right?" Dana asked herself. She had a growing sense of unease and suddenly felt completely out of the loop. Starting to become irritated, she replied, "Photos? Of what? Where did you see photos, Mrs. Sampson?"

Mrs. Sampson smirked. "You obviously don't have a Facebook account, do you Ms. Hajjar? May I use your computer for a moment?"

Dana stepped away from the desk long enough to let Mrs. Sampson log on to her Facebook account. Mrs. Sampson was right; Dana had never gotten around to joining this "Facebook." She had heard plenty of things about it, including both positive and negative stories in the news and from friends. It seemed mostly like a student yearbook program that she wasn't really interested in being a part of. She was starting to wonder if she should be. She watched as Mrs. Sampson pulled up her Facebook homepage and then her "friend list." To Dana's surprise, Mr. Kang was on Mrs. Sampson's friend list. It sort of made sense, she supposed. They lived on the same side of town. He had had Mrs. Sampson's two oldest children in class and now had Frankie. She guessed that they could be considered "friends."

Mrs. Sampson clicked on to Mr. Kang's homepage. There, on his page, was posted a brand-new photo album entitled "After-school Antics: Ms. Hajjar's Mandatory Fun." Dana exhaled and the blood rushed to her cheeks. This was not right: mandatory fun? Was that what he really thought of it? Dana considered Mr. Kang to be an ally. Now it seemed he was making fun of her.

As Mrs. Sampson scrolled through the pictures in Mr. Kang's photo album, Dana saw that many of them seemed harmless enough, friendly teachers smiling together, having dinner, laughing . . . possibly karaoke? And then, as the evening progressed, so did the photos in the album, until finally Mrs. Sampson rested on the picture that had put her in such a state. There, in the background of a picture of Mr. Kang and his wife, was Ms. Voortmann, her son's second-grade teacher, sitting on top of a table, drinking a shot of what looked like tequila.

"And what do you plan to do about that? My son's second-grade teacher is an alcoholic. And doing this in public! Is this how you promote togetherness in your staff? Mandatory drunkenness? Maybe that was fine when you were in your big city schools, but here, we take our teachers a little more seriously. They are supposed to be role models for our children, aren't they?"

Dana was speechless. This was not the kind of team building that she was supporting, was it? She guessed she never really asked questions, and happy hour does imply alcohol, doesn't it? But no, this is not what she meant, and they knew better. "I appreciate you bringing this to my attention Mrs. Sampson. I will . . . get on it."

"I should hope so. This is not acceptable behavior, Ms. Hajjar. And I will not let my son be in a class with a woman like this. She obviously has very little control over herself, so I can imagine how irresponsible she must be with a room full of second graders."

Dana seemed finally to calm Mrs. Sampson down with her promise to take care of things, but as she escorted the parent from her office, Dana realized that she had no idea how to fulfill that promise. Gertrude Voortmann was an outstanding educator and an asset to the school. From the little she could tell, Ms. Voortmann didn't even have a Facebook page of her own, and certainly didn't post this picture herself. She wondered if Ms. Voortmann even knew the picture had been posted or, for that matter, had been taken. And Mr. Kang . . . how surprising this was from him! She would have thought he would have known better. As the bell rang signaling the end of the first period of study, she knew she would have to do something, and do something quickly.

Ms. Hajjar suddenly remembered the double-edged sword of working in a small community school. Just as she had been lauding it early that morning, she now realized that the power of the small, close-knit community was going to work against her. This information would make its way through the parent circuit within hours, and the school community even quicker. Time was of the essence.

Questions for Discussion

1. If you were Ms. Hajjar, what would be your first move? Analyze this first move based on the paradigms of justice, care, critique, and the profession for each of the players.

2. Does Ms. Hajjar have the right to talk to Mr. Kang about the pictures he posted on his private Facebook page? Does Ms. Hajjar have the right to ask Mr. Kang to remove pictures from his private website? Does Ms. Hajjar have the right to ask Mr. Kang not to be a "friend" of parents of current students? What recourse does Ms. Hajjar have if Mr. Kang refuses? What happens to allegiances and staff morale if Mr. Kang complies, but then suddenly becomes a vocal opponent of Ms. Hajjar?

3. What are the implications for Gertrude Voortmann? What happens if she didn't realize the picture was being taken and is horrified? Or conversely if she knows and doesn't care—claims that she was at a restaurant on her off-time away from children having a drink and sees nothing wrong with her behavior, the picture, or the posting?

4. Consider the ethic of community as it pertains to this scenario. Can you see the scenario playing out differently in a large city school? If you were Ms. Hajjar, would you handle it differently based on your location? How?

5. Ms. Hajjar stated that she didn't see it as her responsibility to monitor her teachers' behaviors in their off time. Do you agree or disagree with this statement?

CASE STUDY 11.2 ALL'S FAIR IN LOVE AND SCHOOL

Dr. Meena Patel anxiously turned the key in the ignition of her car as she mentally arranged what she was going to say to her school board that evening. She had been principal at Crest Ridge High School for the past ten years and, before that, had taught tenth-grade social studies for 12 years, specifically United States history, a subject near and dear to her heart. Dr. Patel enjoyed her administrative position immensely because she was able to make a real difference in the lives of students, parents, and faculty. Now, she was starting to have second thoughts.

Over the years, her high school, Crest Ridge, had struggled to meet academic standards and maintain a satisfactory level of educational excellence. The mission of Crest Ridge High School was to "provide students with an excellent education while helping each and every child realize his or her full potential to become a productive and responsible citizen and lifelong learner." The school, even though located in a small, rural community, had a diverse faculty and staff which paralleled the diversity that existed among the students. Dr. Patel had worked hard to increase the level of teacher quality in the school by reducing the high teacher turnover rate and attracting new high-quality faculty members who were passionate about teaching. As a result, student achievement had improved dramatically.

With both pride and a profound sense of sadness, Dr. Patel reflected on one of her most impressive hires, now the center of the turmoil she must address that evening. Over the past five years since his hire, David Wilson had gained a reputation among the faculty as a dedicated and well-respected ninth-grade social studies teacher. Beloved by all his students, he was one of the most popular teachers at Crest Ridge. He was known as the teacher who not only challenged and pushed his students academically but also treated them with respect and kindness.

Mr. Wilson had been instrumental in making changes in the curriculum, spearheading the department committee, and taking on various leadership positions within the school. He designed, developed, and piloted an after-school "Literacy for All" program, for which he had recently gained substantial state funding, thus providing desperately needed resources for students in need of extra help with their academic studies. He had also started an intramural basketball program to provide students with a safe, non-academic activity they could enjoy after school.

As a teacher, Mr. Wilson was approachable—always willing to talk to and listen to his students. Despite his open-door policy with students, he liked to keep his own life private including his personal relationships. All the other teachers knew he was single and were constantly trying to "set him up" with one of their friends or relatives. He always declined, stating he believed that it was important to keep his professional life separate from his personal life. This only strengthened people's admiration of his dedication to his profession.

The problems began with a single incident several weeks earlier. As usual, Mr. Wilson was at work early and, that day, was getting ready for first period. As he was making a final check of any text messages or voicemails before complying with the mandatory "phones off while teaching" policy, he remembered that he had left copies of the social studies quiz he needed for his third period on the copying machine in the teachers' lounge. With a few minutes remaining before classes started, he rushed to get the copies as his first few students began trickling into class. In the teachers' lounge he realized that, in his haste, he had forgotten to turn off his phone. When he reached into his jacket pocket, he discovered that the phone was missing and realized that it must have dropped out of his pocket.

While Mr. Wilson was gone, one of his more outgoing students, Tyler, noticed a cell phone lying on the floor. He picked it up and flipped through it, both out of curiosity and to determine the owner. Tyler got much more than he expected. Shocked, he discovered several highly compromising pictures of Mr. Wilson and another man kissing. In the most explicit picture, they were on the beach, one sitting between the other's legs, leaning back and tilting his head up to kiss the other one. Both men had their shirts off so it appeared that they may have been completely nude. Tyler was stunned, not believing what he saw. Shock turned to anger and images of betrayal as Tyler thought back to the times Mr. Wilson had volunteered to privately tutor him and his friends and all the time spent in the locker room under Mr. Wilson's supervision for the after-school basketball program. As more students entered the room, Tyler decided to share his discovery with his classmates. They began passing the cell phone around so that everyone could see the pictures.

As Mr. Wilson walked back to the classroom he noticed quite a bit of commotion the closer he got. The students started whispering when he walked in and, while it seemed odd, he dismissed it as normal teenage drama. He then noticed the furtive glances they were shooting at Tyler and two students who were gathered around his desk. Tyler quickly flipped the cell phone shut as Mr. Wilson approached: "What is going on here? You need to be in your seats so we can start class. Tyler, what is that in your hand?"

Tyler said that he had found this cell phone on the floor. "OK, well, you know cell phones are not allowed in class," David Wilson calmly replied, hiding his impatience well. "Please put it on my desk."

Then Tyler said: "I wanted to see who it belonged to, so I opened it up to see. Turns out it's yours, Mr. Wilson." At that moment, Mr. Wilson realized that not only was the phone his, but it was obvious by his students' faces that they had all seen the pictures in his phone. He felt violated but knew that he had to address the issue immediately.

Deciding that it would be best to be direct and honest with his students, Mr. Wilson took the phone from Tyler and said calmly, "I understand that all of you must be curious about the pictures in my phone, but certain items are private, and I would like to keep it that way and not discuss my personal life." He put the phone in his desk drawer and then asked his students to return to their seats, take out their social studies books, and get ready for class to start. He really did not feel comfortable discussing his personal life with his students and hoped that his students would respect his right to privacy.

Despite his efforts to move on and put the incident behind him, the students in his class continued to carry on about the pictures on the cell phone and Mr. Wilson's sexual orientation. He had a difficult time keeping the students focused on social studies. Throughout the day, Mr. Wilson's students had become increasingly disruptive and frequently acted out. He finally gave up and called Dr. Patel to his classroom because he could no longer facilitate his lessons. The students had become either uneasy and distracted or angry and belligerent about the cell phone incident. He no longer had control and, as the weeks passed, the situation worsened.

Word of the incident spread quickly around the school and throughout the community. Dr. Patel started receiving phone calls from irate parents. Some reacted to the incident itself and a few went so far as to ask that their child be moved out of Mr. Wilson's class. The majority of complaints, however, came from parents who were truly concerned about their children's safety. Since the incident, Mr. Wilson had been unable to control discipline in his classes. Moreover, there were frequent disputes among the students in the class, with some who felt betrayed intimidating those who supported Mr. Wilson's need for privacy and his sexual orientation.

When she was called down to Mr. Wilson's room, Dr. Patel found a situation more serious than she could ever have imagined. She located a substitute teacher and asked Mr. Wilson to join her in her office. Mr. Wilson explained that he had wanted to keep his personal life private but, since the students had seen the picture, he had needed to address the issue. He then detailed what was said and the behavior he had had to deal with after he thought that he had taken care of the incident.

Dr. Patel believed that teachers have a right to privacy and should not be punished based on what they do in their personal lives, especially considering nothing illegal had occurred. She also knew that Mr. Wilson had a right not to be discriminated against based on his sexual orientation. Yet this incident had affected Mr. Wilson's teaching, and the lack of discipline in his classroom was starting to result in safety concerns. She was forced to admit to Mr. Wilson that she had no choice at that point but to put him on leave until the issue could be resolved. Now, with a sad heart, she dreaded the evening's board meeting.

Questions for Discussion

1. Did Dr. Patel make the right decision to put Mr. Wilson on leave? Based on the facts, do you think he had completely lost control or that the students were in danger?

2. As an educational leader, ensuring the safety of the students is important. At what point does a teacher lose his or her right to privacy when it comes to matters of safety?

3. Analyze this dilemma through the ethical lenses of justice, care, and critique. What decision would be in the best interests of the students?

4. What should be expected of Dr. Patel through the lens of the ethic of profession?

5. Discuss the conflicts between personal beliefs and professional ethics in this situation.

CASE STUDY 11.3 CYBERBULLYING IN THE MIDDLE

Dr. Jack Web, principal of Henry Mercer Middle School (HMMS), became involved in a situation three weeks earlier, following a call from a concerned father. Edward Walsh explained that both he and his wife, Rebecca, noticed that Sam, their recently turned 12-year-old, normally reserved, shy, and mild-mannered child, had been acting strangely for about a week. The Walshes had often worried about their sensitive son who frequently reported that he was "unpopular" in school. He was insecure about being overweight, unathletic, too smart, and loving to sing; "Being fat, smart, and in Glee Club," he remarked, "Does not make one popular." But he was a 'straight A' student, and to reward and encourage him, they gave him the birthday present he had been begging for, a new smart phone and tablet.

Soon after, Sam got his first pre-algebra grade of the second marking period, a 53%—a precipitous drop. His parents discussed taking his electronics away from him, but decided against it because he had worked so hard to earn it. However, on Sunday evening, right after Sam's electronic time (or E.T. as they all referred to it) ended, his parents heard him sobbing. They pleaded with him to explain but could only get out of him that he didn't want to go back to school, which wasn't an option they'd entertain. He would not stop crying, which prompted Mrs. Walsh to suggest that her husband check the parental controls set up to view Sam's electronic footprint.

When he did, Edward saw that Sam had been using expected apps—Facebook (for old folks, as Sam stated), Instagram (Insta), and TikTok (one of Sam's favorites), but also ones that hadn't been approved by his parents. They had specifically forbidden him to use Snapchat. And what on earth was Discord? Even the name sounded troublesome! As Edward later related to Dr. Web, he instinctively knew this was the root of the problem, but needed more information, so he returned to Sam's room.

After being presented with the evidence, Sam finally confided in his parents. It had started innocently enough; he had received a direct message (DM) on Insta from a person who identified themselves as a student in his pre-algebra class. The person did not use their real name, but the screen name, Babe-ah-licious555, was provocative enough to pique Sam's curiosity as to the person's real identity. The person had flirted with Sam, who was not yet ready for any of that. The mystery person's DMs grew more and more provocative, sexually explicit, and personal. Sam explained that he simply did not know how to handle the messages and didn't want to involve his parents for fear of losing his E.T. and being bullied even more at school.

Sam had been unable to find out Babe's true identity, but had repeatedly asked them to stop their online harassment. The scorned Babe assured

Sam that they would ruin his reputation at school by telling everyone he didn't "like girls," a point punctuated with a gay epithet. Sam felt distraught at the thought of being labeled by everyone at his school. "And," Sam cried, "Babe says they're in my pre-algebra class and I don't even know who it is!"

After relating the story, Edward asked Dr. Web to address the issue from within HMMS. Clearly, Sam was being victimized, which was distracting him and affecting his pre-algebra grade. He demanded that Dr. Web find the identity of Babe-ah-licious555 and ensure that the student would be properly punished through expulsion from school.

"Mr. Walsh," Dr. Web interjected, "I'm very sorry that Sam has gone through this. However, other than referring Sam to his counselor, I don't believe I can help you. The incident occurred outside school; I can't see how I have any jurisdiction. In fact, with the anonymity of the online world, we can't even be sure that this person is a girl, let alone a student at HMMS. I'm afraid I can't go on a hunt for the person's identity, and even if I found it, I can't suspend a student for things done outside of school." Edward had hung up the phone in frustration.

On reflection, three weeks later, Web wished he had been more involved in helping Sam and his family. He had been thinking about the issue in terms of all students. The faculty had recently brought the issue of cyberbullying to his attention and asked if they could create an acceptable use policy that extended to cyberbullying outside of school. Still, he had felt unprepared to act. Today, however, he wondered if he should have been more proactive. That morning, he had received a surprise visit from the Walsh family.

In the three weeks since Dr. Web had spoken with Edward, things had gotten worse. At first, all seemed better. Sam was more confident because he was no longer alone in the knowledge of Babe's DMs. He had thrown himself into practice for a musical, in which he was the male lead, and was making friends in the cast. In addition, he spoke to his pre-algebra teacher who allowed him to retake his last exam, which he passed with flying colors.

Everything changed, however, on the opening night of his play, when during his "big number" his voice, which had recently begun changing, cracked. Sam left the stage in a state of utter embarrassment, magnified because some of his classmates were in the audience. However, he forged on and seemingly forgot the incident until the next night when his parents granted permission for him to use his tablet to conduct research for a report he was working on in social studies.

When his mother left the kitchen, he clandestinely logged on to "Snap" for a pre-arranged meeting with a co-star, who unfortunately was not the first person to find him. Babe-ah-licious555 wasted no time in continuing the reign of terror over Sam.

"Thought you'd want to see this queer; I'm sending it to everybody at school!" said the message, accompanied by links to the video of Sam's voice crack on several other apps.

"No!" Sam yelled.

When Mrs. Walsh finally convinced Sam to let his parents watch the video, another message popped up on the screen.

"You've been flamed, fag!" it said.

The Walsh parents privately inspected Babe's unprotected Insta account, in which the first and only post was the offending video with about ten derogatory comments under the video from various other accounts, which commented on how poorly Sam dressed, slammed him for being fat, shamed him for lack of masculinity, and explicitly questioned his sexuality.

Sam had refused to attend school the next morning—and truthfully, they couldn't blame him. But his parents accompanied him to Dr. Web's office. Mrs. Walsh confided in Dr. Web that they had entertained the possibility of withdrawing Sam from the school but had decided against it on principle.

Dr. Web replied, "I'm glad. That seems a bit hasty, don't you think?"

Jarringly, Sam's father banged his fist on the desk and yelled, "Web, I asked you to help three weeks ago, and you refused. My son continues to be victimized beyond belief; you're not meeting his needs or keeping him safe. I have contacted a lawyer to discuss our rights in this situation. What do you intend to do? At the very least, this Babe-ah-licious555 has to be identified then punished."

The worst part for Dr. Web was the end of the conversation. Sam had looked him right in the eye and quietly begged, "You have to stop this, sir. You just have to. Please help me." Jack Web had no idea what to do next.

Questions for Discussion

1. In this situation, none of the bullying has actually occurred in the school. As such, do school officials have an ethical responsibility to get involved? Why or why not?

2. Through which ethical paradigms does Dr. Web seem to make his decisions? Has he demonstrated the ethics of care and the profession to Sam and his parents? If so, in what ways?

3. Does the responsibility of the school rest on whether or not the offender attends the school? What if the identity cannot be ascertained?

4. How can the school, through the ethics of justice, care, and profession, help its students develop a healthy online identity?

5. Although he is repeatedly labeled as gay, Sam's sexual identity is unknown. If Sam identified himself as a gay student, would that make a difference in how to deal with the situation? Why or why not? What is a school leader's responsibility to care for those whose identities come from a place of oppression/resistance? How might the ethic of critique come into play here?

CASE STUDY 11.4 SCHOOL DISCIPLINE, CRIMINAL COMPLAINT, OR COMPASSIONATE INTERVENTION?

In the office of her middle school, morning coffee still hot in her hand, Principal Rondell hung up the phone and stared blankly at Assistant Principal Park and said simply, "Please get Grace from class." Seeing her Principal's expression, Ms. Park asked no questions and returned a few minutes later with a confident eighth grader who could not quite hide the embarrassment and awkwardness she knew she was about to encounter.

Despite her twenty years in public education, and eight as principal of the school she and Ms. Park turned into the most sought-after middle school in this urban district, Principal Rondell was facing an old problem with new challenges. Social media is an established fact of life with her students, and she has grown accustomed to young students discovering how to navigate all its positive and negative uses. Often, it is the parents who struggle more than their children with making balanced judgements about how much supervision and control is needed, welcomed or possible when it comes to students on social media. As principal, she has grown accustomed to counselling students as well as parents about making safe and appropriate choices online. Aware of how such technology opens up delicate challenges to the district disciplinary code, she has managed to address those past instances through quiet conversations with students and parents about respect, privacy and the school's culture of personal responsibility.

The poised eighth grader stood opposite the table with Principal Rondell and Assistant Principal Park.

"Hi, Grace," the principal began. "I just got off the phone with your mother. You knew she was going to call?" Grace sat down and nodded almost invisibly. "Do you have your phone with the picture?" Grace nodded again as she handed over her phone. "Will Ms. Park be able to find the picture herself or do you have to open it for her?"

"I deleted all the others. You'll see it. It has the date and time it was received. But I don't think you really want to see it. I mean, it must be weird for you to see an eighth-grade boy naked."

Ms. Park held her breath for a moment as she finally realized what the situation entailed. She had navigated plenty of incidents about inappropriate postings on social media or messaging apps, but they weren't beyond the kinds of bullying that middle school students have engaged in forever, regardless of the tools and means to exercise social power.

"Don't worry, Grace," said Ms. Park, "I've dealt with enough bad behavior by schoolboys that you might be surprised what I've seen."

Grace looked up, stared Ms. Park straight in the eyes for a moment without speaking. She broke the silence in a low, exactingly clear voice, "I hope you haven't seen a student this way. Close up. Hard."

Ms. Park saw no way around having to see the picture that Bob, Grace's classmate had sent to her. Once the evidence had been confirmed and Grace told her side of the story, she was sent back to class, leaving the leadership team alone to form a plan of action. After she interviewed Bob, and another eighth grader, Rachel, the story seemed to come together quite clearly. No one was debating the actual events and how they unfolded.

The story matched what Grace's mother had explained on the phone. Two days earlier, Bob had made a sexually inappropriate comment to Grace while they were in art class which insinuated that she show him her breasts. Grace tried to deflect the comment with humor by responding flippantly, "Yeah, you first." That evening, Grace received on her phone a photo message from Bob of his erect penis.

Grace would later report being quite disturbed by this, but out of fear and anxiety had not at first told anyone about it. She discussed it the next day in school with her friend, Rachel, who convinced Grace to send her the photo that evening. Unknown to Grace, Rachel sent the photo to most of the eighth-grade class by the end of the next day. Upon discovering this, Grace was horrified and told her mother about the whole episode. The next morning, Grace's mother called Principal Rondell to see that Bob and Rachel's appalling behavior was appropriately addressed.

Ms. Rondell and Ms. Park had difficult decisions to make. These decisions were compounded by the fact that Grace's mother said that she was deciding whether to go to the police precinct to press criminal charges against Bob and Rachel. Ms. Rondell called a Department of Education attorney to discuss the possibility of criminal charges, and she confirmed that there is precedent for children being charged under child pornography laws for photographing and/or distributing nude photographs of themselves or friends. Grace's mother could file a complaint that would not necessarily involve the school. As far as school discipline was concerned, Rondell and Park tried to ascertain whose actions would fit various infractions, including sexual harassment. The situation was complicated by the fact that the picture was taken and sent outside of school and school hours and only with personal devices. They wondered if they were mistaken in even considering this a matter of school discipline.

Principal Rondell and Assistant Principal Park were convinced that they could, legally speaking, wipe their hands clean of the issue and tell Grace's mother that they have no authority over Bob's actions that were taken outside of school. However, they realized that saying that would likely push Grace's mother toward a criminal complaint and create an extremely serious situation for the two families. In addition, it would do nothing to address the fact that the entire eighth grade was now tangentially involved, and the situation might poison the positive school atmosphere that the two school leaders had worked so hard to build over the past eight years. Then again, wouldn't addressing the actions of these students confirm in some parents' minds that it was in fact a school-based disciplinary situation and thus force Rondell's hand at administering consequences?

Also, Principal Rondell and Assistant Principal Park were concerned about Bob's anti-social behavior and how rattled Grace had been. Bob's mother had only recently requested a referral for a full psychological evaluation, and Grace seemed unwilling to fully engage in what impact the episode has had on her. The school leaders were also thinking about how to leverage the situation to spark more courageous conversations with students, teachers, and parents about cyber safety.

Principal Rondell and Assistant Principal Park shut their office door and sat at their conference table to make difficult decisions before students, parents, teachers and possibly the police became further involved. Time was short. The phone would surely start ringing any minute with concerned parents, students are still in class with the picture on their phones, stories will be shared in the teachers' lounge, police may be getting called and the superintendent is bound to hear soon enough.

Questions for Discussion

1. Should Principal Rondell have left viewing the picture to Assistant Principal Park? Was Park obligated to see the picture as evidence?

2. Since the incident did not happen in school, should the Principal encourage Grace's mother to work things out directly with Bob's parents? How should the Principal respond if Grace's mother asks for advice on whether to report the incident to the Police?

3. How do Bob, Grace and Rachel's action compare from an ethical standpoint, being that they all sent the picture? How do they compare insofar as school discipline? Are all three subject to school punishments? How should the principal respond to accusations of one receiving more or less punishment than the other(s)?

4. If Grace's mother were president of the PTA, would it change the principal's response? Should it? What if the PTA president was one of Bob or Rachel's parents? What if Grace or Rachel had a history of suspensions due to bad behavior, and Bob was a popular, straight "A" student? And vice versa?

5. What advice would you give the school leaders? What would be in the best interests of the students while also balancing the school leaders' professional and legal ethics?

CASE STUDY 11.5 GAMING ETIQUETTE OR VIRTUAL BULLYING?

Principal Smith was well versed in the topic of bullying and committed to providing students a safe place to learn. Throughout her career as a teacher and an administrator, she had worked to prevent bullying in her school environment and developed several anti-bullying educational materials and campaigns for Fairweather Middle School. She had done quite a bit of research on what is a violation of free speech when the students' actions may take place after school hours or off campus.

She was well aware that if the actions took place off campus or after hours and the school attempted to address it, they could potentially be sued for exceeding their authority or violating the students' freedom of speech. That said, she formed the school committee that created the off-campus clause in the school's acceptable use policy. This provision would enable school administrators to address possible acts of bullying among their students regardless of where and when the potential bullying took place. It should also be noted that Fairweather had a zero-tolerance policy when it came to bullying, with acts being punished with expulsion from the school.

Principal Smith felt confident in her knowledge on bullying, so she was completely taken aback at the situation that the assistant vice principal, Mr. Johnson, brought to her attention. Earlier that day, Mr. Johnson had been approached by Tom, a seventh-grade student. Tom was very good friends with Steve and Ryan who were characteristically good students, though they did seem to get in some trouble now and again. Apparently, a few weeks ago, Steve, Ryan, and Tom were playing some online, chat-based video games against some of their other classmates. While they were online, they created a request, to Patrick, another of their classmates. Patrick accepted the request and the boys continued playing the game against each other.

During the course of the gameplay, it was apparent that Patrick was very good at the game. He was definitely in a "virtual" position of power—which is something he never experienced within the classroom. Patrick was typically one of the shy, quiet students who kept to himself. Steve and Ryan, who were not used to being displaced by Patrick, began saying things to Patrick such as: "You may be good at this game, but you are a loser in school" and "You might as well just stay home tomorrow—even though you can beat us in this game, we will beat you up for real the next time we see you."

While all of this was going on, Tom was using the recording device on his electronic tablet to record what the boys were saying to Patrick. He recorded about 5 minutes' worth of dialogue between Steve and Ryan and the comments that they were making to Patrick. Steve and Ryan had no idea that they were being videoed during this time. Tom thought it might be funny to share the video later to get a rise out of Patrick. Eventually, Patrick beat Steve and Ryan in the virtual game and the session ended.

Patrick was absent from school for the next few days. Feeling guilty about the comments that were made by his friends and thinking that perhaps this was what was driving Patrick's absence, Tom brought the video to Mr. Johnson and showed him what happened. He felt that reporting the bullying was the right thing to do. Mr. Johnson now had proof that Patrick had been bullied by Steve and Ryan but was hesitant to use the video since it was taken without the boys' knowledge. He also wondered whether he should include Tom as one of the bullies since he was with Steve and Ryan during the occurrence. Finally, at this point, he had not heard from Patrick's parents as to why he was absent and was deciding whether he should reach out to them and try to get information or just let things settle and see what happened. Perhaps his absence was simply a coincidence.

Mr. Johnson discussed the situation with Principal Smith since she was so knowledgeable about the topics of bullying and the acceptable use policy of the school. Principal Smith was now faced with the dilemma of what to do with the students and the issues presented.

Questions for Discussion

1. What alternative actions might Principal Smith consider if she were coming from an ethic of justice? (Remember that justice also includes fairness.)
2. What elements of this dilemma lend themselves to a caring approach? An analysis using the ethic of critique?
3. What would the profession expect of Principal Smith?
4. What would you do if you were Mr. Johnson? Principal Smith? Why?

REFERENCES

Aziz, N., & Mohamad Amin, N. S. (2020). Cyberbullying among children: A cross jurisdictional perspective. *International Islamic University Malaysia Law Journal, 28* (S1), 325–349. Retrieved from https://doi.org/10.31436/iiumlj.v28i(S1).588

Bhat, C.S., Ragan, A., Selvaraj, P.R., & Shultz, B.J. (2017). Online bullying among high-school students in India. *International Journal for the Advancement of Counselling, 2017* (39), 112–124. DOI:10.1007/s10447-017-9286-y

DeMitchell, T.A., Eckes, S.E., & Fossey, R. (2009). Sexual orientation and the public school teacher. *Boston University Public Interest Law Journal, 19*, 65–79.

Decker, J.R. (2014). Facebook phobia! The misguided proliferation of restrictive social networking policies for school employees. *Northwestern Journal of Law and Social Policy, 9*(2), 163–205.

Eckes, S.E., DeMitchell, T.A., & Fossey, R. (2018). Teachers' careers up in smoke and viral: Off-duty conduct in modern times. *West's Education Law Reporter, 355*, 633–640.

Gorman, K. & Pauken, P. (2003). The ethics of zero tolerance. *Journal of Educational Administration, 41*(1), 24–36.

Noddings, N. (1992). *The challenge to care in schools: An alternative approach to education.* New York, NY: Teachers College Press.

Noddings, N. (2013). *Caring: A relational approach to ethics and moral education* (2nd ed.). Oakland, CA: University of California Press.

Shariff, S. (2009). *Confronting cyberbullying: What schools need to know to control misconduct and avoid legal consequences.* London, England: Cambridge University Press.

Shariff, S. (2015). *Sexting and cyberbullying.* London, England: Cambridge University Press.

Shariff, S. & Churchill, A. (Eds.). *Truths and myths of cyberbullying: International perspectives on stakeholder responsibility and children's safety.* New York, NY: Peter Lang.

Starratt, R.J. (2003). *Centering educational administration: Cultivating meaning, community, responsibility.* Mahwah, NJ: Lawrence Erlbaum Associates.

Stefkovich, J.A. (2006). *Best interests of the student: Applying ethical constructs to legal cases in education.* New York, NY: Routledge.

Stefkovich, J.A. (2014). *Best interests of the student: Applying ethical constructs to legal cases in education (2nd ed.).* New York, NY: Routledge.

Stefkovich, J.A. & Frick, W.C. (2021). *Best interests of the student: Applying ethical constructs to legal cases in education* (3rd ed.). New York, NY: Routledge.

Stefkovich, J.A., Crawford, E.R., & Murphy, M.P. (2009). Legal issues related to cyber-bullying [sic]. In S. Shariff & A. Churchill (Eds.), *Truths and myths of cyberbullying: International perspectives on stakeholder responsibility and children's safety* (pp. 139–158). New York: Peter Lang.

Willard, N. (2000). Legal and ethical issues related to the use of the internet in K-12 schools. *Brigham Young University Education and Law Journal, 2000*(2), 225–263.

TEACHING AS SCHOLARLY WORK

Part III is meant to assist anyone who might be teaching or who would like to teach ethics to educators. We begin by focusing on instructors, and in this particular case on ourselves as professors of ethics in educational leadership. We take the reader on a reflective journey. During this journey, we describe how we thought through our own personal and professional codes of ethics, and we reflect on the critical incidents in our lives that shaped our teaching. This self-reflective process helped us determine what readings we privileged in our classrooms. This section also deals with our approaches to teaching ethics, the issues we faced, the theoretical underpinnings behind our pedagogy, and the delivery systems we have used to impart knowledge in an internet era. In addition, we discuss the acceptance of our writings on ethical decision making internationally and why they seem to resonate so well abroad.

In this part of the book, we provide one model to illustrate the concept of scholarly teaching that was introduced by Boyer (1990), in the Carnegie Foundation's report, *Scholarship Reconsidered: Priorities of the Professoriate.* Through a form of self-reflection and peer review that we developed during a 27-year period, we began to define our teaching of ethics as scholarly work. In fact, some of our published writings on ethics contain sections where we speak of our pedagogy and what we have learned through self-reflection and peer review. This concept of teaching as scholarly work was introduced by Shulman (1997, 1999, 2008) and continued by Hutchings (1998, 2000, 2002; Hutchings, Huber & Ciccone, 2011) of The Carnegie Foundation for the Advancement of Teaching. It is a concept that we take seriously.

Part III also covers our experiences in teaching ethics to diverse educational practitioners in different ways. For example, Joan has used a hybrid

DOI: 10.4324/9781003022862-14

teaching format that included both on-line and in-person teaching and Jackie has taught professional development courses through distance learning, using interactive technology. With the emergence of a global pandemic, we discuss how we have come to believe that the ability to teach well on-line is essential for educators. Finally, we mention the translation of our book into Korean, and we discuss why this book, its conceptual framework, and ethical dilemmas have increasingly attracted an international audience.

REFERENCES

Boyer, E.L. (1990). *Scholarship reconsidered: Priorities of the professoriate.* San Francisco, CA: Jossey-Bass.

Hutchings, P. (1998). Building on progress. *AAHE Bulletin, 50*(6), 10–11.

Hutchings, P. (Ed.). (2000). *Opening lines: Approaches to the scholarship of teaching and learning.* Menlo Park, CA: Carnegie Foundation for the Advancement of Teaching.

Hutchings, P. (Ed.). (2002). *Ethics of inquiry: Issues in the scholarship of teaching and learning.* Menlo Park, CA: Carnegie Foundation for the Advancement of Teaching.

Hutchings, P., Huber, M.T., & Ciccone, A. (2011). *The scholarship of teaching and learning reconsidered: Institutional integration and impact.* San Francisco, CA: Jossey-Bass.

Shulman, L.S. (1997). The advancement of teaching. *AAHE Bulletin, 50*(1), 3–7.

Shulman, L.S. (1999). Taking learning seriously. *Change Magazine, 31*(4), 10–17.

Shulman, L.S. (2008). "Send me in, coach!" Ruminations on the ethics of mentoring in teaching and research. *The New Educator, 4*(3), 224–236.

Chapter 12

Ethics, Ourselves, and Our Pedagogy

Although scholars may recognize the importance of ethics for educational leaders, they have not yet been able to resolve how this subject can or should be taught. For example, should ethics be infused throughout the curriculum or should it be a discrete course? Alternatively, should both approaches be utilized? It should be noted that little research has been conducted on these questions (Beck & Murphy, 1994; Shapiro & Gross, 2017). Not only is there no consensus on how ethics should be taught, but also there is very little written about those who teach this discipline. As Starratt (1994a) wrote:

> We know precious little about how professors balance the academic ideal of rigorous scholarship with what might be called a core pastoral concern to nurture and challenge the ethical values and world view of their students. Furthermore, we know precious little about the attitudes, beliefs, and personal journeys of educators practicing in educational administration programs. (p. 100)

However, it is exciting to note that more and more writings, both nationally and internationally, are appearing in the areas of ethical educational leadership, moral leadership, and values and leadership (e.g., Arar et al., 2016; Bartels, et al., 2014; Bass, Cherkowski, Walker & Kutsyuruba, 2015; Bass, Frick & Young, 2018; Begley & Johansson, 2003; Berkovich & Eyal, 2018; Branson & Gross, 2014; Covaleskie, 2016; Duignan, 2007; Gurley & Dagley, 2020; Hammersley-Fletcher, 2015; Langlois & LaPointe, 2010; Mullen, 2017; Murphy, 2011, 2017; Shapira-Lishchinsky, 2018; Shapiro, 2015; Shapiro & Gross, 2013; Starratt, 2004, 2009; Stefkovich, 2014; Stefkovich & Frick, 2021; Vogel, 2012.)

DOI: 10.4324/9781003022862-15

THE TEACHING OF ETHICS: OUR PERSPECTIVES

In this age of division and uncertainty, with all the problems that confront us, we think it is extremely important for those of us carrying out instruction in ethics to have a sense of who we are and what we believe in both personally and professionally. In our case, we realized inasmuch as we ask our students to embark on difficult soul-searching assignments, such as developing their own personal and professional codes, it is important that we do the same.

Furthermore, as two professors who taught basically the same content in an ethics course in different academic years to similar educational leadership doctoral cohort groups, we feel that such exploration may have profound effects, enabling us to compare and contrast how we teach such a course and why we choose to teach it in the ways we do.

We tend to believe what Witherell and Noddings (1991) have written: "To educate is to take seriously both the quest for life's meaning and the meaning of individual lives" (p. 3). We have been affected by the works of Beck (1994), Belenky et al. (1986), Brasof (2015), Gilligan (1982), Gilligan, Ward, and Taylor (1988), Ginsberg, Shapiro, and Brown (2004), Mitra (2018), Noddings (1992, 2002, 2003, 2012, 2013), Shapiro and Smith-Rosenberg (1989), and others who have stressed the importance of developing a voice, and have come to realize that life stories and personal experiences can be powerful. Such stories can help determine who we are today both personally and professionally.

We have also been affected by the work of Bakhtin (1981), Buber (1965), Freire (1970, 1993, 1998), Giroux (2020), Kohlberg (1981), McLaren (2020), Purpel (1989, 2004), and others in their quest for dialogue and knowledge of "self" in relation to others. Difficult dialogue leading to self-disclosure can be a most trying process, but it can also assist us in making our hidden ethical codes explicit. Furthermore, it can take what might be deemed a selfish process of focusing on the "self" and use it to serve and care for others by helping them find their voices and their values.

Before we discuss our course and its pedagogical implications in more detail, we would like to spend a little time providing an overview of our backgrounds and a few critical incidents that have shaped our lives. After considerable reflection, we believe that these stories have led to the development of both our personal and professional ethical codes. We also believe that such self-disclosures are needed to assist us in a better understanding of our pedagogical approaches and how we influence our students (Stefkovich & Shapiro, 1994).

THE PROFESSORS' STORIES

On the surface, the two of us seem to be quite similar. We are both White females; we are both from the North Eastern seaboard; we both have doctoral degrees in educational administration from Ivy League institutions; and we are both middle class and about the same age. However, that is as far as our similarities go.

In fact, we are very different individuals. Part of the difference is explained in our education and professional preparation, but this formal education and its socialization does not tell enough. Our stories and the critical incidents within them have tended to shape who we are. We have chosen parts of our lives that we feel have had an impact on how we came to approach the same ethics course in different ways. Rather than pretend that we came to the course with open minds, we think it is important to indicate some of the experiences and perspectives we brought with us.

Joan's Story

When I reflect on my own personal ethical code, I know that I have been shaped by my religious roots as a Jew, and by the area where I grew up, in the North Eastern part of the United States, which stressed the Puritan work ethic and a form of Social Darwinism in which individual hard work and competition were thought to be healthy values. The notion seemed clear at that time, growing up as a middle-class child in Connecticut, that we all had opportunity, if only we worked hard.

However, I know that my code of values and ethics has been deeply shaped by the years I spent in college—a time when the Civil Rights Movement was growing. While in college, I gave considerable thought to the concept of discrimination, and I remember many a holiday having verbal battles with my parents about the Civil Rights Movement and civil disobedience. In fact, soon after graduation, during my honeymoon, my 18-year-old British brother-in-law accompanied my husband and myself in singing peace and Civil Rights songs. The three of us were so keen that we were the only Whites attending a rally in Washington, D.C., at which Martin Luther King Jr. spoke. My family and friends thought that I had had a very strange honeymoon indeed.

My ethical code was also shaped by teaching British history in London, England for a few years to working-class children who had little chance to advance because they had not passed the 11+ exam, a high stakes test that determined if they were university material or not at the tender age of 11 or so. I taught in a secondary modern girls' school composed of students who were either from working-class, White, Anglo-Saxon families or from working-class families of color from diverse Commonwealth countries. The options for students in this school were generally to become hairdressers, shop assistants, or, at best, secretaries in the high street nearby. Even when we "went comprehensive" under the Labour government, a tracking system prohibited my students from having opportunities to move toward higher education. In England's secondary schools, I saw injustices based primarily on the intersection of social class with race, ethnicity, or both.

Some years later, I returned to the United Kingdom to spend a post-doctoral year at the University of London's Institute of Education. There I was exposed to the rich tradition of the philosophy of education that seemed to permeate all my studies. The philosophical works of Peters (1973) and Hirst (1974), for example, were held in high regard. Peters and Hirst were able to combine the liberal tradition of justice with more of an emotional and caring quality. Their respect for both the cognitive and affective domains had a positive effect on me.

Most importantly, beyond the formal classroom, during the four years I lived in the United Kingdom, I was impressed by British society's ability to combine socialism with the *noblesse oblige* spirit derived from the concept of chivalry in the Middle Ages. The government provided national health care, generous university grants for poor students, and welfare benefits that did not stigmatize people. Unlike many Americans schooled in Social Darwinism, I began to feel that society had an obligation to look after its people in appropriate ways, if at all possible, from the cradle to the grave.

Thus far in my life, my consciousness had been raised in the areas of religion, race, and social class, but it took a critical incident for me to focus on the category of gender discrimination. It was Uncle Max's funeral that was the turning point for me in the area of gender.

Uncle Max's funeral took place in the northern part of England, in which a very fundamentalist sect of Jews lived. When my husband and I arrived at Uncle Max's home, the women were moaning and wailing around a hearse that waited outside the door. This seemed strange to me because Uncle Max was well into his eighties and had not suffered unduly before his death. Accompanied by my husband, I went to the burial grounds for the ceremony. At the grounds, much to my surprise, I turned out to be the only woman present and was told not to leave the car. Apparently, women were not allowed on the burial grounds lest they "sully the soil."

This was a painful experience for me. I had only recently buried my father in the conservative Jewish tradition, and my mother, sister, and I had been free to mourn publicly and on the cemetery grounds. It seemed to me that the humiliation for women continued that day when the Rabbi told Auntie Minnie, Uncle Max's wife of 55 years, that she missed an excellent speech he had given dedicated to her husband on the burial grounds.

All the women around me seemed to accept, without comment, what I perceived to be an insult, but I was never the same. Gender became an overriding category of difference and discrimination in my life, making me into a feminist.

Seven years of co-directing a women's studies program at the University of Pennsylvania continued to raise my consciousness toward injustices—not just in the area of sexism but also in the realms of race, ethnicity, social class, sexual orientation, and disability. In reflecting on patriarchy, power, and hierarchy, I began to realize the great impact of society and how it can manage to keep diverse groups in their place. Dealing with issues of oppression, victimization, and difference, I began to understand how groups have been socially constructed by those in power and the effect of that construction on individuals within the group. Collectivity, social responsibility, and care of others were concepts that struck a chord with me, moving me away from "rugged individualism" and Social Darwinism. Thanks to studying feminist scholarship, I began to question abstract justice, rights, and law.

My background, the numerous critical incidents in my life, the years I spent in England and in the area of women's studies, led me to focus heavily on the underdog in society. I seem to care deeply about injustices of all kinds. I ask constantly: Who has been omitted? Whose voice is missing? Whose ethical values am I privileging? Whose ethical values is society privileging? I often think about the good of the whole community as well as the good of different groups within the community.

However, my code of ethics, I now realize, is not simplistic. On issues related to one's body and one's life, I am very much committed to individual liberty and privacy. Thus, in all cases, I do not disdain the rights of the individual. I am, then, a situational ethicist, who leans toward a belief in our need to have a moral commitment beyond self toward those less fortunate and those who are different from us—toward the concepts of social justice and social responsibility.

Privilege

> Leaders need to be deeply reflective, actively thoughtful, and dramatically explicit about their core values and beliefs. (Bolman & Deal, 1991, p. 449)

Initially, I tried to make certain that the graduate students in my course had some introduction to traditional ethics. I provided an overview of the major Western thinkers in the field, focusing on utilitarianism, consequentialist and non-consequentialist theory, and basic liberal tenets of Western philosophy based on individual rights.

The language of rights was further discussed as we sorted out moral dilemmas raised by Strike, Haller, and Soltis (1988), and I asked the students to use the step-by-step process advocated in their book. This process moved from case presentation, to the establishment of the dispute, to the setting forth of different arguments, and finally to resolving the dilemma. Although the aforementioned framework was used, I spent considerable time critiquing the arguments put forth within it. It seemed to me important for students to see that a basic text was not the gospel and that there were other approaches that could be used to answer the dilemmas discussed in the book. In many ways, I sought to raise questions that would challenge the liberal democratic philosophy espoused in this text.

Although I did not leave out the language of rights, justice, and law, I had my students listen to other voices and turn to the language of critique and possibilities as well as the language of care, concern, and connectedness over time. These models of ethics were presented by non-traditional ethicists.

In particular, to introduce the students to diverse paradigms, I spent considerable time in class focusing on the work of Purpel. In his book, *The Moral and Spiritual Crisis in Education,* Purpel (1989) described a complex form of ethics that made an excellent bridge from traditional to non-traditional ethics. Purpel himself indicated that he borrowed from "two ancient traditions, the Socratic and the Prophetic and two theological movements: Liberation Theology and Creation Theology" (p. xi). This mix enabled students to move from liberal democratic ethics focused on law and justice to areas of social justice and compassion.

Throughout his work, Purpel challenges us to deal with the complexities and the contradictions of the modern world and leave behind any simplistic notions of right and wrong or good and bad. He introduces important paradoxes, and, in so doing, highlights areas of miscommunication that frequently lead to misunderstandings. These paradoxes include concepts of control versus democracy, individuality versus community, worth versus achievement, equality versus competition, and compassion versus sentimentality. These paradoxes are maintained by society and they trickle down to our schools. Although Purpel does not classify himself as a critical theorist, he does set the stage for those who challenge the current system, and he makes us reflect on the important concepts of democracy, social justice, privilege, and power as they relate to schooling. Through Purpel's work, I was able to turn to the writings of critical theorists as I felt that the class and I were ready to discuss the writings of Giroux (1991, 1992, 1994) who not only challenged the system, but also offered promise through the concept of "the language of possibilities."

Under the concept of the language of possibilities, a number of critical theorists recommend activism and social change. Collective effort, learning through service, and local involvement—what Welch (1991) might call working toward solidarity within one's own community—are parts of the message. In many ways, Purpel, as well as the critical theorists, moves away from the remote, neutral, seemingly objective discussions of rights, law, and justice that tend to be ethical arguments of the traditional liberal democracies and towards the inclusion of feeling, emotion, and compassion in ethics.

Other non-traditional education ethicists I privileged in my teaching were feminist ethicists. To illustrate feminist ethics, I turned primarily to the works of Gilligan (1982; Gilligan, Ward, & Taylor, 1988) and to a study (Shapiro & Smith-Rosenberg, 1989) carried out when my colleague, Carroll Smith-Rosenberg, and I taught a women's studies ethics course. Prior to examining the works of feminist ethicists—in particular, Gilligan—I spent time discussing the writings of Kohlberg. I discussed Kohlberg's (1981) ground-breaking work based on an analysis of 84 children's (boys') responses to moral dilemmas over a 20-year period and his design of six stages of moral development.

Although I admire Kohlberg's work, I tended to use his scholarship as a way to introduce Gilligan and her inclusion of girls into the moral development stage theory. I then turned to Gilligan as a scholar who was able to critique Kohlberg's stage theory. In so doing, she revealed responses not taken into account by Kohlberg. She introduced us to the voice of concern, connectedness, relatedness over time, and caring. She felt this voice to be important and yet, in Kohlberg's stage theory, it was invisible—hence, many girls and boys who were caring young people often received low scores using his stages.

Gilligan's critique and the work of scholars such as Noddings (1984, 1992), Belenky et al. (1986), and others made me aware that all voices need not be categorized in traditional ethical ways focusing on justice, law, and rights. There are indeed other voices that are important in this society and should be valued. My own experiences in the three years I taught ethics to undergraduates with Carroll Smith-Rosenberg led me to believe that what Gilligan and Noddings had written had meaning.

Furthermore, in Shapiro and Smith-Rosenberg (1989), we discovered in our own classes many illustrations of alternative ethical thinking. We were able to give examples of students' approaches to solving moral dilemmas through their writings in journals that showed how powerful the voice of care, concern, and connectedness was within our women's studies classroom.

On reflection, then, it seems clear to me that I tended to privilege the voice of critique and possibilities and the voice of care, concern, and connectedness over the voice of abstract rights, law, and justice. Nevertheless, it also became clear that although most of the graduate students could hear all these voices, some could not. This proved to be somewhat disappointing. However, judging from the course evaluations, the journal entries, the personal and professional codes, the ethical dilemmas, and the comments in and out of class, overall, I noted that most of the graduate students were able to at least stand back and reflect on the concepts of the "rugged individual," individual rights, and abstract justice that previously many of them accepted, without question, as the best principles for our current society.

Owing to terrorism, wars, and financial instability, Steven Jay Gross, now an Emeritus Professor of Educational Leadership from Temple University, and I began to explore links between the Multiple Ethical Paradigms, that Jackie and I developed, and Steve's model of Turbulence Theory (Gross, 1998, 2004, 2006, 2014, 2020). This theory, using the pilot's metaphor of light, moderate, severe, and extreme turbulence, worked well with the paradigms in an educational setting. Too often, school administrators did not consider the emotional level in their building. Using a turbulence gauge, an educational leader could bring the level down if there were a lot of chaos in the school and move it upwards if the staff was too complacent. As Steve and I talked, we realized that his theory and Jackie's and my paradigms worked well together. As a result of this interesting combination, Steve and I published two editions of the book, *Ethical Educational Leadership in Turbulent Times: (Re)Solving Moral Dilemmas* (Shapiro & Gross, 2008, 2013), combining Turbulence Theory and the Multiple Ethical Paradigms with authentic ethical dilemmas from the field.

Beyond work on turbulence and ethics, Steve and I created an educational community network. It all began when Steve called me in the summer of 2004 because he was upset with the constant focus on high stakes testing and accountability in the U.S. educational system. Steve wanted much more emphasis on democracy in the hopes of creating an educated citizenry. I agreed with the need for a renewed emphasis on civics in schools and the importance of working with educational leaders in this area. However, I believed that there was also a need for ethics preparation for instructional leaders and for their students. He agreed with me.

Both of us admired FDR and Eleanor and decided to name our movement the New DEEL (Democratic Ethical Educational Leadership). With core values emanating from democracy and ethics, the New DEEL has attracted faculty from over 30 universities and colleges, and practitioners from Canada, England, Australia, Taiwan, Sweden, and Jamaica. Many of them attended the eight New DEEL Conferences held over the years at Temple University's College of Education. As our community grew, we joined the University Council of Educational Administration (UCEA) as a

New DEEL Center. This New DEEL Center also worked together well with the Consortium for the Study of Leadership and Ethics in Education (CSLEE), another center affiliated with UCEA.

A major thrust of the New DEEL is to reintroduce ideals that were meaningful to many of us when we first became educators. Hopefully, the effects of returning to our roots will enable us to critically evaluate external standards, high stakes testing, and accountability, and to reinvigorate the values of civic responsibility, social and racial justice, and ethics. In addition, this movement offers guidance towards developing new courses and programs as well as research and scholarship. In 2016, Steve Gross and I co-authored *Democratic Ethical Educational Leadership: Reclaiming School Reform*, published by Routledge, in which New DEEL members contributed chapters containing stories of courageous exemplars, from around the world, facing and surmounting challenging experiences to educate students and society.

Additionally, a New DEEL Community team has been mentoring teachers and principals in Pennsylvania and in New Jersey to help develop democratic and ethical educational leaders. Most recently, this group has created videos and podcasts in an effort to assist educational administrators in making challenging decisions during a time of a pandemic. To make certain that the New DEEL survives and thrives, two new co-directors, Kevin Peters, a principal in the Dallastown School District in Pennsylvania and Susan Shapiro, a professor from Touro University in New York City, are taking on the leadership.

It is also interesting to note that the Multiple Ethical Paradigms have not only been used in education, but also in the healthcare area. In 2017, the University of Pennsylvania's Dental School created units on ethics to be taught each year to their students. The Multiple Ethical Paradigms have served as a model for the development of these units. Also, there is interest in Jefferson Medical School in teaching its Residents about ethics using the paradigms. So, while focused primarily on educational leadership, the Multiple Ethical Paradigms has become broader in scope and seems to have appeal to health educators. It is exciting that the paradigms have resonated so well beyond its original field.

Jackie's Story

My own values and ethical code have evolved through the years. I was raised in a Catholic working-class family in a rural community in western Pennsylvania. It was here that I learned the importance of honesty, respect for others, and hard work. Mine was the first generation in that town that went to college, and my family viewed an education as the most important goal that one could achieve—both as an end in itself and as a way up and out of a tough life.

In the 1920s, the community where I grew up had been a bustling coal town, but the Great Depression hit hard and the mines closed. Most of the men in the town—those of my parents' generation—turned to labor jobs in neighboring steel mills while their wives stayed at home raising the children. The men of my generation—if not college-bound—took on the hard and often dangerous life of an iron worker. The women married young and became hairdressers or, if they were lucky enough to be educated, teachers. There was a definite pecking order in this town. Those who had been fortunate enough to immigrate first, namely the English and the Welsh, owned farms with large houses and a great deal of land. The Irish came next and often had jobs working for the township. At the bottom of this ladder were those who carried with them the stigma of long, funny last names—the Italians and the Eastern Europeans. These were the majority, and I was one of them.

"You have really got to get that name changed," the town pharmacist said to an 11-year-old me as he stumbled over the name while filling my prescription. "Perhaps you will marry someone with a shorter last name." That was the first time I remember the sting of discrimination. It always struck me as odd that my grandmother—who came from Czechoslovakia in 1914, played the piano, spoke five languages, and raised seven children alone after her young husband was killed in a mine cave-in—was somehow inferior because she carried the badge of a long last name. I also shared that disdain from others—and that limitation—because of my name and my ethnicity. This was only one of a number of similar childhood incidents, but it remains most vivid in my mind because it was the first time I came head to head with the painful realization that I might be limited because of something I could not help—because of who I was. Even at age 11, I realized that to be considered as good as other people I would need to do more than change my name; I would need to deny my identity, my culture, my background, and my family.

This denial of self was something that I have never been prepared to do—either then or now, decades later. But I always carried that memory with me and vowed that I would never, at least intentionally, impose that pain or stigma on any other human being. It was not until I attended college in the late 1960s that I was exposed to people of other races and other cultures and, after hearing their stories, realized how insignificant my pain must have been compared to that of so many others.

Thus, a respect for human dignity and a focus on the worth of each person as a unique individual have always been important values for me. These values began early on but took shape during my college years. I majored in psychology at a time and at a university where a strong liberal arts education was stressed. And, quite by accident, I happened to be attending one of the few universities in this country that approaches psychology from the European tradition of existentialism. So, instead of running rats in mazes, I studied Kant and Sartre and pondered the meaning of existence, something that, at the time, seemed quite exotic for a first-generation, college-educated female from a blue-collar background. Nonetheless, this experience greatly influenced my present view of life as well as my approach to teaching.

Formal education as a personally enriching experience, as a key to open doors of opportunity, and as compensation to counter perceived shortcomings (regarding ethnicity and gender) has always figured large in my life. I earned a master's degree in counseling immediately following undergraduate school and, after some 13 years of working in public schools and in state bureaucracy, I quit what my family perceived as a "good" (meaning "stable") job to attend graduate school full time. During the next seven years, I completed a doctorate as well as a law degree.

Each of these educational experiences taught me important lessons, and each shaped my values in different ways. It was through my counseling program that I learned the meaning of empathy, a key concept in the profession. "It's not the same as sympathy," I remember my professors saying. "It's being able to put yourself in someone else's shoes, to feel as they feel." It is no wonder that today one of my favorite contemporary philosophers is John Rawls, who believes that a just outcome is one that a person would arrive at having no idea which role he or she played in any given moral dilemma.

The summer before entering my doctoral program, I took a course with Larry Kohlberg and learned about the longitudinal studies that gave rise to his theory of moral development as well as Carol Gilligan's feminist challenge of this work. The following year, 1983, I enrolled in Harvard's doctoral program in Administration, Planning, and Social Policy. One of my first required courses, Organizational Theory, was taught by Lee Bolman. He was working on the Bolman and Deal textbook, *Reframing Organizations* (1991) and shared drafts with our class. It was here that I learned how to write case studies and recognized them as a vital tool for instruction. At the time, this instructional method was popular in the Harvard Business School but was new to education. Professor Bolman subsequently hired me to co-author a case study for his summer Institute for Professional Education. Dr. Bolman's analytical approach inspired my ideas for this book's use of different lenses to analyze ethical dilemmas.

I came to the doctoral program aspiring to become a central office administrator. Knowing that most states required a course in school law for certification, I took a deep breath, fearing the content might be more difficult than I could handle. Little did I realize that this decision would change my entire career focus and my life's work.

Rosemary Salomone, who taught education law, helped me to understand the fundamentals of law as well as its policy implications. I learned about issues of equity and inequity and about the power of the law in remedying social injustices. Dr. Salomone was an incredible mentor who nurtured and inspired my love of the law. Still yet, I cite much of her research (Salomone, 1996, 2000, 2003, 2010).

After Professor Salomone left Harvard for a position at St. John's Law School, I was fortunate to work as a graduate assistant for Jay Heubert, who kindly agreed to chair my doctoral dissertation. An exemplar of excellent teaching, Dr. Heubert explained the law from a human perspective. He helped me to understand that plaintiffs and defendants were real people grappling with serious, sometimes heart-wrenching, problems and that the U.S. Supreme Court's rulings were carefully considered solemn decisions rendered with the knowledge of their far-reaching consequences.

At Penn Law School, I learned about justice or at least what I have come to realize as a man-made version of justice. I took courses with Lani Guinier and worked as her graduate student studying the Voting Rights Act and pondering the mechanisms of our democratic system. It was also in law school when I began to realize that my long-held beliefs in individual rights could come into conflict with my concerns about equity. This intersection of civil liberties and civil rights continues to influence my teaching, my research, and my personal and professional values.

Although I have alluded to gender, I mention it this late in my story because I never perceived it as an influential or limiting factor in my early years. I was the older of two children—3½ years older than my brother. Expectations for me, as with all first children, were high. Obviously, I was female, but I never viewed it as a limitation. I felt competent and respected, both at home and at school. My parents' attitudes about hard work and education to improve social class influenced me deeply. These aspirations affected me no less, yet differently, than my entrepreneurial brother probably because I was the first-born and more interested in academics. It was only as I grew older and entered the workforce that I saw my gender as a limiting factor. It was with some dismay, and a great deal of incredulity, that I realized an individual's worth could be diminished and opportunities determined solely because of X and Y chromosomes.

Thus, I entered the teaching of ethics coming from a background in psychology and law that stresses a traditional, liberal democratic philosophy combined with values that have shaped my thinking. The latter include, above all, a respect for an individual's worth and contribution, a desire for justice, fairness, and equity, and a high regard for the ability to empathize.

Privilege

I am guided by Starratt's quotation:

> Ethical education is not a simple training in the predisposition to be ethical, the lessons of which, once learned guarantee an ethical adulthood. Ethical education is lifelong education. It takes place simultaneously with our efforts to be human. (Starratt, 1994b, p. 135)

I began my class much the same as Joan had with an overview of traditional ethics and an exploration of the concepts of utilitarianism as well as consequentialist and non-consequentialist theories. In the beginning, my students were confused when we discussed traditional ethics; they asked for more—more readings, more clarification, more discussion. After all, we had condensed the whole of Western philosophy into one or two short lessons. To compensate for what I saw as an overly brief introduction and to make sure that students would feel grounded in the traditional approach, I stressed these theories throughout my teaching and tried to reinforce their significance in relation to the more modern, less traditional works of Foster (1986), Gilligan (1982), and Purpel (1989).

I also used several dilemmas set forth by Strike, Haller, and Soltis (1988) as a starting point for discussion. Unlike Joan, I did not follow the step-by-step process set forth in the text, but instead made up my own questions. These inquiries generally focused on issues of "What does all this mean?" and "What does it mean to you, personally?" This approach to ethics is advocated by Starratt (1994b) in *Building an Ethical School.*

Although Strike, Haller, and Soltis (1988) come from the same type of liberal democratic tradition that I espouse, I did not always agree with their analysis or with the way the dilemma was constructed. This was particularly true with respect to one situation that involved a principal stopping by a bar on the way home from a meeting only to find his prim English teacher working there as a topless dancer to support her sick mother. The principal was not even sure that it was she until the teacher came up to him later to talk, still dressed in her "costume," a sequined G-string.

The overall situation seems conceivable, but this type of "Marian the Librarian" story in which a woman sheds her conservative clothing and turns into a vamp, although interesting, struck me as lacking verisimilitude. In addition, as several students in my class pointed out, Strike neglected to broach the ethical issue of what the principal was doing in a topless bar. If there was an ethical problem here, was not the principal as ethically bound as the dancer? Would the situation have been different if the principal had been a woman and the teacher a man? In a later edition of their book, Strike and colleagues addressed this issue, but at the time of their first edition these questions prevailed.

Despite the differences in our approaches and analyses, I was fascinated by the dilemmas that Strike et al. presented in that they often included important legal issues. Indeed, the authors pointed out that ethical problems and legal problems are often the same. When I first read this statement, it did not quite ring true to me, but I was not sure why. However, after thinking long and hard, I have come to at least a tentative resolution.

Court opinions often talk about justice, a concept that Kohlberg (1981) characterizes as a higher stage of moral development. Indeed, the symbol for the legal system is a blindfolded woman holding evenly balanced scales. Consequently, legal opinions handed down by the courts are assumedly just decisions. This interpretation makes sense to me in relation to Strike et al.'s statement. As a lawyer as well as an educator, I believe in the power of the law and witness its justice. I see the good that has come from important legal decisions, such as *Brown v. Board of Education* (1954), the U.S. Supreme Court's famous school desegregation decision, and *Brown's* progeny, as well as subsequent federal legislation, which secured the rights of women, linguistic minorities, and persons with disabilities.

However, as Starratt (1994c) pointed out: "What happens when the law is wrong?" Indeed, the law is sometimes wrong, as evidenced by the Jim Crow laws requiring racial segregation and the *Plessy v. Ferguson* (1896) decision which upheld the notion that separate is equal. Moreover, sometimes the law is left open to interpretation and consequently leaves government officials (e.g., public school administrators) with a great deal of discretion in carrying out legal mandates. Therefore, I agree with Starratt and ask a related question that can be easily applied today to court decisions following *Brown* as well as to many students' rights cases: "What happens when the law does not go far enough?"

This last question is one I posed to the second ethics class I taught in one of their final lessons. Here, I diverted from Joan's original syllabus and added the facts only (not the legal analysis) of *Cornfield by Lewis v. Consolidated School District No. 230* (1993), a court opinion that I often include in my legal research. This case involved a total nude strip search of a male high school student for drugs. I gave my class the following instructions: "Here are the facts of a court decision. Assume the actions the school officials took were legal. (The federal appeals court for the seventh circuit said they were legal in that jurisdiction.) Are they ethical? And, given similar circumstances, how would you act if you were the school administrator?"

I used this exercise as a vehicle to encourage students to explore traditional conceptions of justice as well as to apply non-traditional views such as feminist and critical theory. Unlike Joan, I spent little time lecturing on critical theory. Early on, I assigned the same chapters in Foster's (1986) and Purpel's (1989) books that Joan did, but only used them as starting points for discussion of students' personal and professional codes, and ultimately for analysis of the strip-search case. As time went on, I replaced these chapters with articles on social justice, particularly those emphasizing servant leadership and authenticity.

Conversely, I spent a great deal of time on Gilligan's work, but approached it only after an extensive overview of Kohlberg's theory and his stages of moral development. In addition, I encouraged my class to discuss caring, especially the work of Nel Noddings (2002, 2003, 2013) and how this concept fits with notions of justice.

My latest teaching and research efforts emphasize issues related to the intersection of law and ethics, particularly as it applies to the best interests of the student, a concept that lies at the center of our paradigm of the profession. This is the focus of my book, *Best Interests of the Student: Applying Ethical Constructs to Legal Cases,* now in its third edition from Routledge Press (Stefkovich & Frick, 2021).

Starting in 2007 and extending for ten summers, I had the privilege of team-teaching a course in law and ethics as part of the Summer Principals' Academy (SPA) at Teachers College, Columbia University. During this first summer, I had the delightful experience of teaching with Tom Sobol, former Commissioner of Education for New York State, former Superintendent of the Scarsdale School District, and faculty member at Teachers College. His knowledge and wisdom gained from years of study and practical experience at the highest levels of education resulted in a truly memorable experience both for our students and for myself.

In subsequent years, I team-taught this course with many excellent instructors, all of whom added their perspective and depth to the course. A few of these individuals, teaching with me for multiple years, include: Mario Torres, Endowed Professor and Department Head at Texas A&M University; Anthony (Tony) Normore, Emeritus Professor and former Graduate Education Division Chair at California State University, Dominguez Hills; Lawrence (Larry) Rossow, Professor Emeritus at the University of Oklahoma and former Dean and Associate Vice Provost at the University of Houston–Victoria; and Kevin Brady, Professor at the University of Arkansas.

The SPA students were recruited from all over the United States, with many working in the New York City Public Schools. Some had come from "Teach for America," a program that prepares non-education majors to teach in high-need areas. A large number worked in charter schools and/or had started their own schools. As with my courses at Temple and Penn State, I learned as much (or more) from the students in the SPA program as they learned from me.

ETHICS DELIVERY AND TECHNOLOGY

Initially, our teaching of ethics involved a seven-week course, required of all doctoral educational administration students at Temple University. Since many of the students felt that one half of the semester was not sufficient, this course was changed to 14 weeks in duration.

From 2014–2016, online instruction greatly influenced the teaching of ethics at Temple. Joan's ethics course was taught in a hybrid format. She met with her students in the classroom four times a semester. The rest of the sessions were online. Discussion Board was utilized effectively to examine ethical dilemmas. Unlike classroom interactions, where too frequently only a handful of students are active, on Discussion Board all students were required to add their opinions and understandings of the ethical dilemmas presented and of questions raised. In this way, all voices were valued. Joan has also served as the Ethical Threader for the planning process of Temple University's Academic Strategic Compass. This role's objective was to infuse ethics throughout the entire planning process of the university.

Like Joan, Jackie taught the seven-week course and a 14-week course. At Penn State, she taught a hybrid course in ethics, which was approved for continuing education credits through the Pennsylvania State Department of Education. This course met five times and had outside required readings and on-line assignments; it was also available for graduate credit if students completed additional rigorous written work and readings.

We have always been reluctant to include a sample syllabus in this book because, through the years, we have constantly updated our syllabi to adjust to the needs of our students and to include new, relevant information. As we discussed "privilege" in our stories, we noted that while our courses were quite similar, readings and discussions have varied based on our strengths, training, and life/professional experiences, and sometimes on weaker areas where we wanted to compensate. We assume that, after reflection, those teaching ethics with this book will also want the freedom to focus the course in their own special and unique ways. To support these efforts, we have included references to many readings that instructors may want to consult/assign.

In addition, there are key assignments that we have used in teaching the course. These have been specifically mentioned and/or alluded to in our stories but are reiterated here as a guide for instructors. They include: a) lecture and/or discussion to facilitate students' understanding of the multi-paradigm approach in order to apply it to our thinking and to other assignments; b) ample case studies (in this text) that allow for discussions and analyses through the paradigms; c) weekly journal entries of participants' reflections on readings, class discussion, and/or class activities; d) a personal code of ethics; e) a critical incident that shaped one's ethical beliefs; f) a professional code of ethics unique to each individual; g) comparisons of personal and professional codes of ethics as individuals and with classmates; h) comparison of students' professional codes of ethics with those codes developed by professional associations; and i) a written assignment involving an ethical dilemma unique to each student (i.e., either happened to the student or something the student had heard about with names and details disguised to ensure anonymity) and an analysis of this dilemma using the multiple paradigm approach.

We believe that teaching ethics readily lends itself to various modes of delivery. As indicated above, ethical decision making can easily be taught in person as seven- and 14-week classes. The latter might include several sessions where students present their dilemmas to the class and receive immediate feedback from others. If completed as a hybrid class, we suggest that the instructor devote at least one in-person session reviewing the various paradigms and answering questions to ensure that all students thoroughly understand the paradigms before applying them to the cases and written assignments. Other assignments can be presented on-line with discussion groups. In addition, the readings and other assignments we have suggested easily lend themselves to a totally on-line course; however, we must warn instructors that any on-line course requires extensive (and often time-consuming) preparation.

Finally, as mentioned earlier, ethics may be infused into the curriculum with one caveat. Although we believe that ethics may be taught effectively in many ways, we have found that dealing with the issues we have come to face—concerns about diversity and an ever-evolving view of ethics as a process requiring self-reflection—are handled more easily when adequate time is allotted.

Diversity as a Strength and a Challenge

During the period from 1990 to 1999, when we worked together at Temple University, we taught more than 150 graduate students as part of their doctoral cohort requirement. Joan continued to teach the ethics course at Temple from 2000 to 2016, and during that same period, Jackie taught courses in ethical leadership and "law and ethics" to undergraduate, masters, and doctoral students at Penn State University.

Probably what has been most striking about our students is their diversity. Temple is an urban university and has been fortunate in attracting students from a variety of racial and ethnic backgrounds. At Temple, some students come from Philadelphia, the location of the university, in the sixth largest city in the United States. Others come from smaller Pennsylvania cities, such as Harrisburg and Scranton or from other states such as New Jersey, Delaware, and Maryland.

Some students commuted from very rural areas, whereas others lived in wealthy suburbs. In one class at Temple, there was a woman from Trinidad, a man from Ethiopia, a relocated New Yorker, and a student born and raised in Pennsylvania Dutch Country (home of the state's substantial Amish and Mennonite populations). Temple also had three cohorts of educational administration students in Jamaica. At Penn State, one student observed that he was the only white male in a class of 20 with American Indians, an American woman born in Puerto Rico, and international students from Asia, Africa, and South America. He enjoyed this experience but was surprised at such diversity in an educational leadership course.

At Penn State, on this rural campus, Jackie taught a variety of students as well. Many students were from Central Pennsylvania, others commuted two to three hours to attend classes, and a substantial number of full-time students came from across the country and the world, representing a wide range of racial, ethnic, and religious backgrounds. Penn State has a well-established Comparative International Education (CIED) dual-degree program and for years has hosted mid-career professionals from emerging nations as part of the Hubert H. Humphrey Fellowship Program. Jackie's ethics classes attracted international students from both programs as well as from more traditional majors. Her international students often came directly from their home countries with the intention of returning to serve in their schools, universities, or ministries of education or, sometimes, to seek positions in the United States.

For 40 years, Penn State was home to an American Indian Leadership Program (AILP) where students earned masters' and doctoral degrees in educational leadership. These students, most of whom returned to work in their tribal schools or held high positions in state and federal government, brought perspectives that greatly enriched Jackie's classes; some of these students wrote dilemmas that appear in this book.

Besides having racial and ethnic diversity, students in our ethics classes have also been different in many other ways. During her years at Penn State, Jackie taught classes with (to name only a few) American Indian teachers and administrators from tribal schools; students representing ministries of education in countries as diverse as Saudi Arabia, Chile, and Korea; educators from Colombia, Guam, Cyprus, Turkey, India, Kazakhstan, and various African countries; teachers from China, Korea, Japan, and Taiwan; as well as many teachers and administrators born and raised in central Pennsylvania, and educators relocated from cities such as New York and Philadelphia.

Turning to religious diversity, although primarily Christian or Jewish, our students represented a variety of factions within these religions, which we believe, tend to influence students' personal and professional codes (that often sounded like some version of the Ten Commandments). Some students belonged to Philadelphia's Black Baptist churches. Others were White Christian fundamentalists from a Bible Belt part of Pennsylvania. We taught Catholic nuns and a priest, Orthodox, Conservative, and Reform Jews, Muslims from Middle-Eastern countries and Black Muslims from Philadelphia, Hindus, and Mennonites as well as individuals who never mentioned religion as part of their identity or who practiced different forms of spiritualism.

Graduate students at both universities ranged in age from the mid-twenties to almost 60, and their professional experiences were often just as diverse. As might be expected, we had our share of public schoolteachers and administrators; however, others came from higher education, business, the military, or other "non-traditional" settings. They were school counselors, psychologists, biologists, athletic trainers, physical therapists, professional athletes, and teachers from all grade levels and subjects, ranging from English to physics, working in traditional public schools, charter schools, private schools, and adult evening schools. And, just as we, the professors, came to this experience with certain predilections, so did our students. It was through our pedagogy that both we and our students came to understand our values and the critical incidents in our lives that shaped them.

We believe this quality of diversity accounted for the classes' greatest strength and greatest challenge in that it enabled different perspectives on ethical issues to be discussed. We could never really resolve the differences among our students, nor should we. What we could do, though, was employ strategies that would draw students out and force them to reflect on their own ethical codes as well as the perspectives of others in the class. As one of our students reflected on the diversity she encountered:

> A course such as this, with the participants we have in class, would be beneficial to everyone. How many of us get the opportunity to really "hear" the beliefs and thoughts of people different from ourselves in an academic, nonthreatening atmosphere? In truth, this . . . cohort is the first time that I've encountered such diverse people in all my graduate courses. I am constantly amazed at the responses of some of the people in class because they are so different from my own experience and way of thinking. This is truly energizing, and I am enjoying the exchange a lot.

In teaching ethics, we also had to be very careful to guard against stereotypes of any kind, not just the most obvious—for example, along race and gender lines—but also the more subtle stereotypes based on religion, culture, sexual orientation, geographical location, profession, and previous training. We not only had to check ourselves, but our students, always challenging preconceived assumptions and ingrained notions. We found ourselves grappling with clashes of culture regarding diverse student populations and ultimately acting as translators for our students, crossing borders of gender, race, social class, and other categories of difference to make meaning of others' values, morals, and ethical codes. Through this process, we, too, benefited, growing—as teachers and as human beings—from these experiences.

Beyond U.S. Classrooms and Institutions

As early as the 1990s, we began to attend annual national conventions of the University Council of Educational Administration (UCEA). This organization has been extremely important to us. Michelle Young, Dean of Education at Loyola Marymount University in Los Angeles, California and UCEA's Executive Director from 2001–2019, was particularly welcoming to us. In fact, in 2002, we were delighted to hear that the then President of UCEA, Gail Furman, a scholar in the ethics of community, highlighted the first edition of our ethics book in her presidential speech, later published in the *UCEA Review* (Furman, 2003). It was a thoughtful and knowledgeable introduction to our writings.

UCEA not only had national conventions, but it also had several affiliated centers. Early on, we joined UCEA's Center for the Study of Leadership and Ethics (CSLE). We started by attending and presenting papers at the Center's annual conferences in 2000. In 2003, the Center's director, Paul Begley, moved from the University of Toronto to Penn State. Through Paul's leadership and annual conferences, we were able to work with educational ethicists from around the world and directly expose our students to cutting-edge work in professional ethics.

In 2009, with Paul's return to Canada, the UCEA ethics center expanded to include Penn State's Willower Center, Penn State's Rock Ethics Institute, Temple's New DEEL Community Network and other ethics groups from Australia, Canada, Hong Kong, and Sweden. Currently, we present our work at conferences sponsored by the Center for the Study of Leadership and Ethics in Education (CSLEE), directed by Hollie Mackey, Associate Professor at North Dakota State University, as well as in other professional venues.

We are pleased that the third edition of our ethics book was translated into Korean (Shapiro & Stefkovich, 2011) and various editions have been utilized in diverse English-speaking locations such as Canada, New Zealand,

Australia, Hong Kong, and countries where English is not the native language, including Sweden, China, and Colombia.

Jackie has, upon request, conducted a series of workshops based on our book in Croatia where she served as a Fulbright Fellow for five months and in Colombia, South America where she has consulted with The Vermont School in Bogota and the Ethics and Citizenship Education Center at Rosario University. Also, Jackie has taught classes on ethical decision making in Sydney and Melbourne, Australia.

Joan was invited to keynote our work at the Berlin Conference for teachers in Germany and to school administrators in England. She was also asked to share her ethics syllabus by colleagues in Sweden. However, Joan was very clear to indicate that this was probably not the most appropriate syllabus for Sweden, and it would need to be reworked utilizing Swedish educational references as well as authentic, local cases.

This interest world-wide is something both of us want to explore with our international colleagues. We would like to know: How is the book utilized in other countries? Do the ethical dilemmas all resonate with diverse populations or do we need to modify the cases so that they make meaning better beyond our borders? In furtherance of this pursuit, we have begun to include more international dilemmas in our book. For example, a new dilemma in this 2021 edition addresses an issue specific to Sweden and its immigrants, but the basic themes and dilemma might easily resonate with countries in a comparable situation. This scenario joins existing contributions from Canada and Guam.

IN CONCLUSION

Throughout this chapter, we have stressed the importance of conversations with colleagues, focusing on issues such as who they are and what and how they teach. Such conversations can lead to careful content analysis of what readings and resources are privileged in the classroom. They can also help identify what pedagogical approaches are employed to make certain that the content is delivered to all students. We feel that in-depth, thoughtful, and provocative discussions will help us assess what voices we tend to emphasize when we teach—the voice of justice, rights, law; the voice of critique and possibilities; the voice of care, concern, and connectedness; or, alternatively, a combination of these voices. It was also through this experience that we were able to recognize the need for an additional paradigm—the ethic of the profession. Thus, we see ethics teaching as an on-going process, one that necessitates continual reflection and discussion by the instructors and by their students.

REFERENCES

Arar, K, Haj, I, Abramovitz, R, Oplatka, I. (2016). Ethical leadership in education and its relation to ethical decision-making: The case of Arab school leaders in Israel. *Journal of Educational Administration 54*(6), 647–660.

Bakhtin, M. (1981). *The dialogic imagination.* Austin, TX: University of Texas Press.

Bartels, D.M., Bauman, C.W., Cushman, F.A., Pizarro, D.A., & McGraw, A.P. (2014). Moral judgment and decision making. In G. Keren & G. Wu (Eds.). *The Wiley Blackwell handbook of judgment and decision making,* pp. 478–515. Chichester, UK: Wiley.

Bass, L., Frick, W.C., & Young, M.D. (Eds.). (2018). *Developing ethical principles for school leadership: PSEL standard two.* New York, NY: Routledge.

Beck, L.G. (1994). *Reclaiming educational administration as a caring profession.* New York, NY: Teachers College Press.

Beck, L.G. & Murphy, J. (1994). *Ethics in educational leadership programs: An expanding role.* Thousand Oaks, CA: Corwin Press.

Begley, P.T. & Johansson, O. (Eds.) (2003). *The ethical dimensions of school leadership.* Boston, MA: Kluwer.

Belenky, M.F., Clinchy, B.M., Goldberger, N.R., & Tarule, J.M. (1986). *Women's ways of knowing.* New York, NY: Basic Books.

Berkovich, I. & Eyal, O. (2018). Ethics education in leadership development: Adopting multiple ethical paradigms. *Educational Management, Administration, and Leadership, 48*(2), 270–285.

Bolman, L.G. & Deal, T.E. (1991). *Reframing organizations: Artistry, choice, and leadership.* San Francisco, CA: Jossey-Bass.

Branson, C.M. & Gross, S.J. (Eds.) (2014). *Handbook of ethical educational leadership.* New York, NY: Routledge.

Brasof, M. (2015) *Student voice and school governance: Distributing leadership to youth and adults.* New York, NY: Routledge.

Brown v. Board of Education, 347 U.S. 483 (1954).

Buber, M. (1965). Education. In M. Buber (Ed.), *Between man and man* (pp. 83–103). New York, NY: Macmillan.

Cherkowski, S., Walker, K.D., & Kutsyuruba, B. (2015). Principal's moral agency and ethical decision making towards a transformation of ethics. *International Journal of Education Policy and Leadership, 10*(5), 1–17.

Cornfield by Lewis v. Consolidated School District No. 230, 991 F.2d 1316 (7th Cir. 1993).

Covaleskie, J.F. (2016). Moral vision in a world of diversity. *Values and Ethics in Educational Administration, 12,* 1–8.

Duignan, P. (2007). *Educational leadership: Key challenges and ethical tensions.* Cambridge, England: Cambridge University Press.

Foster, W. (1986). *Paradigms and promises: New approaches to educational administration.* Buffalo, NY: Prometheus Books.

Freire, P. (1970). *Pedagogy of the oppressed* (M.B. Ramos, Trans.). New York, NY: Continuum.

Freire, P. (1993). *Pedagogy of the city* (D. Macedo, Trans.). New York, NY: Continuum.

Freire, P. (1998). *Pedagogy of freedom: Ethics, democracy, and civic courage* (P. Clarke, Trans.). Lanham, MD: Rowman & Littlefield.

Furman, G.C. (2003). The 2002 UCEA presidential address: Toward a new scholarship of educational leadership. *UCEA Review, 45*(1), 1–6.

Gilligan, C. (1982). *In a different voice.* Cambridge, MA: Harvard University Press.

Gilligan, C., Ward, J., & Taylor, J. (1988). *Mapping the moral domain: A contribution of women's thinking to psychology and education.* Cambridge, MA: Harvard University Graduate School of Education.

Ginsberg, A.E., Shapiro, J.P., & Brown, S.P. (2004). *Gender in urban education: Strategies for student achievement.* Portsmouth, NH: Heinemann.

Giroux, H.A. (Ed.) (1991). *Postmodernism, feminism, and cultural politics: Redrawing educational boundaries.* Albany, NY: State University of New York Press.

Giroux, H.A. (1992). *Border crossings: Cultural workers and the politics of education.* New York, NY: Routledge.

Giroux, H.A. (1994). Educational leadership and school administrators: Rethinking the meaning of democratic public culture. In T. Mulkeen, N.H. Cambron-McCabe, & B. Anderson (Eds.). *Democratic leadership: The changing context of administrative preparation* (pp. 31–47). Norwood, NJ: Ablex.

Giroux, H.A. (2020). *On critical pedagogy* (2nd ed.). London, England: Bloomsbury Academic.

Gross, S.J. (1998). *Staying centered: Curriculum leadership in a turbulent era.* Alexandria, VA: Association for Supervision and Curriculum Development.

Gross, S.J. (2004). *Promises kept: Sustaining innovative curriculum leadership.* Alexandria, VA: Association of Supervision and Curriculum Development.

Gross, S.J. (2006). *Leadership mentoring: Maintaining school improvement in turbulent times.* Lanham, MD: Rowman & Littlefield.

Gross, S.J. (2014). Using turbulence theory to guide actions. In C.M. Branson & S.J. Gross (Eds.), *Handbook of ethical leadership* (pp. 246–262). New York, NY: Routledge.

Gross, S.J. (2020). *Applying turbulence theory to educational leadership in challenging times: A case-based approach.* New York, NY: Routledge.

Gurley, D.K. & Dagley, A. (2020). Pulling back the curtain on moral reasoning and ethical leadership development for K-12 school leaders. *Journal of Research on Leadership Education.* Retrieved from https://doi.org/10.1177/1942775120921213

Hammersley-Fletcher, L (2015). Value(s)-driven decision-making: The ethics work of English headteachers within discourses of constraint. *Educational Management Administration and Leadership, 43*(2), 198–213.

Hirst, P.H. (1974). *Moral education in a secular society.* London, England: University of London Press.

Kohlberg, L. (1981). *The philosophy of moral development: Moral stages and the idea of justice* (Vol. 1). San Francisco, CA: Harper & Row.

Langlois, L. & LaPointe, C. (2010). Can ethics be learned? Results from a three-year action-research project. *Journal of Educational Administration, 48*(2), 147–163.

McLaren, P. (2020). *Life in schools: An introduction to critical pedagogy in the foundations of education* (6th ed.). New York, NY: Routledge.

Mitra, D. (2018). Student voice in secondary schools: The possibility for deeper change. *Journal of Educational Administration, 56*(5), 473–487.

Mullen, C.A. (2017). What's ethics got to do with it? Pedagogical support for ethical student learning in a principal preparation program. *Journal of Research on Leadership Education, 12*(3), 239–272.

Murphy, J. (2011). *Essential lessons for leaders.* Thousand Oaks, CA: Corwin Press.

Murphy, J.F. (2017). *Professional standards educational leaders: The empirical, moral, and experiential foundations.* Thousand Oaks, CA: Corwin.

Noddings, N. (1984). *Caring: A feminine approach to ethics and moral education.* Berkeley, CA: University of California Press.

Noddings, N. (1992). *The challenge to care in schools: An alternative approach to education.* New York, NY: Teachers College Press.

Noddings, N. (2002). *Educating moral people: A caring alternative to character education.* New York, NY: Teachers College Press.

Noddings, N. (2003). *Caring: A feminine approach to ethics and moral education* (2nd ed.). Berkeley, CA: University of California Press.

Noddings, N. (2012). The caring relation in teaching. *Oxford Review of Education, 38*(6), 771–781.

Noddings, N. (2013). *Caring: A relational approach to ethics and moral education* (2nd ed.). Oakland, CA: University of California Press.

Peters, R.S. (1973). *Reason and compassion.* London, England: Routledge & Kegan Paul.

Plessy v. Ferguson, 163 U.S. 537 (1896).

Purpel, D.E. (1989). *The moral and spiritual crisis in education: A curriculum for justice and compassion in education.* New York, NY: Bergin & Garvey.

Purpel, D.E. (2004). *Reflections on the moral and spiritual crisis in education.* New York, NY: Peter Lang.

Salomone, R.C. (1996). Common schools, uncommon values: Listening to the voices of dissent. *Yale Law and Policy Review, 14,* 169–235.

Salomone, R.C. (2000). *Visions of schooling: Conscience, community, and common education.* New Haven, CT: Yale University Press.

Salomone, R.C. (2003). *Same, different, equal: Rethinking single-sex schooling.* New Haven, CT: Yale University Press.

Salomone, R.C. (2010). *True American: Language, identity and the education of immigrant children,* Cambridge, MA: Harvard University Press.

Shapira-Lishchinsky, O. (2018). *International aspects of organizational ethics in educational systems.* Bingley, England: Emerald Publishing Limited.

Shapiro, J. (2015). What is ethical educational leadership? In Griffiths, D. & Portelli, J.P. (Eds.), *Key questions for educational leaders.* (p. 91). Toronto, Canada: Word & Deed Publishing Inc. & Edphil Books.

Shapiro, J.P. & Gross, S.J. (2013). *Ethical educational leadership in turbulent times: (Re) solving moral dilemmas* (2nd ed.). New York, NY: Routledge.

Shapiro, J. & Gross, S.J. (2017). Ethics and professional norms. In Murphy, J.F. *Professional standards for educational leaders: The empirical, moral and experiential foundations.* (pp. 21–37). Thousand Oaks, CA: Corwin.

Shapiro, J.P. & Smith-Rosenberg, C. (1989). The "other voices" in contemporary ethical dilemmas: The value of the new scholarship on women in the teaching of ethics. *Women's Studies International Forum, 12*(2), 199–211.

Shapiro, J.P. & Stefkovich, J.A. (2011). *Ethical leadership and decision making in education* (3rd ed.). Mapogu, Seoul Korea: Hakjisa Publisher, Inc.

Starratt, R.J. (1994a). Afterword. In L.G. Beck & J. Murphy (Eds.), *Ethics in educational leadership programs: An expanding role* (pp. 100–103). Thousand Oaks, CA: Corwin Press.

Starratt, R.J. (1994b). *Building an ethical school: A practical response to the moral crisis in schools.* London, England: Falmer Press.

Starratt, R.J. (1994c, April 6). Preparing administrators for ethical practice: State of the art. Presentation at the annual meeting of the American Educational Research Association, New Orleans.

Starratt, R.J. (2004). *Ethical leadership.* San Francisco, CA: Jossey-Bass.

Starratt, R.J. (2009). Ethical leadership. In B. Davies (Ed.). *The essentials of school leadership* (2nd ed.) (pp. 74–90). London, England: Sage.

Stefkovich, J.A. (2014). *Best interests of the student: Applying ethical constructs to legal cases in education* (2nd ed.). New York, NY: Routledge.

Stefkovich, J.A. & Frick, W.C. (2021). *Best interests of the student: Applying ethical constructs to legal cases* (3rd ed.). New York, NY: Routledge.

Stefkovich, J.A. & Shapiro, J.P. (1994). Personal and professional ethics for educational administrators. *Review Journal of Philosophy and Social Science, 20*(1&2), 157–186.

Strike, K.A., Haller, E.J., & Soltis, J.F. (1988). *The ethics of school administration.* New York, NY: Teachers College Press.

Vogel, L.R. (2012). Leading with hearts and minds: Ethical orientations of educational leadership doctoral students. *Values and Ethics in Educational Administration, 10*(1), 1–12.

Welch, S. (1991). An ethic of solidarity and difference. In H. Giroux (Ed.), *Postmodernism, feminism, and cultural politics: Redrawing educational boundaries* (pp. 83–99). Albany, NY: State University of New York Press.

Witherell, C. & Noddings, N. (1991). *Stories lives tell: Narrative and dialogue in education.* New York, NY: Teachers College Press.

About the Contributors

AUTHORS

Joan Poliner Shapiro is Professor Emerita of Higher Education at Temple University's College of Education and Human Development. Previously, she served as Associate Dean for Research and Development, and she was Chair of the Educational Leadership and Policy Studies Department at Temple. She has also been Co-Director of the Women's Studies Program at the University of Pennsylvania, taught middle school and high school in the United States and the United Kingdom, and supervised intern teachers. More recently, she served as the President of Temple University's Faculty Senate. Currently, she is the Co-Director Emerita of an educational community network, called the New DEEL (Democratic Ethical Educational Leadership), with Steven Jay Gross. She holds a doctorate in Educational Administration from the University of Pennsylvania; in addition, she completed a postdoctoral year at the University of London's Institute of Education. Among her honors are the Lindback Distinguished Teaching Award, the University Council for Educational Administration's Master Professor Award, and Temple University's Great Teacher Award. In the area of scholarship, she has co-authored the following books: *Reframing Diversity in Education* with Trevor E. Sewell and Joseph P. DuCette (Rowman & Littlefield, 2001); *Gender in Urban Education: Strategies for Student Achievement* with Alice E. Ginsberg and Shirley P. Brown (Heinemann, 2004); *Educational Ethical Leadership in Turbulent Times* (2nd ed.) with Steven Jay Gross (Routledge, 2013); and *Democratic Ethical Educational Leadership* with Steven Jay Gross (Routledge, 2016). She has also written many journal articles and book chapters focusing on gender issues in education and on ethical leadership.

Jacqueline A. Stefkovich, Professor Emerita of Educational Leadership at the Pennsylvania State University, is an independent consultant and researcher. Formerly, she was Associate Dean for Graduate Programs, Research, and Faculty Development at Penn State, and Head of the Department of Education Policy Studies. She holds a doctoral degree in Administration, Planning, and Social Policy from Harvard University's Graduate School of Education and a J.D. from the University of Pennsylvania Law School. She is licensed to practice law in Pennsylvania, New Jersey, and the District of Columbia. She has worked as a teacher, school counselor, and state-level administrator. Dr. Stefkovich's research interests focus on the law and ethics as related to students' rights and school leaders' responsibilities to keep schools safe. In addition to this book, she has co-authored: *The Best Interests of the Student: Applying Ethical Constructs to Legal Cases* (3rd ed.) (Routledge, 2021) with William Frick; *The Law and Education: Cases and Materials* (4th ed.) (Carolina Press, 2021) with Kevin Brady, Traci Ballard, and Lawrence Rossow; *Search and Seizure in the Public Schools* (4th ed.) (Education Law Association, 2014) with Lawrence Rossow; and *Ethics for School Business Officials* (Scarecrow Press, 2005) with William Hartman. She has published over 75 book chapters and journal articles. Her most recent research focuses on legal and ethical aspects of school discipline and students' rights from an international perspective. She has taught courses in Sydney and Melbourne, Australia and Tokyo, Japan, held a Fulbright fellowship in Croatia, and consulted for two months in Bogota, Colombia.

CONTRIBUTORS

Carly Ackley is a higher education professional with over 15 years of administrative and teaching experience in business schools in the Mid-Atlantic. As both a university administrator and instructor, she has spent her career researching and teaching leadership development. She currently works in executive education at Johns Hopkins Carey Business School where she teaches leadership coaching and manages customized leadership development programs. Carly earned her Ph.D. and M.Ed. from the The Pennsylvania State University and is a certified career and executive coach.

Aisha Salim Ali Al-Harthi is an associate professor and the head of department for the Education Foundations and Administration (DEFA) at the College of Education in Sultan Qaboos University, Oman. Her research interests include the following areas: distance education, Massive Open Online

Courses (MOOCs), cultural issues, learner self-regulation, learner characteristics, learning strategies, vocational secondary education, and entrepreneurship. She publishes in both distance education and educational leadership journals and leads/ participates in many funded research projects. She supervises both Masters' and Doctoral students. She received the Milldred and Charles Wedemyer Award for Outstanding Scholar in Distance Education in 2011.

Jennifer Antoni is a full-time professional school counselor as well as an assistant adjunct professor in the Psychological Studies in Education program at Temple University. Dr. Antoni is also Co-Coordinator for Community Engagement for the New DEEL (Democratic Ethical Educational Leadership). She holds an Ed.D. in Educational Leadership. Her main research interest centers around the way educational leadership responses influence student decision making regarding the attainment of a high school diploma and chronic absenteeism. Apart from spending countless hours with her family and two dogs, she enjoys volunteering as a leader with Girl Scouts and writing creatively.

Peter Brigg is the principal of Sabold Elementary in Springfield School District in Pennsylvania. He has been an administrator for more than nine years after seven years in the classroom. In 2019, Sabold Elementary was recognized by the United States Department of Education as a National Blue Ribbon School under Dr. Brigg's leadership. Dr. Brigg earned his undergraduate degree at Widener University, a Masters' degree in Educational Leadership from Villanova University, and a Doctoral degree from Temple University. Dr. Brigg is an inspirational leader who is committed to excellence for his school and community.

Amelia Foy Buonanno is a transgender educator from Philadelphia, PA, dedicated to finding solutions to the many leadership challenges and policy dilemmas in public schools. Her focus has been improving educational equity for children that have been historically marginalized. Dr. Buonanno received her Bachelors' degree in Media Studies at Temple University. She then continued her education at Arcadia University and Penn State University, earning a Masters' in Education. Dr. Buonanno later became a Principal Fellow at Harvard University's Graduate School of Education and completed her doctoral studies at Temple University, focusing on ethics, policy, and organizational psychology.

Joseph A. Castellucci is Superintendent of Lower Cape May Regional School District in New Jersey. He has been a Director of Curriculum and Instruction, Principal, Assistant Principal, and teacher of Social Studies. He received his B.S. from Penn State University, M.A. from New Jersey City University, and advanced graduate courses at Temple University. He has worked to increase access to Career and Technical Education in comprehensive high schools, serves on the Healthy Youth Coalition combating the opiate epidemic, and has supported the Resiliency Initiative, raising awareness of the effects of Adverse Childhood Experiences (ACE's) and toxic stress on young people.

Lynn A. Cheddar serves as Supervisor of Federal Programs, Assessment and Professional Development in Saucon Valley School District in Hellertown, Pennsylvania. During her career, she has worked as an elementary school teacher, Reading Specialist, Coordinator of Academic Services and Assistant Principal. Presently, she partners with the district's instructional and technology integration coaches as part of a district-wide initiative to implement personalized learning. She also works as an Adjunct Professor at DeSales University in Center Valley, PA. Additionally, she provides professional development and training at various educational conferences and school districts in the mid-Atlantic region.

Tara H. Collice has been an educator for 24 years, beginning her career in Philadelphia after graduating from Temple University with a B.S. in Early Childhood and Elementary Education. She joined Colonial School District in 2002 where she now serves on the Colonial Middle School administrative team. Tara additionally served as an adjunct faculty member at Holy Family University from 2002 to 2012. She holds a Masters' degree with Reading Certification from Holy Family University as well as a M.Ed. in Educational Leadership with Principal Certification.

Taryn J. Conroy is a school counselor and serves on her school's administration team. She is the Co-Coordinator of Community Engagement for the New DEEL (Democratic Ethical Educational Leadership) Community Network. Dr. Conroy's work focuses on ethical educational leadership, particularly educational leaders working from an ethic of care. She has presented her work at a number of national conferences. Dr. Conroy received a Paul Begley award at CSLEE's Values and Leadership Conference for her contribution to the field of ethics, values, and leadership education.

Emily R. Crawford is an Associate Professor in the Department of Educational Leadership & Policy Analysis at the University of Missouri,

Columbia. Emily's research agenda examines how school leaders respond to the impact of immigration policy on undocumented and mixed-legal status students and families. She is the co-editor of *Educational Leadership of Immigrants: Case Studies in Times of Change* (Routledge) and has published in *Educational Administration Quarterly*, the *Journal of School Leadership, Equity & Excellence in Education,* and the *International Journal of Qualitative Studies in Education.*

Robert L. Crawford, Ed.D., M.S., LPC, NCC is a Licensed Professional Counselor and Nationally Certified Counselor practicing privately for over fifteen years in southern New Jersey. During his career, Dr. Crawford has taught at several universities and is a frequent keynote speaker for regional and national conferences. Personally, Dr. Crawford parents his three children with passionate delight—a pre-teen, teenager, and twenty-something—in their journeys to becoming beautiful human beings.

Addie Daniels-Lane currently serves as a member of the Trenton Board of Education in Trenton, New Jersey. She is a retired educator who served the Trenton School District for 37 years in many capacities, the last of which was Principal of Trenton Central High School West. Ms. Daniels-Lane's many experiences as an educator include elementary principal, middle school principal, vice principal, whole school reform facilitator, social studies teacher, and reading teacher. She received a B.S. degree from Seton Hall University, and an M.A. in Counseling and a M.Ed. in Educational Leadership, both from the College of New Jersey. Ms. Daniels-Lane engaged in post-graduate studies at Temple University.

Daniel L. Dukes is a Special Education Director from Abilene, Texas. He received his undergraduate degree from Texas Christian University, Master's degree from the University of Texas at Arlington, and doctoral degree in Educational Leadership from George Washington University. He is the former principal of the Model Secondary School for the Deaf in Washington, D.C. He has an extensive background in gifted and talented and deaf education programs. Dr. Dukes resides in Abilene, TX, with his wife and four children.

James C. Dyson is a retired music educator. He received a B.S. from West Chester University of Pennsylvania and an Elementary Education Certification, a Masters' degree in Secondary Education, and Elementary and Secondary Principal Certifications from East Stroudsburg University of Pennsylvania. He completed his doctorate in Educational Administration from Temple University.

Omar X. Easy, Superintendent of Wayland (MA) Public Schools, has experience as a professional athlete, school leader, and Spanish teacher. Starting in 2002, he played four seasons in the NFL with the Kansas City Chiefs and (former) Oakland Raiders. He then earned an M.B.A. from the University of Phoenix and an M.Ed. and a Ph.D. in Educational Leadership from The Pennsylvania State University. He served as Director of Organizational Assessment for the City of Everett (MA), Vice-Principal and Executive Director of the Parent Information Center for the Everett Public School System, and a Teaching Assistant/ Director of Player Development at Penn State.

Patricia A.L. Ehrensal is an independent scholar. Prior to retiring from academia, she was on faculty of Fordham University, George Washington, and Cabrini University. Dr. Ehrensal has published articles and book chapters examining ethics, school organizations, and the social construction of children. She is also a Co-Editor of the book, *Legal frontiers in education: Complex issues for leaders, policymakers, and policy implementers.* Dr. Ehrensal is currently the Director of the 3rd Street Gallery, and artist cooperative, in Philadelphia. In addition to the directorship, she now divides her time between photography and her ongoing research agenda.

Toni Faddis, Ed.D. has served as a public-school educator for the past twenty-six years as a teacher, principal, and district leader. She also teaches leadership courses at San Diego State University for teachers who aspire to become principals. Toni's passion for educational excellence, equity, and ethical school leadership led to the publication of *The Ethical Line: 10 Strategies for Effective Decision Making* (Corwin Press, 2019).

Susan C. Faircloth (an enrolled member of the Coharie Tribe of North Carolina) is Professor and Director of the School of Education at Colorado State University. Dr. Faircloth's research interests include: Indigenous education, the education of culturally and linguistically diverse students with special educational needs, and the moral and ethical dimensions of school leadership. She has published widely in such journals as *Educational Administration Quarterly, Harvard Educational Review, The Journal of Special Education Leadership, International Studies in Educational Administration, Values and Ethics in Educational Administration, Tribal College Journal of American Indian Higher Education, Rural Special Education Quarterly,* and *Journal of Disability Policy Studies.*

David M. Gates is a retired Temple University adjunct professor who taught graduate courses in educational administration and research design.

He is a former English Department chair with 30 years' experience teaching high school English. Additionally, he served as a "Classrooms for the Future" coach facilitating the integration of technology and the internet into secondary education curriculum and pedagogy. Dr. Gates received his B.S. degree in secondary education from Indiana University of Pennsylvania and his Ed.M. and Ed.D. degrees from Temple University.

Steven Jay Gross is Professor Emeritus of Educational Leadership at Temple University and Founding Director of the New DEEL (Democratic Ethical Educational Leadership). His books include: *Applying Turbulence Theory to Educational Leadership in Challenging Times* (2020); *Democratic Ethical Educational Leadership* (2016) (co-authored with Joan Poliner Shapiro); *The Handbook on Ethical Educational Leadership* (2014) (co-edited with Christopher Branson); *and Ethical Educational Leadership in Turbulent Times* (with Joan Poliner Shapiro) (2013, 2nd ed). He received the Willower Award for Excellence, UCEA's Master Professor Award, and is a member of the Golden Key International Honour Society, and the Horace Mann League.

Loree P. Guthrie retired as Assistant Superintendent at the Pocono Mountain School District in Swiftwater, Pennsylvania. Prior to entering the field of administration, she taught advanced placement senior English for 15 years. Dr. Guthrie was also involved in an educational partnership, housed within her district, for professional development as well as a transitions program for school-phobic children with East Stroudsburg University. She received her doctorate in Educational Administration from Temple University.

Kathrine J. Gutierrez is an associate professor in the School of Education at the University of Guam, having started January 2021. Prior to this position, she served as a faculty member at the University of Oklahoma for 14 ½ years, teaching and advising graduate students. Dr. Gutierrez earned a Ph.D. in Educational Leadership and M.Ed. in Higher Education from The Pennsylvania State University. She is also an alumna of the University of Guam having earned B.B.A. and M.P.A. degrees. Her higher education work experience includes research (scholarly publications and national/international conference presentations), teaching (graduate coursework) and service activities (national/international).

Jane Harstad is the state Director of Indian Education and Tribal Liaison to Minnesota's eleven Tribal Nations at the Minnesota Department of

Education. She is an enrolled member of the Red Cliff band of Lake Superior Anishinaabe. She graduated from the University of Minnesota with a Bachelors' degree in Elementary Education with a concentration in American Indian Studies. and received her Masters' and doctoral degrees in Educational Leadership from Penn State University. Ms. Harstad served as principal of the Nay Ah Shing and Pine Grove Tribal Schools on the Mille Lacs Reservation and taught elementary students for 11 years in St. Paul, Minnesota.

James K. Krause is a former special education teacher, administrator, and university faculty member. He recently retired from Bloomsburg University of Pennsylvania after 23 years of service. During his tenure, he served as faculty, Department Chair, Assistant Dean, Dean, Assistant Provost, and Provost. His research interests include inclusive practices for students with disabilities, special education (SE) administration, SE clinical education, adult services, and attitudinal issues related to disabilities. He completed his Doctoral degree in Educational Leadership and Policy Studies at Temple University.

Mary Beth Kurilko is the Director of Online Programs at Thomas Jefferson University's East Falls campus. Her love of all things higher education developed when she began as an admissions counselor with Temple University in 1995. She worked her way to Associate Director of Undergraduate Admissions, managing the tour guide program, along with print and e-marketing campaigns for freshman recruitment. She was also part of a team that read over twenty thousand admissions applications each year. She earned her undergraduate and Masters' degrees at Temple. Her graduate work in educational administration focused on standardized test score differentials in non-Asian minorities.

Amy Lavin is an assistant professor and academic director at the Fox School of Business at Temple University. She earned her Ed.D. and MBA from Temple University. Dr. Lavin's focus and interests include Management Information Systems, User Experience, Business Intelligence, student engagement and the delivery, and success of online education.

Kuan-Pei Lin is an associate professor in the Graduate Institute of Educational Administration at the National Pingtung University in Taiwan. She completed her Ph.D. in Educational Leadership from Penn State University. She earned her M.S. in Counseling and Counselor Education from Indiana University. Her research interests include educational leadership, school principal and teacher evaluation, and multicultural education.

Jeannette McGill-Harris has 25 years of experience in the field of education. She is currently the principal of Gregory Elementary School in Trenton, New Jersey. Jeannette is a former teacher, teacher trainer, and vice principal. She received her B.S. in elementary education from SUNY New Paltz College and her Masters' degree from the University of Pittsburgh.

Hollie J. Mackey (Northern Cheyenne) is an Associate Professor at North Dakota State University. Her research examines structural inequity of Indigenous and other marginalized populations in educational leadership/public policy through multiple critical frameworks and methodologies. She received the Willower Award for Excellence (ethics in leadership) and the Culbertson Award for outstanding accomplishments as a junior professor of educational leadership. Dr. Mackey serves as the Executive Director for the Consortium for the Study of Leadership and Ethics in Education (CSLEE), and the Associate Director for the Barbara L. Jackson Scholars Network.

Patricia A. Maloney is Assistant Superintendent at Dover Area School District in Dover, Pennsylvania. She is a former classroom teacher, high school guidance counselor, assistant high school principal, and supervisor of student support services. Dr. Maloney served as an educational leader for over 34 years. She received her undergraduate and Masters' degrees from Millersville University and her doctorate in Educational Administration from Temple University. Dr. Maloney's research interests are in the areas of alternative education and underserved youth. She has served as an adjunct professor for Temple University, Penn State University, and Cabrini College.

Liza Meiris has been an educator for fourteen years while fulfilling many roles within Philadelphia's public and charter schools, as well as in alternative education. While teaching at the secondary level, she has worked as a curriculum writer, student activities director, instructional coach, data analyst, fundraising coordinator, and counselor. She earned both her Bachelors' and Masters' degree in Educational Administration degrees from Temple University. She holds a Principal Certification in addition to certifications to teach English, Math, and Social Studies 7-12.

Beatrice H. Mickey is the Executive Director of the Pennsylvania Division of the Lost Children Foundation. Formerly, Dr. Mickey was a school principal. She earned her Masters' in English Education and Doctorate in Educational Administration from Temple University. Dr. Mickey has a broad teaching background including elementary school as a reading specialist, to the graduate level, as an adjunct professor of education. Her research interests include student-centered instructional practices, instructional leadership, and the technology of teaching.

Angela Duncan Montgomery is the Assistant Dean and Executive Director of Graduate Admissions at Drexel University. Her career focuses on higher education admissions and administration, the study of ethics and decision making in public and private schools, academic advising, and student affairs at the Graduate level. She has spent the last 15 years in top universities, including Penn State, Georgetown University, and Johns Hopkins, and remains passionate about access and equity in higher education. Dr. Montgomery earned an undergraduate degree in Music Education from Millikin University, a Masters' degree in Educational Leadership and Policy from American University, and a Ph.D. in Educational Leadership from Penn State.

James F. Montgomery is a corporate strategist. He is a United States Army veteran with over 20 years of service, retiring as a Lieutenant Colonel. He completed his Masters' degree in Educational Leadership in 2005 at The Pennsylvania State University. James was named a research associate for the D.J. Willower Center in 2006 and was published in the U.S. Army's *Cyber Defense Review*. James has served in numerous leadership and managerial positions in civilian and military positions including three combat tours in Southwest Asia. He is currently working corporate strategy for a U.S. based defense contractor.

Katarina Norberg is an Associate Professor in Education at the Centre for Principal Development, Umeå University, Sweden. Dr. Norberg received the D.J. Willower Center for the Study of Leadership and Ethics Award of Excellence in 2016. Her research interest is the ethical dimension of schooling linked to schools' democratic assignment. She is especially focused on issues concerning ethics and values in multicultural schools and school leadership for social justice. Her latest publications highlight how school leaders handled the situation in 2015 when the number of asylum seekers increased dramatically in Sweden.

C. Esteban Pérez is Vice Principal and Director of Professional Development for the Vermont School in Bogota, Colombia, where in addition to other duties, he works to promote research in the classrooms and has provided faculty with in-service programs on ethical decision making.

Prior to this position, he was administrative director at the Vermont School, CEO of Celumusica, LTDA, Country Manager at Telemedia, LTDA, and a Junior Analyst at Colombia Movil. He earned a PhD in Curriculum and Instruction and a Masters' degree in Educational Leadership from Penn State. He holds Bachelors' and graduate specialist (strategic planning) degrees in business.

Kevin A. Peters is a middle school principal in the Dallastown Area School District (Pennsylvania). He is Co-Director of the New DEEL (Democratic Ethical Educational Leadership) Community Network. Dr. Peters has published articles on mentoring and presented his work at several state, national, and international conferences. He earned his undergraduate degree from York College of Pennsylvania, a Masters' degree in special education from McDaniel College, and a doctorate in educational leadership and policy studies from Temple University.

Tamarah Pfeiffer, of the Bitterwater clan (To'dichinii) born for the Metal Hat People, is the Chief Academic Officer for the Bureau of Indian Education. Her long career in American Indian Education includes that of a high school teacher, principal and curriculum specialist at the Rough Rock Community School and Principal/Superintendent of the Alamo Navajo Community School for ten years. Dr. Pfeiffer holds a B.A. in Education from the University of New Mexico, a Masters' degree in English from the Bread Loaf School of English, and a Ph.D. in Educational Leadership specializing in American Indian education from the Pennsylvania State University.

Leon Poeske is the Administrative Director at Bucks County Technical High School, located outside of Philadelphia. He has served as an administrator in various schools and capacities since 1997. Before moving into administration, Dr. Poeske was a secondary school teacher for eleven years; one of his more memorable experiences was teaching in West Africa as a Peace Corps Volunteer. Dr. Poeske completed his graduate degrees at Temple University and earned his undergraduate from the University of Wisconsin. In 2015, Dr. Poeske was named the Pennsylvania Administrator of the Year from the Pennsylvania Association for Career and Technical Education.

Dipali Puri received her Ph.D. in Educational Leadership from Penn State University. She is currently a faculty member and certification director at Juniata College in Huntingdon, Pennsylvania. Before that, she was an Associate Professor of Education at Lincoln University in Chester County, PA with a campus in Philadelphia where she taught childhood courses at both the undergraduate and graduate levels in the Education department. Dr. Puri's research interests include pre-service teacher identity development, high impact practices for English language learners, and enhancing social justice through teacher education programs.

Laura L. Randolph earned an MS in College Student Personnel from Miami University and an Ed.D. in Educational Leadership from Temple University. She has held positions in residence life for a several years before transitioning to the area of new student orientation. Dr. Randolph's research interests include exploring a sense of belonging in a college environment for minorities populations. She is currently the Director for New Student Orientation and Family Programs at Rutgers University in New Brunswick, New Jersey.

Susan A. Rosano is a retired educator. Before retiring, Ms. Rosano spent over two decades serving Philadelphia schools as a teacher, teacher coach and Peer Assistance and Review Consulting Teacher supporting new and struggling teachers. She is continuing to follow her passion to serve children in her new home state (Arizona) as an active member of Optimist International Club dedicated to "Bringing Out the Best in Kids" through community service programs and using her Masters' degree in Counseling to mentor public school students struggling with behavioral challenges in the classroom.

Jason Rosenbaum has worked in New York City public schools since 2000. He is currently an assistant principal and previously taught middle school English and Social Studies. He graduated from Middlebury College and holds Masters' degrees from Bank Street College of Education and Columbia University. Throughout his career he has focused on fostering inclusive classrooms and schools and exploring the ethical dilemmas that flow from the pursuit of educational equity.

Hector L. Sambolin, Jr. currently serves as the Associate Dean for Academic Affairs, Academic Success & Assessment at Pomona College in Claremont, California. He is also the Director of the Mellon Mays Undergraduate Program for the Claremont Colleges and Director of the Sage Fellows Peer Academic Coaching Program. Dr. Sambolin's areas of expertise include higher education assessment, ethical leadership, Diversity, Equity & Inclusion, student academic success, student & faculty cohort programming, and data analytics. He received his Ph.D. in educational leadership with an emphasis on higher education from The Pennsylvania State University. His dissertation studied ethical decision making of university presidents.

Elizabeth A. Santoro is Director of Elementary Education for the North Penn School District (NPSD) in Montgomery County, Pennsylvania. She has been an educator for 37 years serving as an elementary teacher, elementary principal, and director of special education/student services. Dr. Santoro holds a B.S. in Elementary Education from Chestnut Hill College, a Masters' degree in Educational Administration from Villanova University, a Superintendent's Letter of Eligibility from Arcadia University, and a Doctorate in Educational Leadership/Policy Studies from Temple University. Most noteworthy is Dr. Santoro's work with the implementation of full-day kindergarten in the NPSD in 2019.

John Schlegel has been an educator for over 40 years as a teacher and administrator. He received his B.S. in Secondary Education from Kutztown University, his M.S.Ed. in Counseling from Millersville University, and his Ed.D. in Educational Administration from Temple University. Dr. Schlegel retired in 2013 as the Director of Secondary Education for the Cornwall-Lebanon School District in Pennsylvania. John was an adjunct instructor at Drexel University. He currently serves in a number of professional capacities in the Cornwall Lebanon School District.

Susan H. Shapiro is Assistant Professor of Early Childhood and Special Education at Touro Graduate School of Education and Co-Director of the New DEEL (Democratic Ethical Educational Leadership). She earned her Bachelor's degree in child psychology from the New School, Eugene Lang College; a Master's degree from Bank Street College of Education; and her Doctorate from the Steinhardt School at New York University in Educational Leadership. She has led early childhood programs and inclusion programs for the past 25 years. She has also been an advocate for early childhood education policy and has authored articles on ethical leadership and compassion.

Stormy Stark holds a Ph.D. in Educational Leadership from Pennsylvania State University. She focuses on rural and Appalachian education allowing her to combine her loves of teaching and helping the people from the Blue Ridge Mountains, the place she holds dearest in her heart. Stormy is also the owner of StonyMan Sheep, a flock of 45 Lincoln and Wensleydale sheep, raised strictly for their wool, which has won National Championships. She combines her joys of teaching and agriculture frequently. You never know when a baby lamb will pop up in her class!

Spencer S. Stober is a Professor of Biology and Leadership Studies at Alvernia University, Reading, PA. In 2005, he received Alvernia's

Christian R. & Mary F. Lindback Foundation Award for Excellence in Teaching, and he was awarded the Neag Professorship in 2011 for excellence in teaching and scholarship. Dr. Stober is an advisory board member for the international "On Sustainability Research Network." He regularly publishes on topics in sustainability and leadership. Dr. Stober's most recent book is a co-edited volume, entitled *Transitions to Sustainability: Theoretical Debates for a Changing Planet*. He has also served in key administrative positions at Alvernia University.

David J. Traini had been in public education since 1978, prior to his retirement in 2007. He holds a Bachelors' degree in Philosophy from Princeton University and a Masters' degree in Educational Administration from Rowan University. He spent 11 years as a physical science teacher before joining the ranks of administration. He served as an administrator at the Cumberland Regional High School in Seabrook, New Jersey, one of the first schools in New Jersey to implement block scheduling. He currently teaches math and science at a small private school in North Carolina.

Monica N. Villafuerte, School Leader and Founding Principal of Cresthaven Academy Charter School, has over two decades of urban public-school experience in New York City and New Jersey. Previously, she was the Founding Assistant School Leader in a Newark (NJ) charter school, a dean, school programmer, staff developer, and adult high school coordinator. She has taught elementary and middle school grades, working with at-risk, special needs, and multicultural students, including English-language learners. She has a B.S. from New York University, and Ed.M. degrees from Columbia University (educational leadership) and Cambridge College.

William W. Watts is an educator in the Council Rock School District in Bucks County, Pennsylvania. He has served in the district for 42 years as a Health and Physical Education instructor, coach, athletic director, and district curriculum coordinator. He has also served on many academic committees and student support programs throughout his tenure. Dr. Watts earned his Bachelors' degree in Health and Physical Education from the University of Pittsburgh and a Masters' and Doctoral degree (Ed.D.) in Education Administration from Rider University and Temple University, respectively. His doctoral study examines student beliefs of violence in schools.

Deborah L. Weaver retired as an elementary school principal in Elizabethtown, Pennsylvania. She received her B.S. from West Chester

University, her M.Ed. degrees from Penn State Harrisburg and Shippensburg Universities respectively, and her doctorate from Temple University. As a 33-year veteran in the field of education, her professional involvement has included classroom teaching at both the elementary and middle school levels, active participation in education-related organizations, and facilitation of workshops on various topics. She currently serves on the "Pennsylvania Administrator" editorial board for PA Principals' Association.

Christopher S. Weiler is an associate professor in the department of Elementary, Middle Level, Library and Technologies Education at Kutztown University of Pennsylvania. Previously, he taught sixth grade in suburban Philadelphia. He received his BA in Elementary Education from Lock Haven University of Pennsylvania, his MS in Educational Technology from Lehigh University, and his EdD in Educational Administration from Temple University. Dr. Weiler's current research interests include middle-grades education; developing equitable, socially just, culturally responsive, and ethically informed pre-service teachers; use of high-leverage practices in teacher education; and inquiry-based methods for teaching of math and science.

Arkadiy Yelman is the founding leader of One Bright Ray's Mansion Adult Campus, an evening school for adult students seeking a high school diploma. Leading from a community-building perspective, he helped establish numerous partnerships as the school rapidly expanded. Mr. Yelman is also the Coordinator of Media/Technology for the New DEEL (Democratic Ethical Educational Leadership). He spent his early career teaching social studies to credit-deficient high school students and maintains democracy, ethics, and citizenship as the basis of his practice. Mr. Yelman's research interests include adult secondary education and adult literacy.

Lindy Zaretsky holds a Ph.D. degree in Education Administration, Theory and Policy Studies from the University of Toronto. Lindy is President of Reaching Education Resolutions Inc., a consulting service supporting families living with disabilities and organizations with barrier-free access to affordable and inclusive programs and services in the education and social service sectors. Lindy serves on the Education Standards Development Committee, supported by the Ontario Ministry of Education and the Ministry of Seniors and Accessibility Ontario. She is also Board President of the SAAAC Autism Centre where she remains committed to supporting families living in under-resourced and culturally diverse communities.

Index

Note: Page locators in *italic* refer to figures.

Made in the USA
Coppell, TX
03 June 2022

78441549R00175